I NEED A VACATION...

叶 恭弘

For those of you buying this book, thank you very much. This is the first volume of *Pretty Face*. For someone who works as slowly as I do, a weekly series was an almost impossible pace, but with the help of my staff and the support of my readers, I've been able to make it this far. Now I really understand what they mean when they say, "Anything's possible when you try!"

...Is that too serious? [laughs]

—Yasuhiro Kano, 2002

Yasuhiro Kano made his manga debut in 1992 with *Black City*, which won *Weekly Shonen Jump*'s Hop★Step Award for new artists. From 1993 to 2001, he illustrated Mugen's serialized novels *Midnight Magic* in *Jump Novel* magazine, and also produced a manga adaptation. *Pretty Face* appeared in *Weekly Shonen Jump* from 2002 to 2003. Kano's newest series, *M x O*, began running in *Weekly Shonen Jump* in 2006.

PRETTY FACE
VOL. 1

The SHONEN JUMP ADVANCED Manga Edition

STORY AND ART BY
YASUHIRO KANO

Translation & English Adaptation/Anita Sengupta
Touch-up Art & Lettering/Eric Erbes
Design/Hidemi Dunn
Editor/Jason Thompson

Editor in Chief, Books/Alvin Lu
Editor in Chief, Magazines/Marc Weidenbaum
VP, Publishing Licensing/Rika Inouye
VP, Sales & Product Marketing/Gonzalo Ferreyra
VP, Creative/Linda Espinosa
Publisher/Hyoe Narita

Printed in the U.S.A.

Published by VIZ Media, LLC
P.O. Box 77010
San Francisco, CA 94107

SHONEN JUMP ADVANCED Manga Edition
10 9 8 7 6 5 4 3
First printing, August 2007
Third printing, June 2008

www.viz.com

www.shonenjump.com

PARENTAL ADVISORY
PRETTY FACE is rated T+ for Older Teen and is recommended for ages 16 and up. Contains strong language, violence, nudity and sexual situations.

RATED T+ FOR OLDER TEEN

ratings.viz.com

Pretty Face

Vol. 1

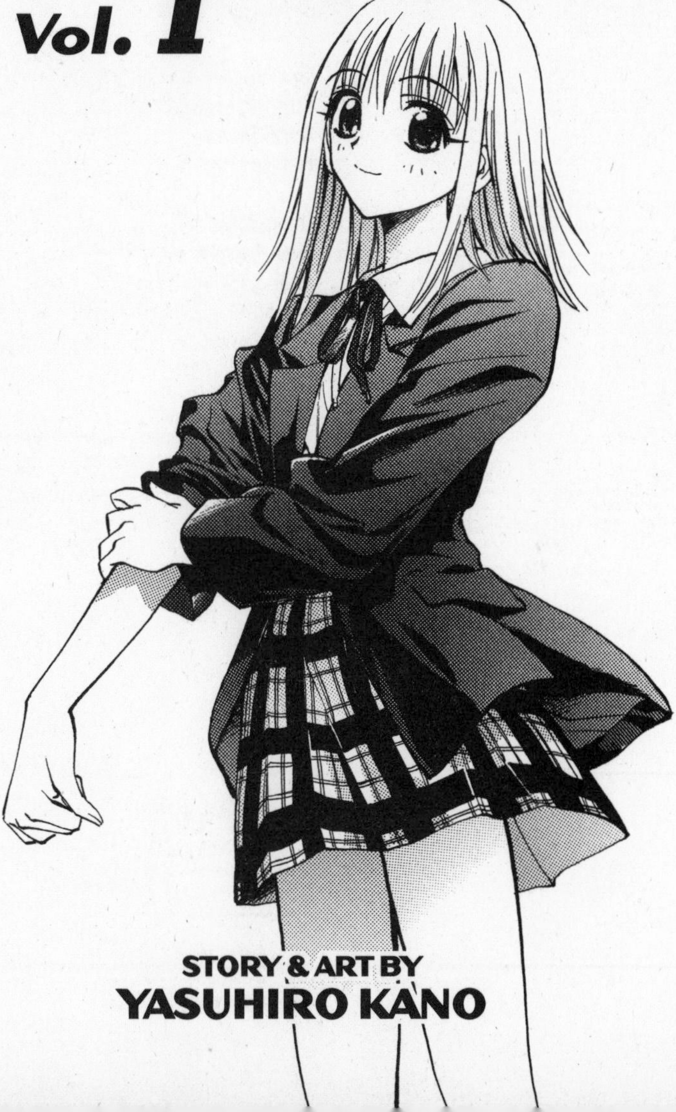

STORY & ART BY
YASUHIRO KANO

PRETTY FACE
Vol. 1
CONTENTS

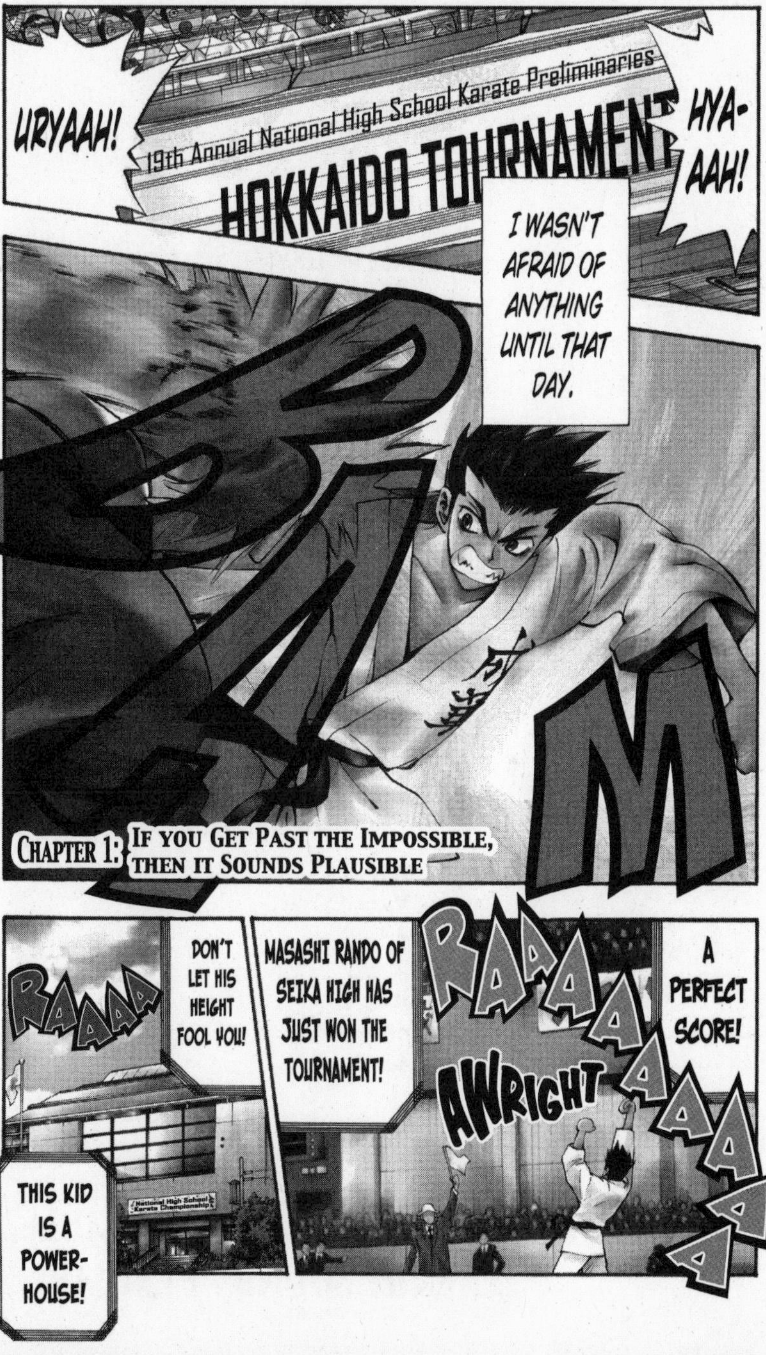
HYA-AAH!
HOKKAIDO TOURNAMENT
19th Annual National High School Karate Preliminaries
URYAAH!
I WASN'T AFRAID OF ANYTHING UNTIL THAT DAY.
BAM
Chapter 1: If you Get Past the Impossible, then it Sounds Plausible
A PERFECT SCORE!
RAAAAAAAAAA
AWRIGHT
MASASHI RANDO OF SEIKA HIGH HAS JUST WON THE TOURNAMENT!
DON'T LET HIS HEIGHT FOOL YOU!
RAAAA
National High School Karate Championship
THIS KID IS A POWER-HOUSE!

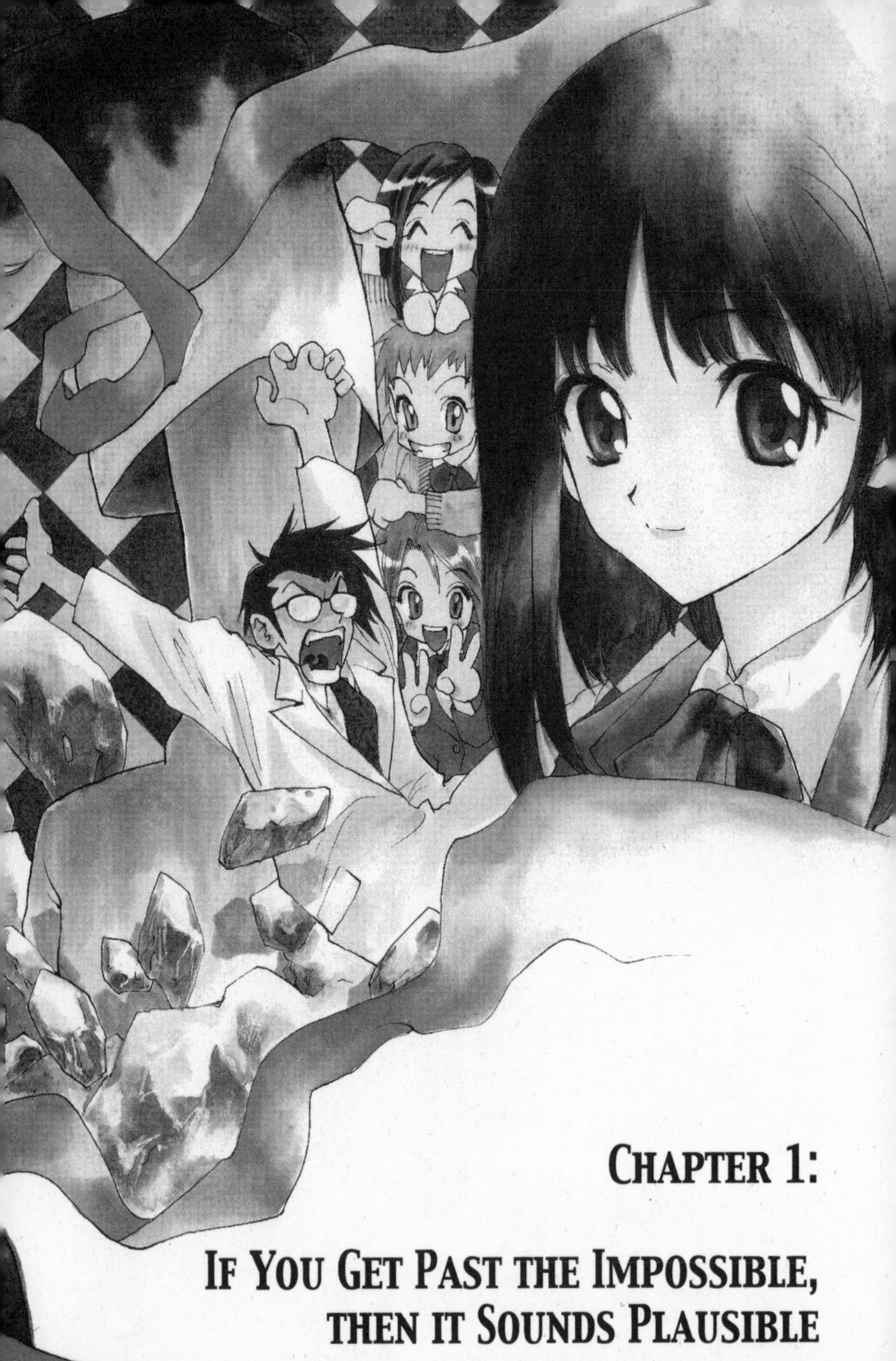

Chapter 1:

If You Get Past the Impossible, then it Sounds Plausible

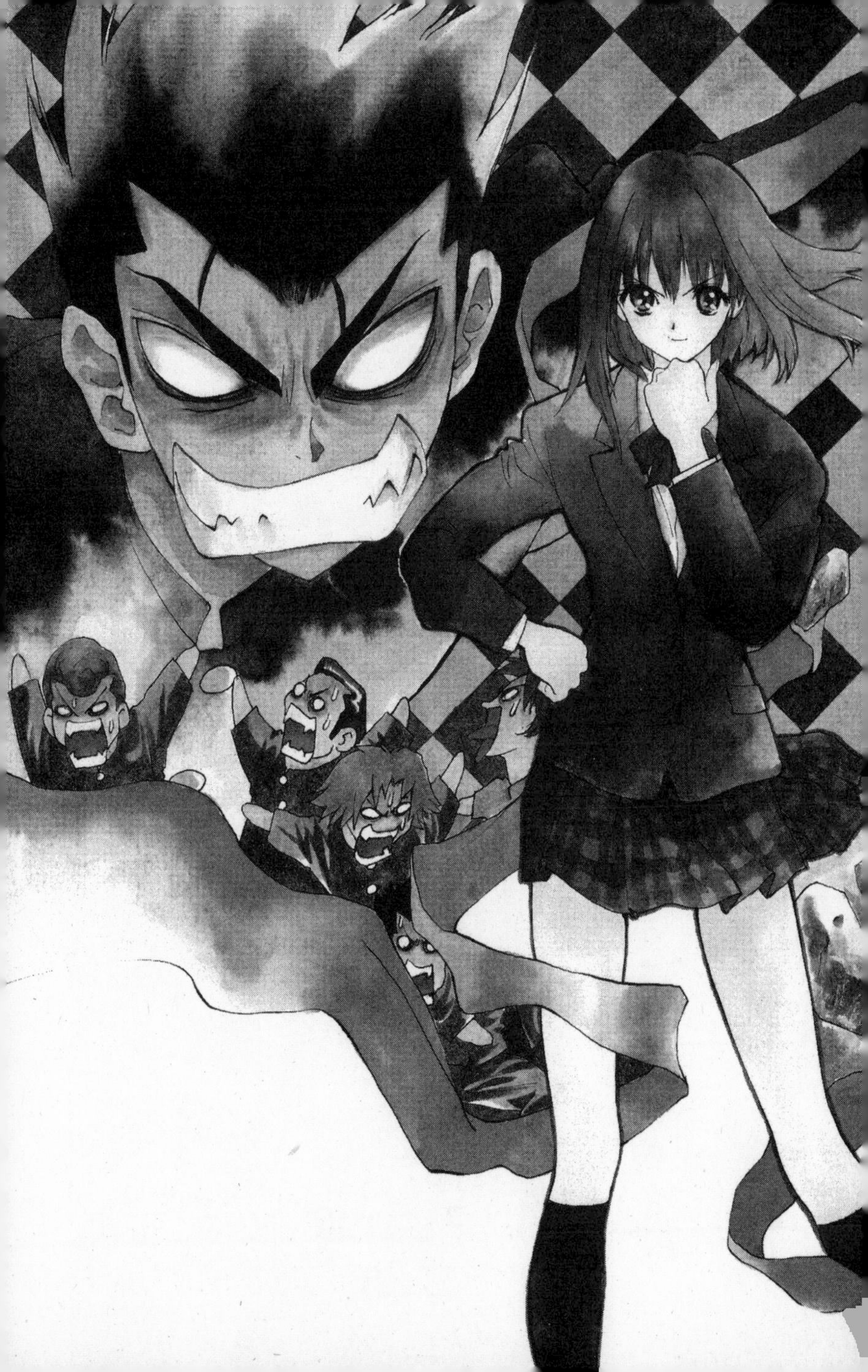

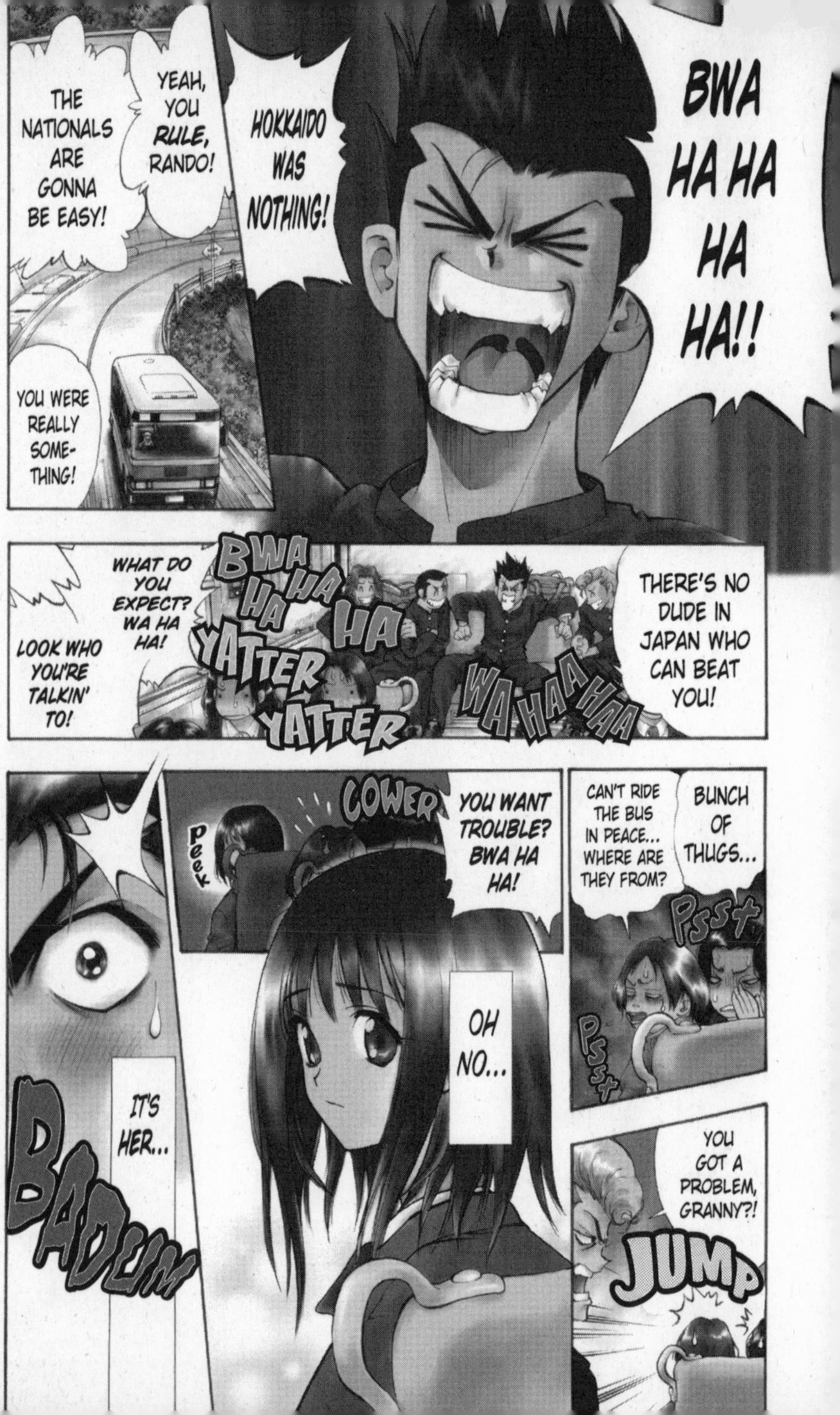
BWA HA HA HA HA!!
HOKKAIDO WAS NOTHING!
YEAH, YOU *RULE*, RANDO!
THE NATIONALS ARE GONNA BE EASY!
YOU WERE REALLY SOME-THING!
THERE'S NO DUDE IN JAPAN WHO CAN BEAT YOU!
WA HAA HAA
BWA HA HA HA
YATTER YATTER
WHAT DO YOU EXPECT? WA HA HA!
LOOK WHO YOU'RE TALKIN' TO!
BUNCH OF THUGS...
CAN'T RIDE THE BUS IN PEACE... WHERE ARE THEY FROM?
Psst
Psst
YOU GOT A PROBLEM, GRANNY?!
JUMP
YOU WANT TROUBLE? BWA HA HA!
COWER
Peek
OH NO...
IT'S HER...
BADUM

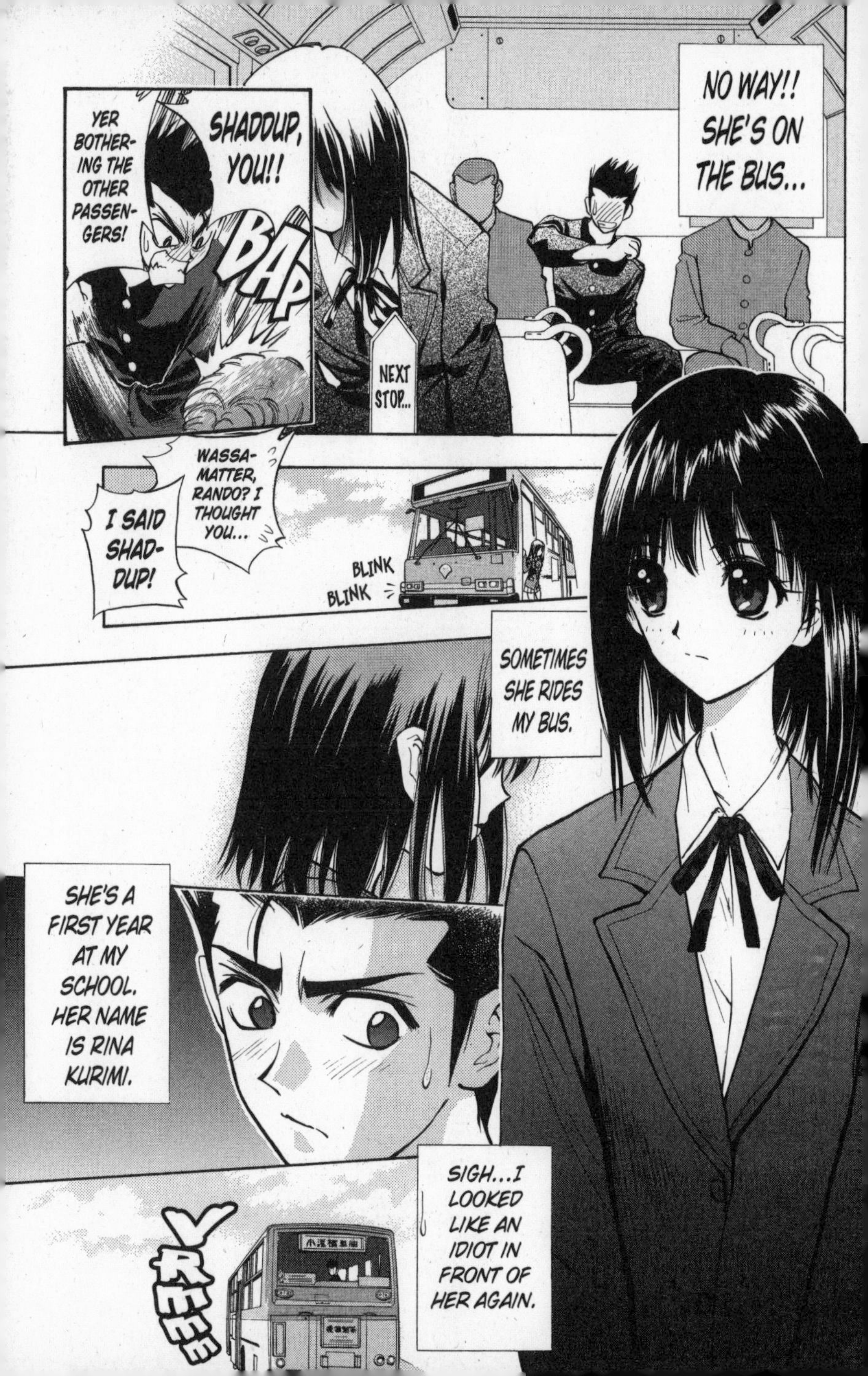
NO WAY!! SHE'S ON THE BUS...
NEXT STOP...
SHADDUP, YOU!!
YER BOTHERING THE OTHER PASSENGERS!
BAP
SOMETIMES SHE RIDES MY BUS.
WASSAMATTER, RANDO? I THOUGHT YOU...
I SAID SHADDUP!
BLINK BLINK
SHE'S A FIRST YEAR AT MY SCHOOL. HER NAME IS RINA KURIMI.
SIGH...I LOOKED LIKE AN IDIOT IN FRONT OF HER AGAIN.
VREEEM

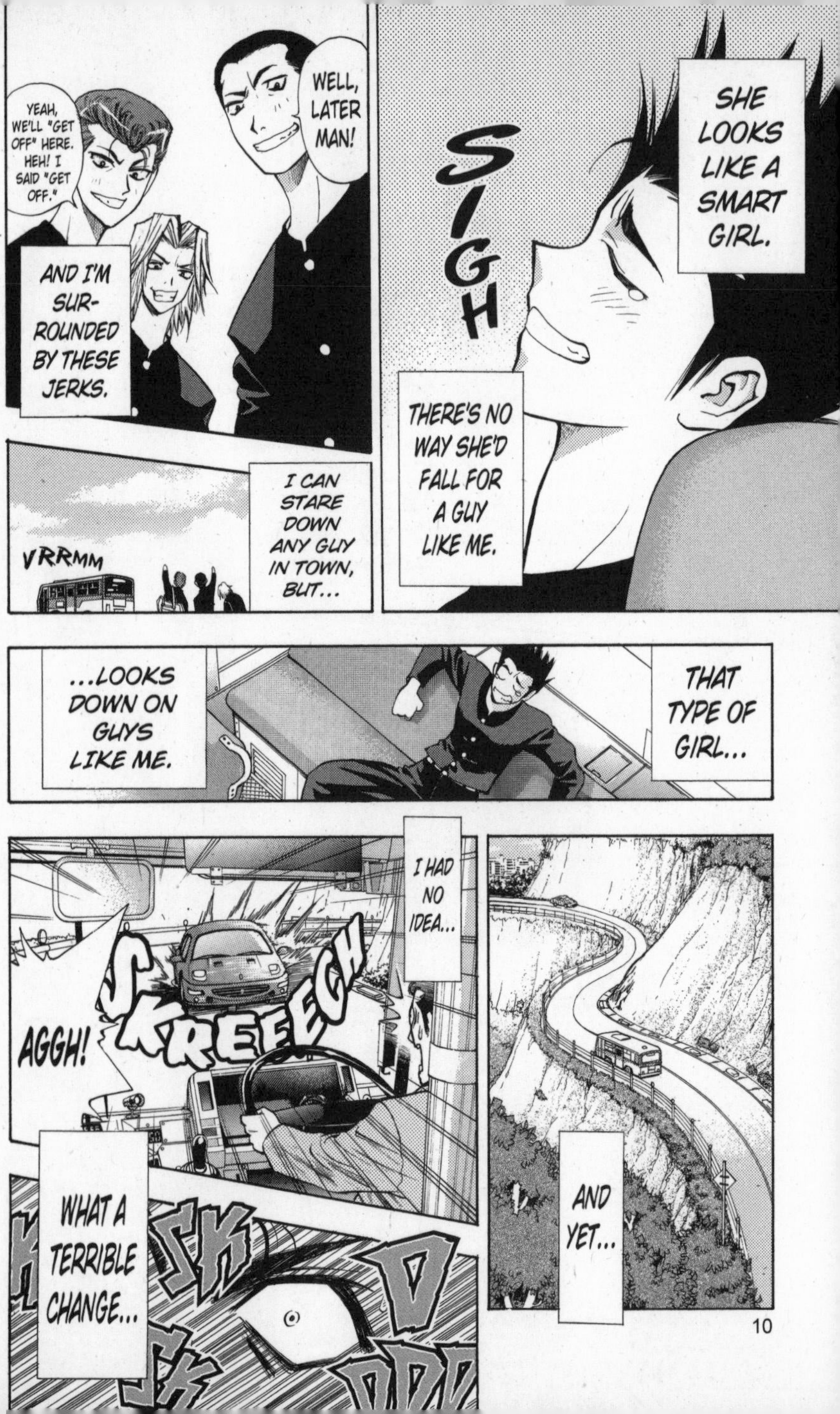
SIGH
SHE LOOKS LIKE A SMART GIRL.
THERE'S NO WAY SHE'D FALL FOR A GUY LIKE ME.
WELL, LATER MAN!
YEAH, WE'LL "GET OFF" HERE. HEH! I SAID "GET OFF."
AND I'M SUR-ROUNDED BY THESE JERKS.
I CAN STARE DOWN ANY GUY IN TOWN, BUT...
VRRMM
THAT TYPE OF GIRL...
...LOOKS DOWN ON GUYS LIKE ME.
AND YET...
I HAD NO IDEA...
SKREEECH
AGGH!
WHAT A TERRIBLE CHANGE...

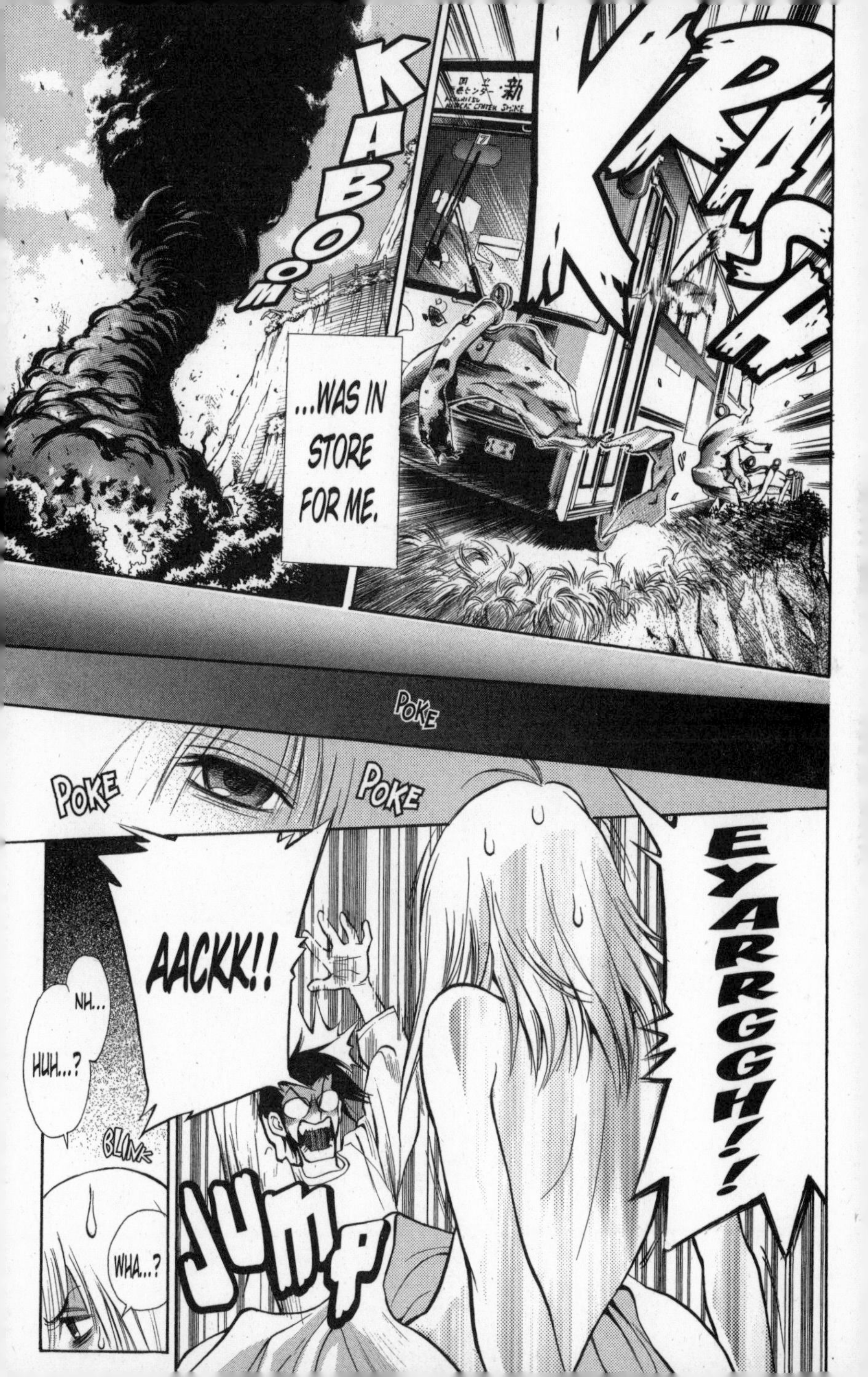
KRASH
KABOOM
...WAS IN STORE FOR ME.
POKE
POKE
POKE
EYARRGGH!!!
AACKK!!
JUMP
NH...
HUH...?
BLINK
WHA...?

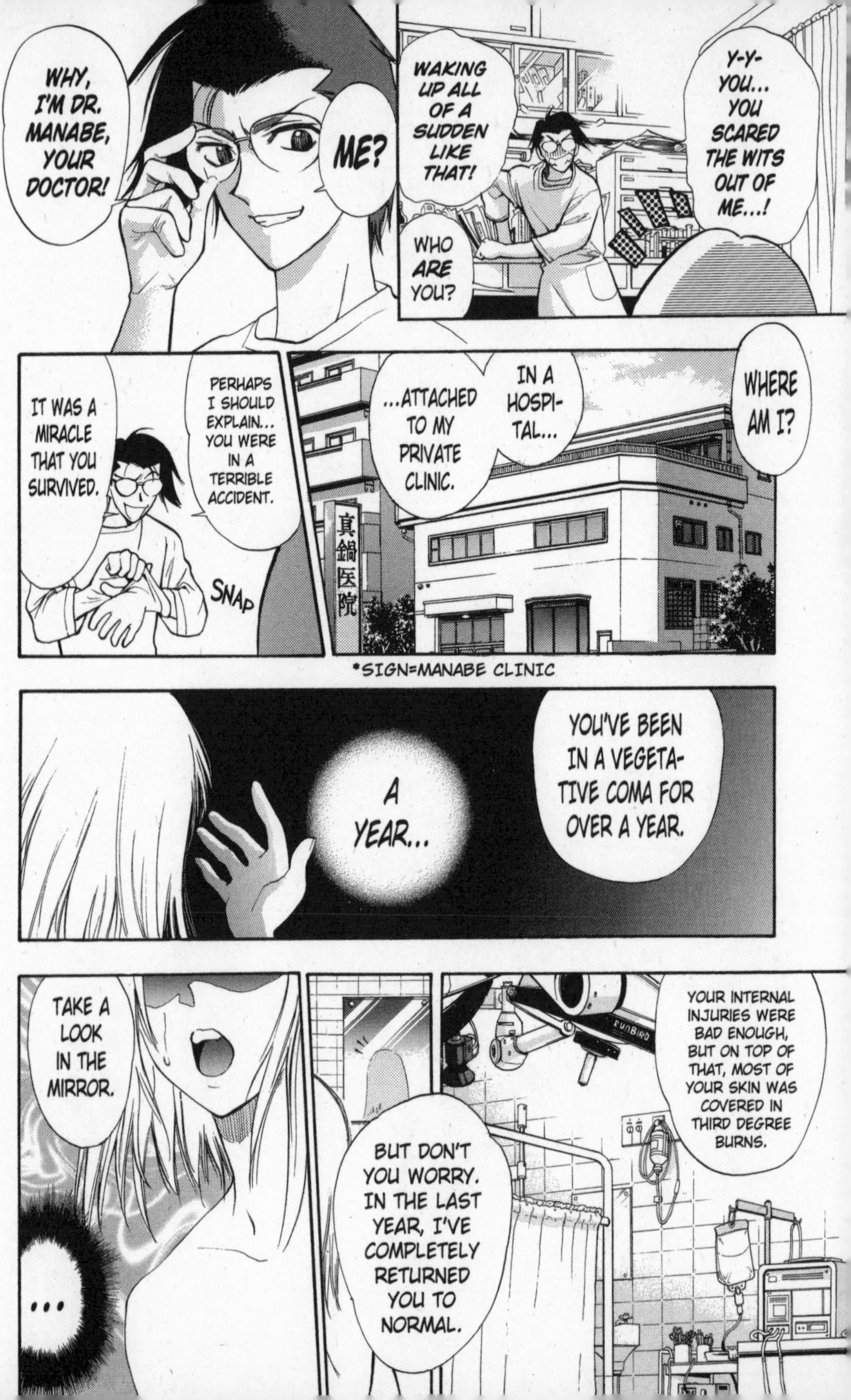
Y-Y-YOU... YOU SCARED THE WITS OUT OF ME...!
WAKING UP ALL OF A SUDDEN LIKE THAT!
WHO ARE YOU?
ME?
WHY, I'M DR. MANABE, YOUR DOCTOR!
WHERE AM I?
IN A HOSPITAL...
...ATTACHED TO MY PRIVATE CLINIC.
真鍋医院
PERHAPS I SHOULD EXPLAIN... YOU WERE IN A TERRIBLE ACCIDENT.
SNAP
IT WAS A MIRACLE THAT YOU SURVIVED.
*SIGN=MANABE CLINIC
YOU'VE BEEN IN A VEGETATIVE COMA FOR OVER A YEAR.
A YEAR...
YOUR INTERNAL INJURIES WERE BAD ENOUGH, BUT ON TOP OF THAT, MOST OF YOUR SKIN WAS COVERED IN THIRD DEGREE BURNS.
BUT DON'T YOU WORRY. IN THE LAST YEAR, I'VE COMPLETELY RETURNED YOU TO NORMAL.
TAKE A LOOK IN THE MIRROR.
...

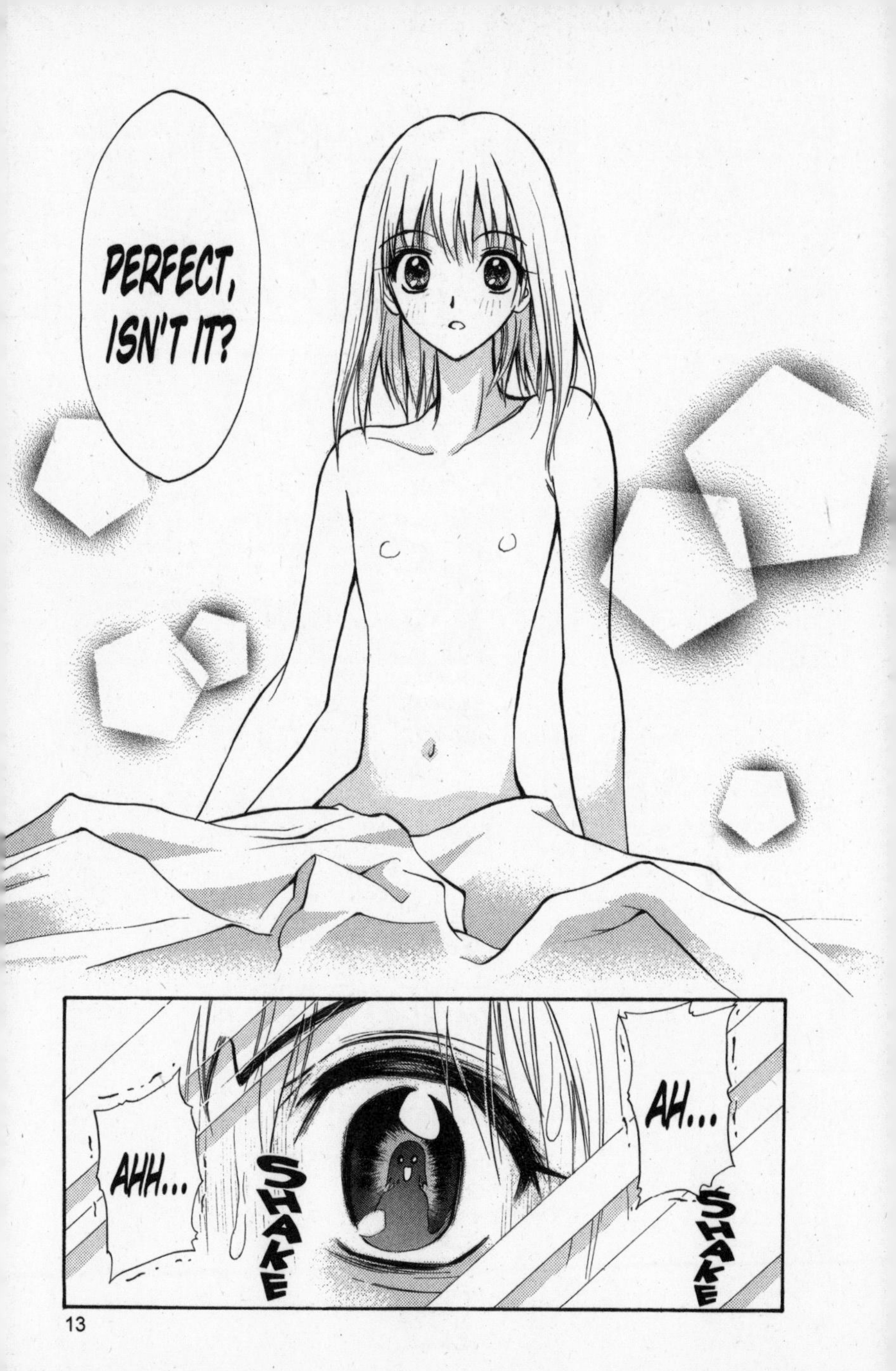
PERFECT, ISN'T IT?
AH...
SHAKE
SHAKE
AHH...

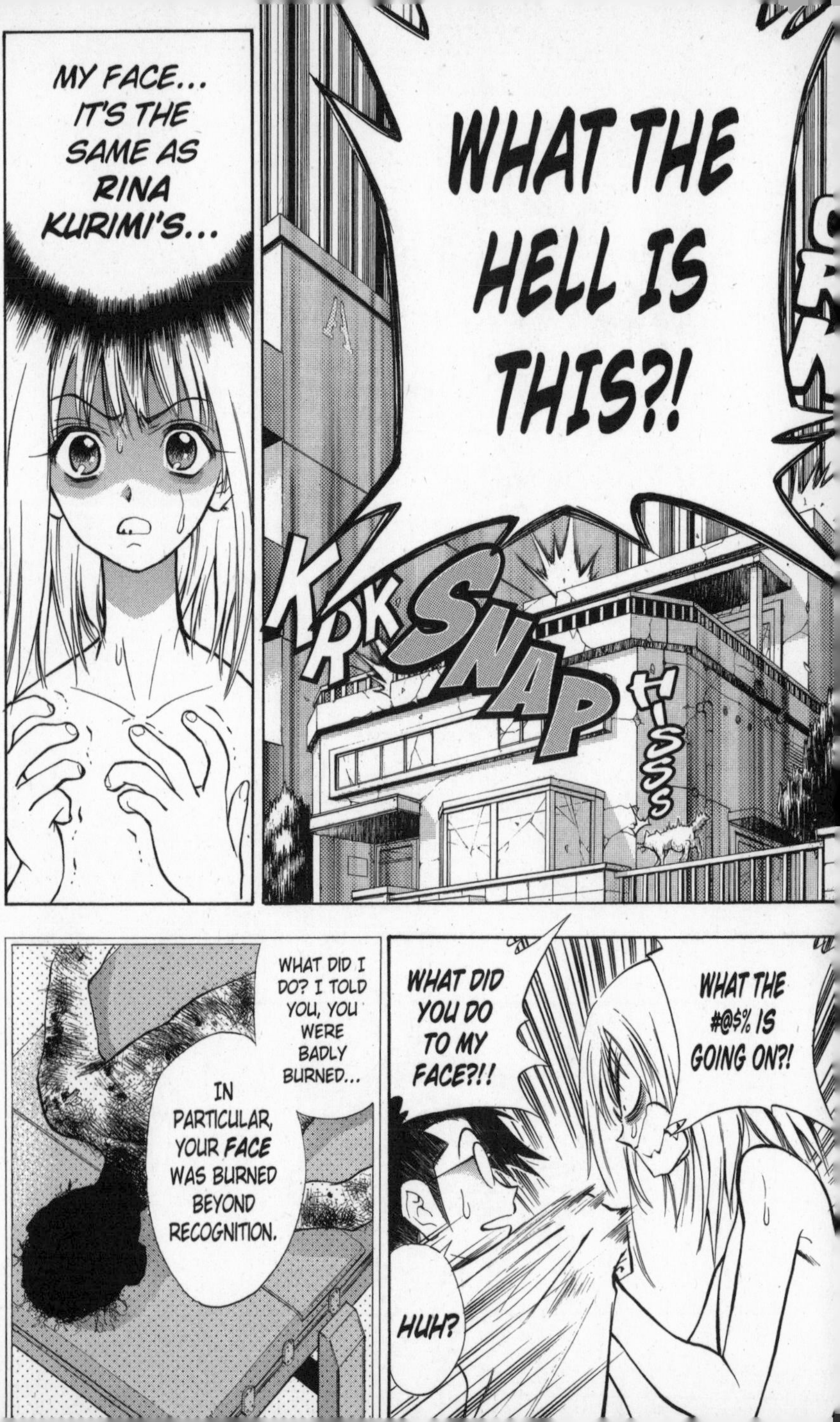
WHAT THE HELL IS THIS?!
KRKK
SNAP
HISSS
MY FACE… IT'S THE SAME AS RINA KURIMI'S…
WHAT THE #@$% IS GOING ON?!
WHAT DID YOU DO TO MY FACE?!!
HUH?
WHAT DID I DO? I TOLD YOU, YOU WERE BADLY BURNED…
IN PARTICULAR, YOUR FACE WAS BURNED BEYOND RECOGNITION.

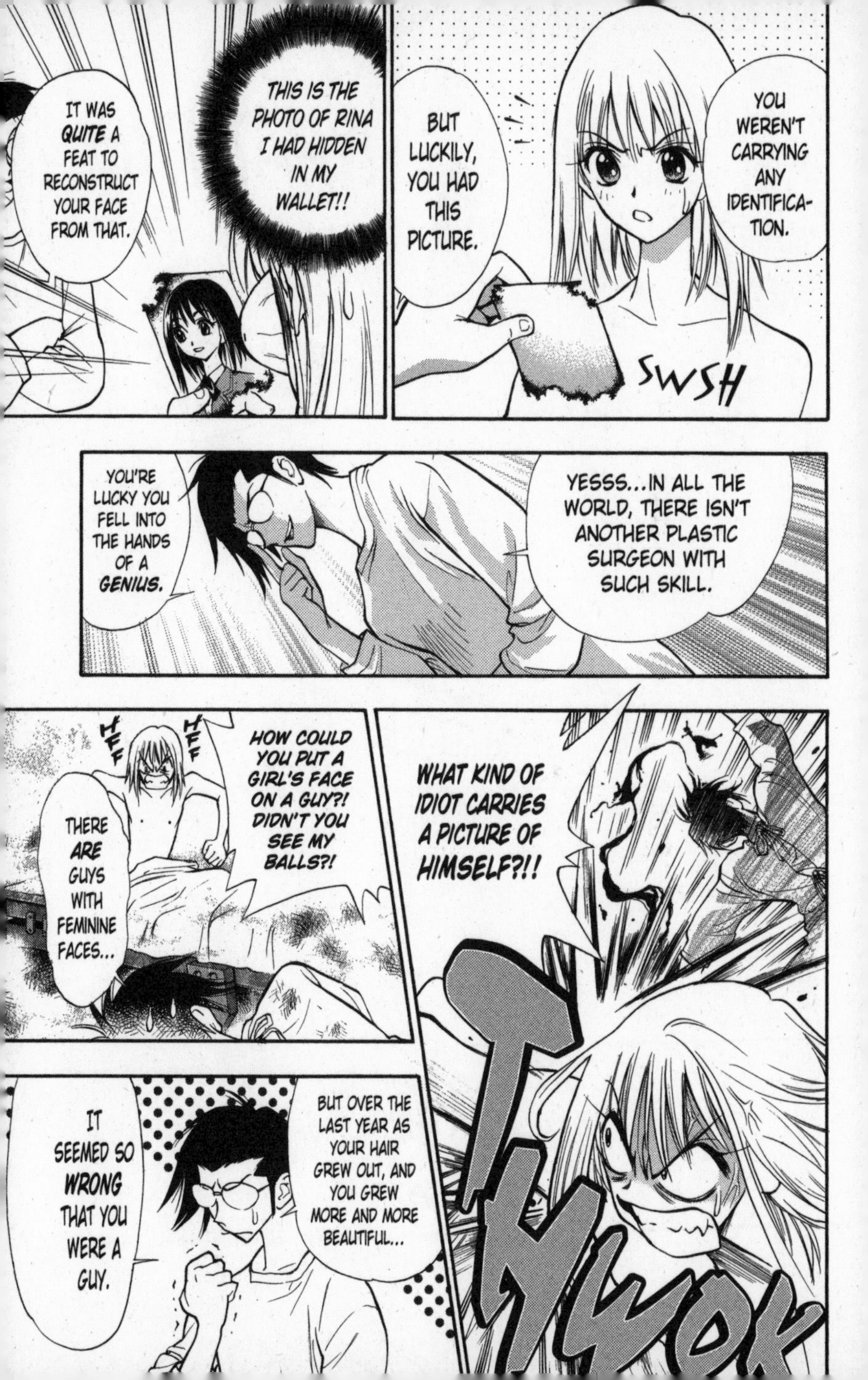
YOU WEREN'T CARRYING ANY IDENTIFICA-TION.
BUT LUCKILY, YOU HAD THIS PICTURE.
SWSH
THIS IS THE PHOTO OF RINA I HAD HIDDEN IN MY WALLET!!
IT WAS QUITE A FEAT TO RECONSTRUCT YOUR FACE FROM THAT.
YESSS...IN ALL THE WORLD, THERE ISN'T ANOTHER PLASTIC SURGEON WITH SUCH SKILL.
YOU'RE LUCKY YOU FELL INTO THE HANDS OF A GENIUS.
WHAT KIND OF IDIOT CARRIES A PICTURE OF HIMSELF?!!
THWOK
HFF HFF
HOW COULD YOU PUT A GIRL'S FACE ON A GUY?! DIDN'T YOU SEE MY BALLS?!
THERE ARE GUYS WITH FEMININE FACES...
BUT OVER THE LAST YEAR AS YOUR HAIR GREW OUT, AND YOU GREW MORE AND MORE BEAUTIFUL...
IT SEEMED SO WRONG THAT YOU WERE A GUY.

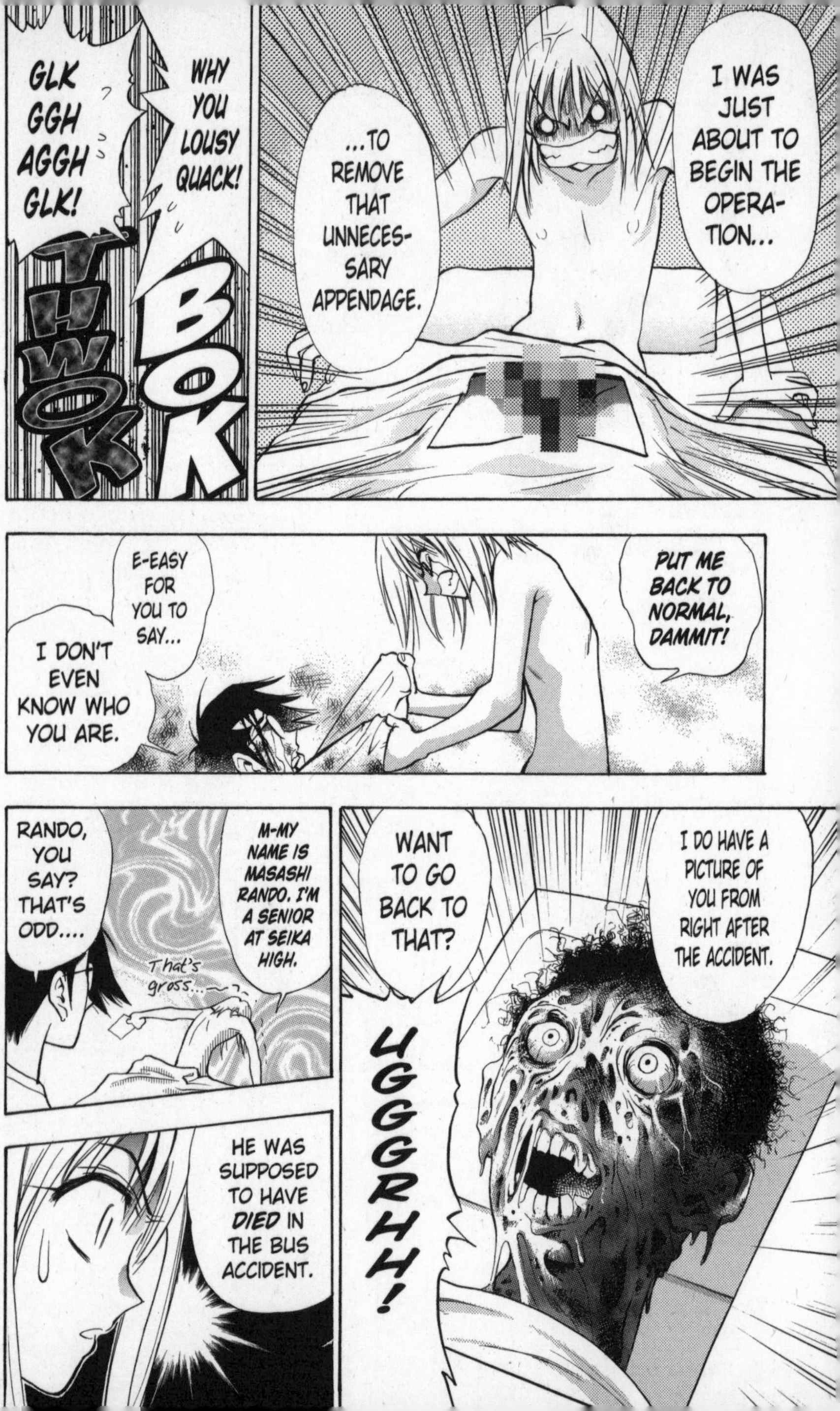
I WAS JUST ABOUT TO BEGIN THE OPERA-TION...
...TO REMOVE THAT UNNECES-SARY APPENDAGE.
WHY YOU LOUSY QUACK!
GLK GGH AGGH GLK!
BOK
THWOK
PUT ME BACK TO NORMAL, DAMMIT!
E-EASY FOR YOU TO SAY...
I DON'T EVEN KNOW WHO YOU ARE.
I DO HAVE A PICTURE OF YOU FROM RIGHT AFTER THE ACCIDENT.
WANT TO GO BACK TO THAT?
UGGGRHH!
M-MY NAME IS MASASHI RANDO. I'M A SENIOR AT SEIKA HIGH.
That's gross...
RANDO, YOU SAY? THAT'S ODD....
HE WAS SUPPOSED TO HAVE DIED IN THE BUS ACCIDENT.

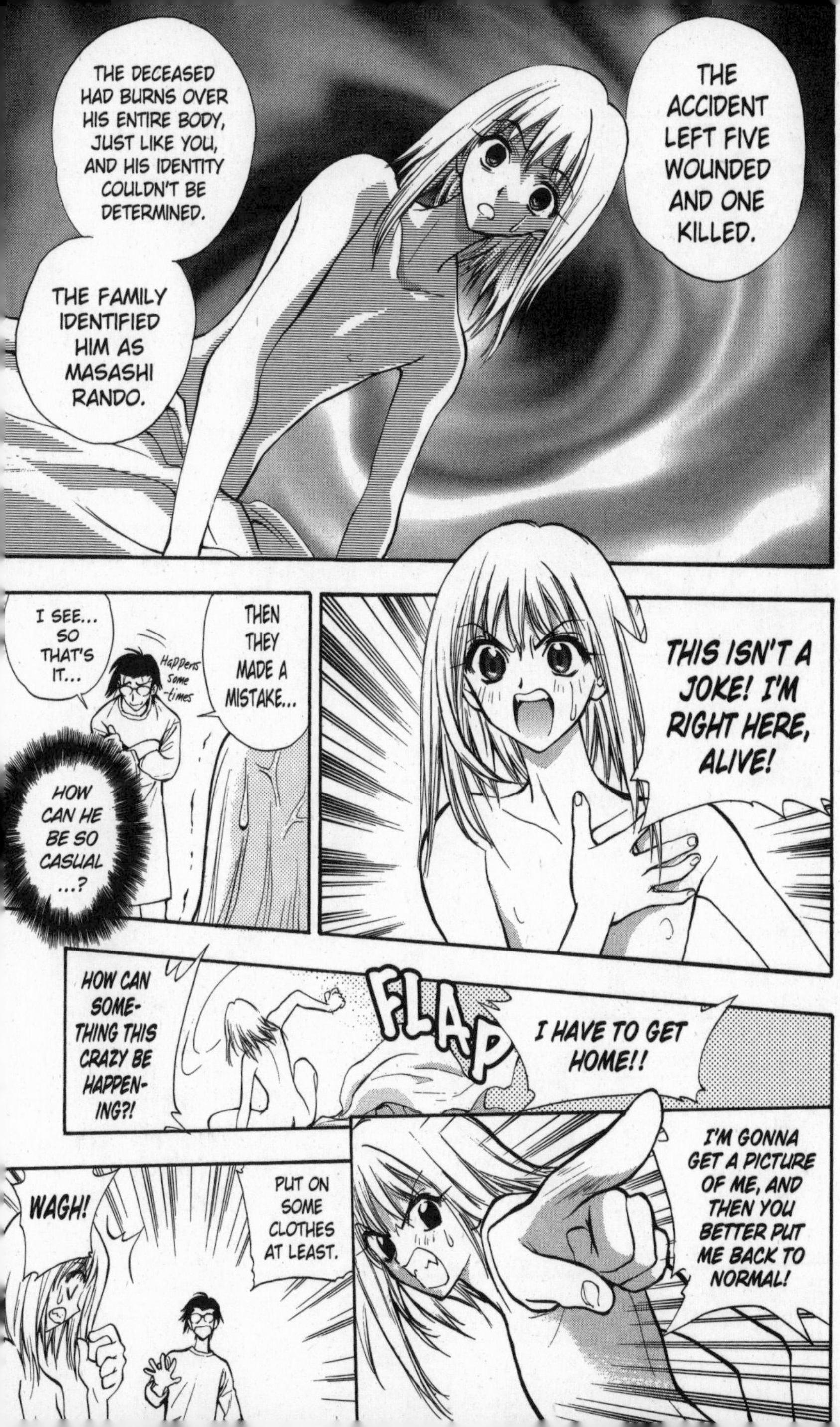
THE ACCIDENT LEFT FIVE WOUNDED AND ONE KILLED.
THE DECEASED HAD BURNS OVER HIS ENTIRE BODY, JUST LIKE YOU, AND HIS IDENTITY COULDN'T BE DETERMINED.
THE FAMILY IDENTIFIED HIM AS MASASHI RANDO.
THIS ISN'T A JOKE! I'M RIGHT HERE, ALIVE!
THEN THEY MADE A MISTAKE...
I SEE... SO THAT'S IT...
Happens some-times
HOW CAN HE BE SO CASUAL ...?
I HAVE TO GET HOME!!
FLAP
HOW CAN SOME-THING THIS CRAZY BE HAPPEN-ING?!
I'M GONNA GET A PICTURE OF ME, AND THEN YOU BETTER PUT ME BACK TO NORMAL!
PUT ON SOME CLOTHES AT LEAST.
WAGH!

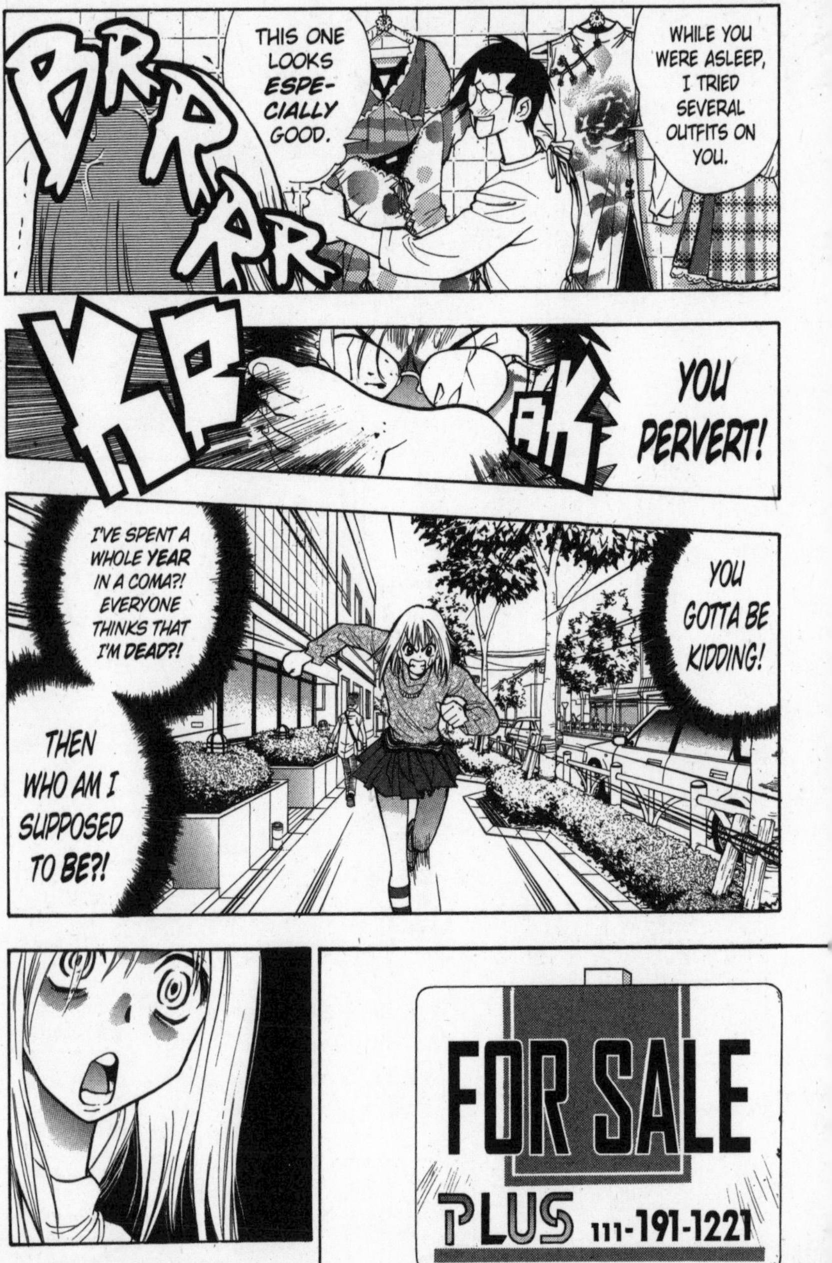
WHILE YOU WERE ASLEEP, I TRIED SEVERAL OUTFITS ON YOU.
THIS ONE LOOKS ESPECIALLY GOOD.
YOU PERVERT!
YOU GOTTA BE KIDDING!
I'VE SPENT A WHOLE YEAR IN A COMA?! EVERYONE THINKS THAT I'M DEAD?!
THEN WHO AM I SUPPOSED TO BE?!
FOR SALE
PLUS 111-191-1221

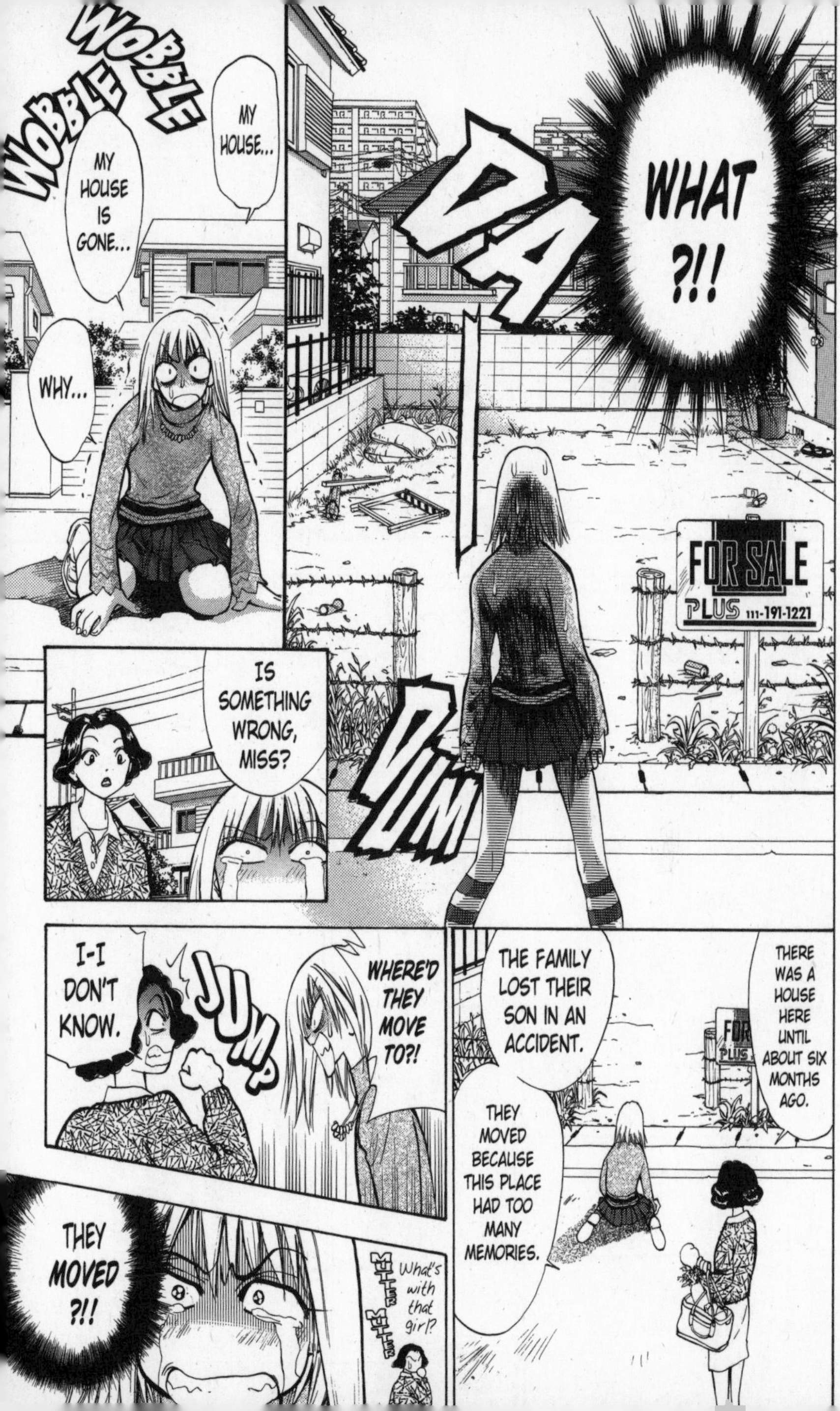
WHAT ?!!
DA
FOR SALE
PLUS 111-191-1221
DUM
MY HOUSE...
WOBBLE WOBBLE
MY HOUSE IS GONE...
WHY...
IS SOMETHING WRONG, MISS?
THERE WAS A HOUSE HERE UNTIL ABOUT SIX MONTHS AGO.
THE FAMILY LOST THEIR SON IN AN ACCIDENT.
THEY MOVED BECAUSE THIS PLACE HAD TOO MANY MEMORIES.
WHERE'D THEY MOVE TO?!
JUMP
I-I DON'T KNOW.
MUTTER MUTTER
What's with that girl!?
THEY MOVED ?!!

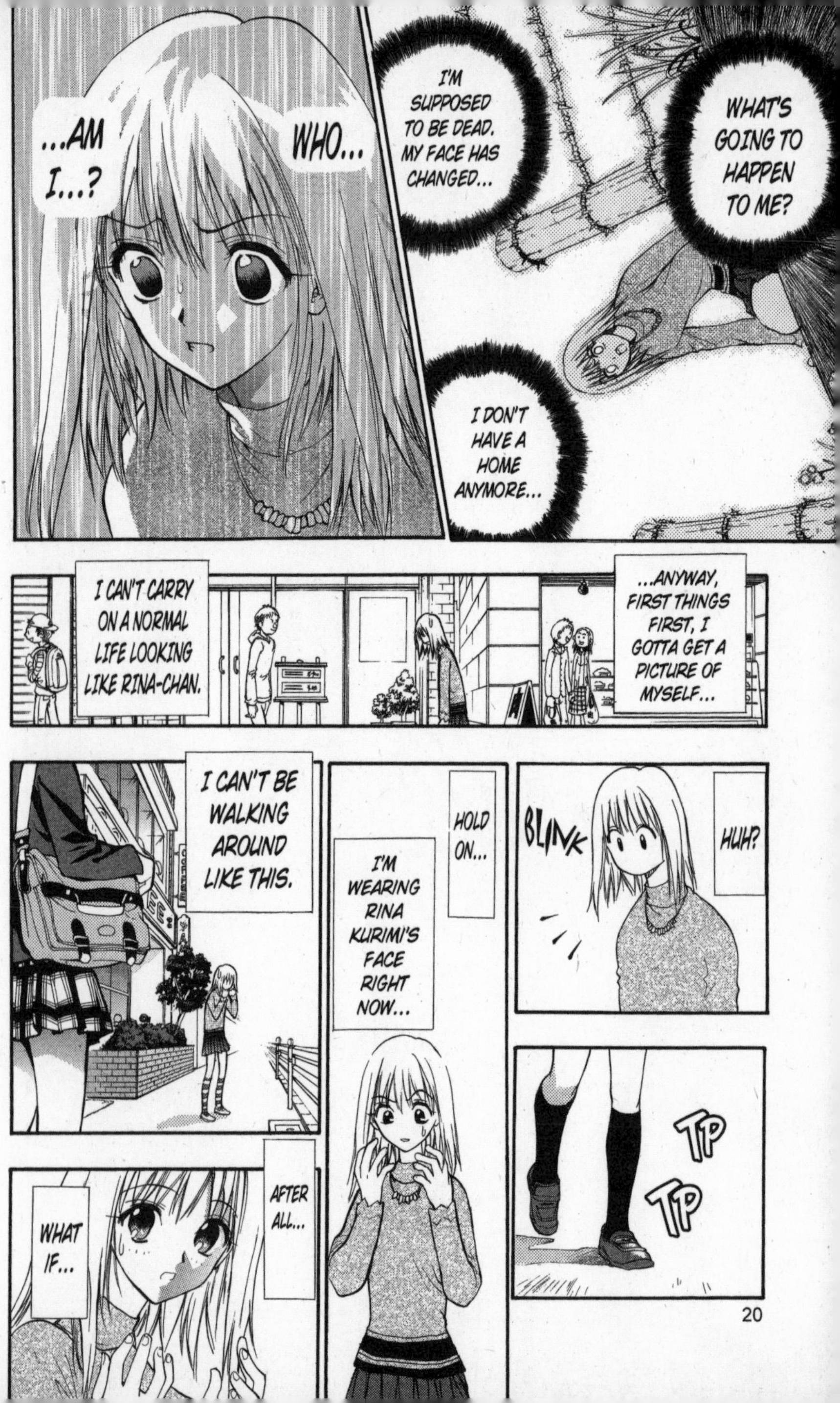
WHAT'S GOING TO HAPPEN TO ME?
I'M SUPPOSED TO BE DEAD. MY FACE HAS CHANGED...
I DON'T HAVE A HOME ANYMORE...
WHO...
...AM I...?
...ANYWAY, FIRST THINGS FIRST, I GOTTA GET A PICTURE OF MYSELF...
I CAN'T CARRY ON A NORMAL LIFE LOOKING LIKE RINA-CHAN.
HUH?
BLINK
TP
TP
HOLD ON...
I'M WEARING RINA KURIMI'S FACE RIGHT NOW...
I CAN'T BE WALKING AROUND LIKE THIS.
AFTER ALL...
WHAT IF...

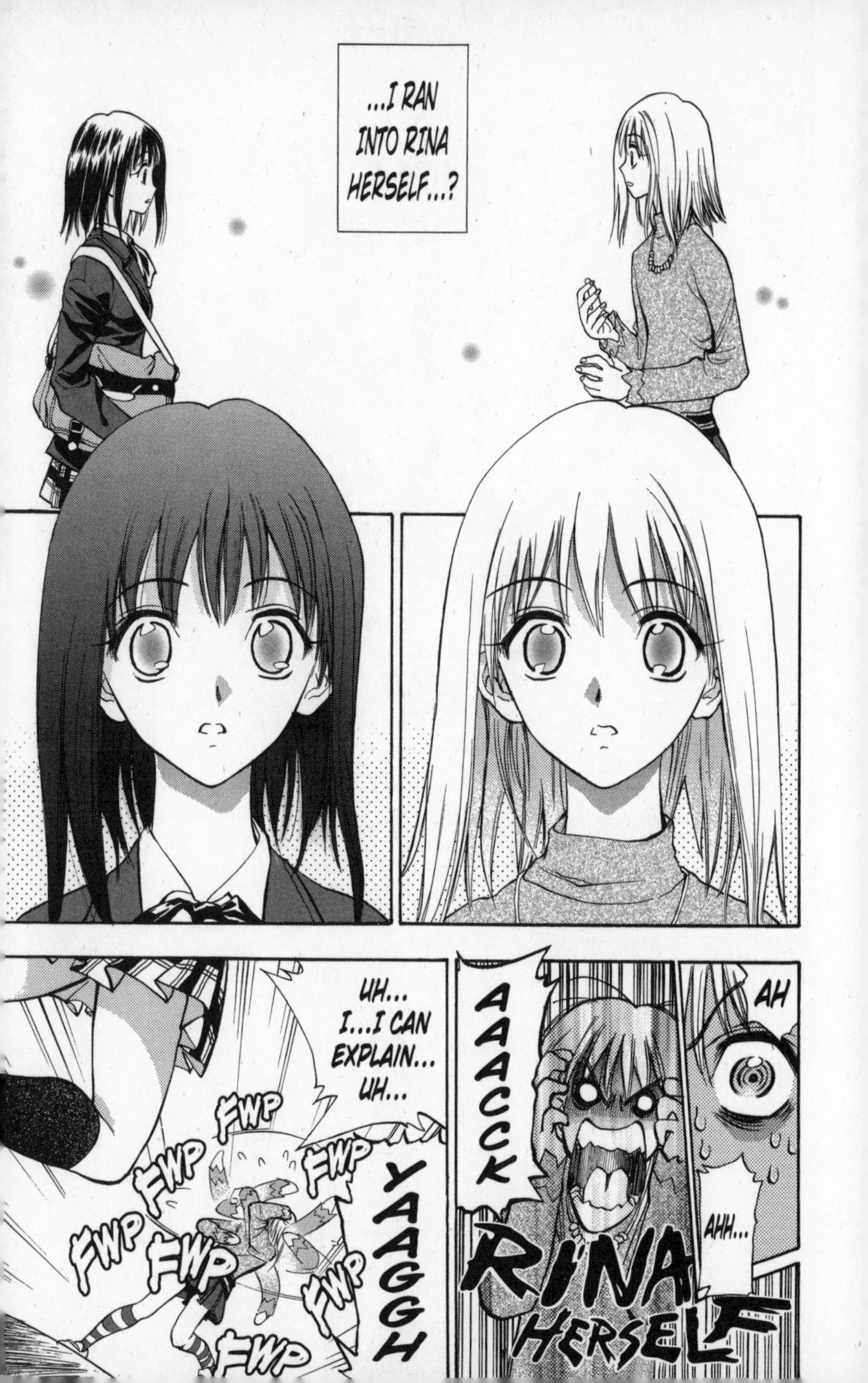
...I RAN INTO RINA HERSELF...?
AH
AHH...
AAAACCK
RINA HERSELF
UH... I...I CAN EXPLAIN... UH...
YAAAGGH
FWP FWP FWP FWP FWP FWP FWP FWP FWP

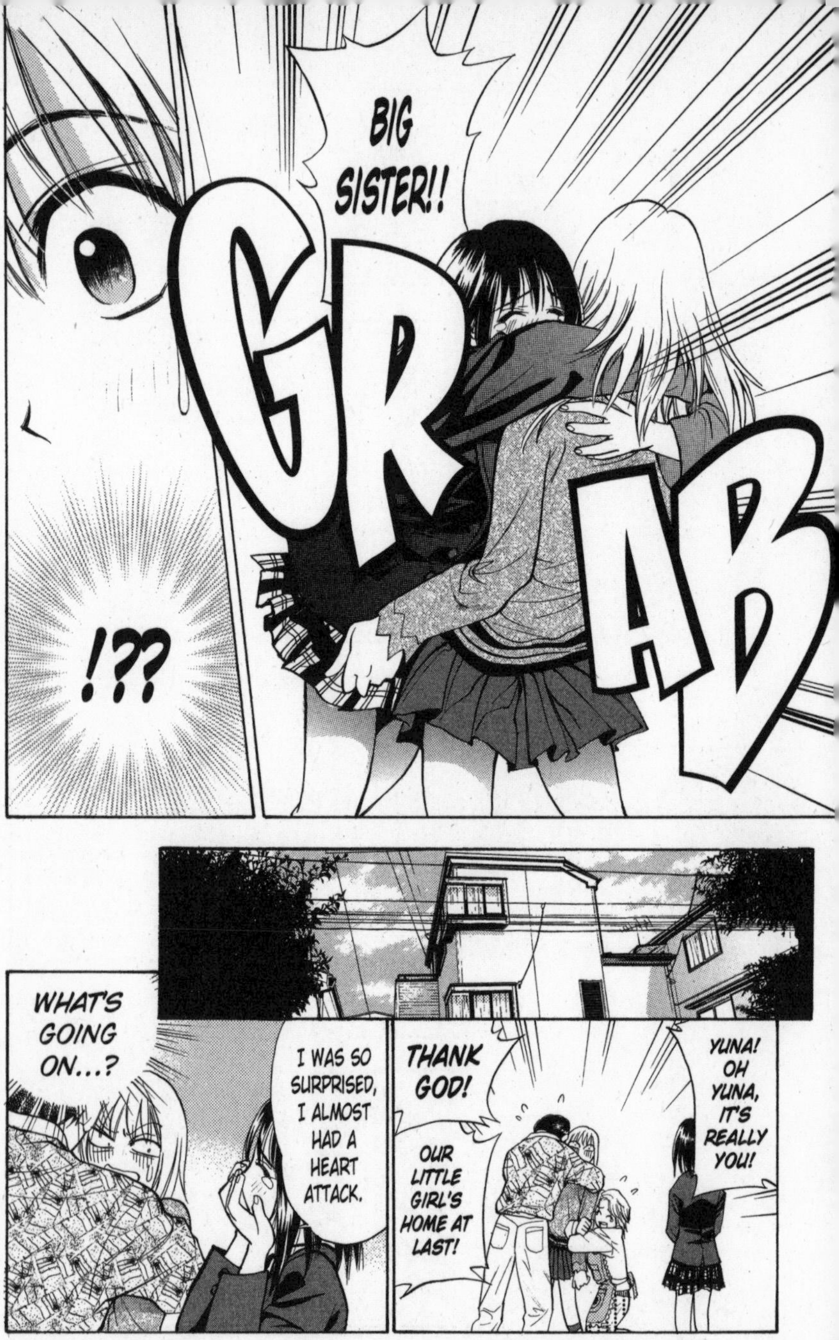
BIG SISTER!!
GRAB
!??
YUNA! OH YUNA, IT'S REALLY YOU!
THANK GOD!
OUR LITTLE GIRL'S HOME AT LAST!
I WAS SO SURPRISED, I ALMOST HAD A HEART ATTACK.
WHAT'S GOING ON...?

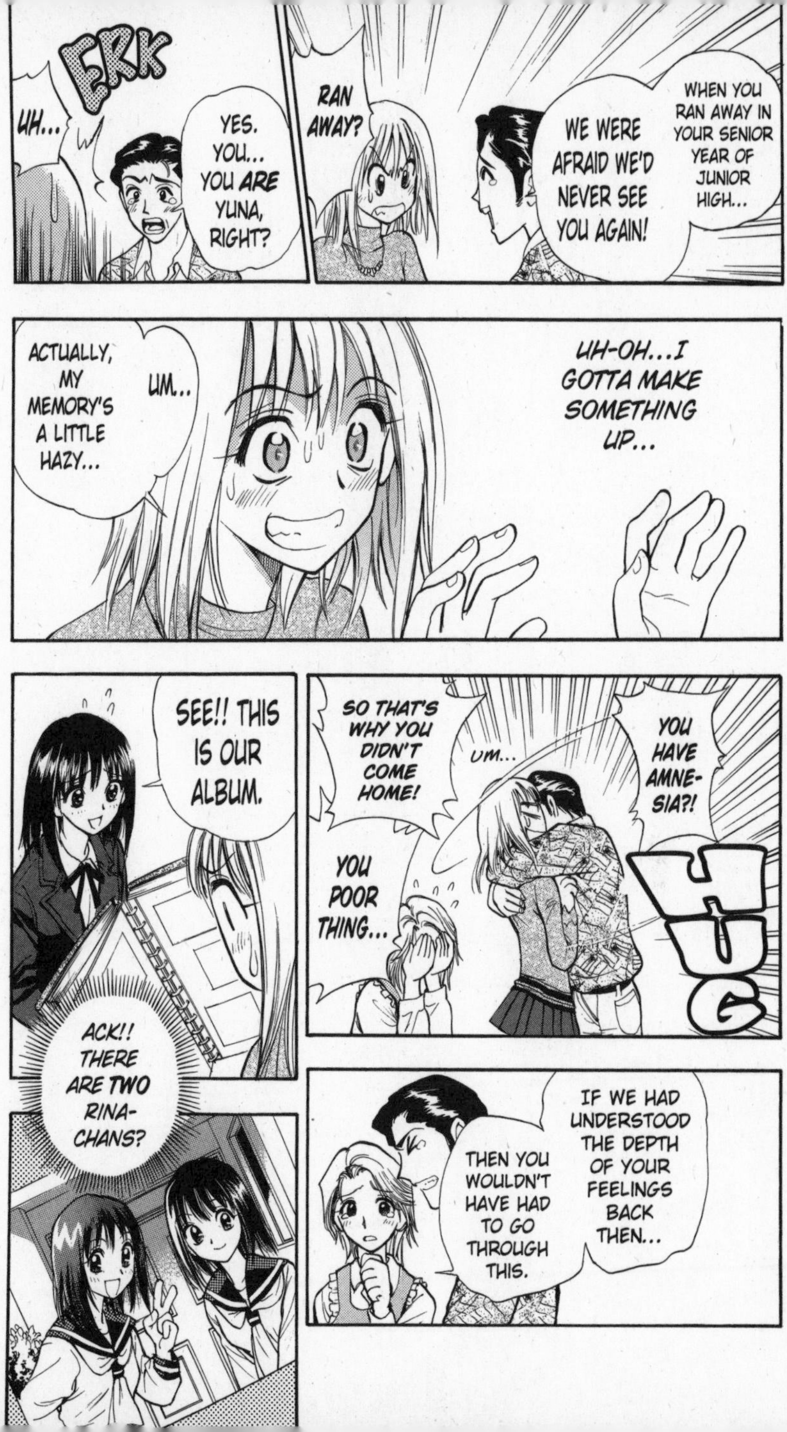
WHEN YOU RAN AWAY IN YOUR SENIOR YEAR OF JUNIOR HIGH...
WE WERE AFRAID WE'D NEVER SEE YOU AGAIN!
RAN AWAY?
ERK
YES. YOU... YOU ARE YUNA, RIGHT?
UH...
UH-OH...I GOTTA MAKE SOMETHING UP...
UM...
ACTUALLY, MY MEMORY'S A LITTLE HAZY...
YOU HAVE AMNESIA?!
HUG
UM...
SO THAT'S WHY YOU DIDN'T COME HOME!
YOU POOR THING...
IF WE HAD UNDERSTOOD THE DEPTH OF YOUR FEELINGS BACK THEN...
THEN YOU WOULDN'T HAVE HAD TO GO THROUGH THIS.
SEE!! THIS IS OUR ALBUM.
ACK!! THERE ARE TWO RINA-CHANS?

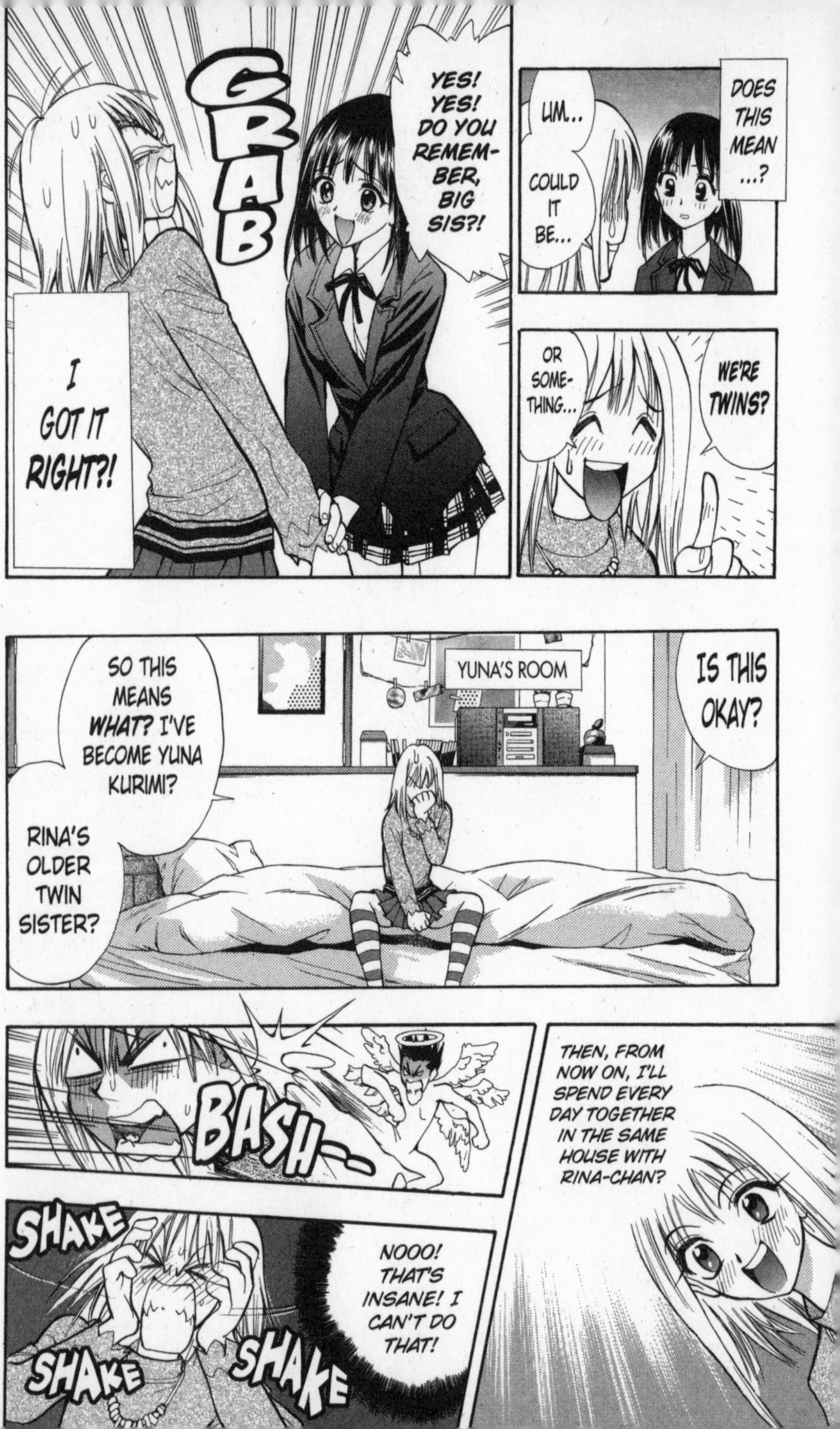
DOES THIS MEAN ...?
UM...
COULD IT BE...
WE'RE TWINS?
OR SOME-THING...
YES! YES! DO YOU REMEM-BER, BIG SIS?!
GRAB
I GOT IT RIGHT?!
IS THIS OKAY?
YUNA'S ROOM
SO THIS MEANS WHAT? I'VE BECOME YUNA KURIMI?
RINA'S OLDER TWIN SISTER?
THEN, FROM NOW ON, I'LL SPEND EVERY DAY TOGETHER IN THE SAME HOUSE WITH RINA-CHAN?
BASH--
SHAKE
NOOO! THAT'S INSANE! I CAN'T DO THAT!
SHAKE
SHAKE

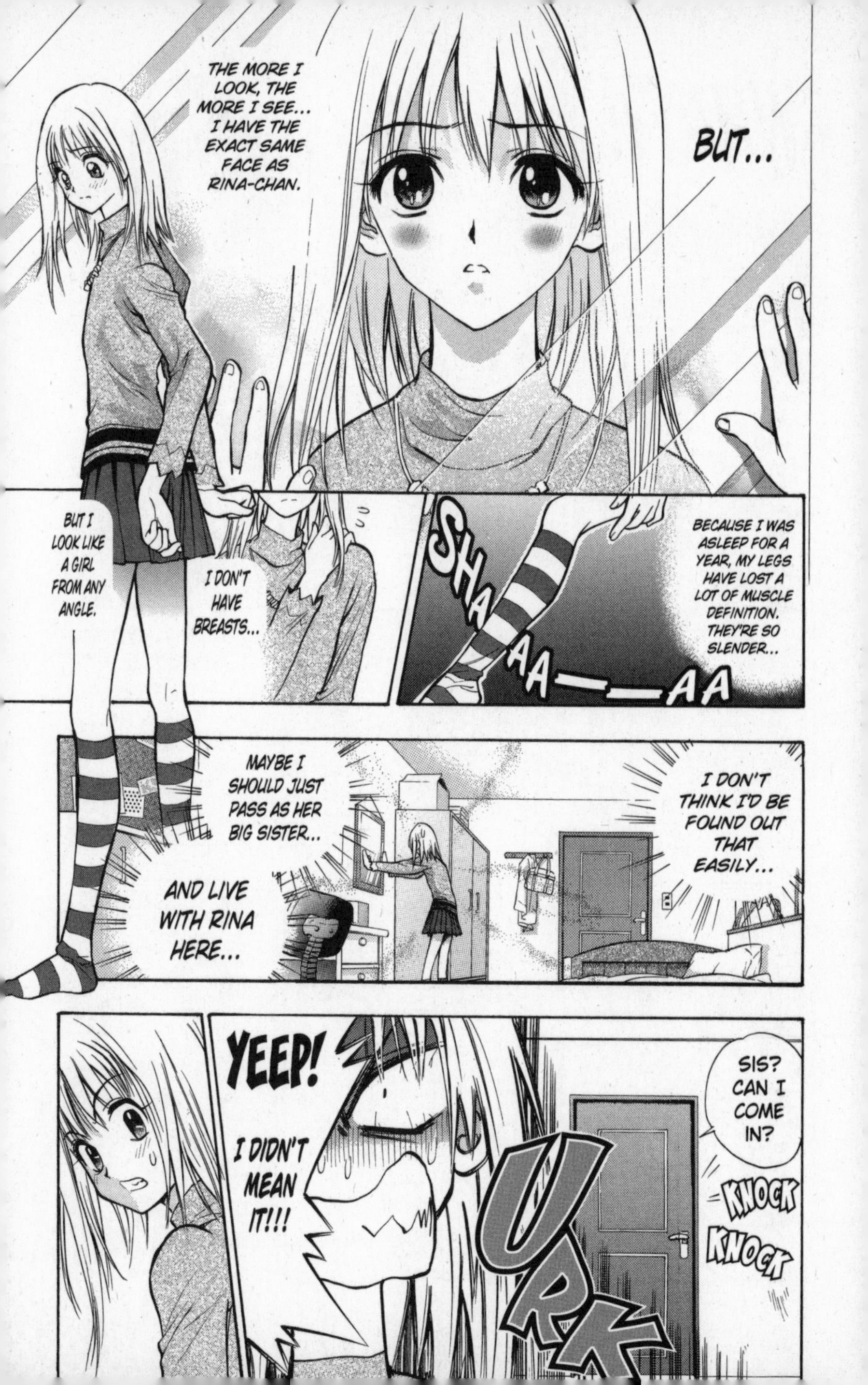
THE MORE I LOOK, THE MORE I SEE... I HAVE THE EXACT SAME FACE AS RINA-CHAN.
BUT...
SHAAA———AA
BECAUSE I WAS ASLEEP FOR A YEAR, MY LEGS HAVE LOST A LOT OF MUSCLE DEFINITION. THEY'RE SO SLENDER...
I DON'T HAVE BREASTS...
BUT I LOOK LIKE A GIRL FROM ANY ANGLE.
I DON'T THINK I'D BE FOUND OUT THAT EASILY...
MAYBE I SHOULD JUST PASS AS HER BIG SISTER...
AND LIVE WITH RINA HERE...
SIS? CAN I COME IN?
KNOCK
KNOCK
URK
YEEP!
I DIDN'T MEAN IT!!!

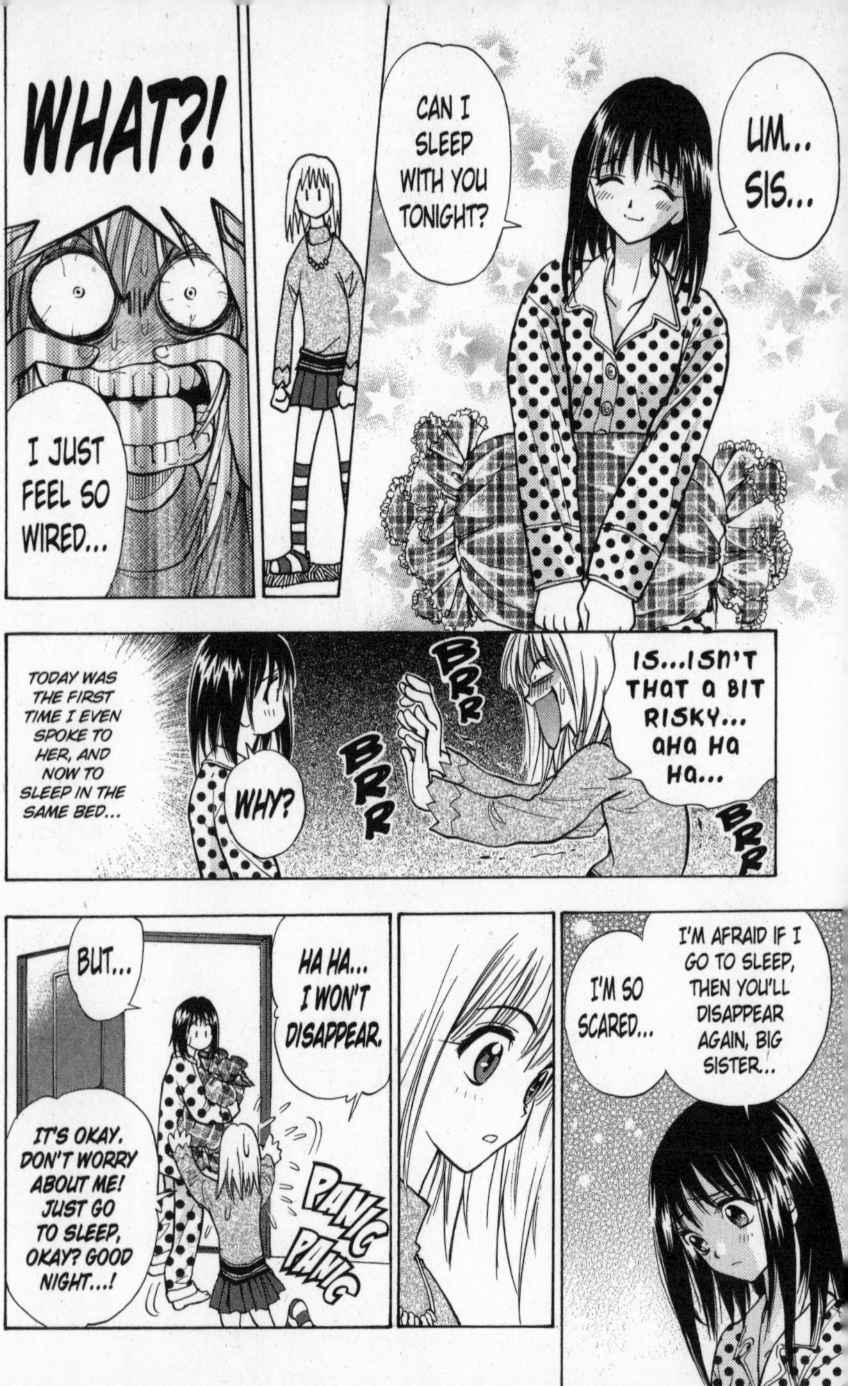
UM... SIS...
CAN I SLEEP WITH YOU TONIGHT?
WHAT?!
I JUST FEEL SO WIRED...
IS...ISN'T THAT A BIT RISKY... AHA HA HA...
BRR
BRR
BRR
WHY?
TODAY WAS THE FIRST TIME I EVEN SPOKE TO HER, AND NOW TO SLEEP IN THE SAME BED...
I'M AFRAID IF I GO TO SLEEP, THEN YOU'LL DISAPPEAR AGAIN, BIG SISTER...
I'M SO SCARED...
HA HA... I WON'T DISAPPEAR.
BUT...
PANIC PANIC
IT'S OKAY. DON'T WORRY ABOUT ME! JUST GO TO SLEEP, OKAY? GOOD NIGHT...!

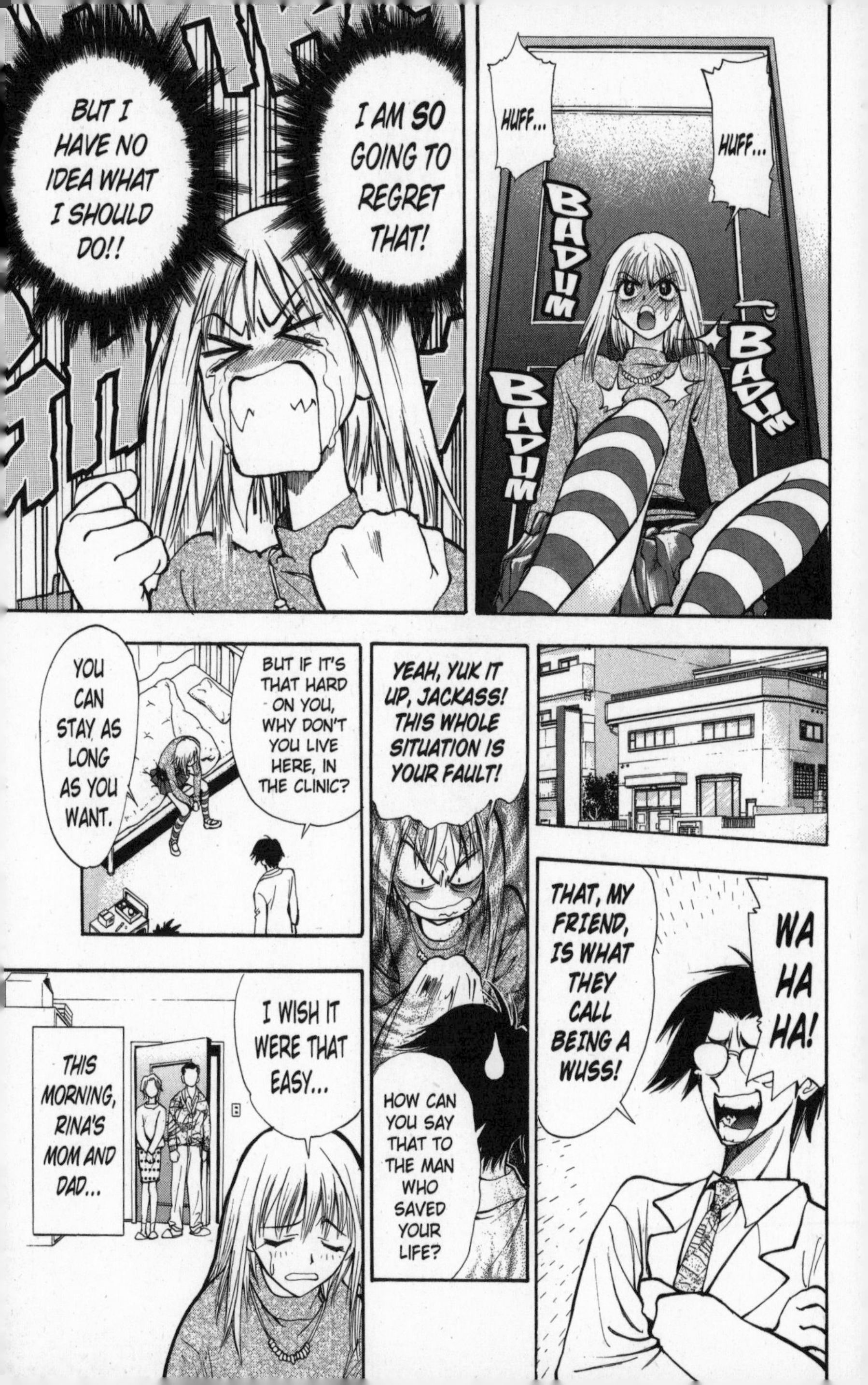
HUFF...
HUFF...
BADUM
BADUM
BADUM
I AM SO GOING TO REGRET THAT!
BUT I HAVE NO IDEA WHAT I SHOULD DO!!
WA HA HA!
THAT, MY FRIEND, IS WHAT THEY CALL BEING A WUSS!
YEAH, YUK IT UP, JACKASS! THIS WHOLE SITUATION IS YOUR FAULT!
HOW CAN YOU SAY THAT TO THE MAN WHO SAVED YOUR LIFE?
BUT IF IT'S THAT HARD ON YOU, WHY DON'T YOU LIVE HERE, IN THE CLINIC?
YOU CAN STAY AS LONG AS YOU WANT.
I WISH IT WERE THAT EASY...
THIS MORNING, RINA'S MOM AND DAD...

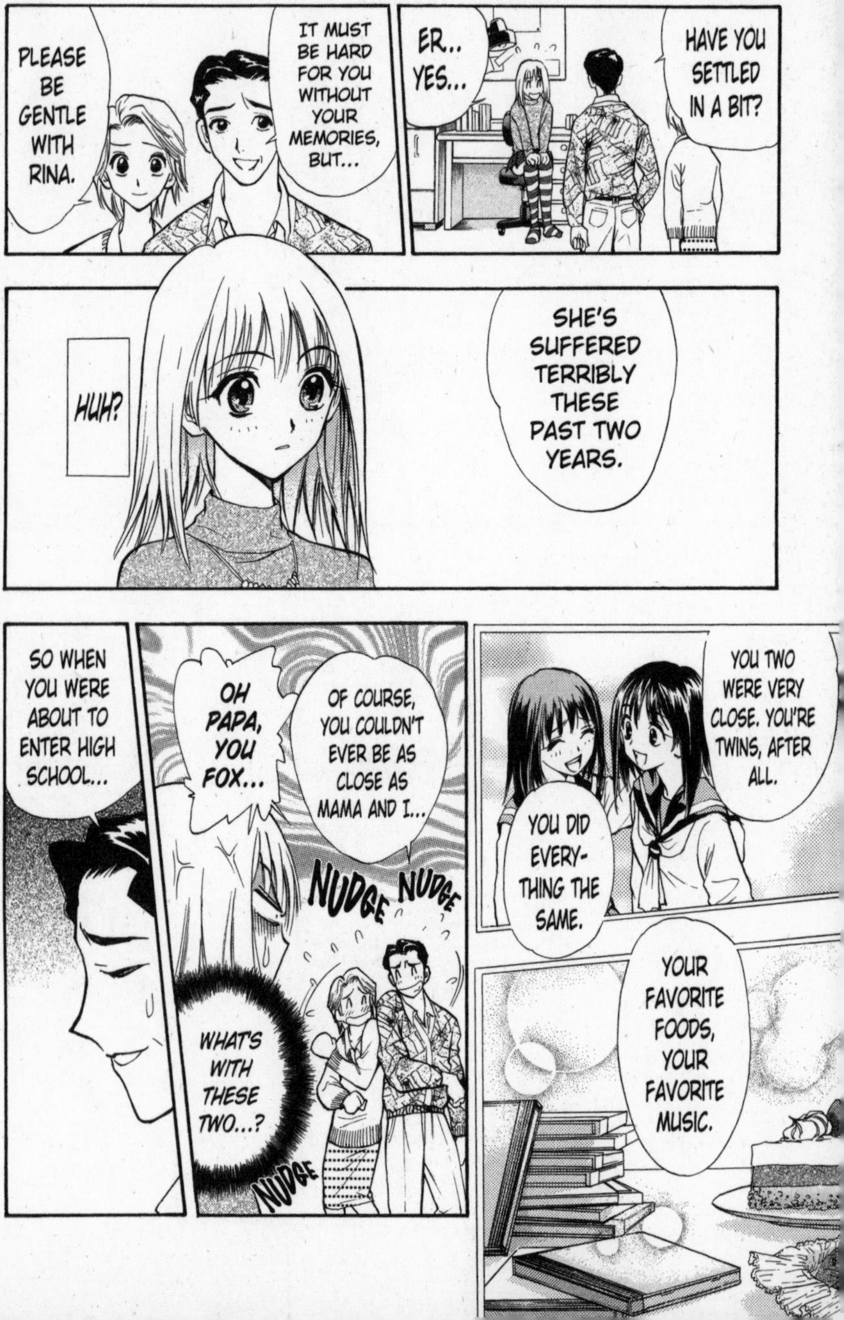
HAVE YOU SETTLED IN A BIT?
ER... YES...
IT MUST BE HARD FOR YOU WITHOUT YOUR MEMORIES, BUT...
PLEASE BE GENTLE WITH RINA.
SHE'S SUFFERED TERRIBLY THESE PAST TWO YEARS.
HUH?
YOU TWO WERE VERY CLOSE. YOU'RE TWINS, AFTER ALL.
YOU DID EVERY-THING THE SAME.
YOUR FAVORITE FOODS, YOUR FAVORITE MUSIC.
OF COURSE, YOU COULDN'T EVER BE AS CLOSE AS MAMA AND I...
OH PAPA, YOU FOX...
NUDGE NUDGE
WHAT'S WITH THESE TWO...?
NUDGE
SO WHEN YOU WERE ABOUT TO ENTER HIGH SCHOOL...

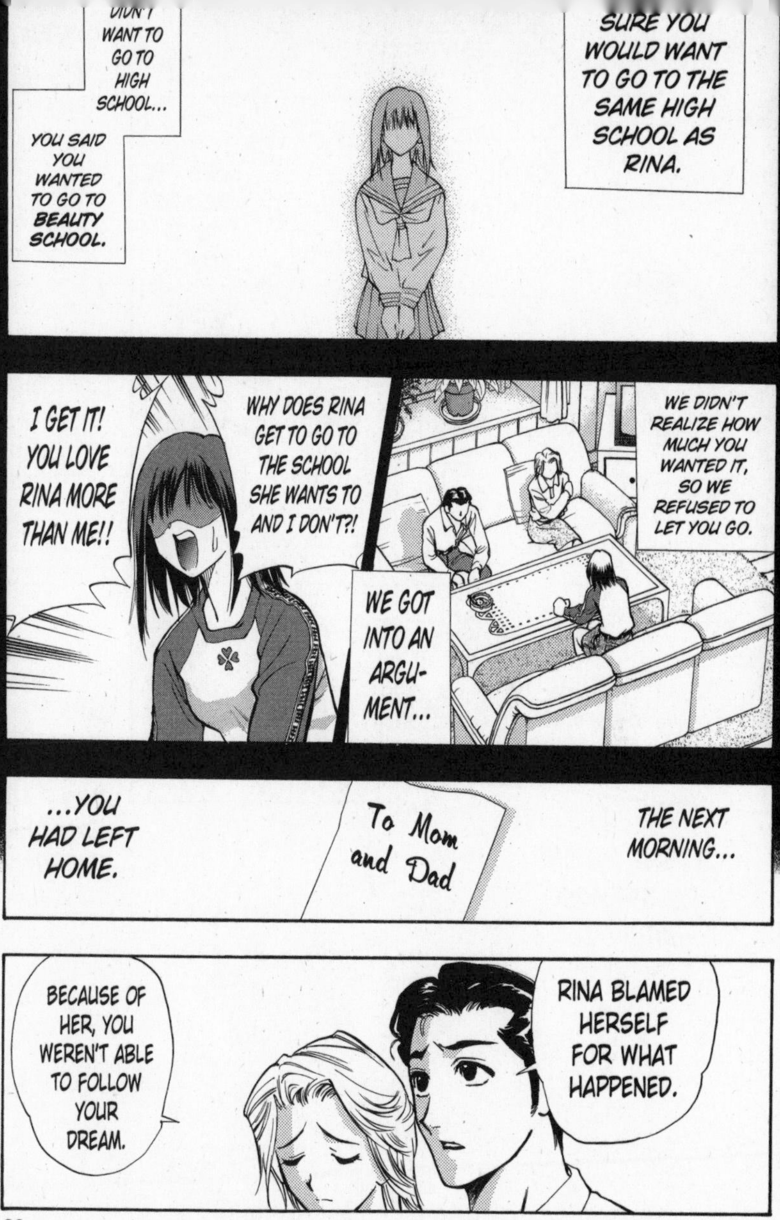
SURE YOU WOULD WANT TO GO TO THE SAME HIGH SCHOOL AS RINA.
WANT TO GO TO HIGH SCHOOL...
YOU SAID YOU WANTED TO GO TO BEAUTY SCHOOL.
WE DIDN'T REALIZE HOW MUCH YOU WANTED IT, SO WE REFUSED TO LET YOU GO.
WE GOT INTO AN ARGUMENT...
WHY DOES RINA GET TO GO TO THE SCHOOL SHE WANTS TO AND I DON'T?!
I GET IT! YOU LOVE RINA MORE THAN ME!!
THE NEXT MORNING...
To Mom and Dad
...YOU HAD LEFT HOME.
RINA BLAMED HERSELF FOR WHAT HAPPENED.
BECAUSE OF HER, YOU WEREN'T ABLE TO FOLLOW YOUR DREAM.

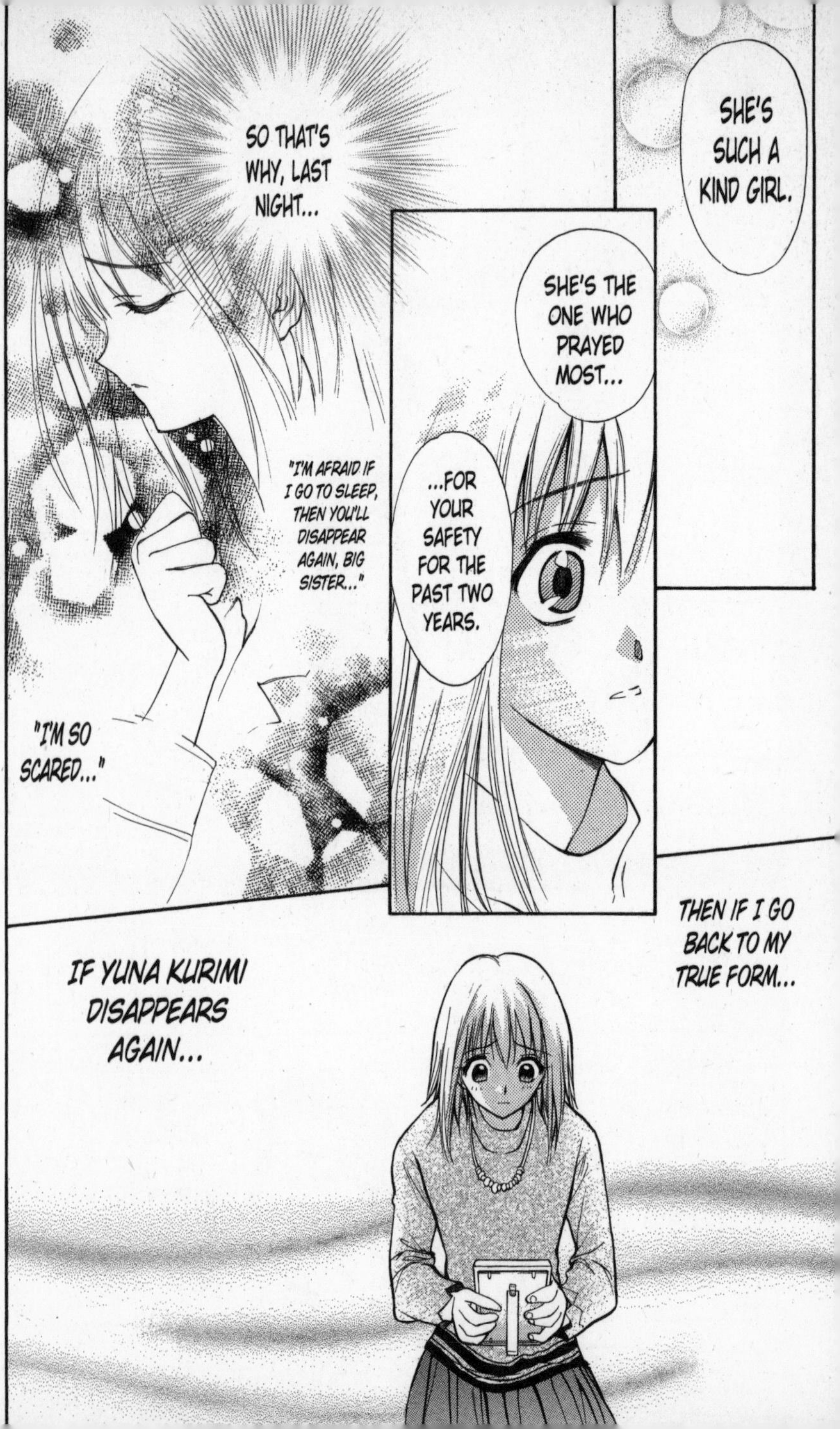
SHE'S SUCH A KIND GIRL.
SHE'S THE ONE WHO PRAYED MOST...
...FOR YOUR SAFETY FOR THE PAST TWO YEARS.
SO THAT'S WHY, LAST NIGHT...
"I'M AFRAID IF I GO TO SLEEP, THEN YOU'LL DISAPPEAR AGAIN, BIG SISTER..."
"I'M SO SCARED..."
THEN IF I GO BACK TO MY TRUE FORM...
IF YUNA KURIMI DISAPPEARS AGAIN...

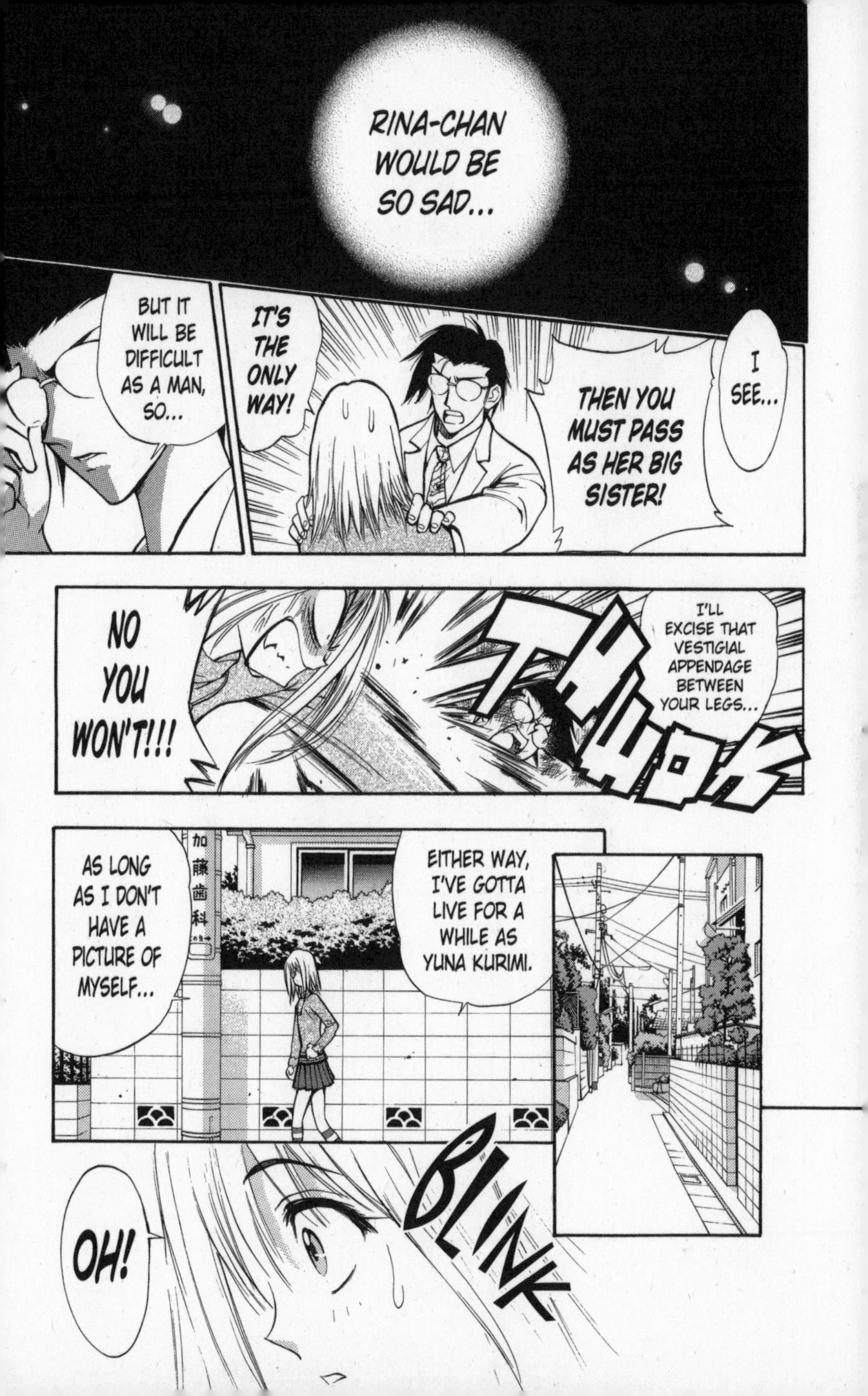
RINA-CHAN WOULD BE SO SAD...
I SEE...
THEN YOU MUST PASS AS HER BIG SISTER!
IT'S THE ONLY WAY!
BUT IT WILL BE DIFFICULT AS A MAN, SO...
I'LL EXCISE THAT VESTIGIAL APPENDAGE BETWEEN YOUR LEGS...
THWACK
NO YOU WON'T!!!
EITHER WAY, I'VE GOTTA LIVE FOR A WHILE AS YUNA KURIMI.
加藤歯科
AS LONG AS I DON'T HAVE A PICTURE OF MYSELF...
BLINK
OH!

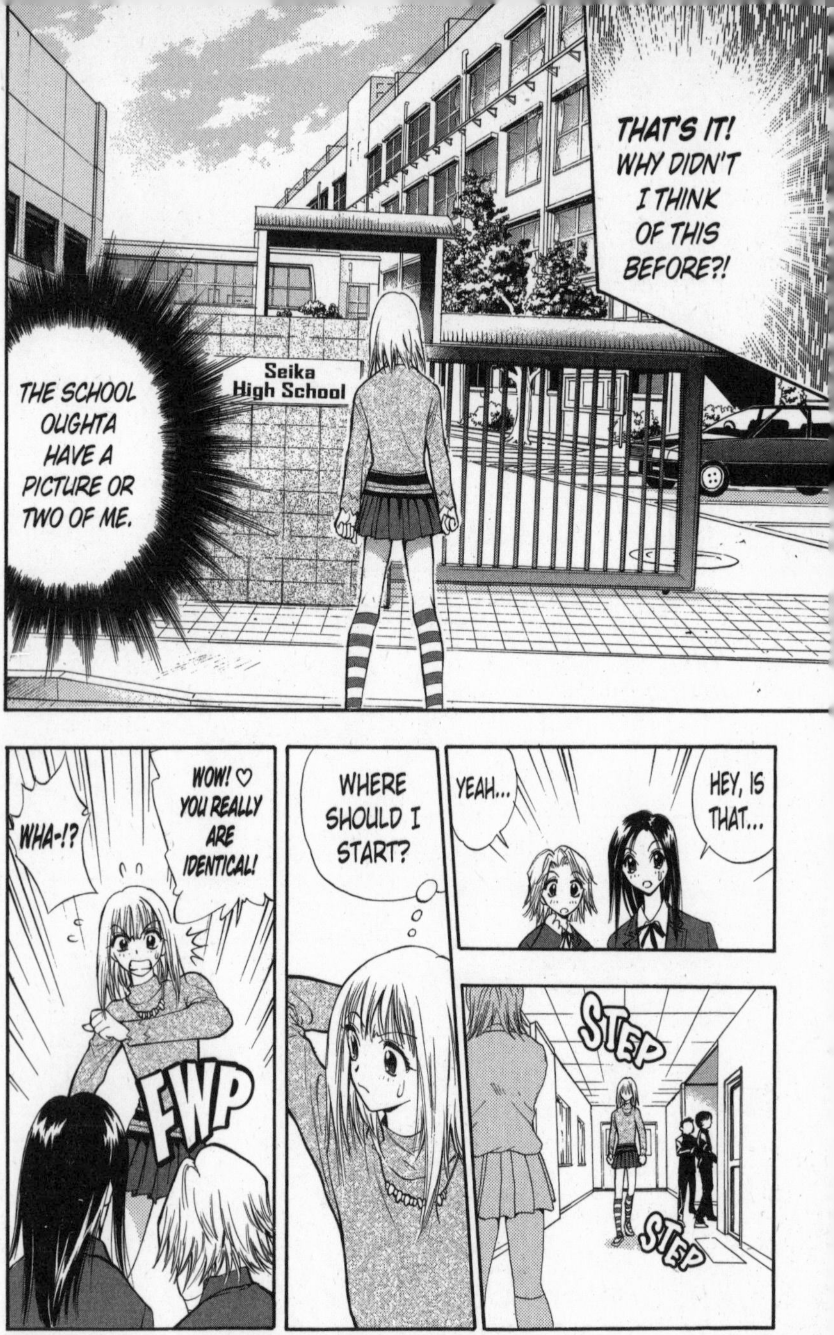
THAT'S IT! WHY DIDN'T I THINK OF THIS BEFORE?!
Seika High School
THE SCHOOL OUGHTA HAVE A PICTURE OR TWO OF ME.
HEY, IS THAT...
YEAH...
STEP
STEP
WHERE SHOULD I START?
WOW! ♡ YOU REALLY ARE IDENTICAL!
WHA-!?
FWP

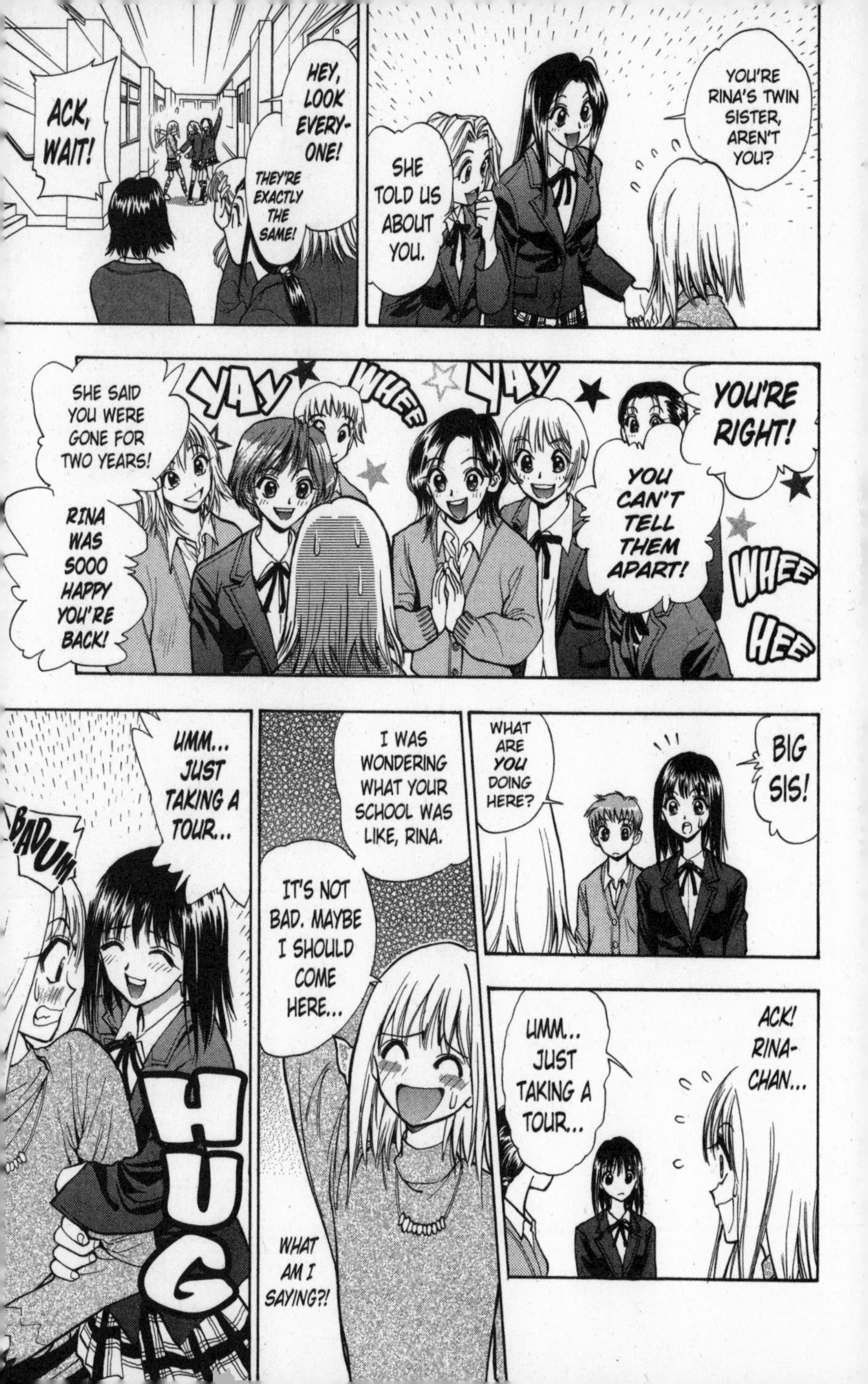

YOU'RE RINA'S TWIN SISTER, AREN'T YOU?
SHE TOLD US ABOUT YOU.
HEY, LOOK EVERYONE!
THEY'RE EXACTLY THE SAME!
ACK, WAIT!
YOU'RE RIGHT!
YAY
WHEE
YAY
YOU CAN'T TELL THEM APART!
WHEE
HEE
SHE SAID YOU WERE GONE FOR TWO YEARS!
RINA WAS SOOO HAPPY YOU'RE BACK!
BIG SIS!
WHAT ARE YOU DOING HERE?
ACK! RINA-CHAN...
UMM... JUST TAKING A TOUR...
I WAS WONDERING WHAT YOUR SCHOOL WAS LIKE, RINA.
IT'S NOT BAD. MAYBE I SHOULD COME HERE...
WHAT AM I SAYING?!
UMM... JUST TAKING A TOUR...
BADUM
HUG

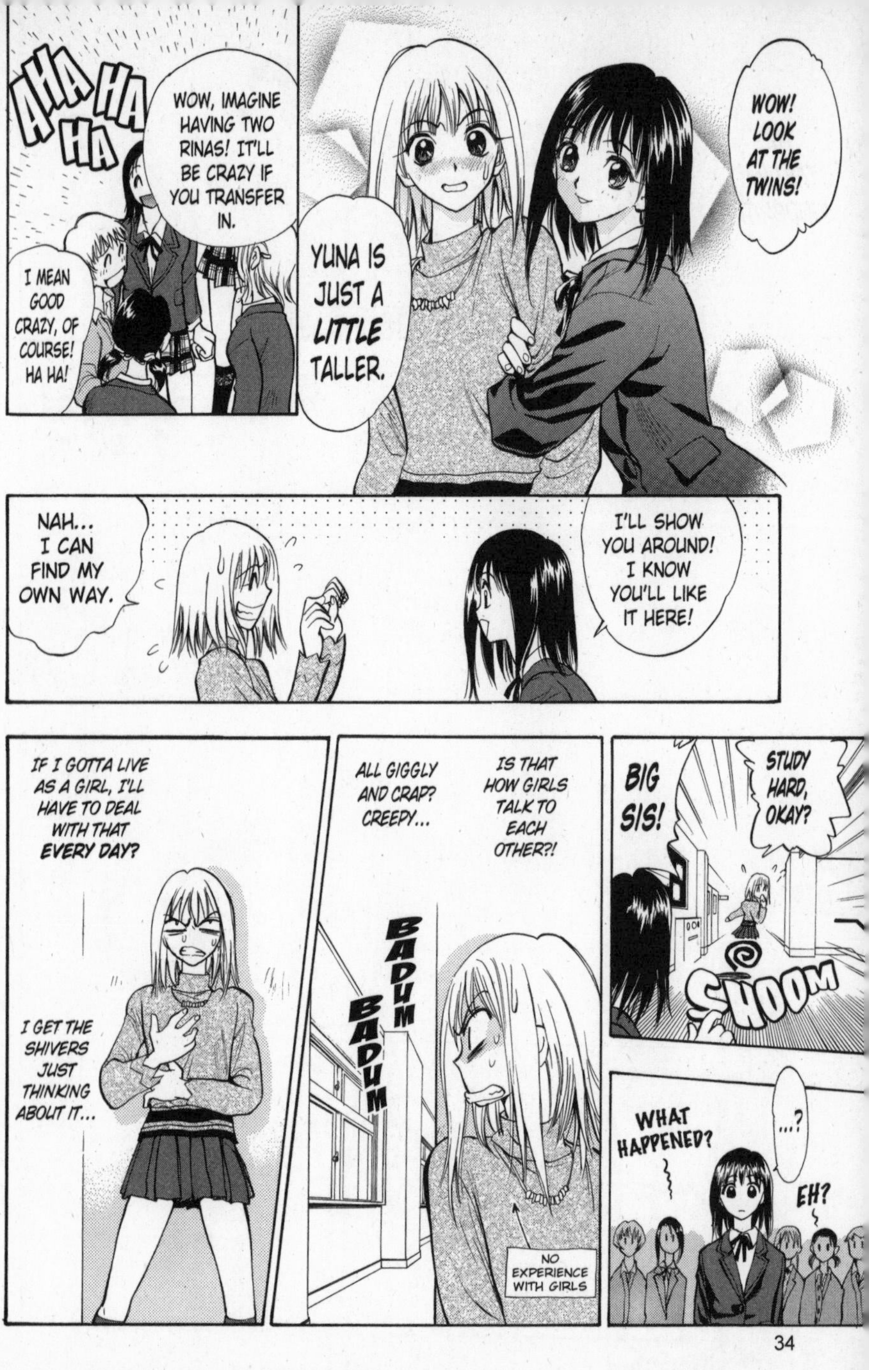
WOW! LOOK AT THE TWINS!
YUNA IS JUST A LITTLE TALLER.
AHA HA HA HA
WOW, IMAGINE HAVING TWO RINAS! IT'LL BE CRAZY IF YOU TRANSFER IN.
I MEAN GOOD CRAZY, OF COURSE! HA HA!
I'LL SHOW YOU AROUND! I KNOW YOU'LL LIKE IT HERE!
NAH... I CAN FIND MY OWN WAY.
STUDY HARD, OKAY?
BIG SIS!
SHOOM
...?
WHAT HAPPENED?
EH?
IS THAT HOW GIRLS TALK TO EACH OTHER?!
ALL GIGGLY AND CRAP? CREEPY...
BADUM
BADUM
NO EXPERIENCE WITH GIRLS
IF I GOTTA LIVE AS A GIRL, I'LL HAVE TO DEAL WITH THAT EVERY DAY?
I GET THE SHIVERS JUST THINKING ABOUT IT...

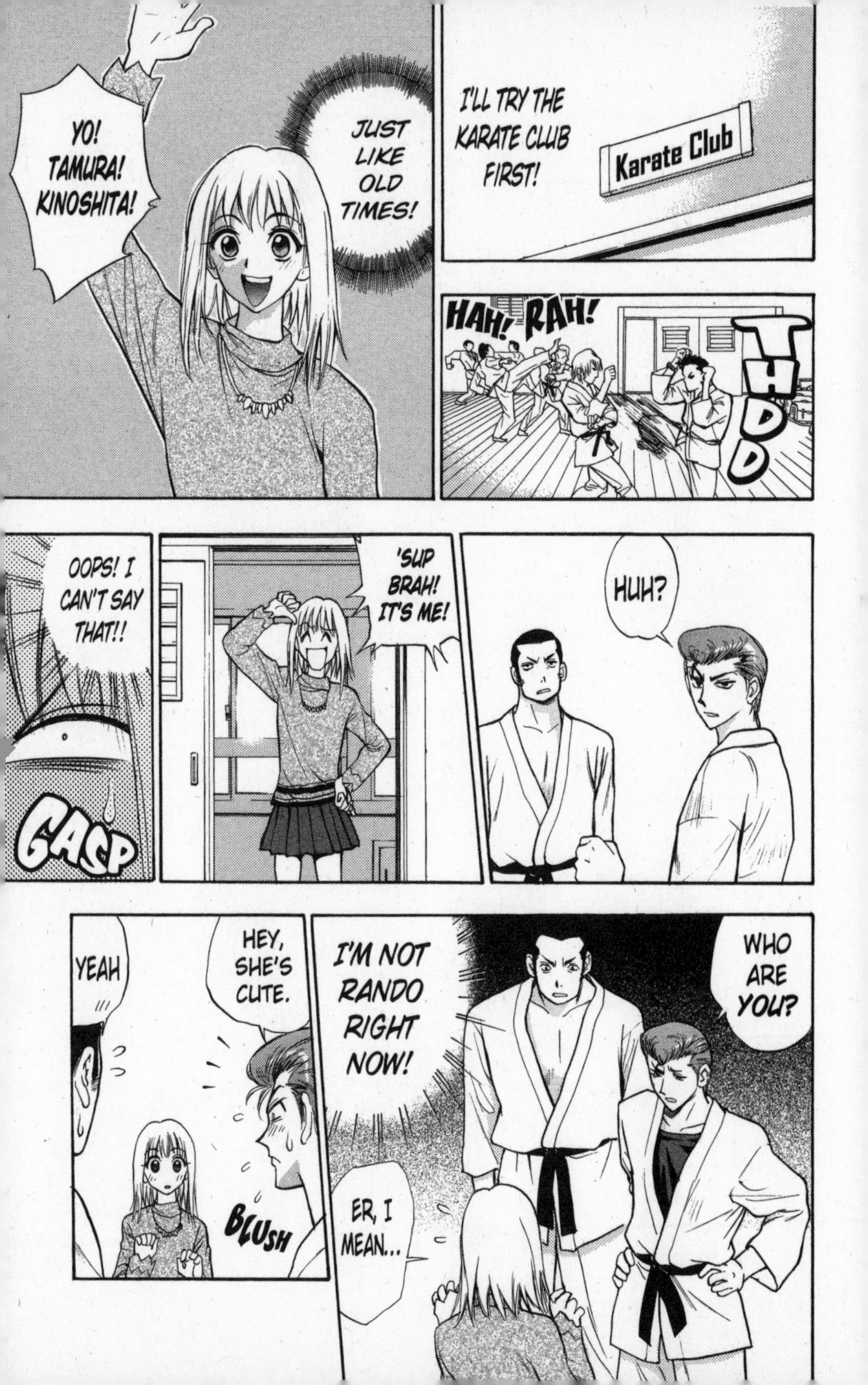

I'LL TRY THE KARATE CLUB FIRST!
Karate Club
HAH! RAH!
THDD
JUST LIKE OLD TIMES!
YO! TAMURA! KINOSHITA!
HUH?
'SUP BRAH! IT'S ME!
OOPS! I CAN'T SAY THAT!!
GASP
WHO ARE YOU?
I'M NOT RANDO RIGHT NOW!
ER, I MEAN...
HEY, SHE'S CUTE.
YEAH
BLUSH

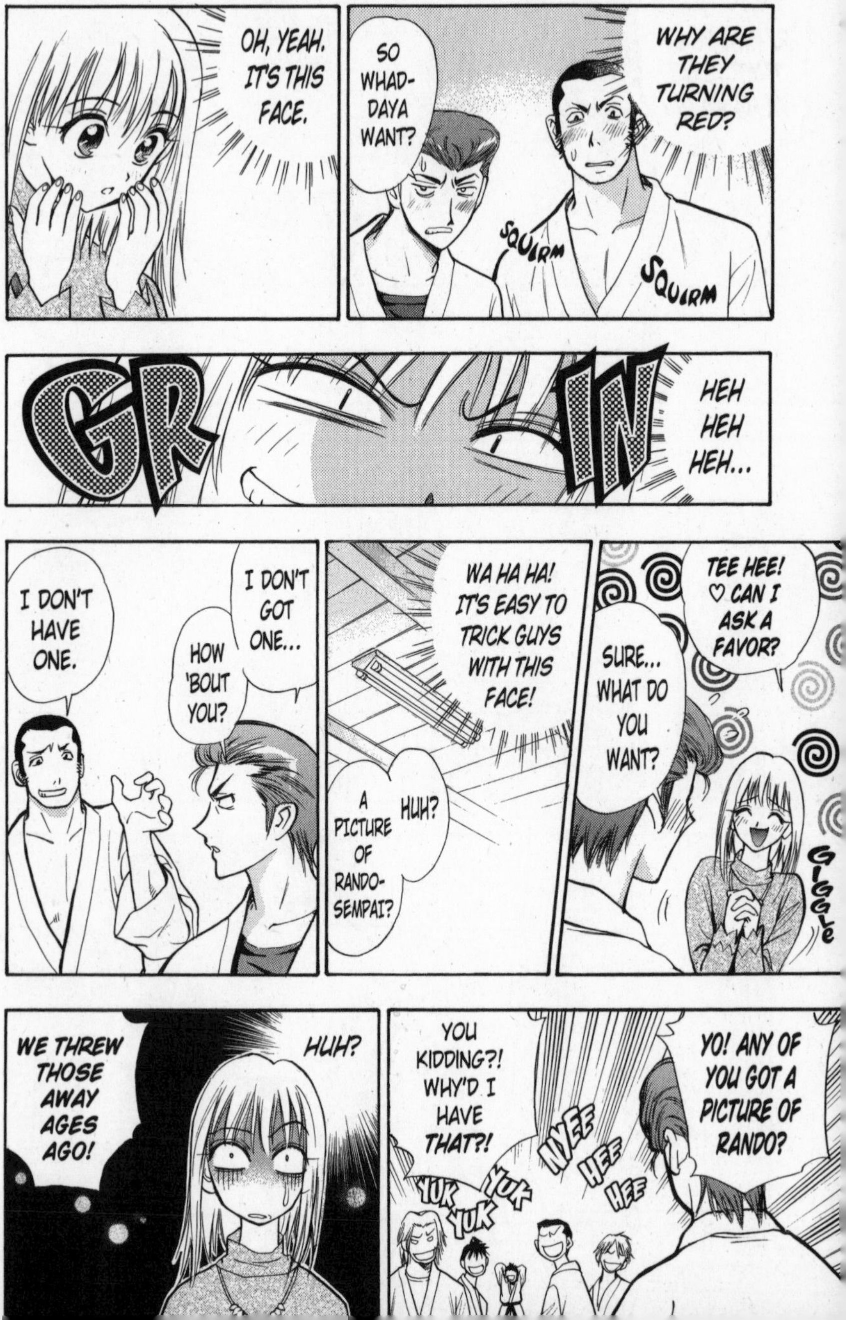
WHY ARE THEY TURNING RED?
SO WHADDAYA WANT?
SQUIRM
SQUIRM
OH, YEAH. IT'S THIS FACE.
HEH HEH HEH...
GRIN
TEE HEE! ♡ CAN I ASK A FAVOR?
SURE... WHAT DO YOU WANT?
GIGGLE
WA HA HA! IT'S EASY TO TRICK GUYS WITH THIS FACE!
HUH?
A PICTURE OF RANDO-SEMPAI?
I DON'T GOT ONE...
HOW 'BOUT YOU?
I DON'T HAVE ONE.
YO! ANY OF YOU GOT A PICTURE OF RANDO?
YOU KIDDING?! WHY'D I HAVE THAT?!
NYEE HEE HEE
YUK YUK YUK
HUH?
WE THREW THOSE AWAY AGES AGO!

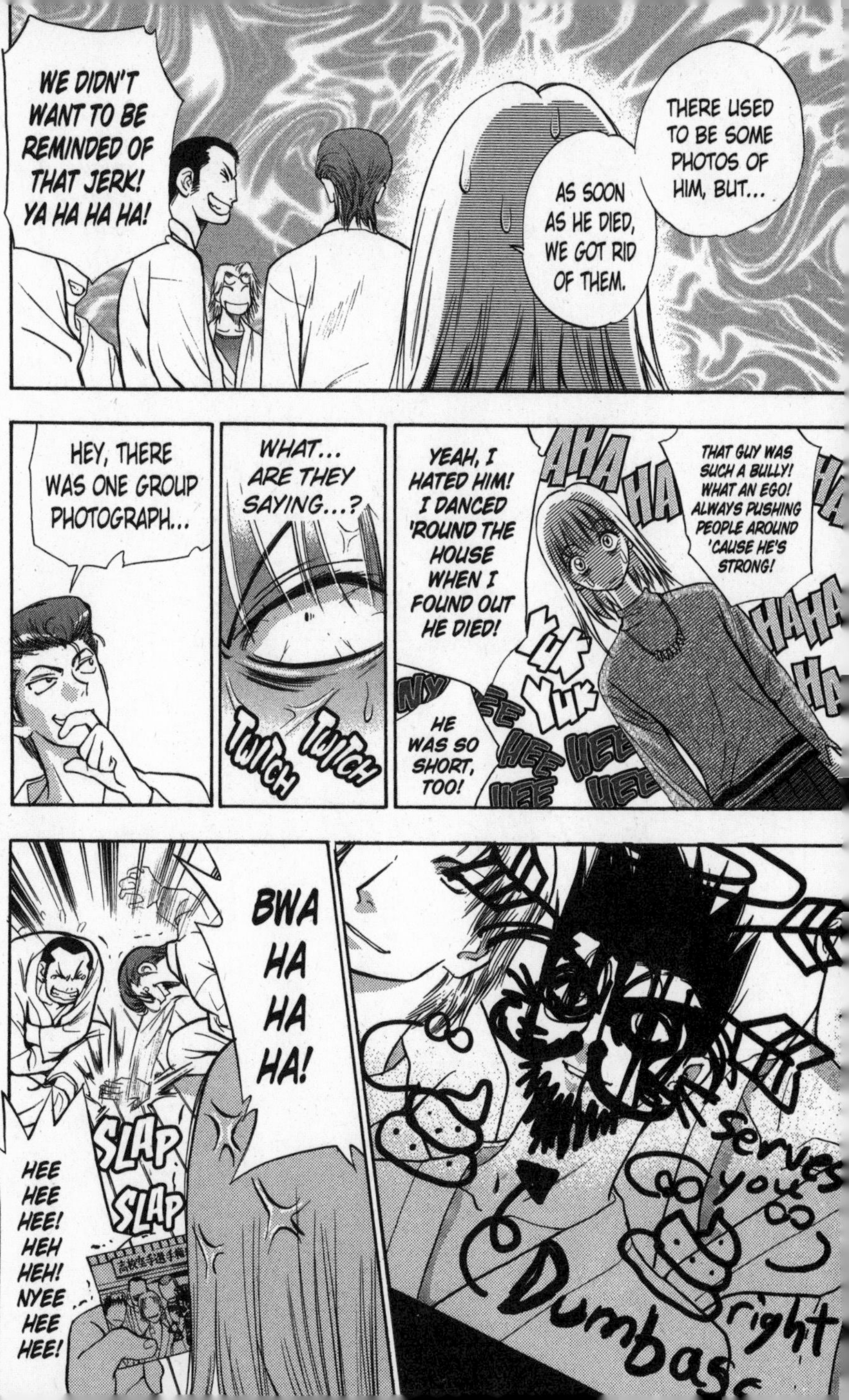
THERE USED TO BE SOME PHOTOS OF HIM, BUT...
AS SOON AS HE DIED, WE GOT RID OF THEM.
WE DIDN'T WANT TO BE REMINDED OF THAT JERK! YA HA HA HA!
THAT GUY WAS SUCH A BULLY! WHAT AN EGO! ALWAYS PUSHING PEOPLE AROUND 'CAUSE HE'S STRONG!
HA
AHAHA
HA
YEAH, I HATED HIM! I DANCED 'ROUND THE HOUSE WHEN I FOUND OUT HE DIED!
HAHA
YUK YUK
HEE HEE HEE
HE WAS SO SHORT, TOO!
WHAT... ARE THEY SAYING...?
TWITCH TWITCH
HEY, THERE WAS ONE GROUP PHOTOGRAPH...
serves you right
Dumbass
BWA HA HA HA HA!
SLAP SLAP
HEE HEE HEE! HEH HEH! NYEE HEE HEE!

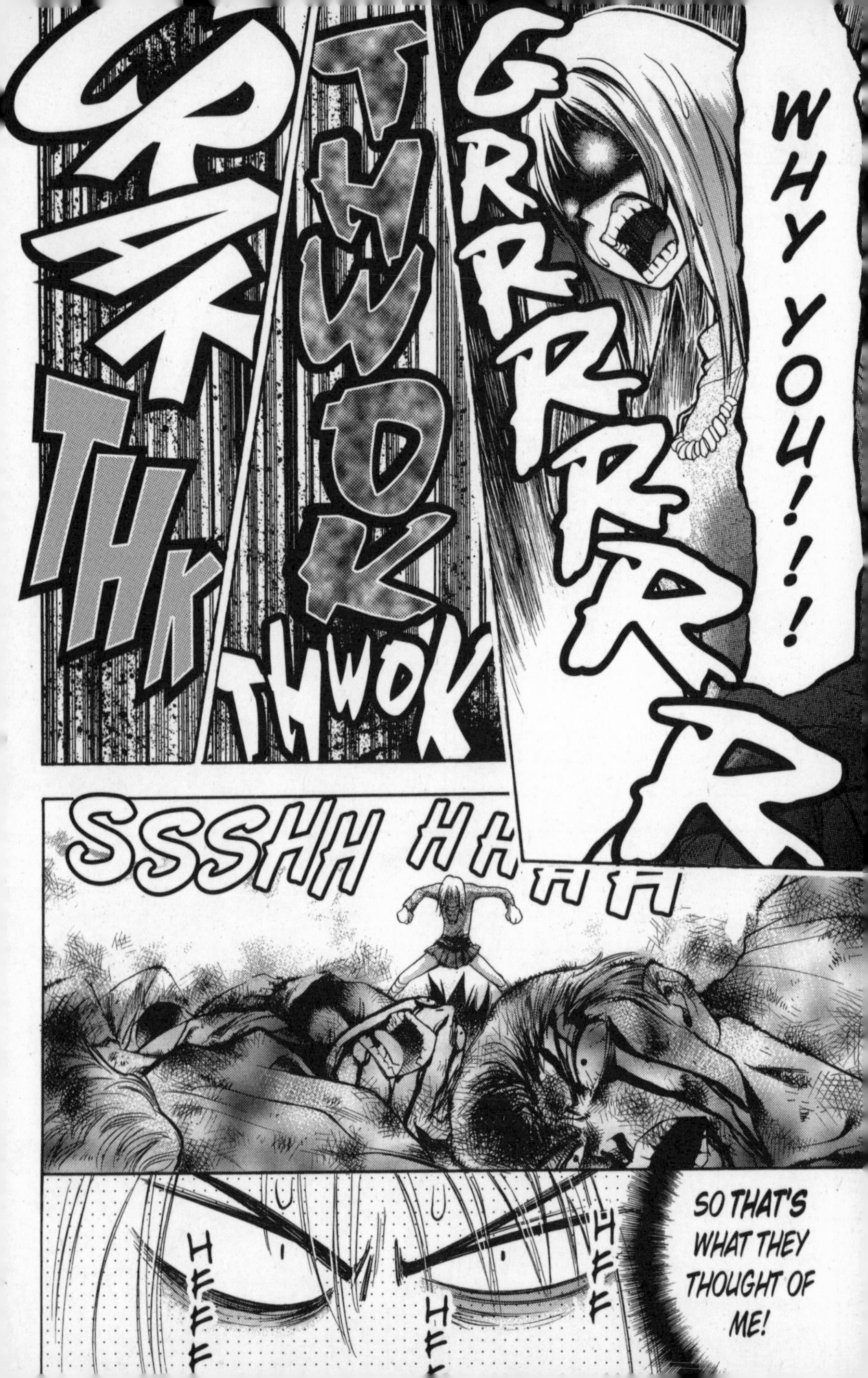
WHY YOU!!!
GRRRRRRR
THWOK
SSSHH HHHHH
SO THAT'S WHAT THEY THOUGHT OF ME!
HEFF
HEFF
HEFF

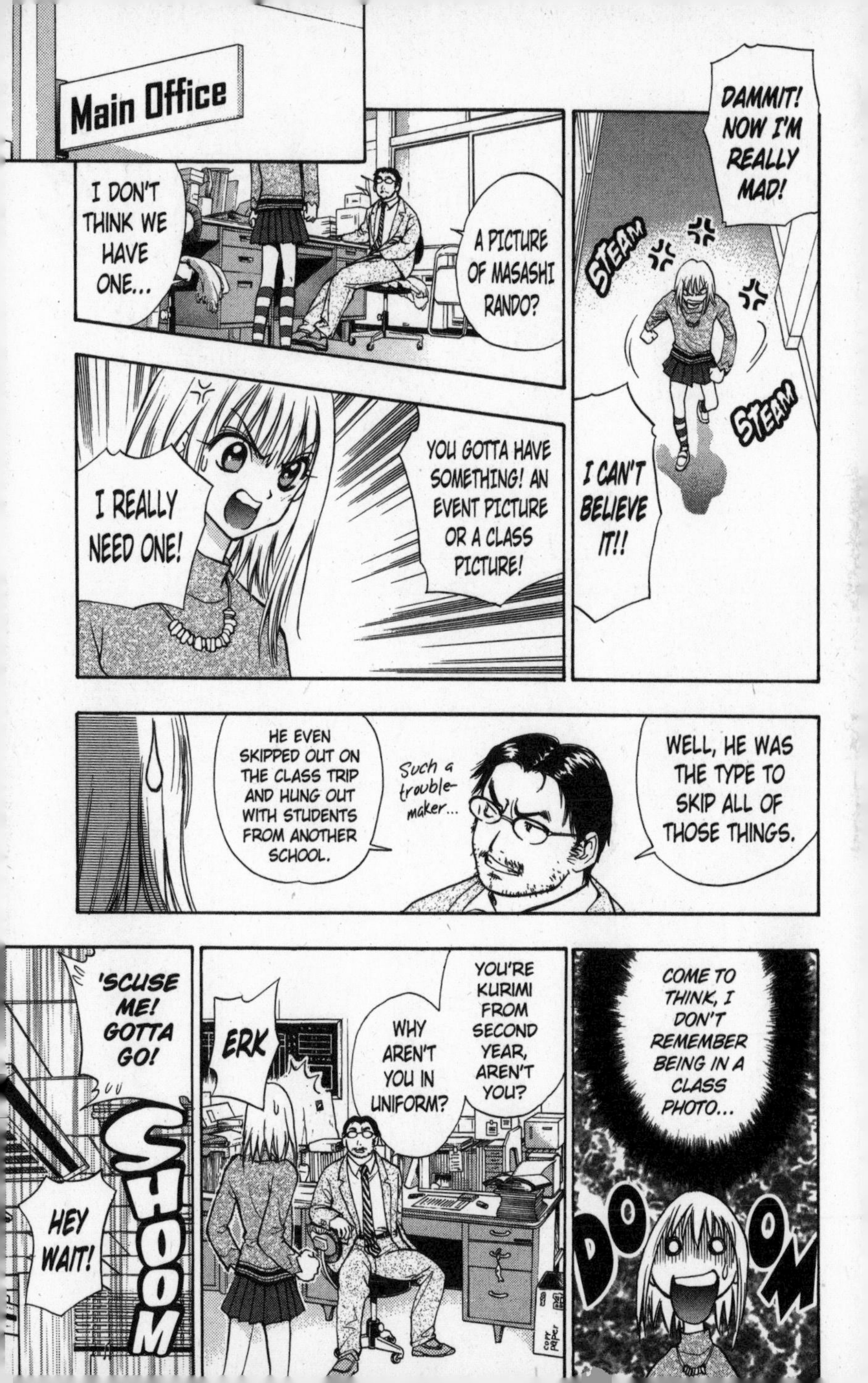
DAMMIT! NOW I'M REALLY MAD!
STEAM
STEAM
I CAN'T BELIEVE IT!!
Main Office
A PICTURE OF MASASHI RANDO?
I DON'T THINK WE HAVE ONE...
YOU GOTTA HAVE SOMETHING! AN EVENT PICTURE OR A CLASS PICTURE!
I REALLY NEED ONE!
WELL, HE WAS THE TYPE TO SKIP ALL OF THOSE THINGS.
Such a trouble-maker...
HE EVEN SKIPPED OUT ON THE CLASS TRIP AND HUNG OUT WITH STUDENTS FROM ANOTHER SCHOOL.
COME TO THINK, I DON'T REMEMBER BEING IN A CLASS PHOTO...
DOOOM
YOU'RE KURIMI FROM SECOND YEAR, AREN'T YOU?
WHY AREN'T YOU IN UNIFORM?
ERK
'SCUSE ME! GOTTA GO!
SHOOM
HEY WAIT!

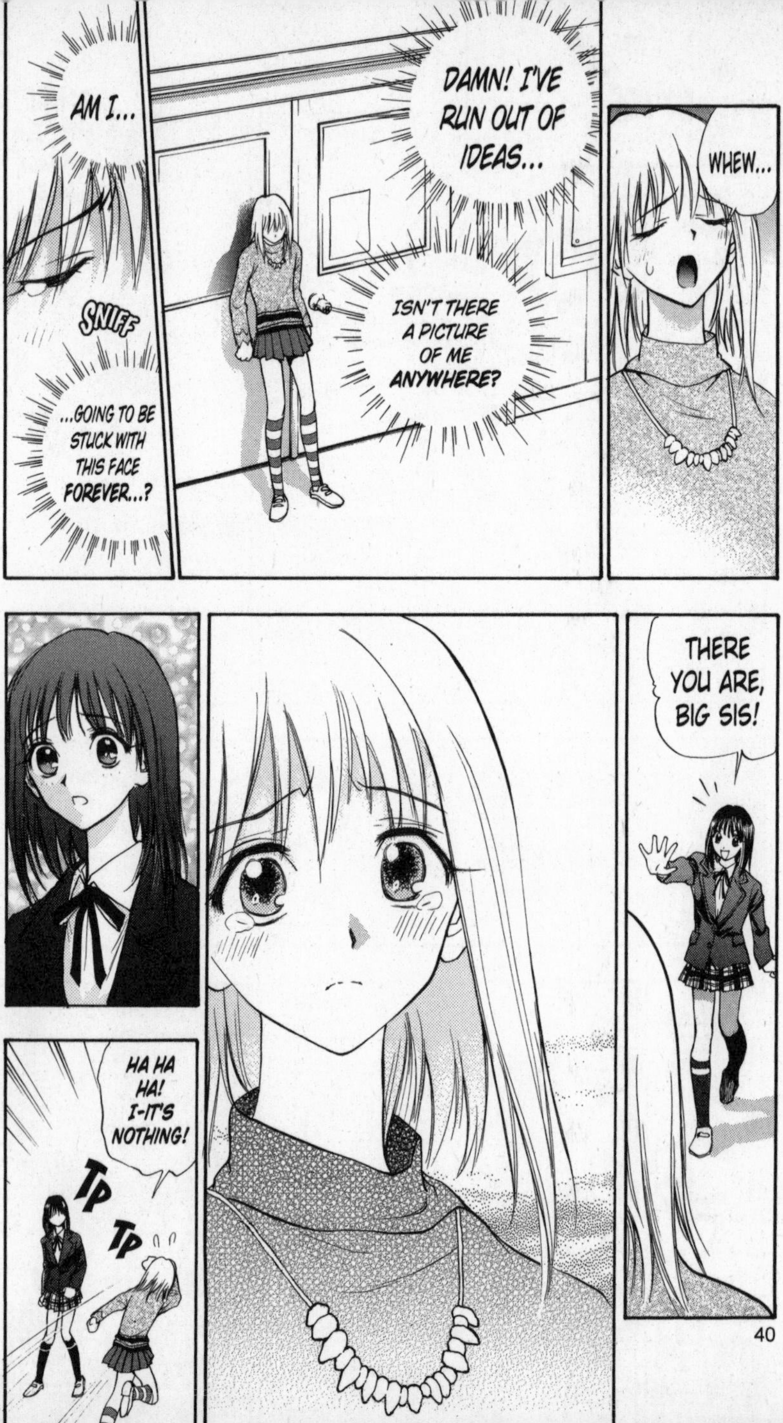
WHEW...
DAMN! I'VE RUN OUT OF IDEAS...
ISN'T THERE A PICTURE OF ME ANYWHERE?
AM I...
SNIFF
...GOING TO BE STUCK WITH THIS FACE FOREVER...?
THERE YOU ARE, BIG SIS!
HA HA HA! I-IT'S NOTHING!
TP TP

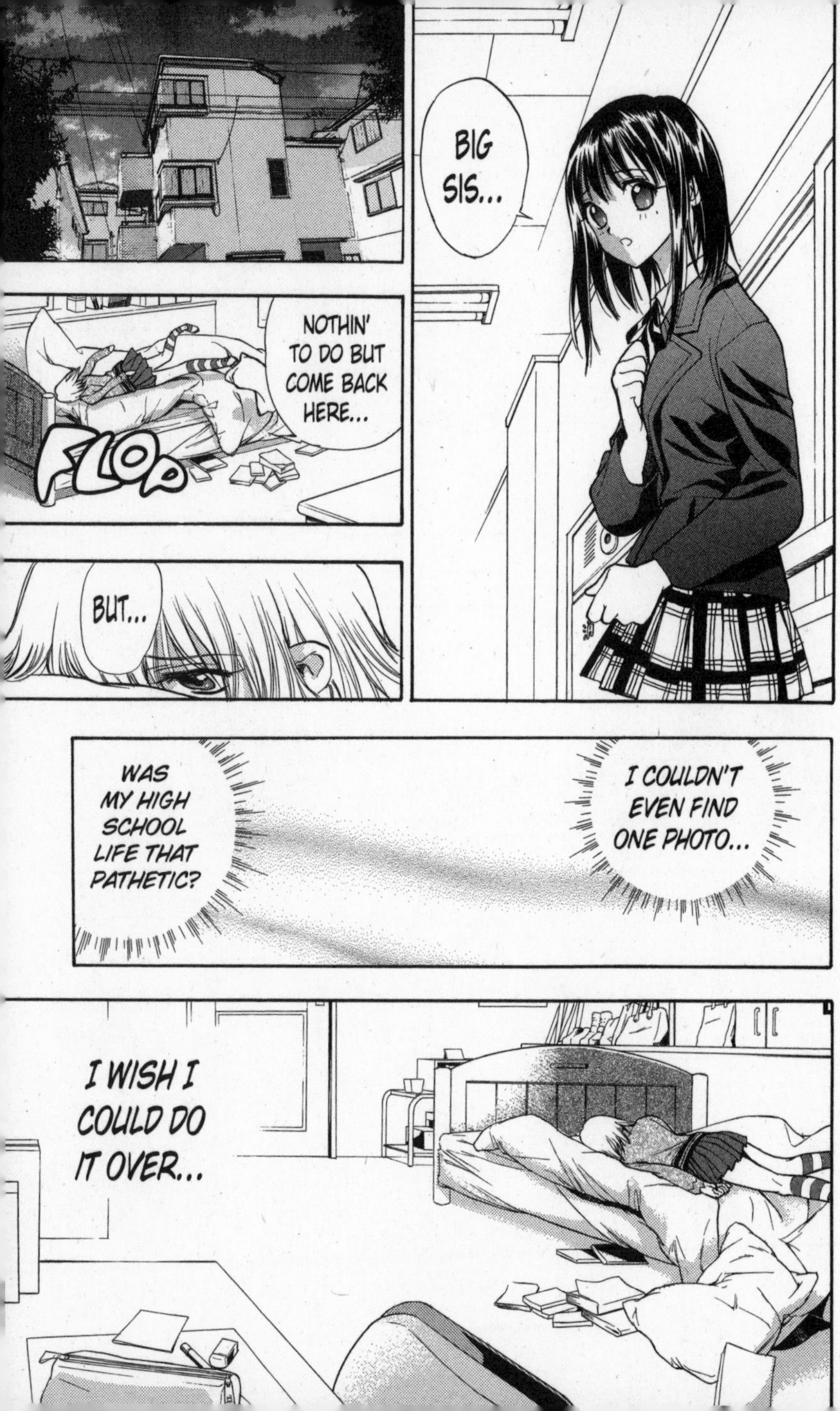
BIG SIS...
NOTHIN' TO DO BUT COME BACK HERE...
FLOP
BUT...
I COULDN'T EVEN FIND ONE PHOTO...
WAS MY HIGH SCHOOL LIFE THAT PATHETIC?
I WISH I COULD DO IT OVER...

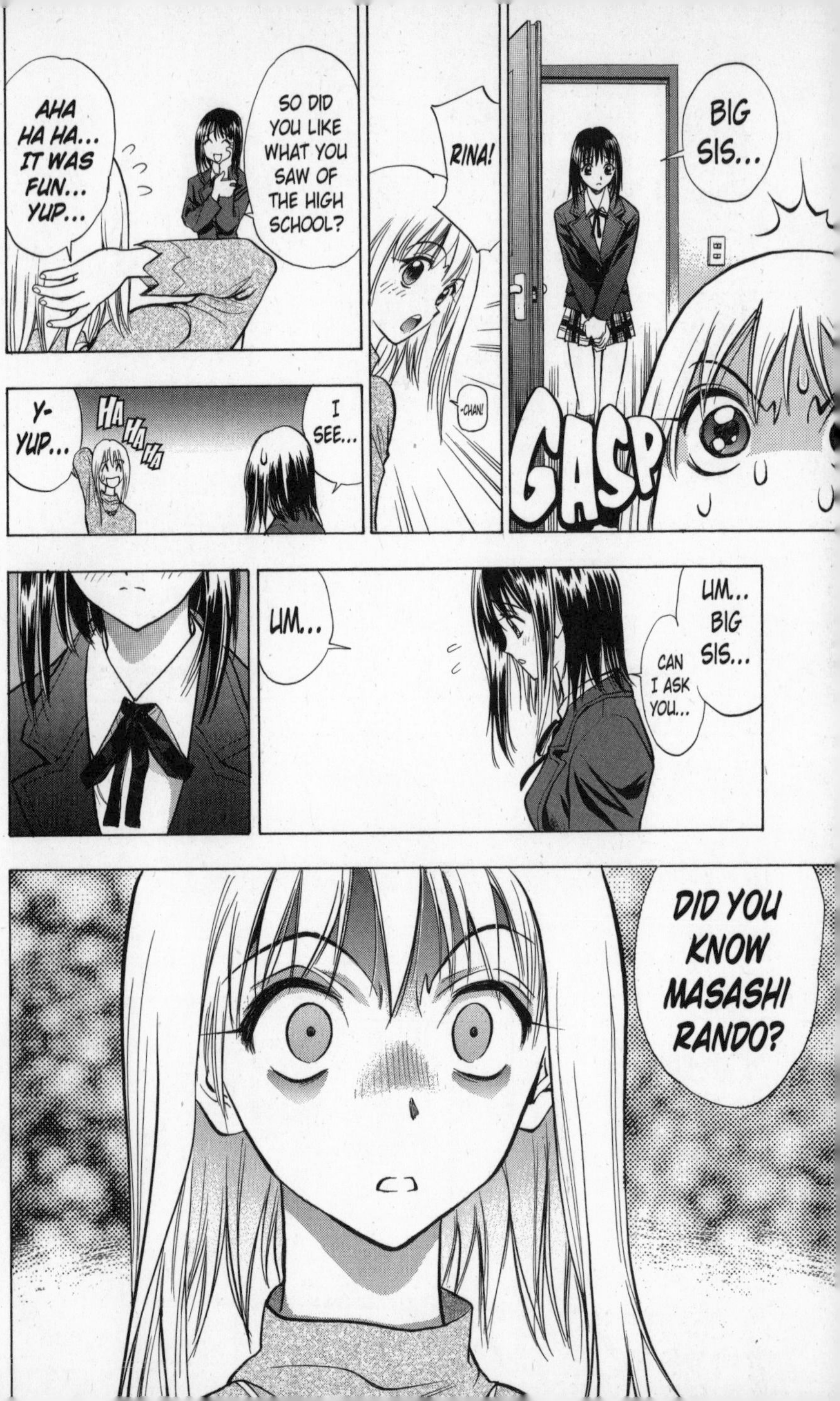
BIG SIS...
GASP
RINA!
-CHAN!
SO DID YOU LIKE WHAT YOU SAW OF THE HIGH SCHOOL?
AHA HA HA... IT WAS FUN... YUP...
I SEE...
Y-YUP...
HA HA HA HA
UM.. BIG SIS...
CAN I ASK YOU...
UM...
DID YOU KNOW MASASHI RANDO?

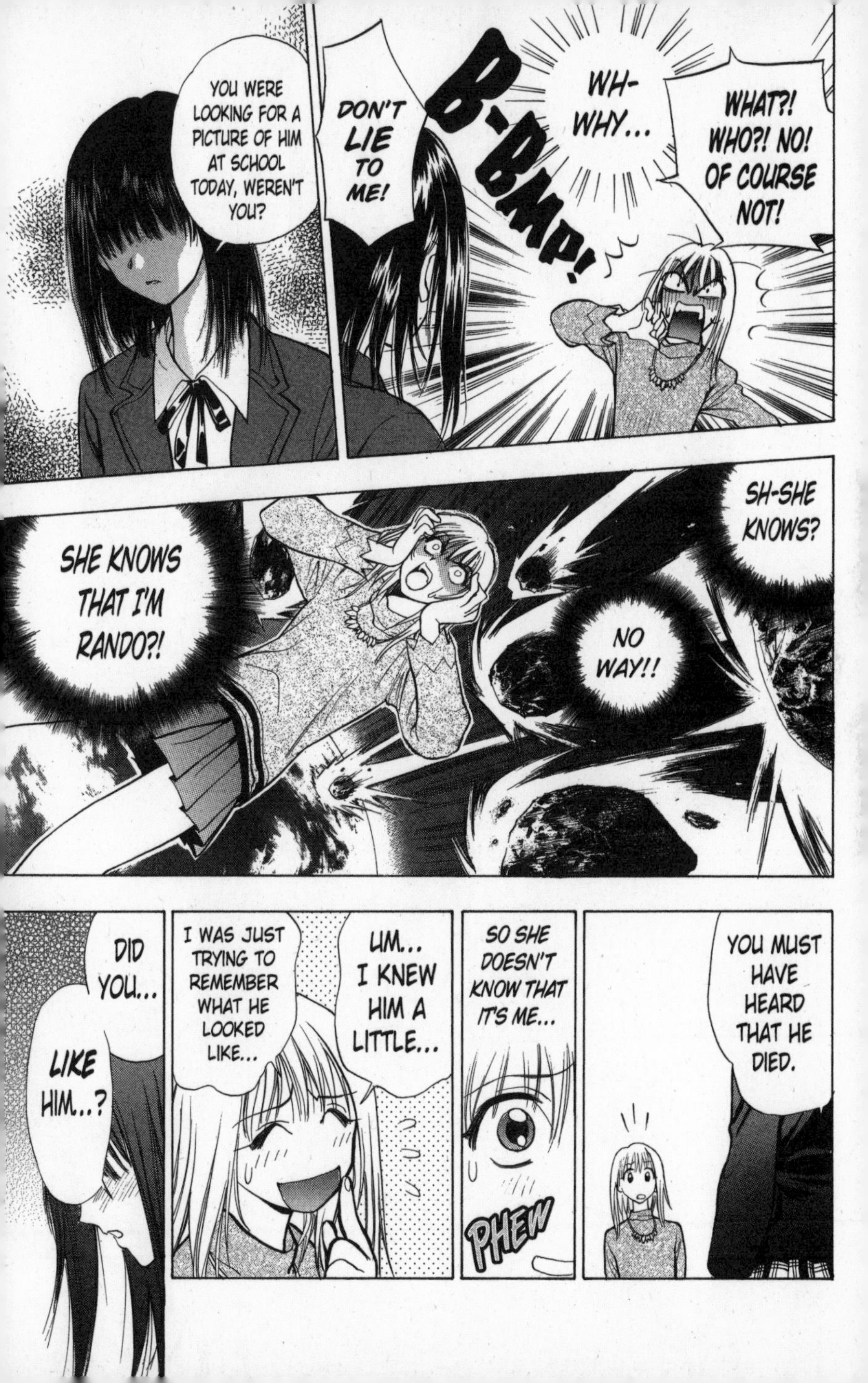
WHAT?! WHO?! NO! OF COURSE NOT!
WH- WHY...
B-BMP!
DON'T LIE TO ME!
YOU WERE LOOKING FOR A PICTURE OF HIM AT SCHOOL TODAY, WEREN'T YOU?
SH-SHE KNOWS?
NO WAY!!
SHE KNOWS THAT I'M RANDO?!
YOU MUST HAVE HEARD THAT HE DIED.
SO SHE DOESN'T KNOW THAT IT'S ME...
PHEW
UM... I KNEW HIM A LITTLE...
I WAS JUST TRYING TO REMEMBER WHAT HE LOOKED LIKE...
DID YOU...
LIKE HIM...?

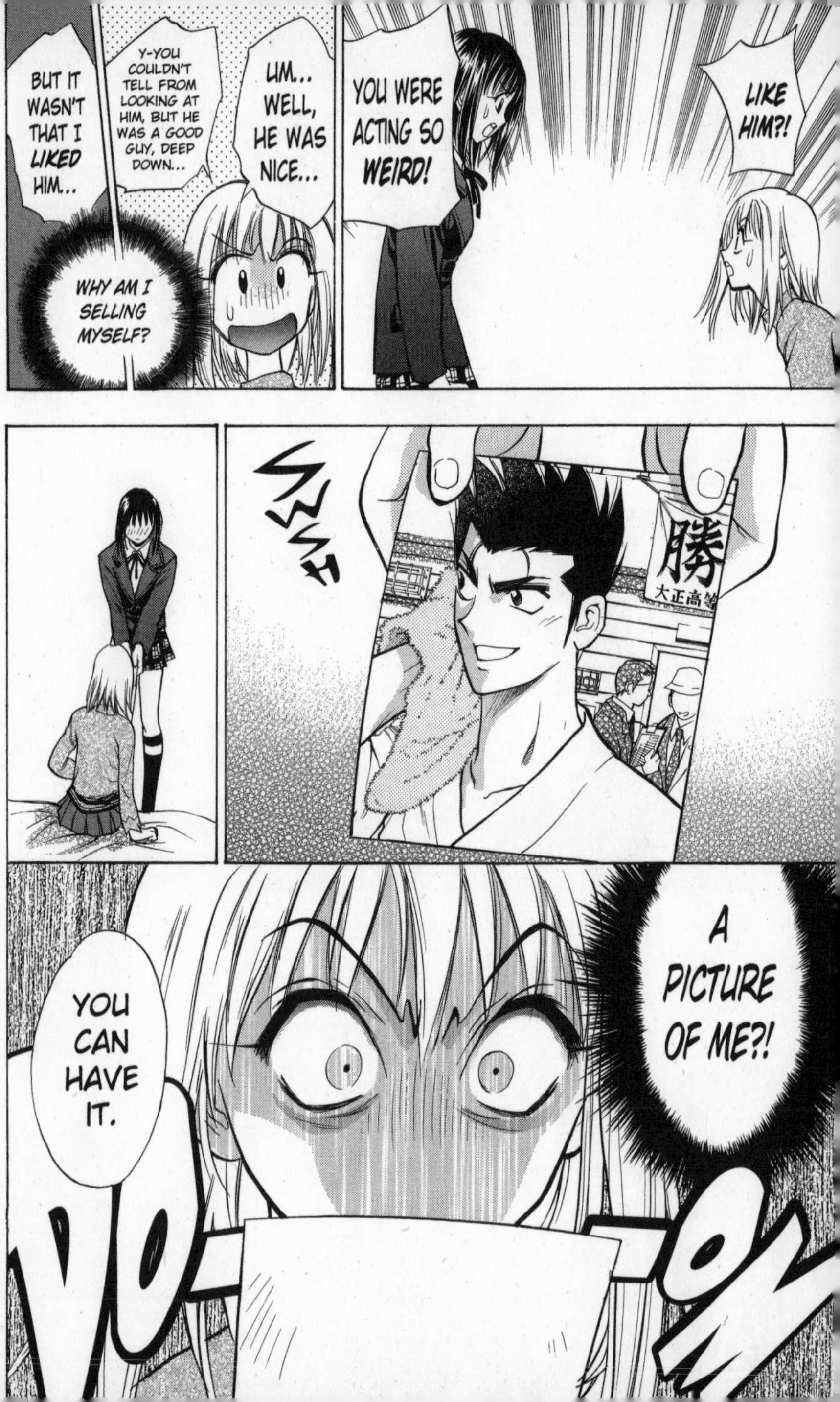
LIKE HIM?!
YOU WERE ACTING SO WEIRD!
UM... WELL, HE WAS NICE...
Y-YOU COULDN'T TELL FROM LOOKING AT HIM, BUT HE WAS A GOOD GUY, DEEP DOWN...
BUT IT WASN'T THAT I LIKED HIM...
WHY AM I SELLING MYSELF?
SWISH
勝
大正高
A PICTURE OF ME?!
YOU CAN HAVE IT.
DO—
—ON

READ THIS WAY

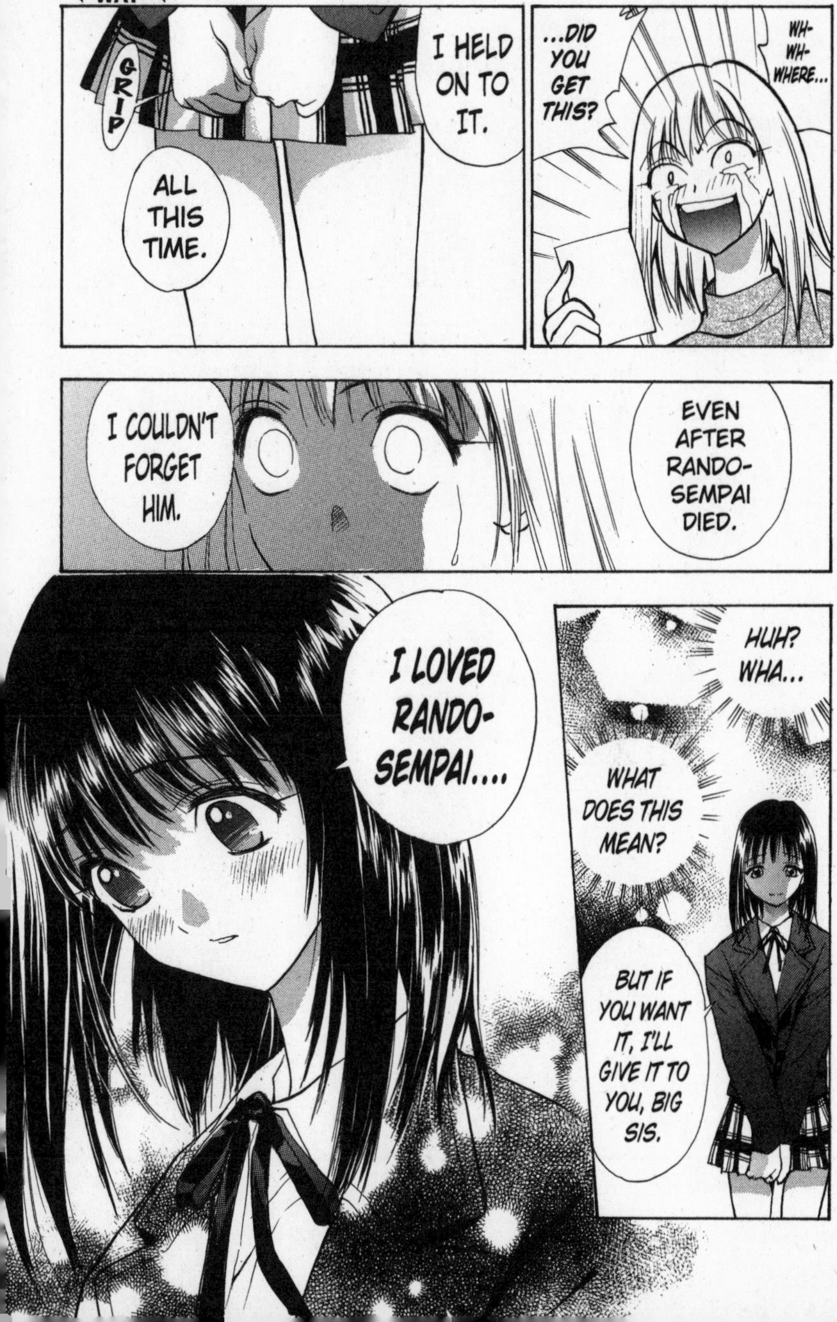
WH-WH-WHERE...
...DID YOU GET THIS?
I HELD ON TO IT.
GRIP
ALL THIS TIME.
EVEN AFTER RANDO-SEMPAI DIED.
I COULDN'T FORGET HIM.
I LOVED RANDO-SEMPAI....
HUH? WHA...
WHAT DOES THIS MEAN?
BUT IF YOU WANT IT, I'LL GIVE IT TO YOU, BIG SIS.

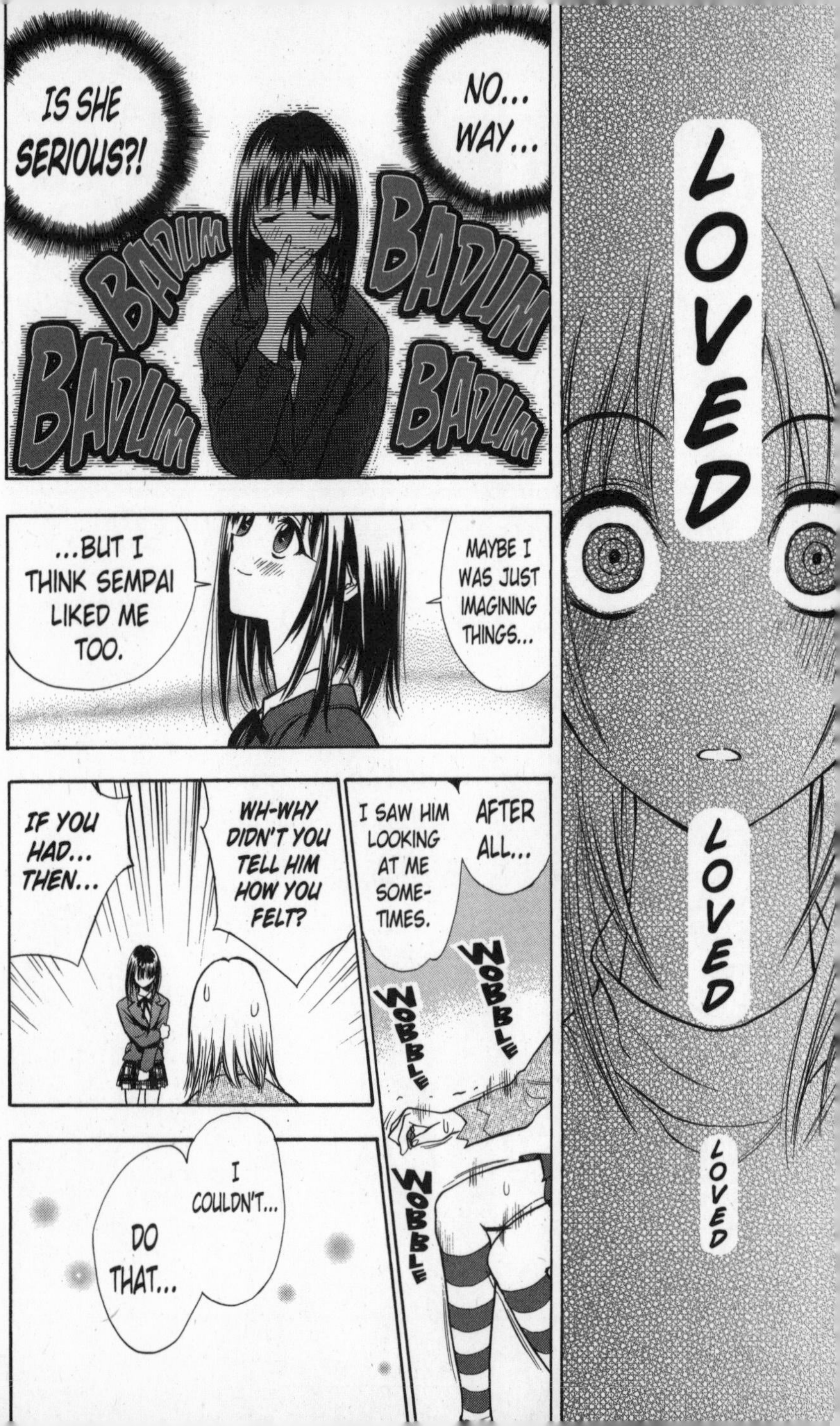
LOVED
LOVED
LOVED
NO... WAY...
BADUM
BADUM
BADUM
BADUM
IS SHE SERIOUS?!
MAYBE I WAS JUST IMAGINING THINGS...
...BUT I THINK SEMPAI LIKED ME TOO.
AFTER ALL...
I SAW HIM LOOKING AT ME SOME-TIMES.
WOBBLE
WOBBLE
WOBBLE
WH-WHY DIDN'T YOU TELL HIM HOW YOU FELT?
IF YOU HAD... THEN...
I COULDN'T...
DO THAT...

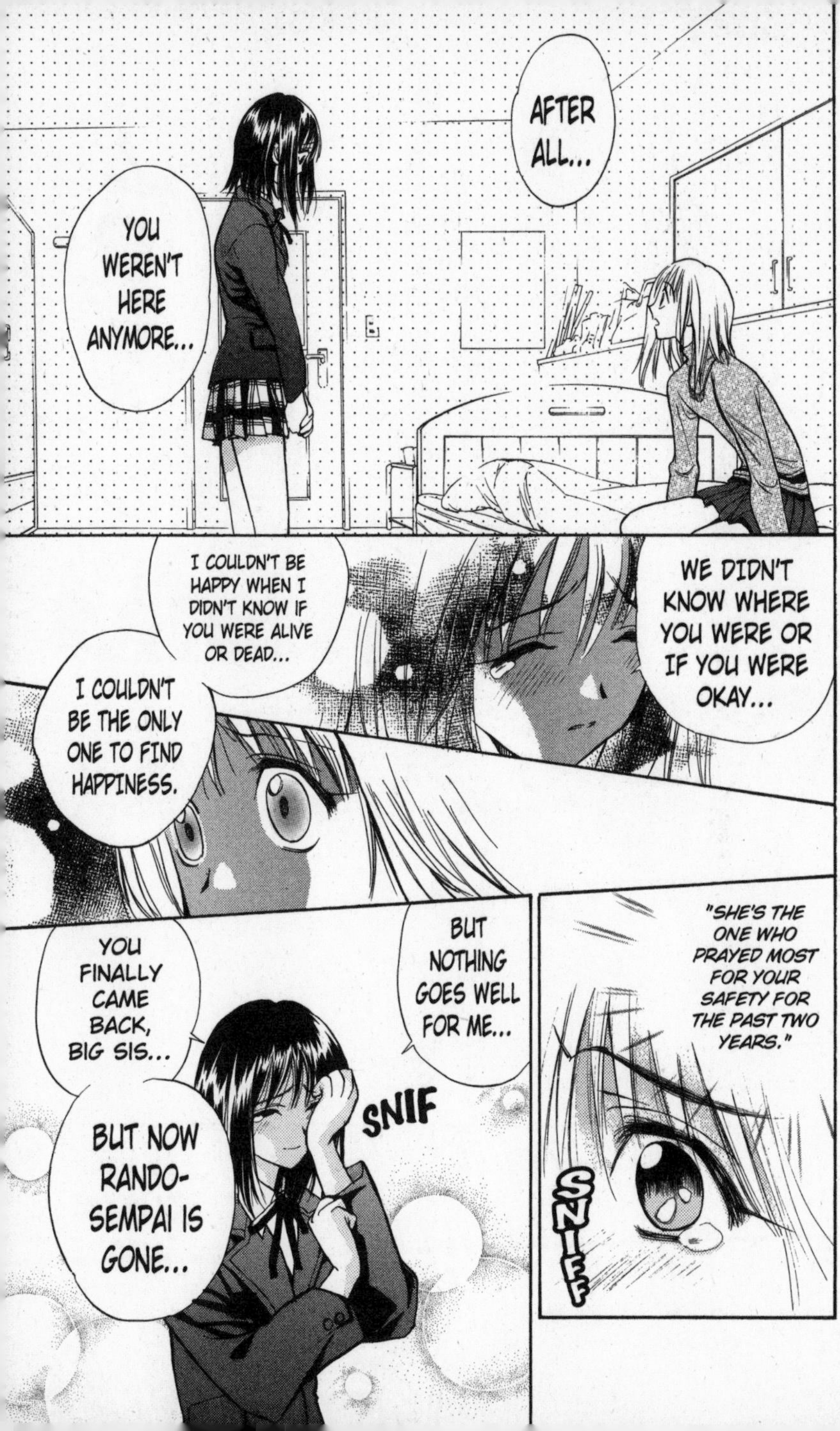
AFTER ALL...
YOU WEREN'T HERE ANYMORE...
WE DIDN'T KNOW WHERE YOU WERE OR IF YOU WERE OKAY...
I COULDN'T BE HAPPY WHEN I DIDN'T KNOW IF YOU WERE ALIVE OR DEAD...
I COULDN'T BE THE ONLY ONE TO FIND HAPPINESS.
"SHE'S THE ONE WHO PRAYED MOST FOR YOUR SAFETY FOR THE PAST TWO YEARS."
SNIFF
BUT NOTHING GOES WELL FOR ME...
YOU FINALLY CAME BACK, BIG SIS...
BUT NOW RANDO-SEMPAI IS GONE...
SNIF

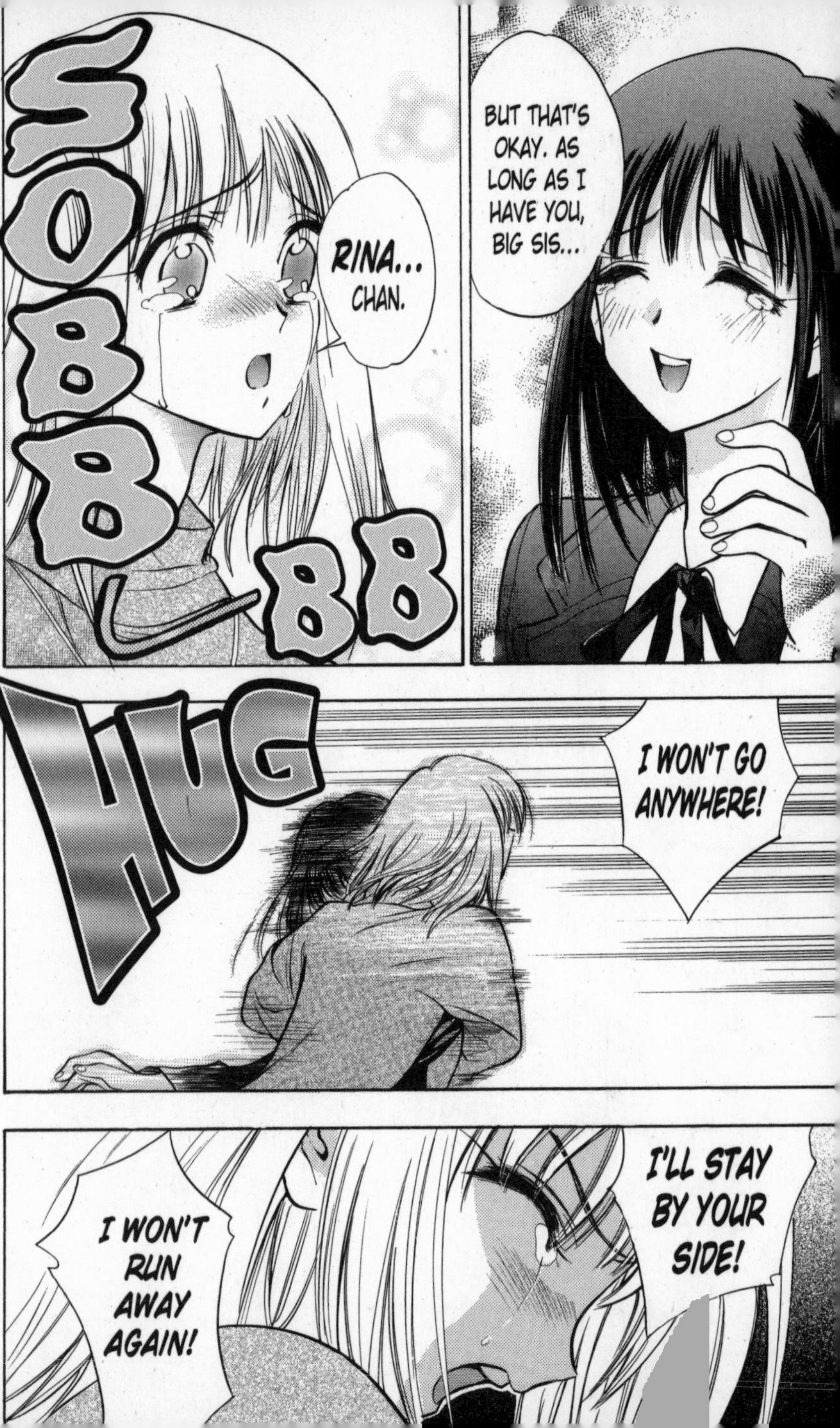

BUT THAT'S OKAY. AS LONG AS I HAVE YOU, BIG SIS...
RINA... CHAN.
SOBBBB
HUG
I WON'T GO ANYWHERE!
I'LL STAY BY YOUR SIDE!
I WON'T RUN AWAY AGAIN!

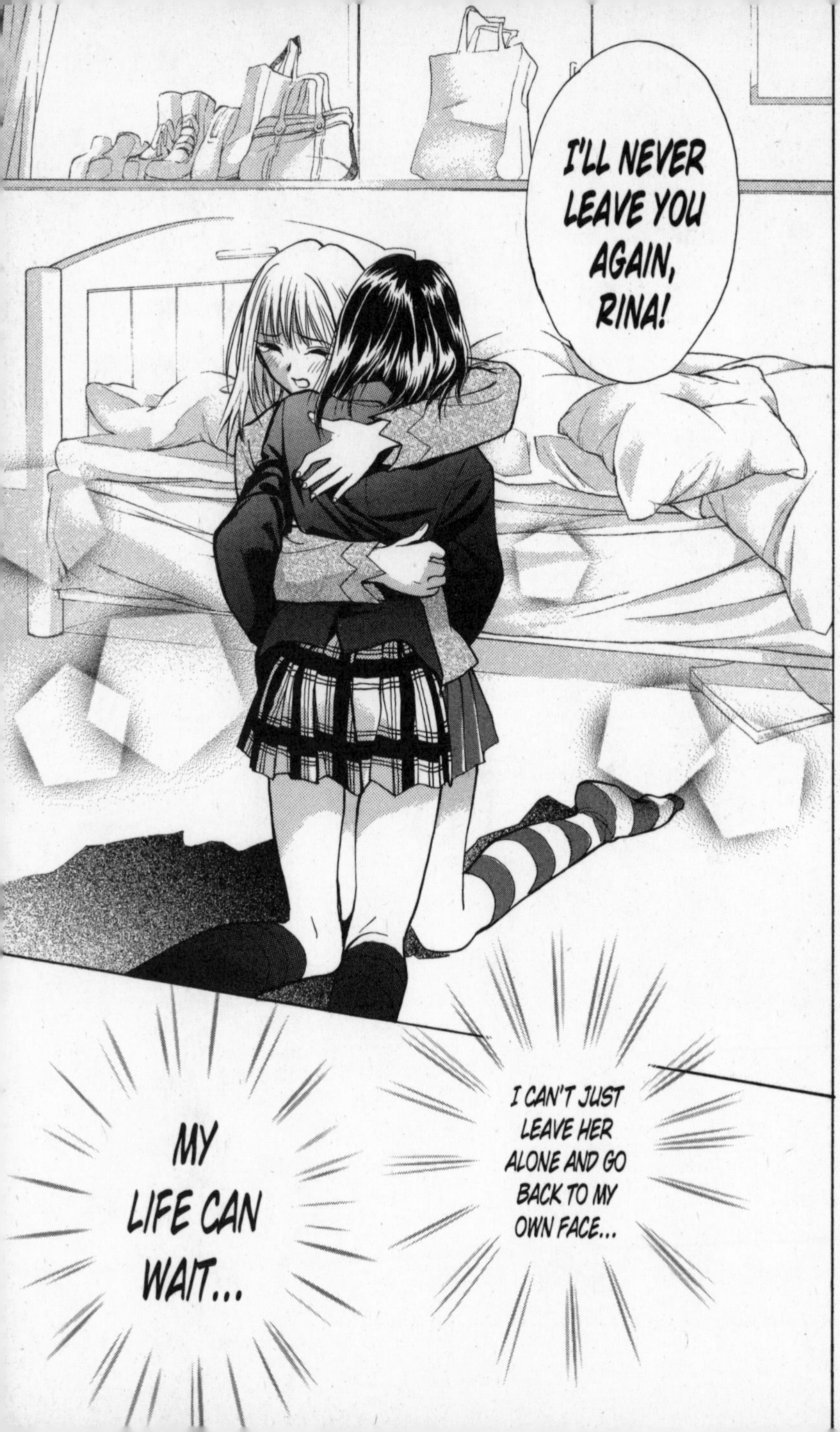
I'LL NEVER LEAVE YOU AGAIN, RINA!
I CAN'T JUST LEAVE HER ALONE AND GO BACK TO MY OWN FACE...
MY LIFE CAN WAIT...

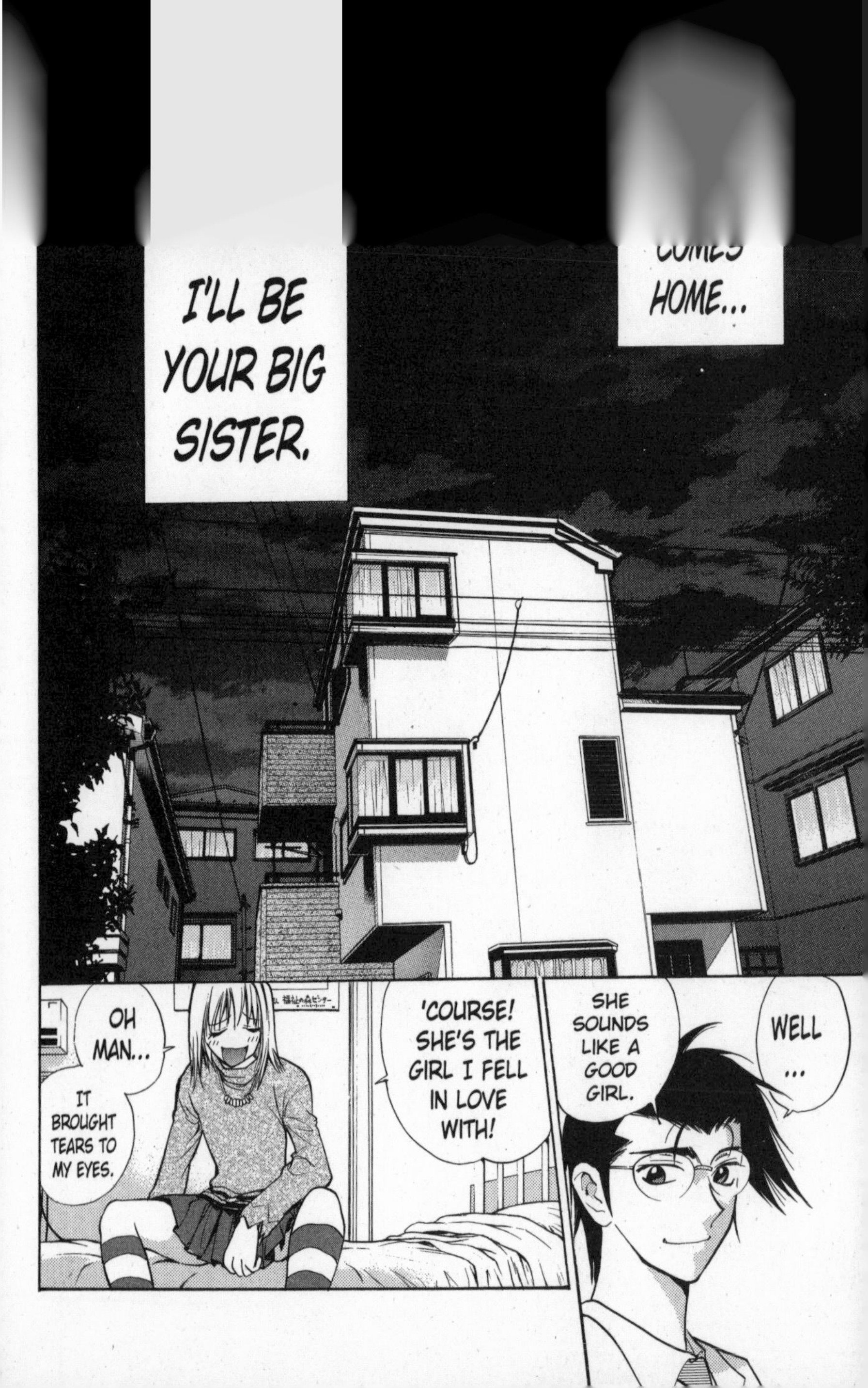
HOME...
I'LL BE YOUR BIG SISTER.
WELL ...
SHE SOUNDS LIKE A GOOD GIRL.
'COURSE! SHE'S THE GIRL I FELL IN LOVE WITH!
OH MAN...
IT BROUGHT TEARS TO MY EYES.

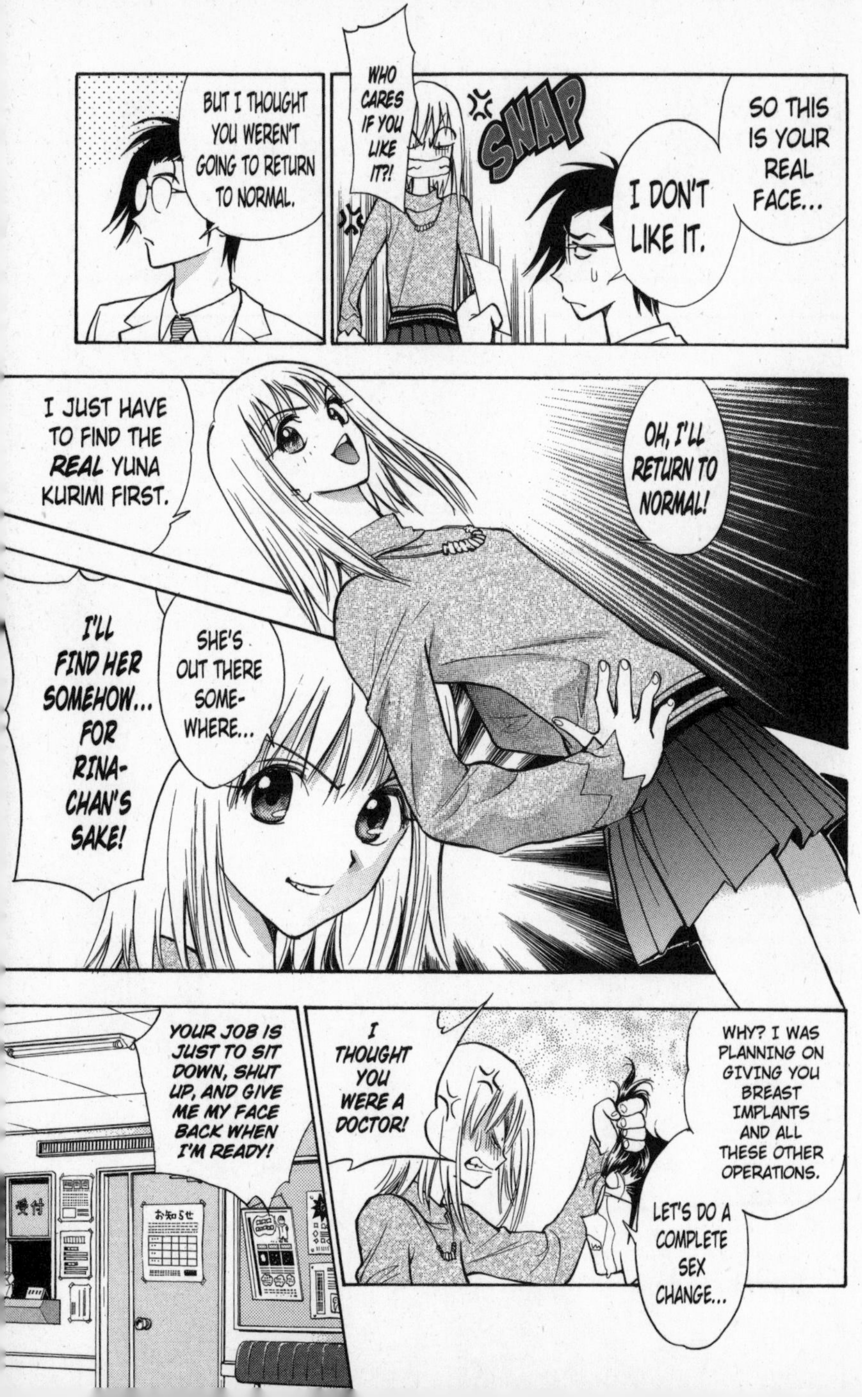
SO THIS IS YOUR REAL FACE...
I DON'T LIKE IT.
SNAP
WHO CARES IF YOU LIKE IT?!
BUT I THOUGHT YOU WEREN'T GOING TO RETURN TO NORMAL.
OH, I'LL RETURN TO NORMAL!
I JUST HAVE TO FIND THE REAL YUNA KURIMI FIRST.
SHE'S OUT THERE SOME-WHERE...
I'LL FIND HER SOMEHOW... FOR RINA-CHAN'S SAKE!
WHY? I WAS PLANNING ON GIVING YOU BREAST IMPLANTS AND ALL THESE OTHER OPERATIONS.
LET'S DO A COMPLETE SEX CHANGE...
I THOUGHT YOU WERE A DOCTOR!
YOUR JOB IS JUST TO SIT DOWN, SHUT UP, AND GIVE ME MY FACE BACK WHEN I'M READY!
受付
お知らせ

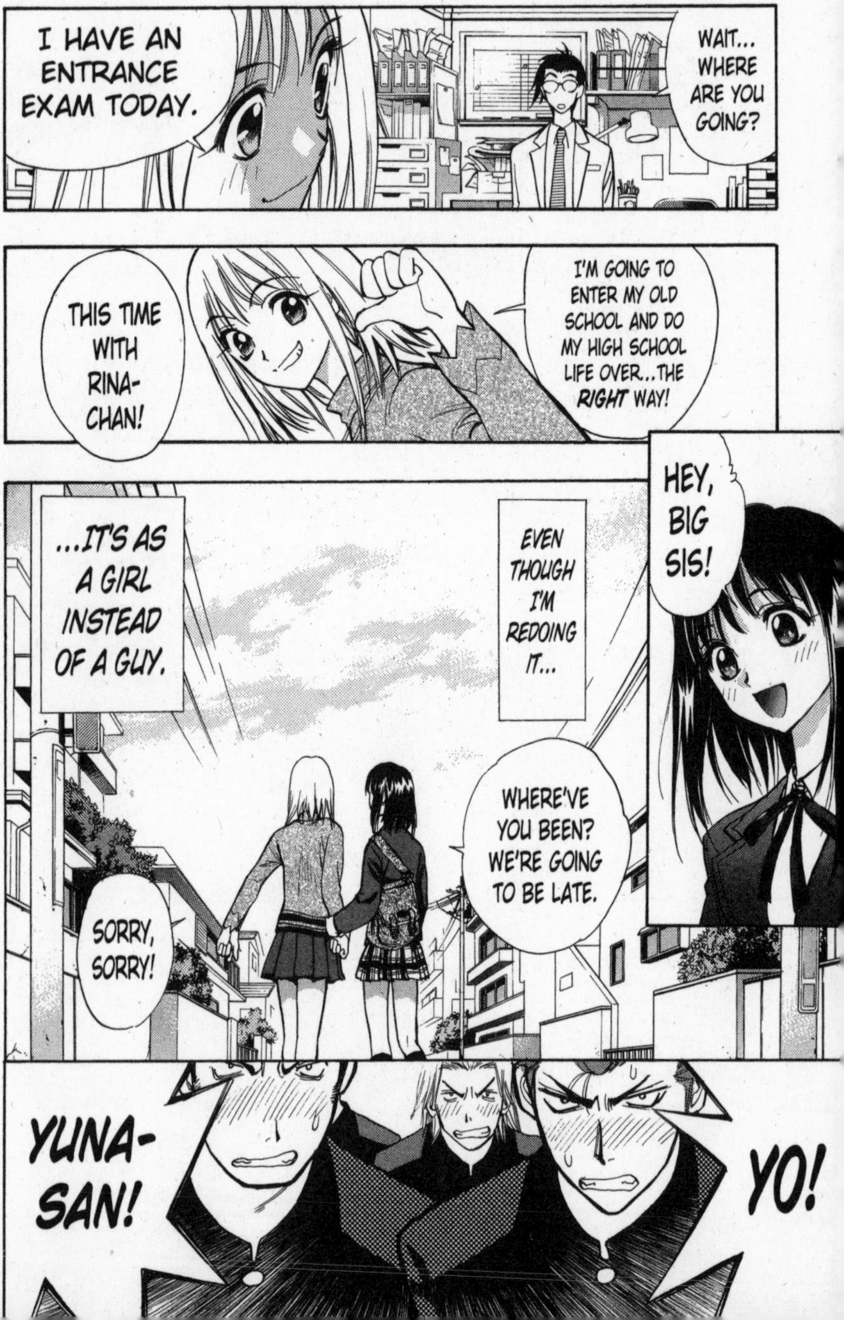
WAIT... WHERE ARE YOU GOING?
I HAVE AN ENTRANCE EXAM TODAY.
I'M GOING TO ENTER MY OLD SCHOOL AND DO MY HIGH SCHOOL LIFE OVER...THE *RIGHT* WAY!
THIS TIME WITH RINA-CHAN!
HEY, BIG SIS!
EVEN THOUGH I'M REDOING IT...
...IT'S AS A GIRL INSTEAD OF A GUY.
WHERE'VE YOU BEEN? WE'RE GOING TO BE LATE.
SORRY, SORRY!
YO!
YUNA-SAN!

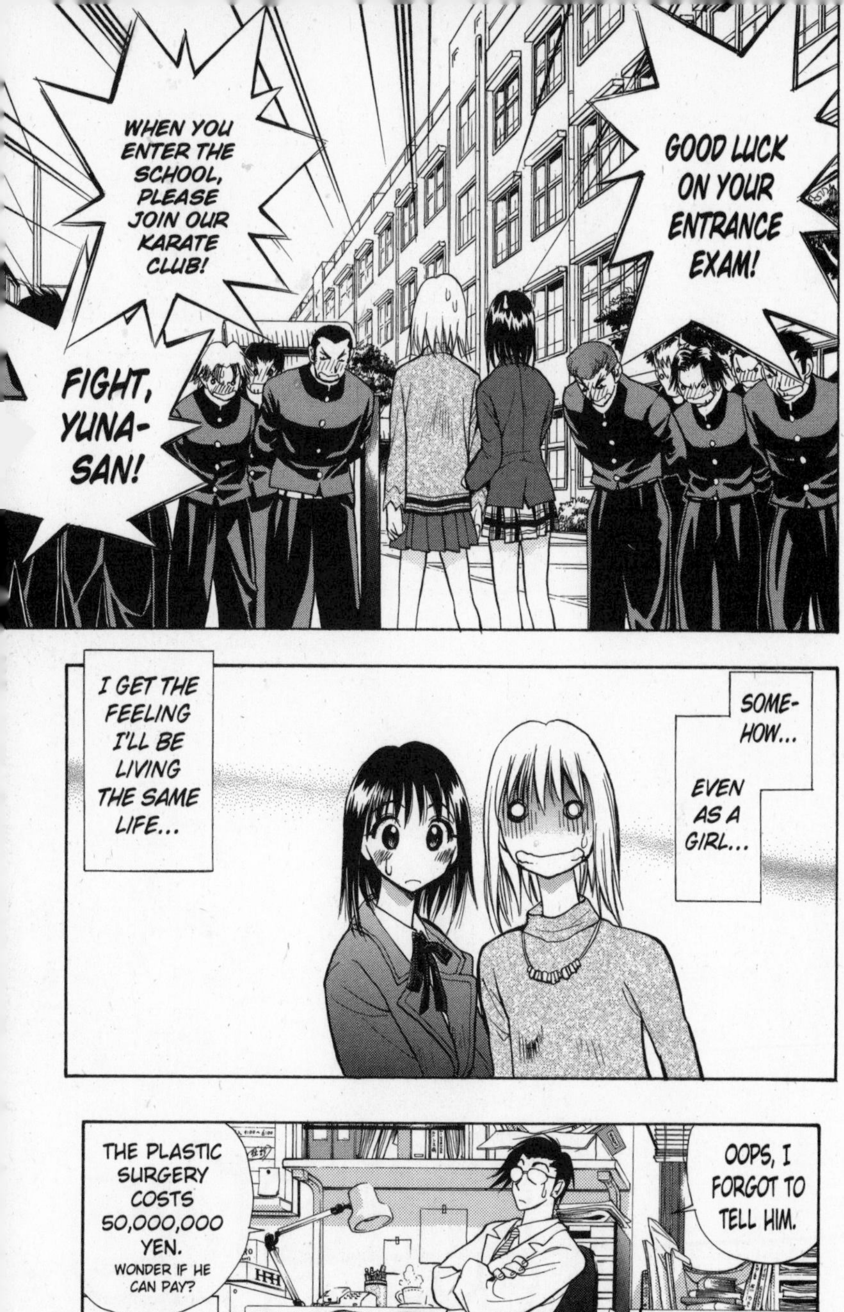
GOOD LUCK ON YOUR ENTRANCE EXAM!
WHEN YOU ENTER THE SCHOOL, PLEASE JOIN OUR KARATE CLUB!
FIGHT, YUNA-SAN!
SOME-HOW...
EVEN AS A GIRL...
I GET THE FEELING I'LL BE LIVING THE SAME LIFE...
OOPS, I FORGOT TO TELL HIM.
THE PLASTIC SURGERY COSTS 50,000,000 YEN.
WONDER IF HE CAN PAY?

*ABOUT $500,000

Pretty Face

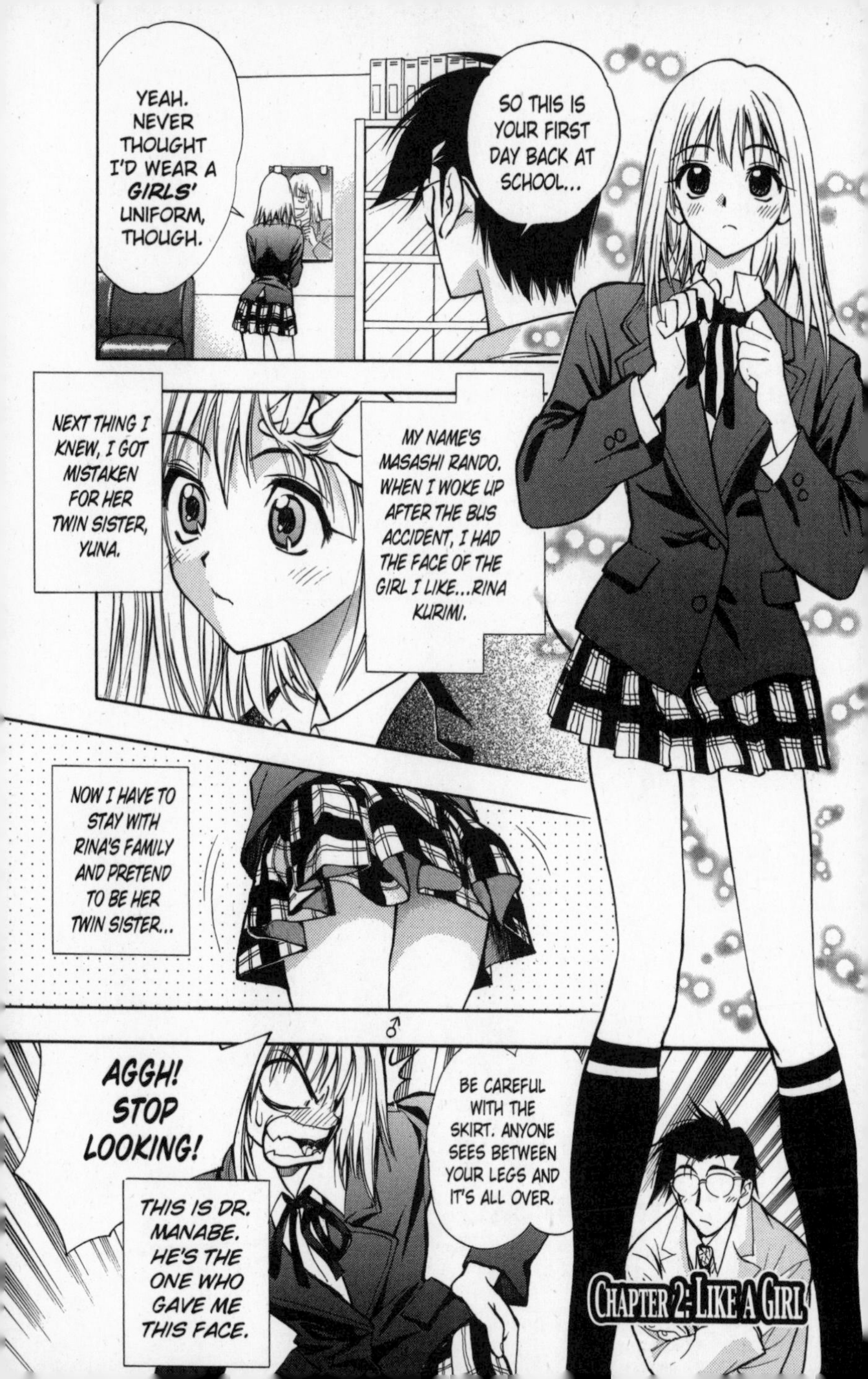
CHAPTER 2: LIKE A GIRL
SO THIS IS YOUR FIRST DAY BACK AT SCHOOL...
YEAH. NEVER THOUGHT I'D WEAR A GIRLS' UNIFORM, THOUGH.
MY NAME'S MASASHI RANDO. WHEN I WOKE UP AFTER THE BUS ACCIDENT, I HAD THE FACE OF THE GIRL I LIKE...RINA KURIMI.
NEXT THING I KNEW, I GOT MISTAKEN FOR HER TWIN SISTER, YUNA.
NOW I HAVE TO STAY WITH RINA'S FAMILY AND PRETEND TO BE HER TWIN SISTER...
♂
BE CAREFUL WITH THE SKIRT. ANYONE SEES BETWEEN YOUR LEGS AND IT'S ALL OVER.
AGGH! STOP LOOKING!
THIS IS DR. MANABE. HE'S THE ONE WHO GAVE ME THIS FACE.

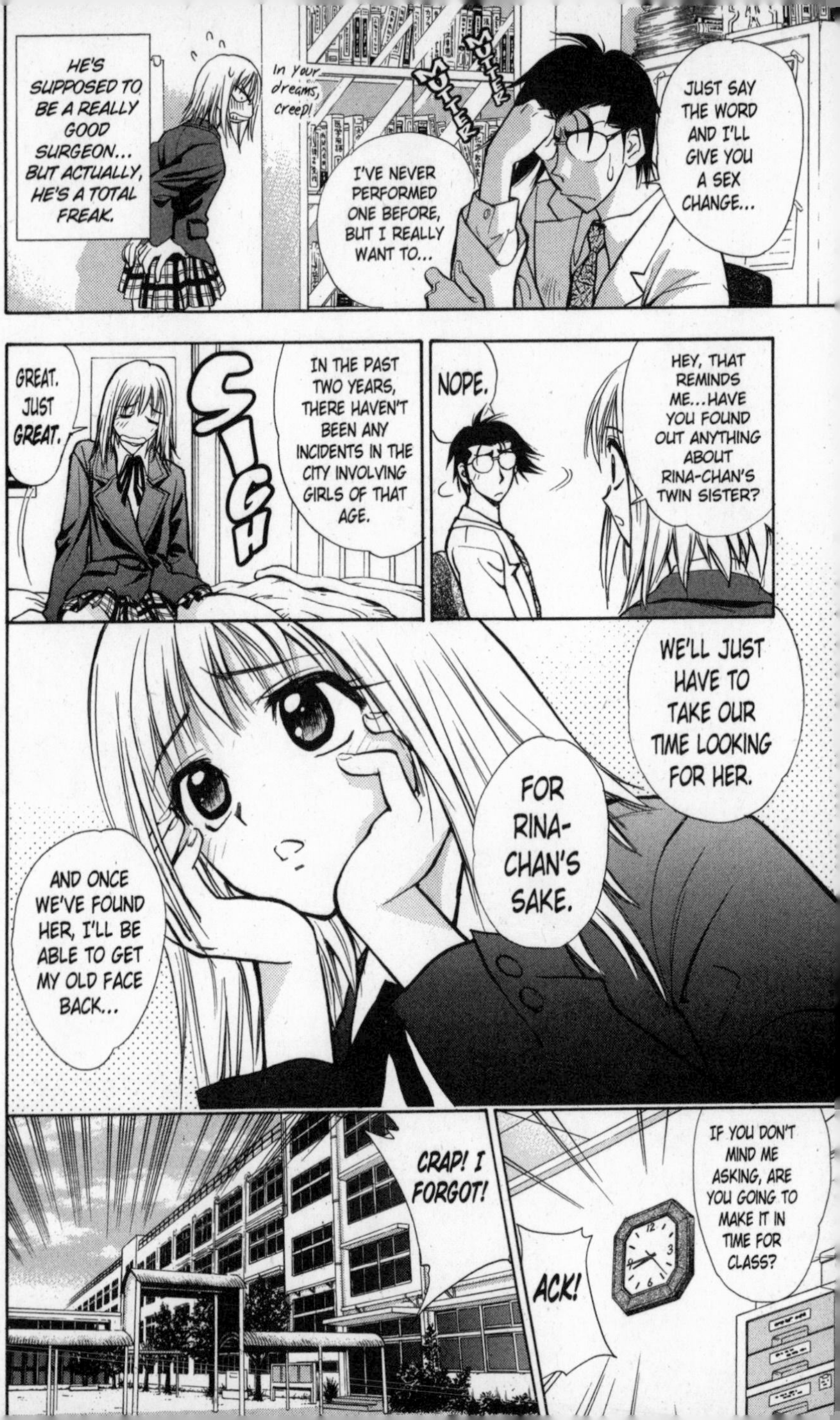
JUST SAY THE WORD AND I'LL GIVE YOU A SEX CHANGE...
MUTTER MUTTER
I'VE NEVER PERFORMED ONE BEFORE, BUT I REALLY WANT TO...
In your dreams, creep!
HE'S SUPPOSED TO BE A REALLY GOOD SURGEON... BUT ACTUALLY, HE'S A TOTAL FREAK.
HEY, THAT REMINDS ME...HAVE YOU FOUND OUT ANYTHING ABOUT RINA-CHAN'S TWIN SISTER?
NOPE.
IN THE PAST TWO YEARS, THERE HAVEN'T BEEN ANY INCIDENTS IN THE CITY INVOLVING GIRLS OF THAT AGE.
SIGH
GREAT. JUST GREAT.
WE'LL JUST HAVE TO TAKE OUR TIME LOOKING FOR HER.
FOR RINA-CHAN'S SAKE.
AND ONCE WE'VE FOUND HER, I'LL BE ABLE TO GET MY OLD FACE BACK...
IF YOU DON'T MIND ME ASKING, ARE YOU GOING TO MAKE IT IN TIME FOR CLASS?
ACK!
CRAP! I FORGOT!

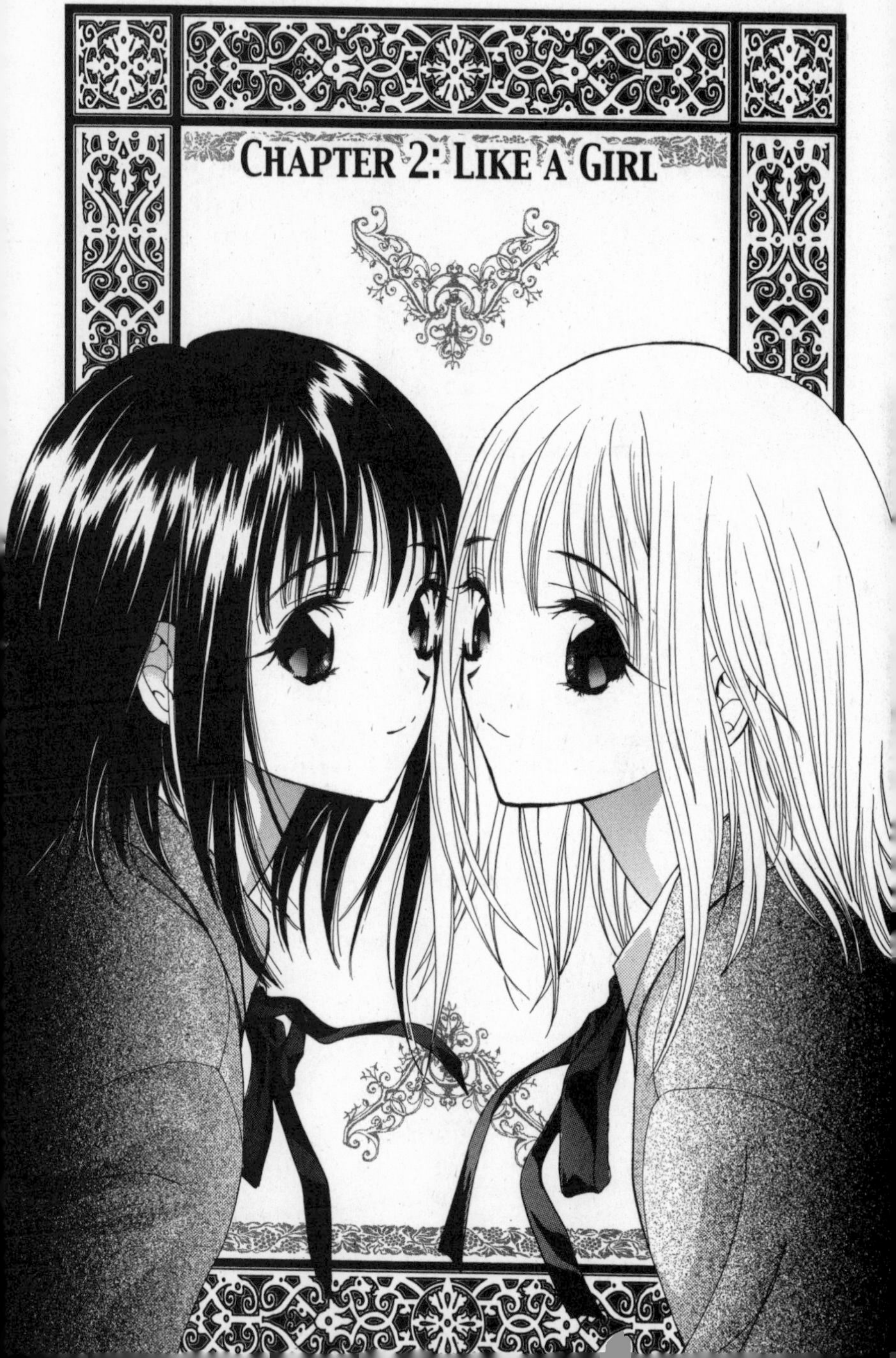
CHAPTER 2: LIKE A GIRL

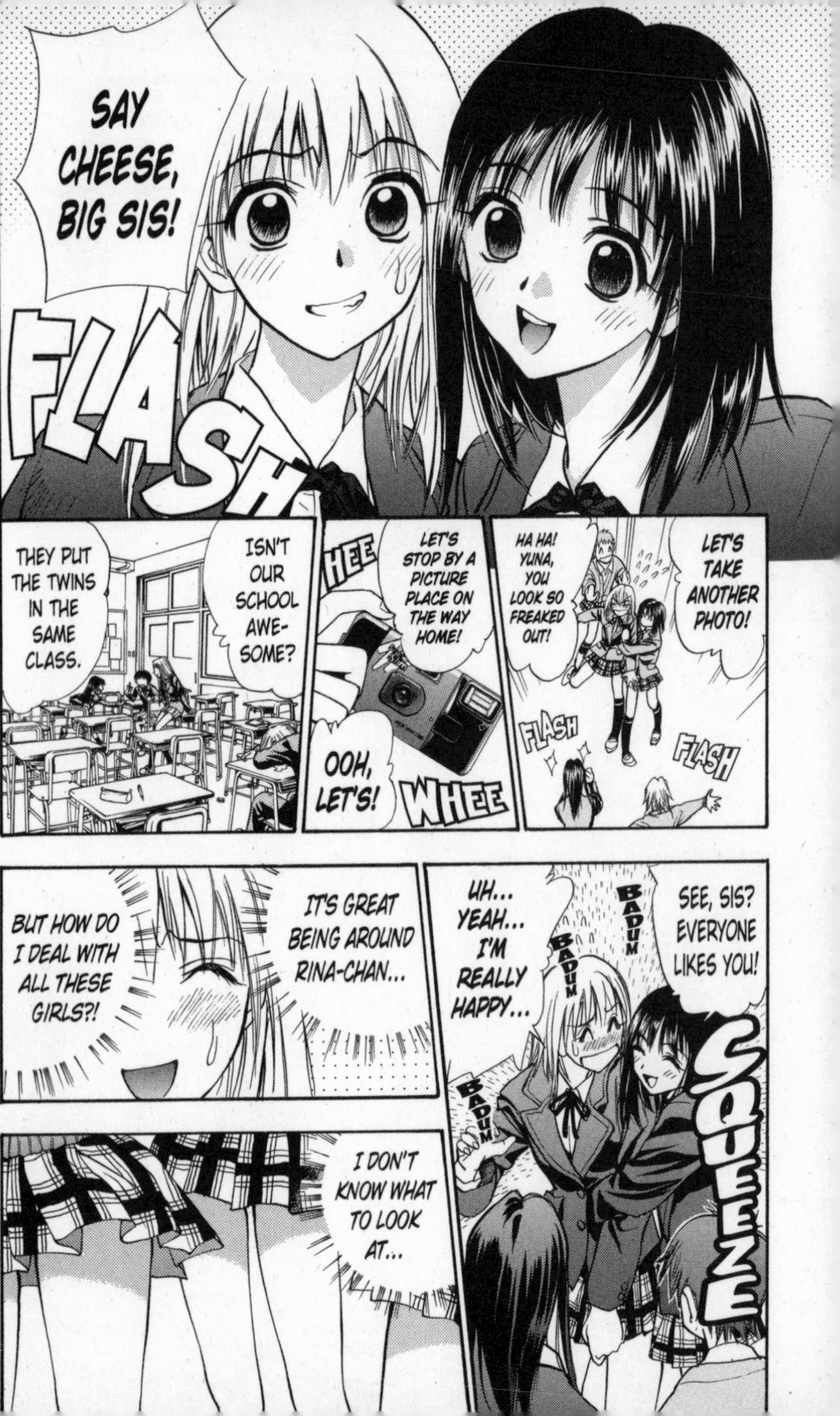
SAY CHEESE, BIG SIS!
FLASH
LET'S TAKE ANOTHER PHOTO!
HA HA! YUNA, YOU LOOK SO FREAKED OUT!
FLASH
FLASH
WHEE
LET'S STOP BY A PICTURE PLACE ON THE WAY HOME!
OOH, LET'S!
WHEE
ISN'T OUR SCHOOL AWESOME?
THEY PUT THE TWINS IN THE SAME CLASS.
SEE, SIS? EVERYONE LIKES YOU!
BADUM
UH... YEAH... I'M REALLY HAPPY...
BADUM
BADUM
SQUEEZE
IT'S GREAT BEING AROUND RINA-CHAN...
BUT HOW DO I DEAL WITH ALL THESE GIRLS?!
I DON'T KNOW WHAT TO LOOK AT...

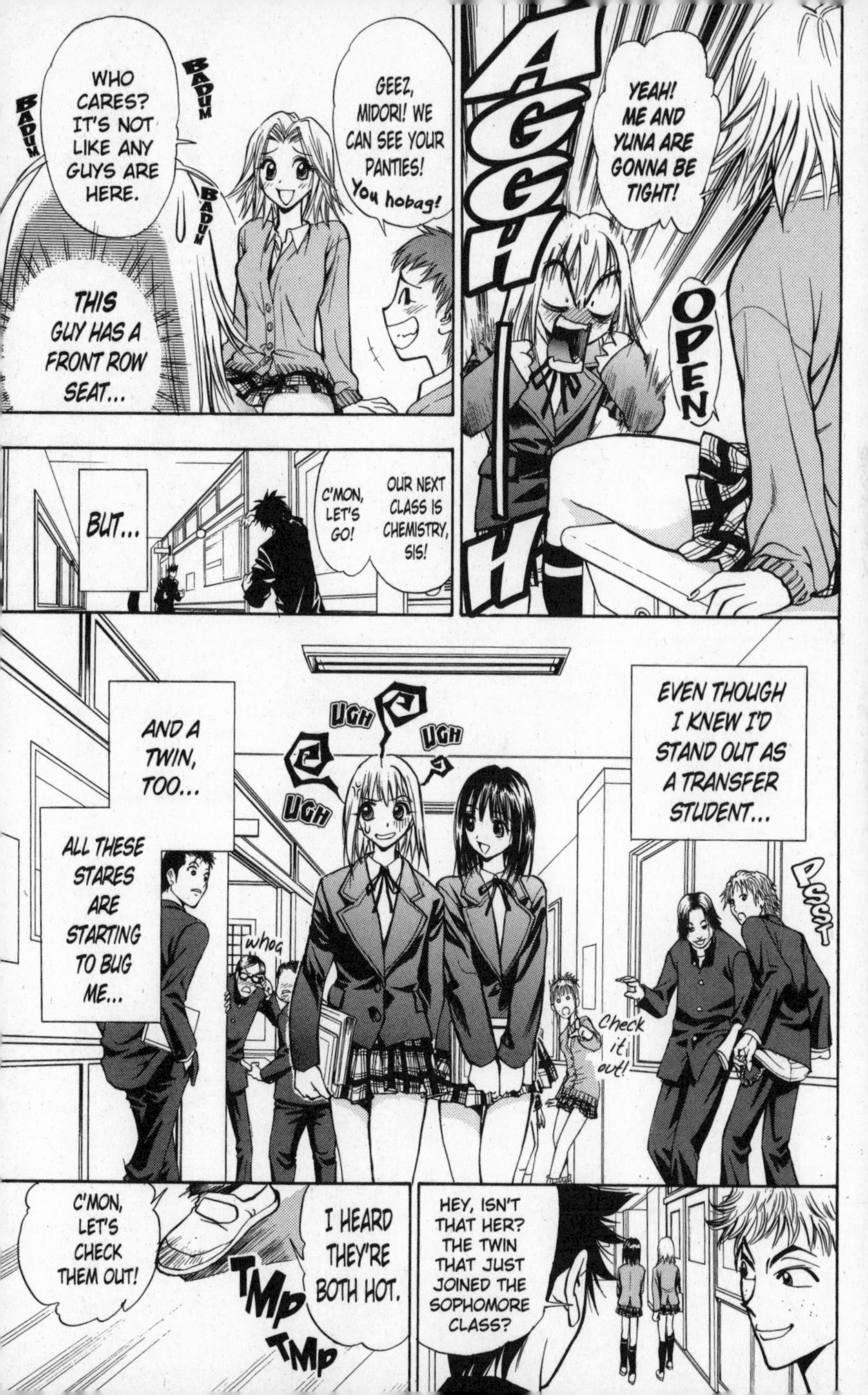
YEAH! ME AND YUNA ARE GONNA BE TIGHT!
OPEN
AGGHH
GEEZ, MIDORI! WE CAN SEE YOUR PANTIES! You hobag!
WHO CARES? IT'S NOT LIKE ANY GUYS ARE HERE.
BADUM
BADUM
BADUM
THIS GUY HAS A FRONT ROW SEAT...
OUR NEXT CLASS IS CHEMISTRY, SIS!
C'MON, LET'S GO!
BUT...
EVEN THOUGH I KNEW I'D STAND OUT AS A TRANSFER STUDENT...
PSST
Check it out!
UGH
UGH
UGH
AND A TWIN, TOO...
whoa
ALL THESE STARES ARE STARTING TO BUG ME...
HEY, ISN'T THAT HER? THE TWIN THAT JUST JOINED THE SOPHOMORE CLASS?
I HEARD THEY'RE BOTH HOT.
C'MON, LET'S CHECK THEM OUT!
TMP
TMP

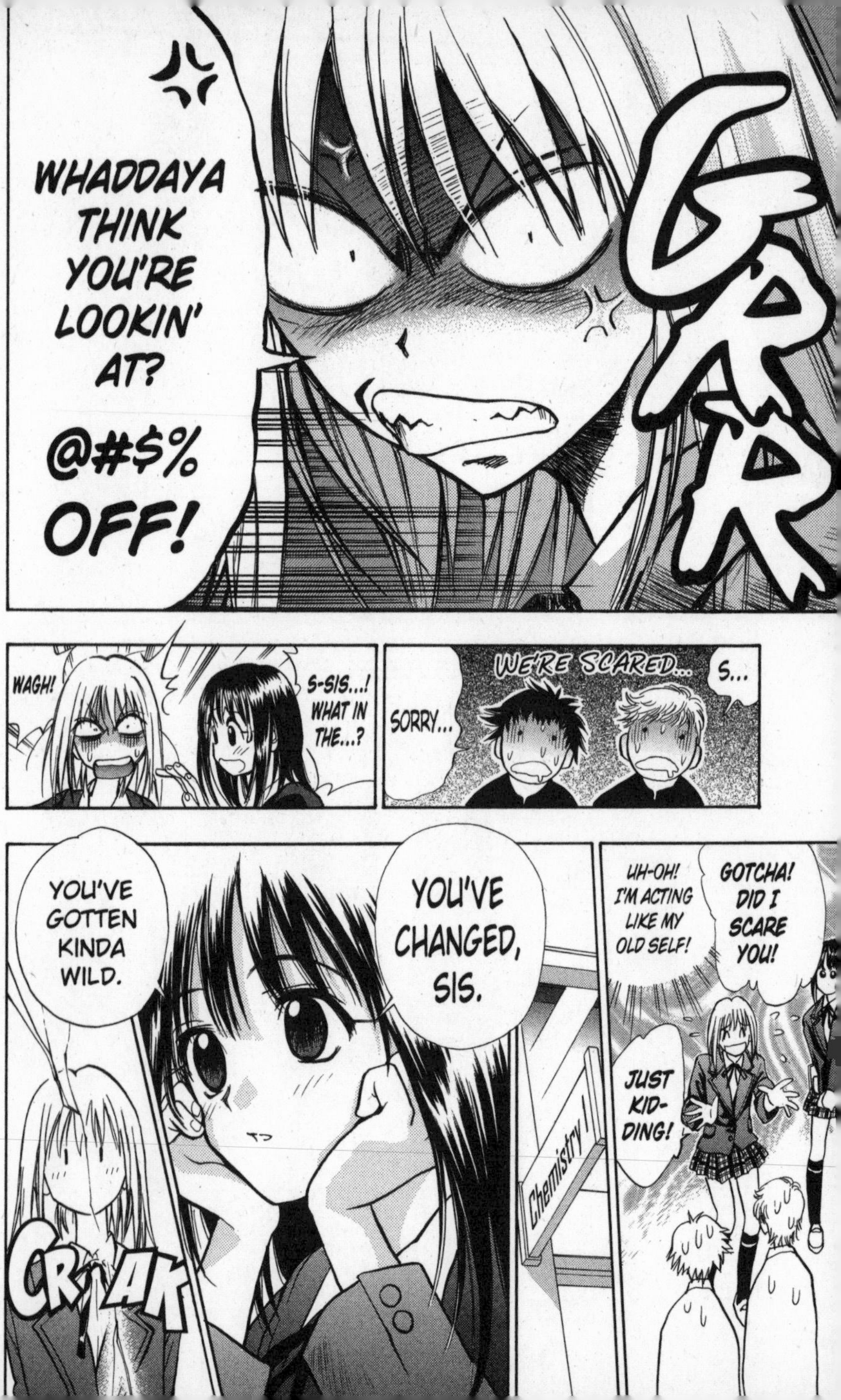
GRRR
WHADDAYA THINK YOU'RE LOOKIN' AT? @#$% OFF!
S...
WE'RE SCARED...
SORRY...
S-SIS...! WHAT IN THE...?
WAGH!
GOTCHA! DID I SCARE YOU!
UH-OH! I'M ACTING LIKE MY OLD SELF!
JUST KID-DING!
YOU'VE CHANGED, SIS.
YOU'VE GOTTEN KINDA WILD.
Chemistry
CRAK

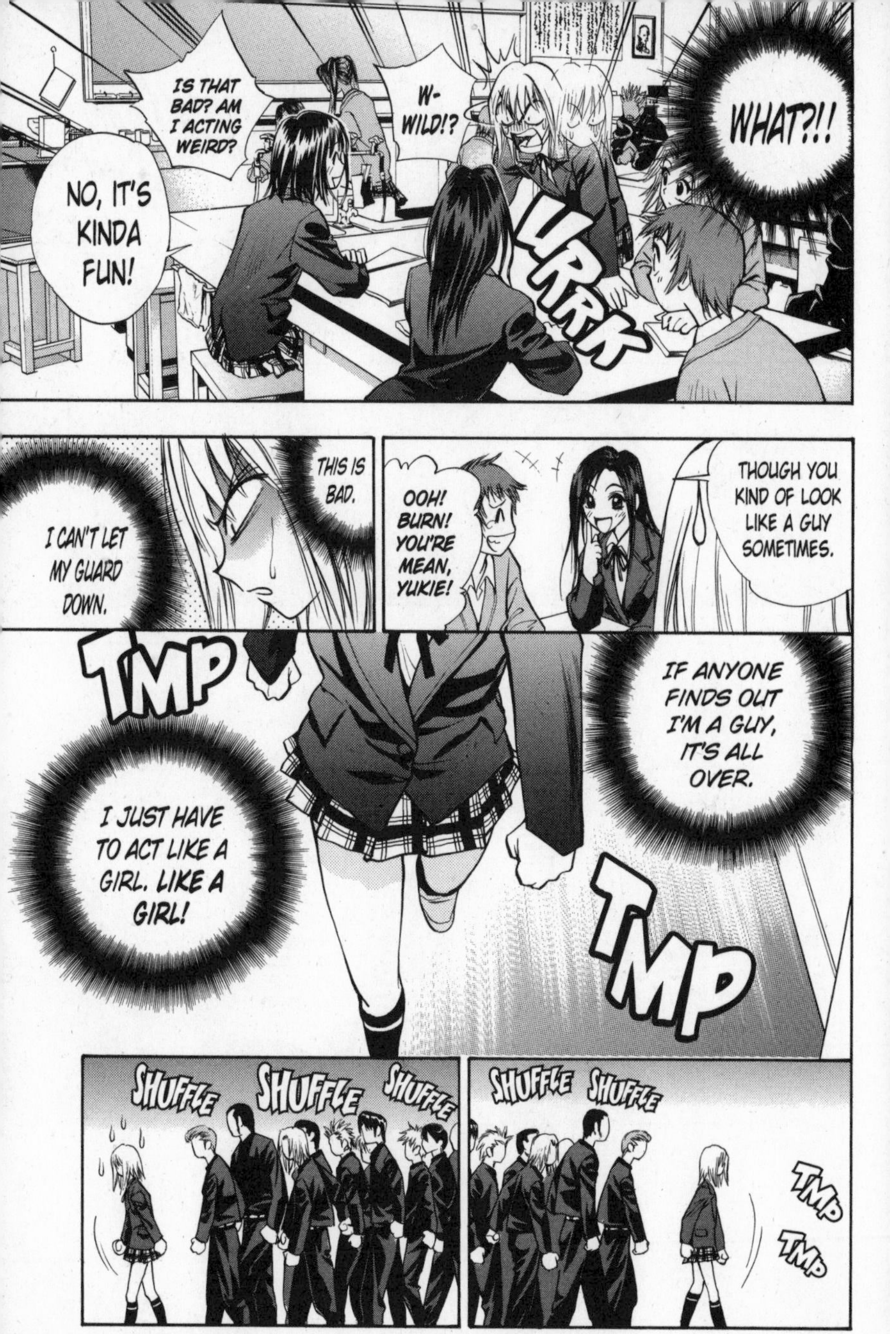
WHAT?!!
W-WILD!?
IS THAT BAD? AM I ACTING WEIRD?
URRK
NO, IT'S KINDA FUN!
THOUGH YOU KIND OF LOOK LIKE A GUY SOMETIMES.
OOH! BURN! YOU'RE MEAN, YUKIE!
THIS IS BAD.
I CAN'T LET MY GUARD DOWN.
IF ANYONE FINDS OUT I'M A GUY, IT'S ALL OVER.
TMP
I JUST HAVE TO ACT LIKE A GIRL. LIKE A GIRL!
TMP
SHUFFLE SHUFFLE
TMP
TMP
SHUFFLE SHUFFLE SHUFFLE

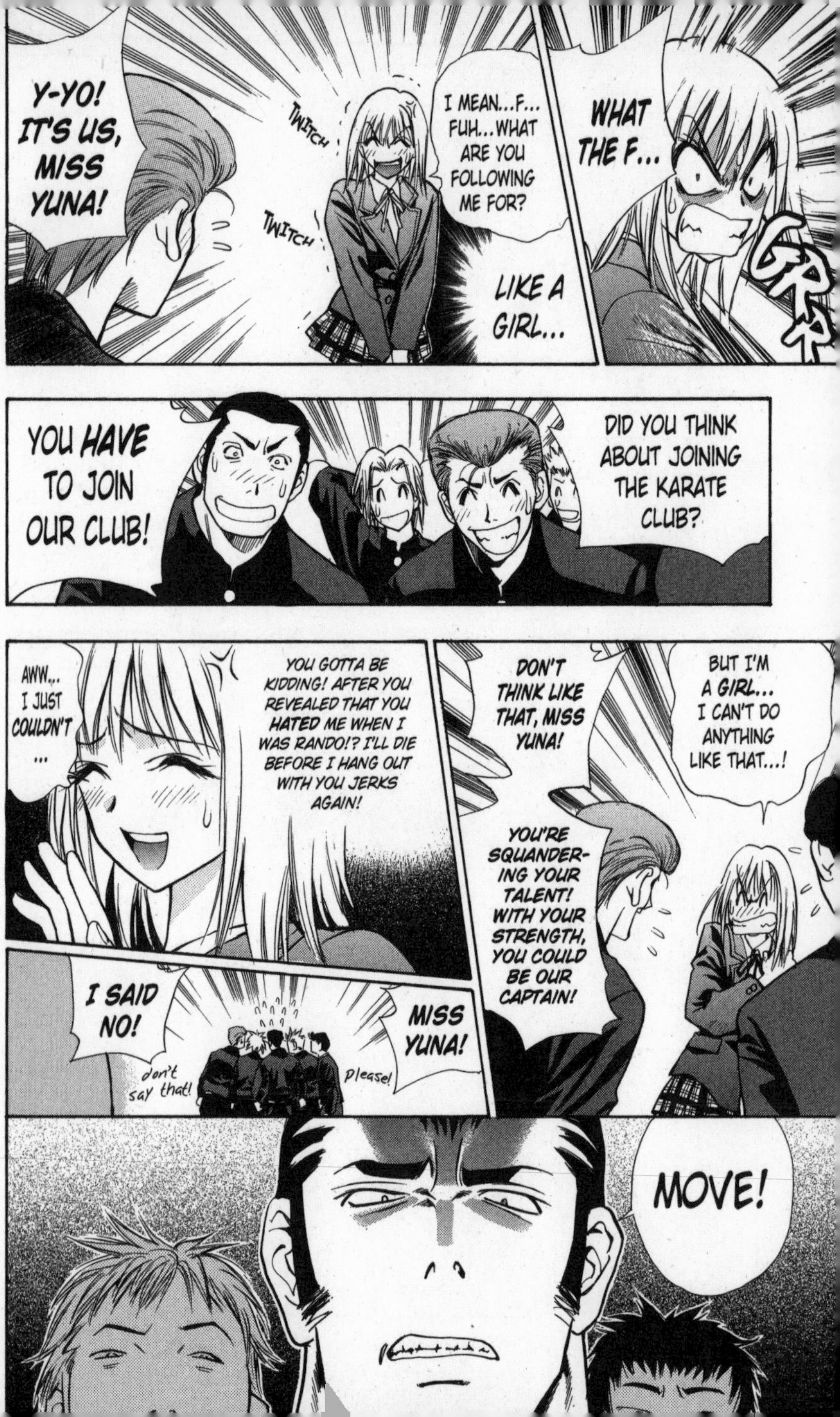
WHAT THE F...
GRR
I MEAN...F... FUH...WHAT ARE YOU FOLLOWING ME FOR?
TWITCH
TWITCH
LIKE A GIRL...
Y-YO! IT'S US, MISS YUNA!
DID YOU THINK ABOUT JOINING THE KARATE CLUB?
YOU HAVE TO JOIN OUR CLUB!
BUT I'M A GIRL... I CAN'T DO ANYTHING LIKE THAT...!
DON'T THINK LIKE THAT, MISS YUNA!
YOU'RE SQUANDER-ING YOUR TALENT! WITH YOUR STRENGTH, YOU COULD BE OUR CAPTAIN!
YOU GOTTA BE KIDDING! AFTER YOU REVEALED THAT YOU HATED ME WHEN I WAS RANDO!? I'LL DIE BEFORE I HANG OUT WITH YOU JERKS AGAIN!
AWW... I JUST COULDN'T ...
MISS YUNA!
Please!
don't say that!
I SAID NO!
MOVE!

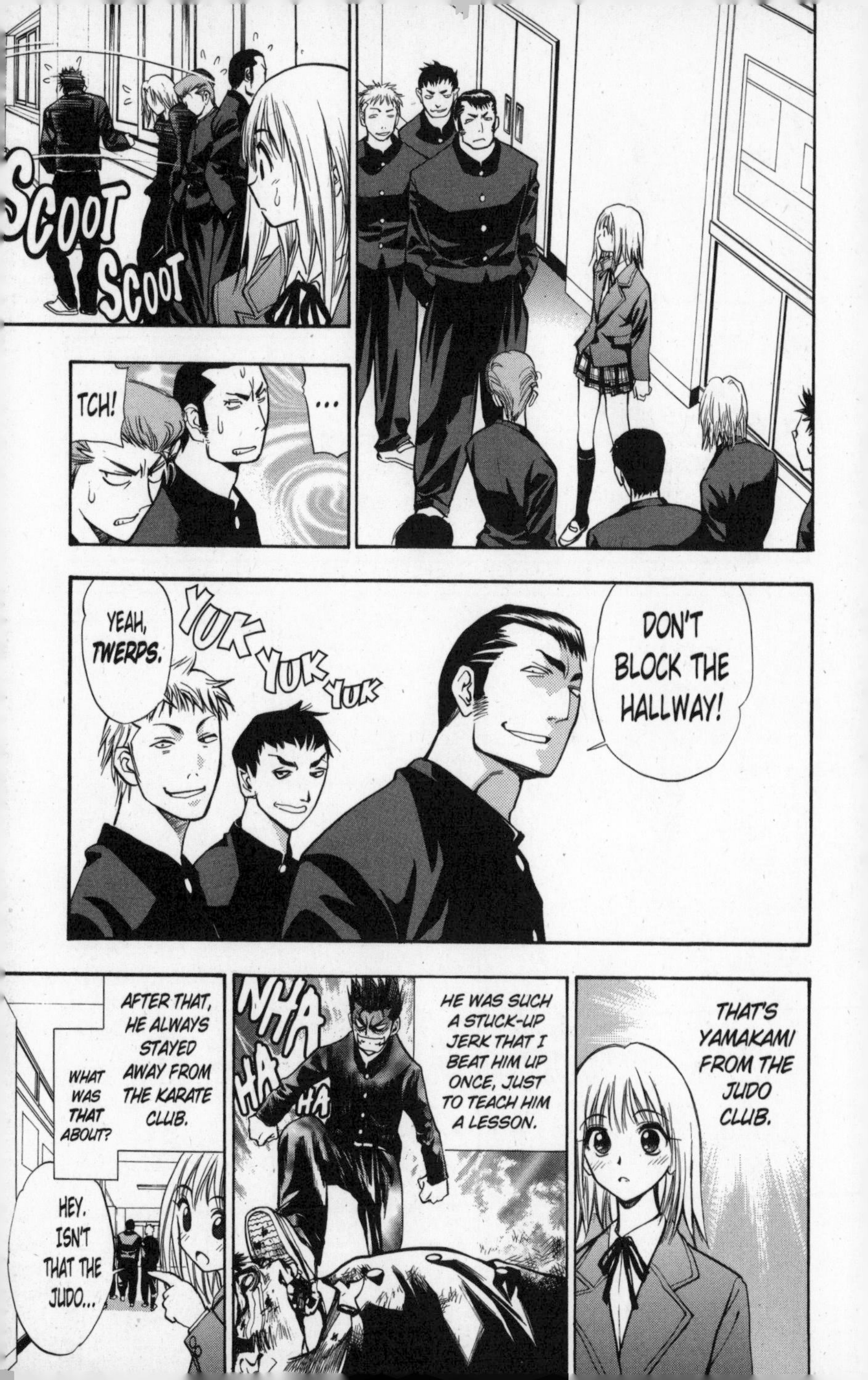
SCOOT
SCOOT
...
TCH!
DON'T BLOCK THE HALLWAY!
YUK YUK YUK
YEAH, TWERPS.
THAT'S YAMAKAMI FROM THE JUDO CLUB.
HE WAS SUCH A STUCK-UP JERK THAT I BEAT HIM UP ONCE, JUST TO TEACH HIM A LESSON.
NHA HA HA
AFTER THAT, HE ALWAYS STAYED AWAY FROM THE KARATE CLUB.
WHAT WAS THAT ABOUT?
HEY. ISN'T THAT THE JUDO...

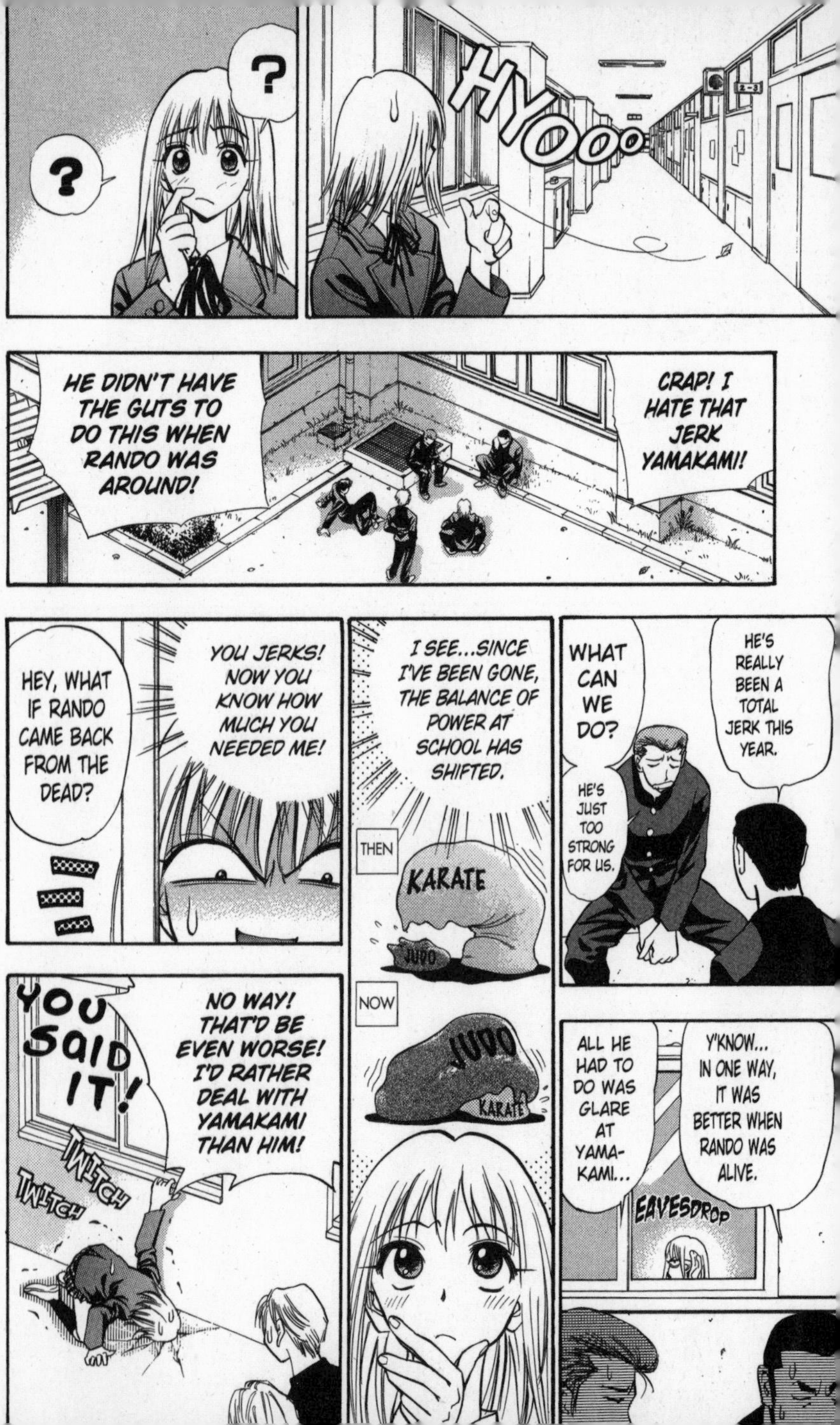
HYOOoo
?
?
CRAP! I HATE THAT JERK YAMAKAMI!
HE DIDN'T HAVE THE GUTS TO DO THIS WHEN RANDO WAS AROUND!
HE'S REALLY BEEN A TOTAL JERK THIS YEAR.
WHAT CAN WE DO?
HE'S JUST TOO STRONG FOR US.
Y'KNOW... IN ONE WAY, IT WAS BETTER WHEN RANDO WAS ALIVE.
ALL HE HAD TO DO WAS GLARE AT YAMA-KAMI...
EAVESDROP
I SEE...SINCE I'VE BEEN GONE, THE BALANCE OF POWER AT SCHOOL HAS SHIFTED.
THEN
KARATE
JUDO
NOW
JUDO
KARATE
YOU JERKS! NOW YOU KNOW HOW MUCH YOU NEEDED ME!
HEY, WHAT IF RANDO CAME BACK FROM THE DEAD?
NO WAY! THAT'D BE EVEN WORSE! I'D RATHER DEAL WITH YAMAKAMI THAN HIM!
YOU SAID IT!
TWITCH
TWITCH

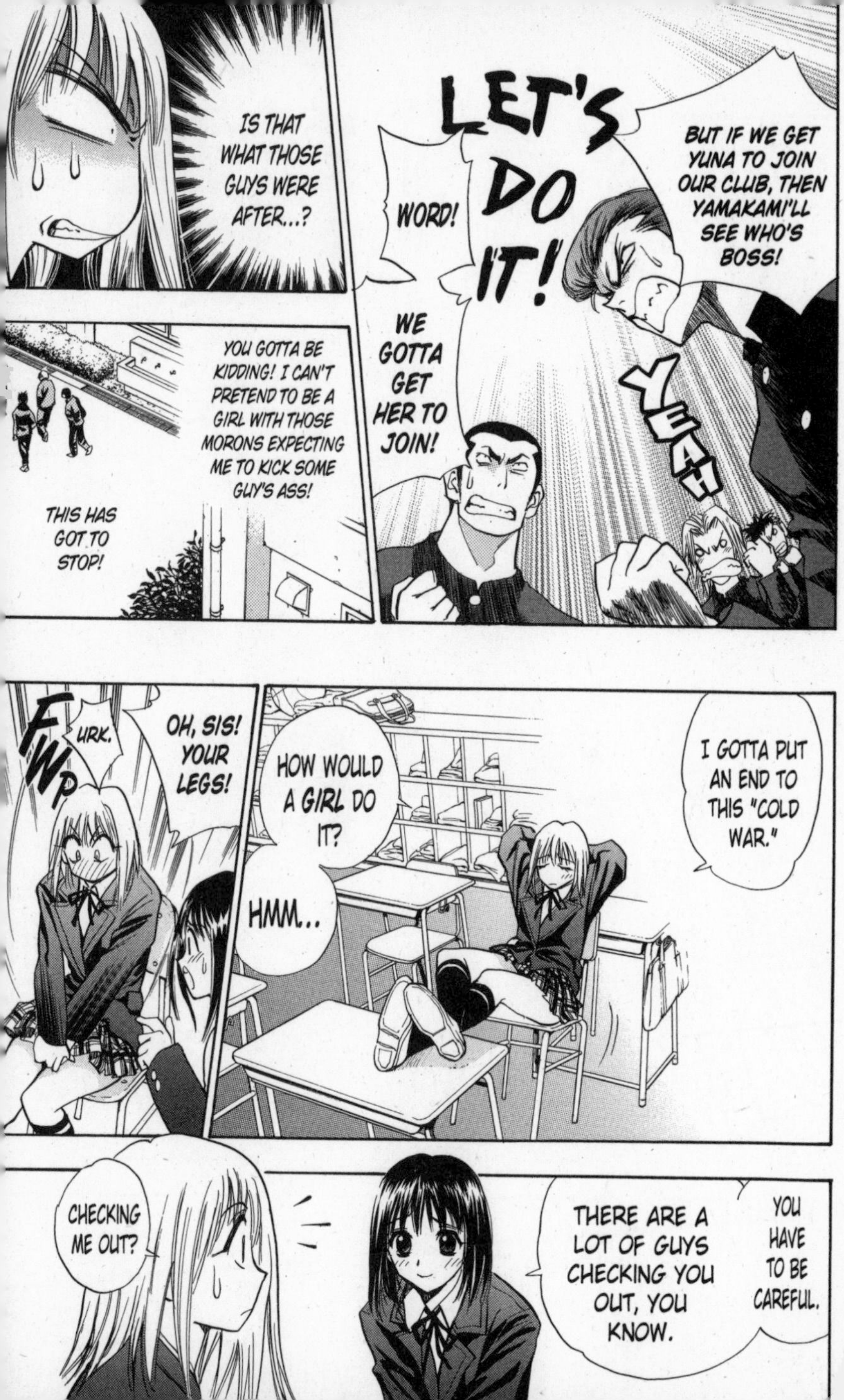
BUT IF WE GET YUNA TO JOIN OUR CLUB, THEN YAMAKAMI'LL SEE WHO'S BOSS!
LET'S DO IT!
WORD!
YEAH
WE GOTTA GET HER TO JOIN!
IS THAT WHAT THOSE GUYS WERE AFTER...?
YOU GOTTA BE KIDDING! I CAN'T PRETEND TO BE A GIRL WITH THOSE MORONS EXPECTING ME TO KICK SOME GUY'S ASS!
THIS HAS GOT TO STOP!
I GOTTA PUT AN END TO THIS "COLD WAR."
HOW WOULD A GIRL DO IT?
HMM..
OH, SIS! YOUR LEGS!
URK.
FWP
YOU HAVE TO BE CAREFUL.
THERE ARE A LOT OF GUYS CHECKING YOU OUT, YOU KNOW.
CHECKING ME OUT?

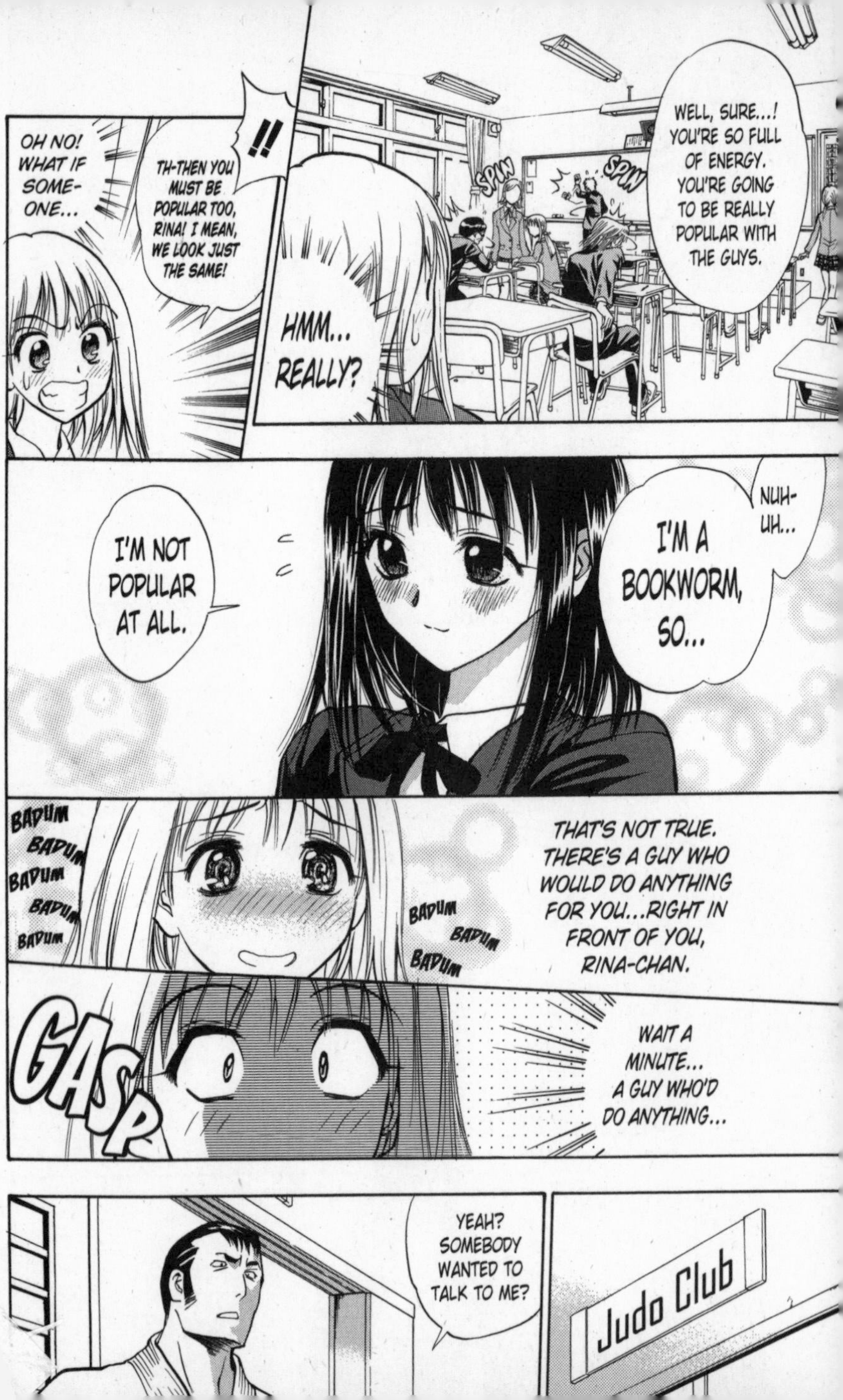
WELL, SURE...! YOU'RE SO FULL OF ENERGY. YOU'RE GOING TO BE REALLY POPULAR WITH THE GUYS.
SPIN
SPIN
HMM... REALLY?
!!
TH-THEN YOU MUST BE POPULAR TOO, RINA! I MEAN, WE LOOK JUST THE SAME!
OH NO! WHAT IF SOME-ONE...
NUH-UH...
I'M A BOOKWORM, SO...
I'M NOT POPULAR AT ALL.
THAT'S NOT TRUE. THERE'S A GUY WHO WOULD DO ANYTHING FOR YOU...RIGHT IN FRONT OF YOU, RINA-CHAN.
BADUM BADUM BADUM
BADUM BADUM BADUM BADUM BADUM
WAIT A MINUTE... A GUY WHO'D DO ANYTHING...
GASP
Judo Club
YEAH? SOMEBODY WANTED TO TALK TO ME?

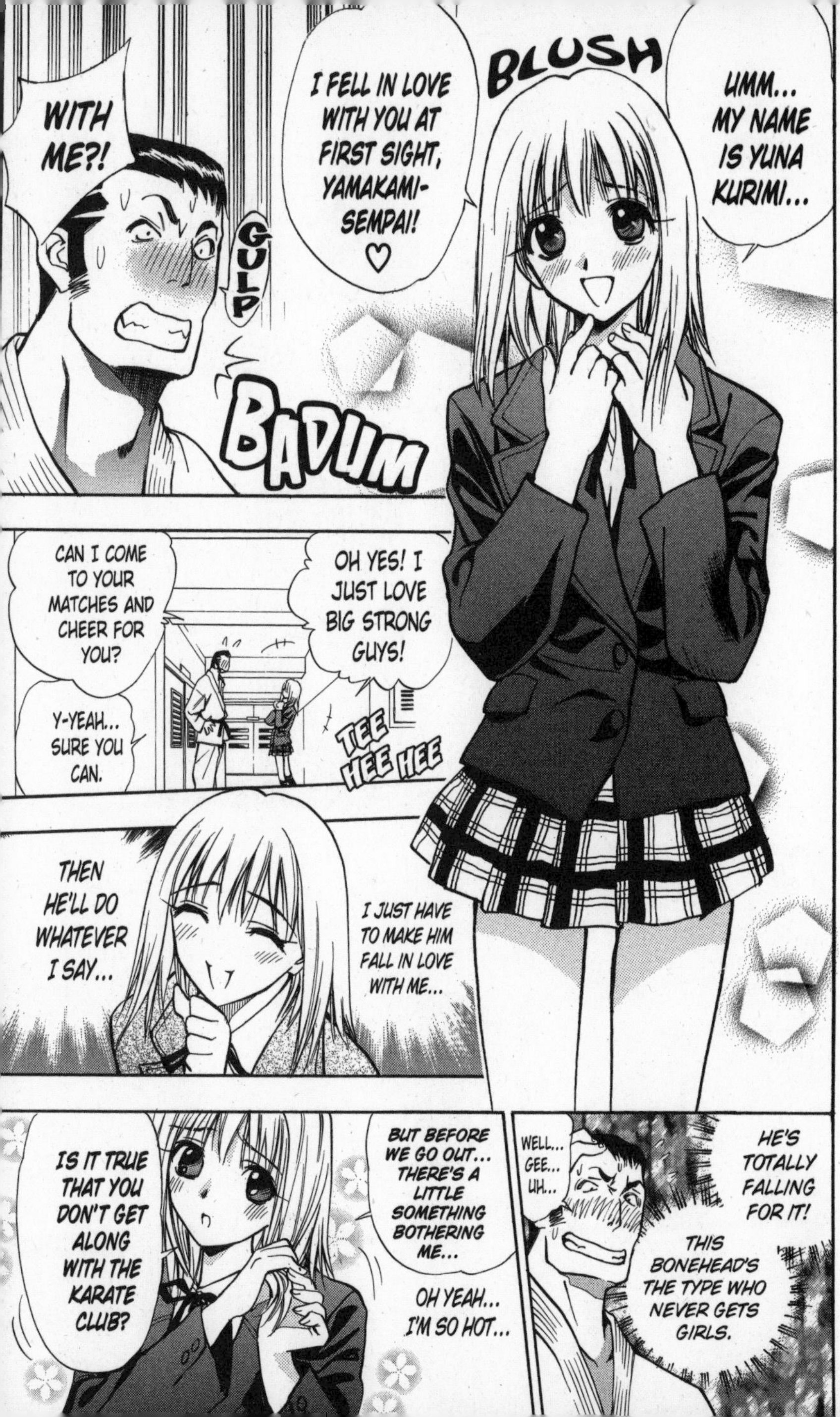
UMM... MY NAME IS YUNA KURIMI...
BLUSH
I FELL IN LOVE WITH YOU AT FIRST SIGHT, YAMAKAMI-SEMPAI! ♡
WITH ME?!
GULP
BADUM
CAN I COME TO YOUR MATCHES AND CHEER FOR YOU?
Y-YEAH... SURE YOU CAN.
OH YES! I JUST LOVE BIG STRONG GUYS!
TEE HEE HEE
I JUST HAVE TO MAKE HIM FALL IN LOVE WITH ME...
THEN HE'LL DO WHATEVER I SAY...
HE'S TOTALLY FALLING FOR IT!
WELL... GEE... UH...
THIS BONEHEAD'S THE TYPE WHO NEVER GETS GIRLS.
OH YEAH... I'M SO HOT...
BUT BEFORE WE GO OUT... THERE'S A LITTLE SOMETHING BOTHERING ME...
IS IT TRUE THAT YOU DON'T GET ALONG WITH THE KARATE CLUB?

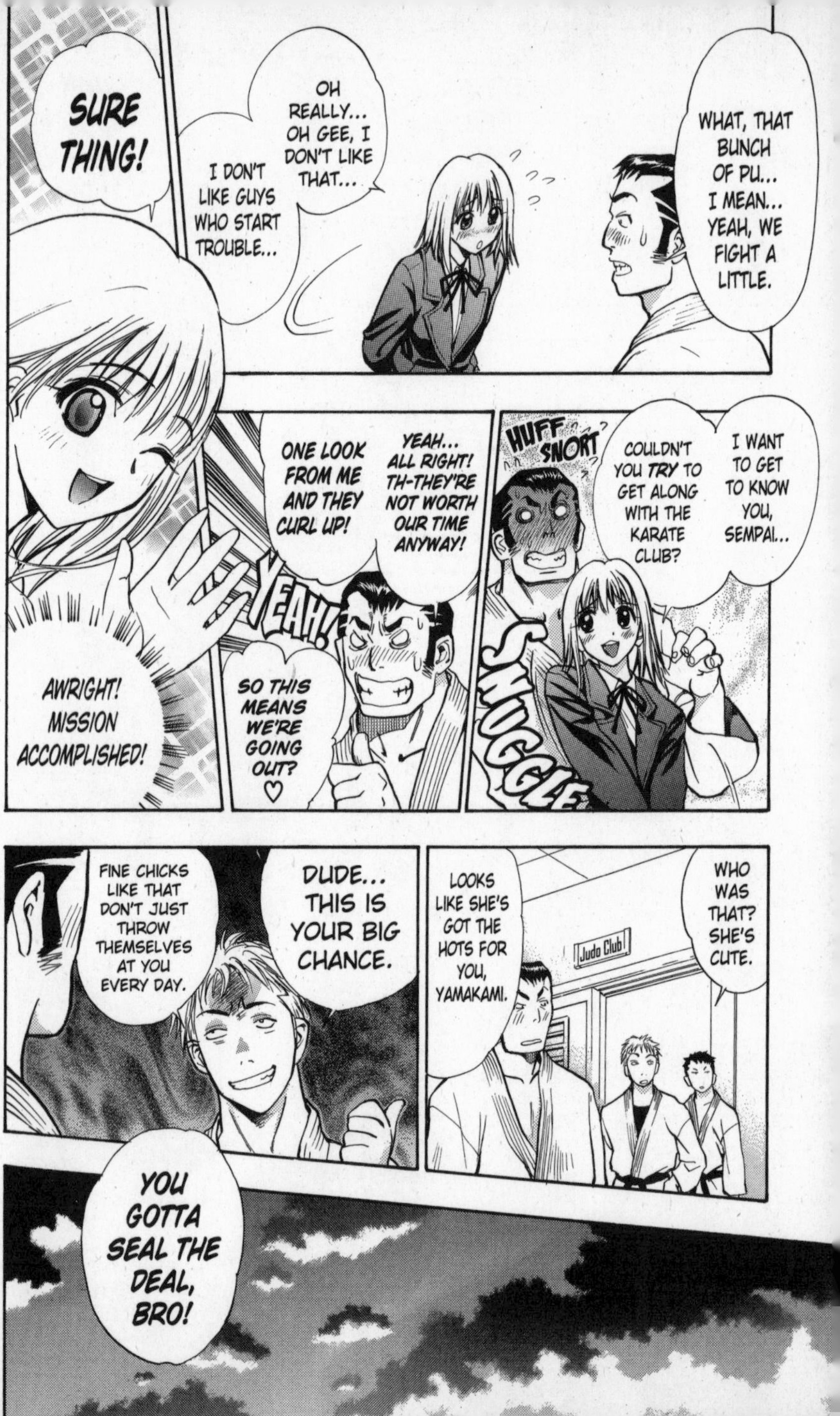
WHAT, THAT BUNCH OF PU... I MEAN... YEAH, WE FIGHT A LITTLE.
OH REALLY... OH GEE, I DON'T LIKE THAT...
I DON'T LIKE GUYS WHO START TROUBLE...
I WANT TO GET TO KNOW YOU, SEMPAI...
COULDN'T YOU TRY TO GET ALONG WITH THE KARATE CLUB?
HUFF SNORT
SNUGGLE
YEAH... ALL RIGHT! TH-THEY'RE NOT WORTH OUR TIME ANYWAY!
ONE LOOK FROM ME AND THEY CURL UP!
YEAH!
SO THIS MEANS WE'RE GOING OUT? ♡
SURE THING!
AWRIGHT! MISSION ACCOMPLISHED!
WHO WAS THAT? SHE'S CUTE.
Judo Club
LOOKS LIKE SHE'S GOT THE HOTS FOR YOU, YAMAKAMI.
DUDE... THIS IS YOUR BIG CHANCE.
FINE CHICKS LIKE THAT DON'T JUST THROW THEMSELVES AT YOU EVERY DAY.
YOU GOTTA SEAL THE DEAL, BRO!

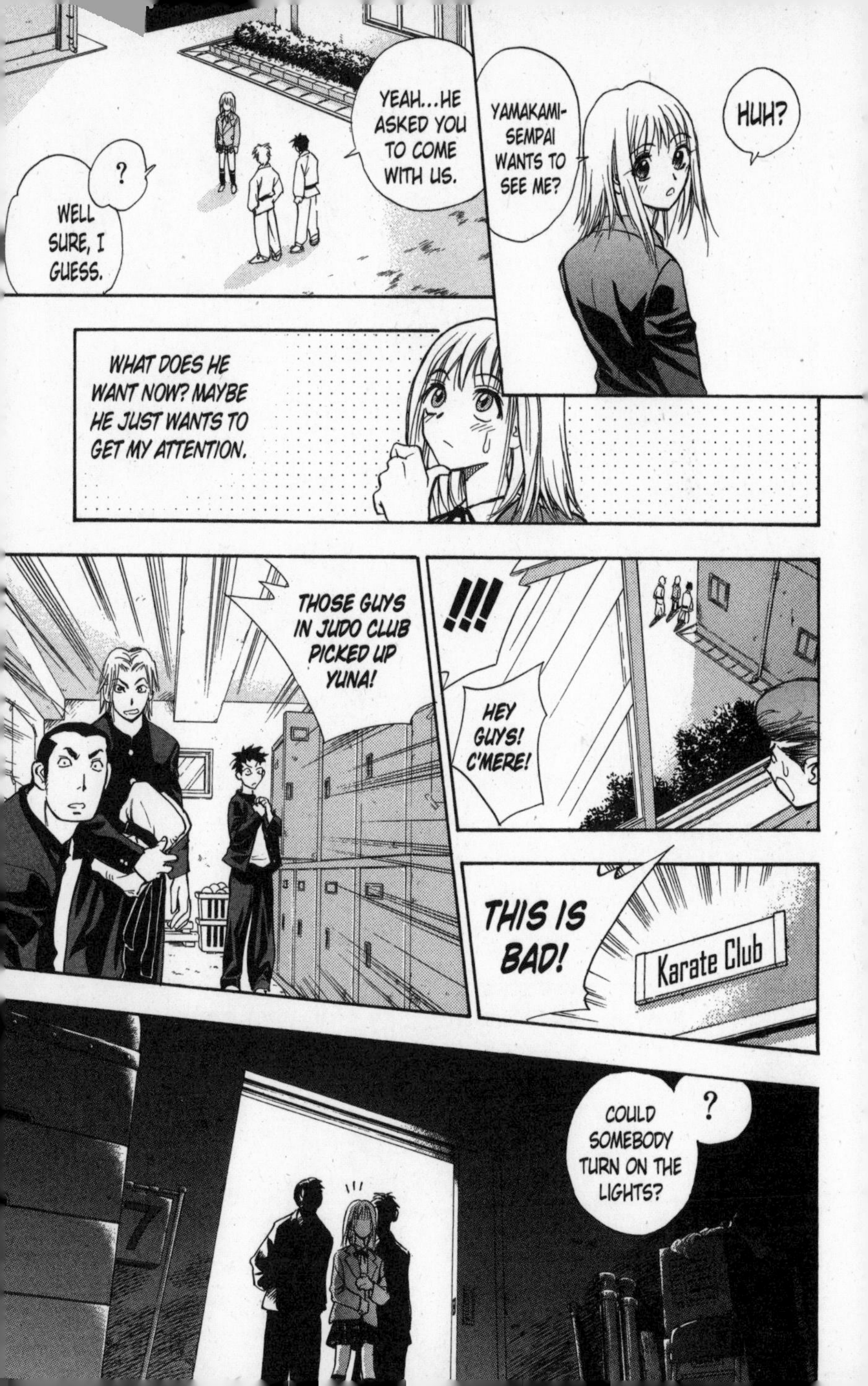
HUH?
YAMAKAMI-SEMPAI WANTS TO SEE ME?
YEAH...HE ASKED YOU TO COME WITH US.
?
WELL SURE, I GUESS.
WHAT DOES HE WANT NOW? MAYBE HE JUST WANTS TO GET MY ATTENTION.
!!!
HEY GUYS! C'MERE!
THIS IS BAD!
Karate Club
THOSE GUYS IN JUDO CLUB PICKED UP YUNA!
?
COULD SOMEBODY TURN ON THE LIGHTS?

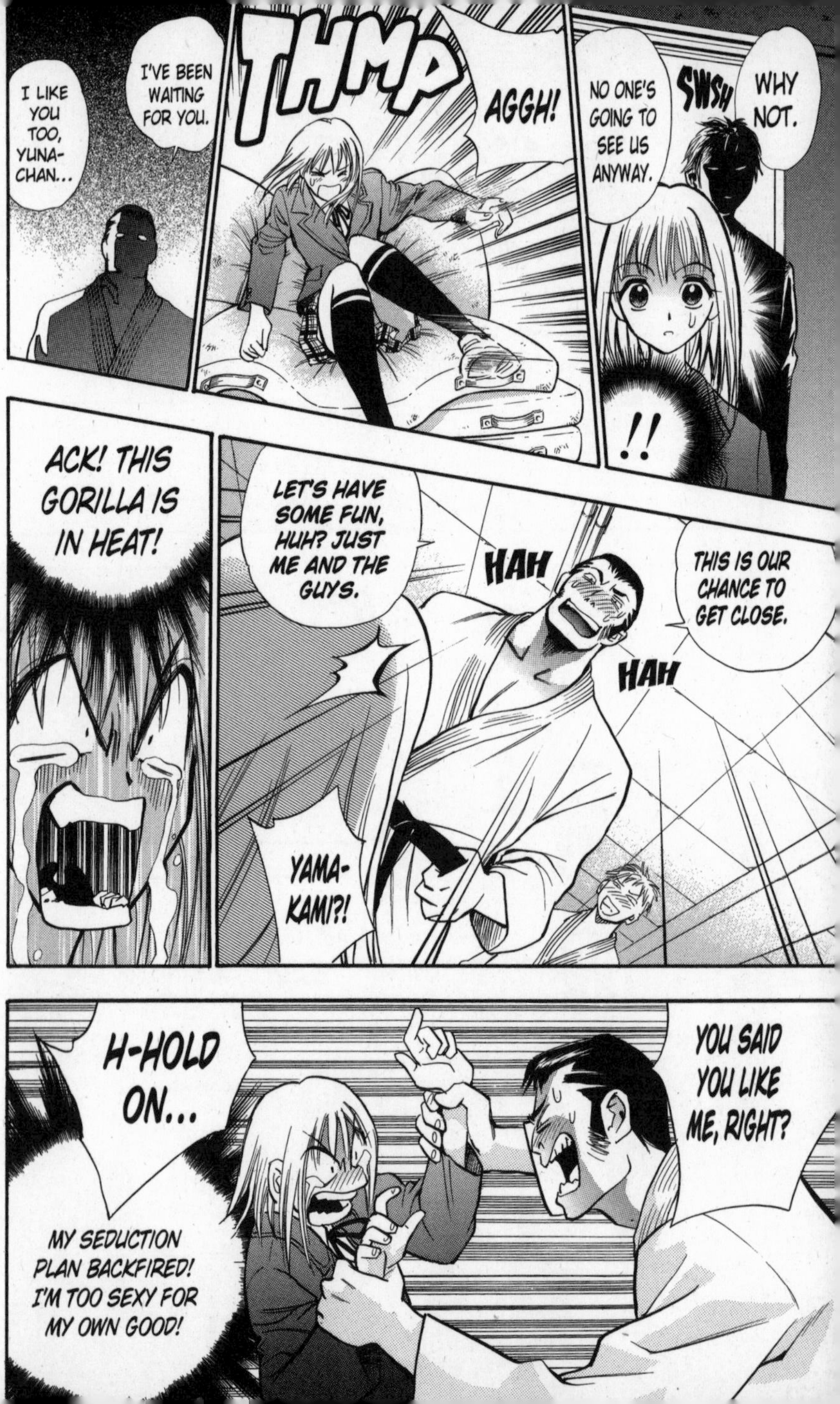
WHY NOT.
SWSH
NO ONE'S GOING TO SEE US ANYWAY.
!!
THMP
AGGH!
I'VE BEEN WAITING FOR YOU.
I LIKE YOU TOO, YUNA-CHAN...
THIS IS OUR CHANCE TO GET CLOSE.
HAH
HAH
LET'S HAVE SOME FUN, HUH? JUST ME AND THE GUYS.
YAMA-KAMI?!
ACK! THIS GORILLA IS IN HEAT!
YOU SAID YOU LIKE ME, RIGHT?
H-HOLD ON...
MY SEDUCTION PLAN BACKFIRED! I'M TOO SEXY FOR MY OWN GOOD!

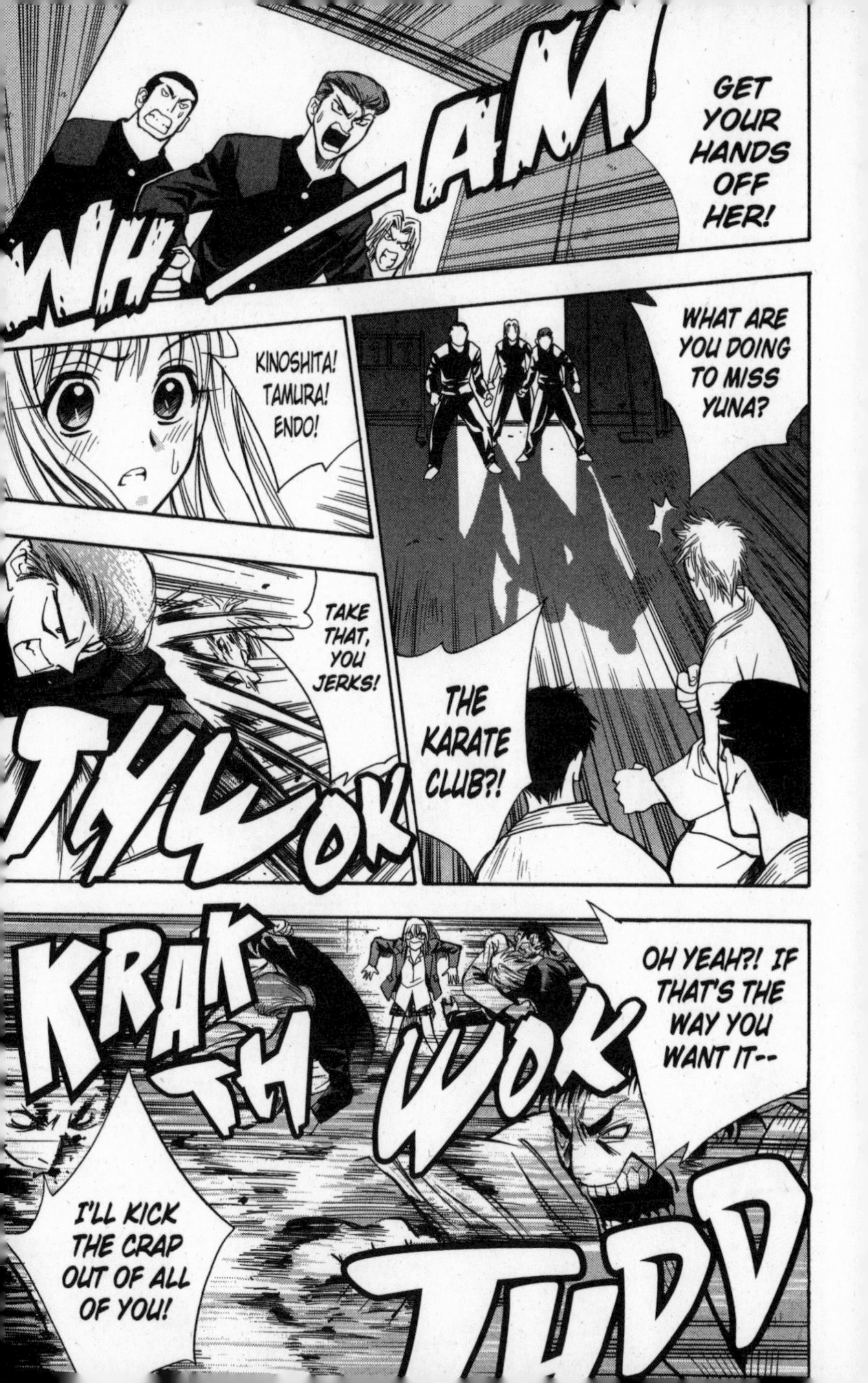
GET YOUR HANDS OFF HER!
WHAM
WHAT ARE YOU DOING TO MISS YUNA?
THE KARATE CLUB?!
KINOSHITA! TAMURA! ENDO!
TAKE THAT, YOU JERKS!
THWOK
OH YEAH?! IF THAT'S THE WAY YOU WANT IT--
THWOK
KRAK
I'LL KICK THE CRAP OUT OF ALL OF YOU!
TUDD

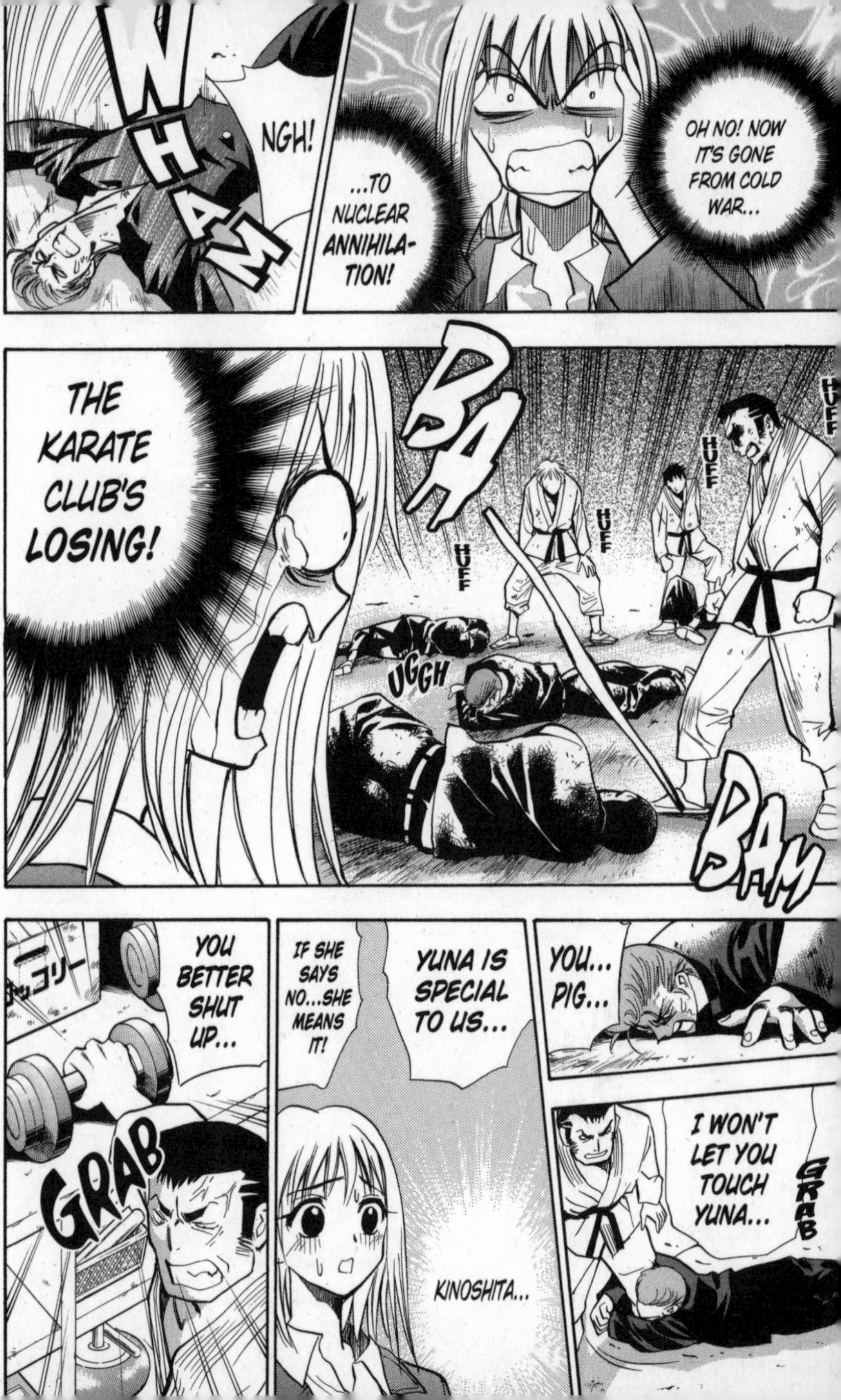
OH NO! NOW IT'S GONE FROM COLD WAR...
...TO NUCLEAR ANNIHILATION!
WHAM
NGH!
BAM
HUFF
HUFF
HUFF
HUFF
THE KARATE CLUB'S LOSING!
UGGH
BAM
YOU... PIG...
I WON'T LET YOU TOUCH YUNA...
GRAB
YUNA IS SPECIAL TO US...
IF SHE SAYS NO...SHE MEANS IT!
KINOSHITA...
YOU BETTER SHUT UP...
GRAB

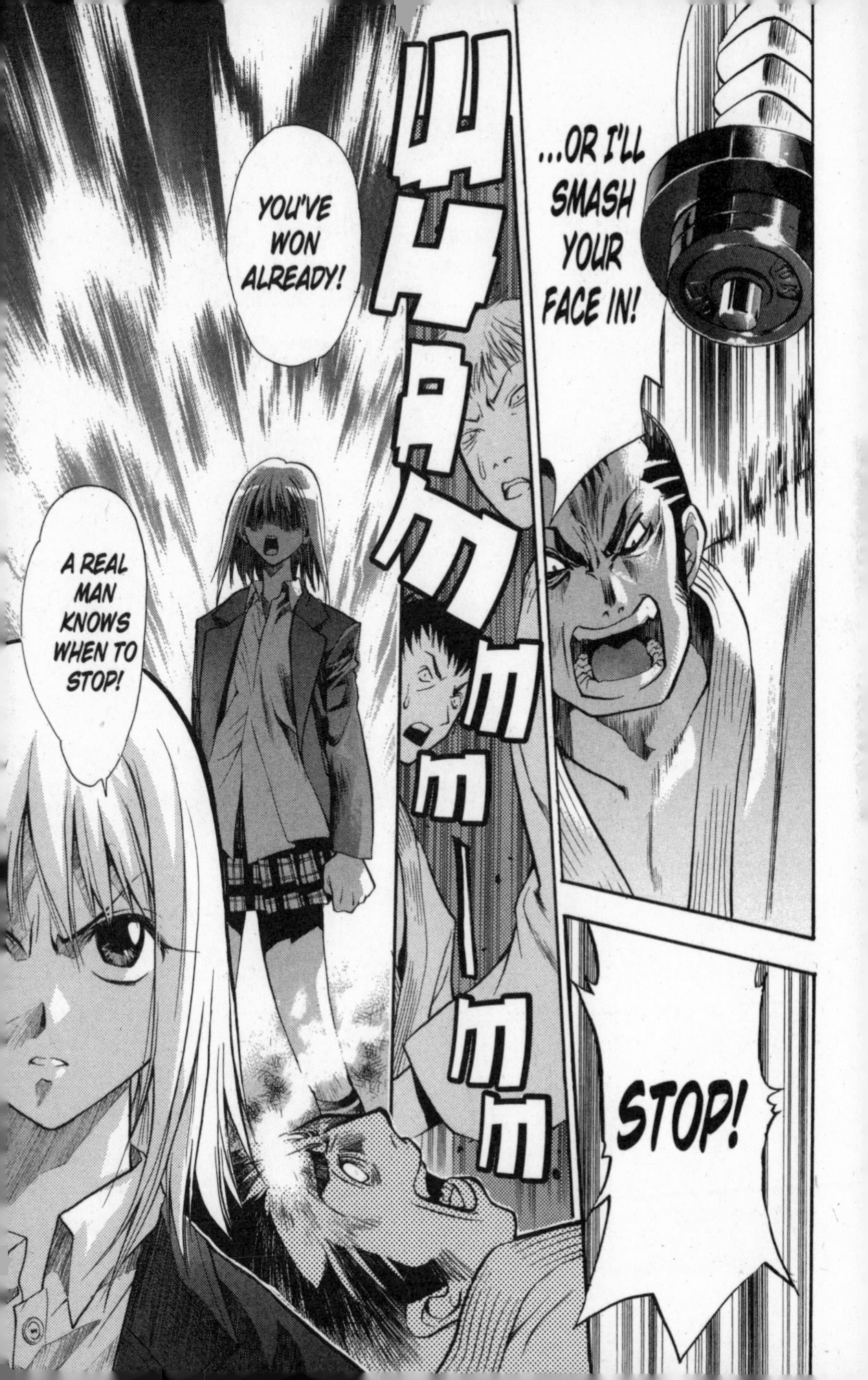
...OR I'LL SMASH YOUR FACE IN!
STOP!
YOU'VE WON ALREADY!
A REAL MAN KNOWS WHEN TO STOP!

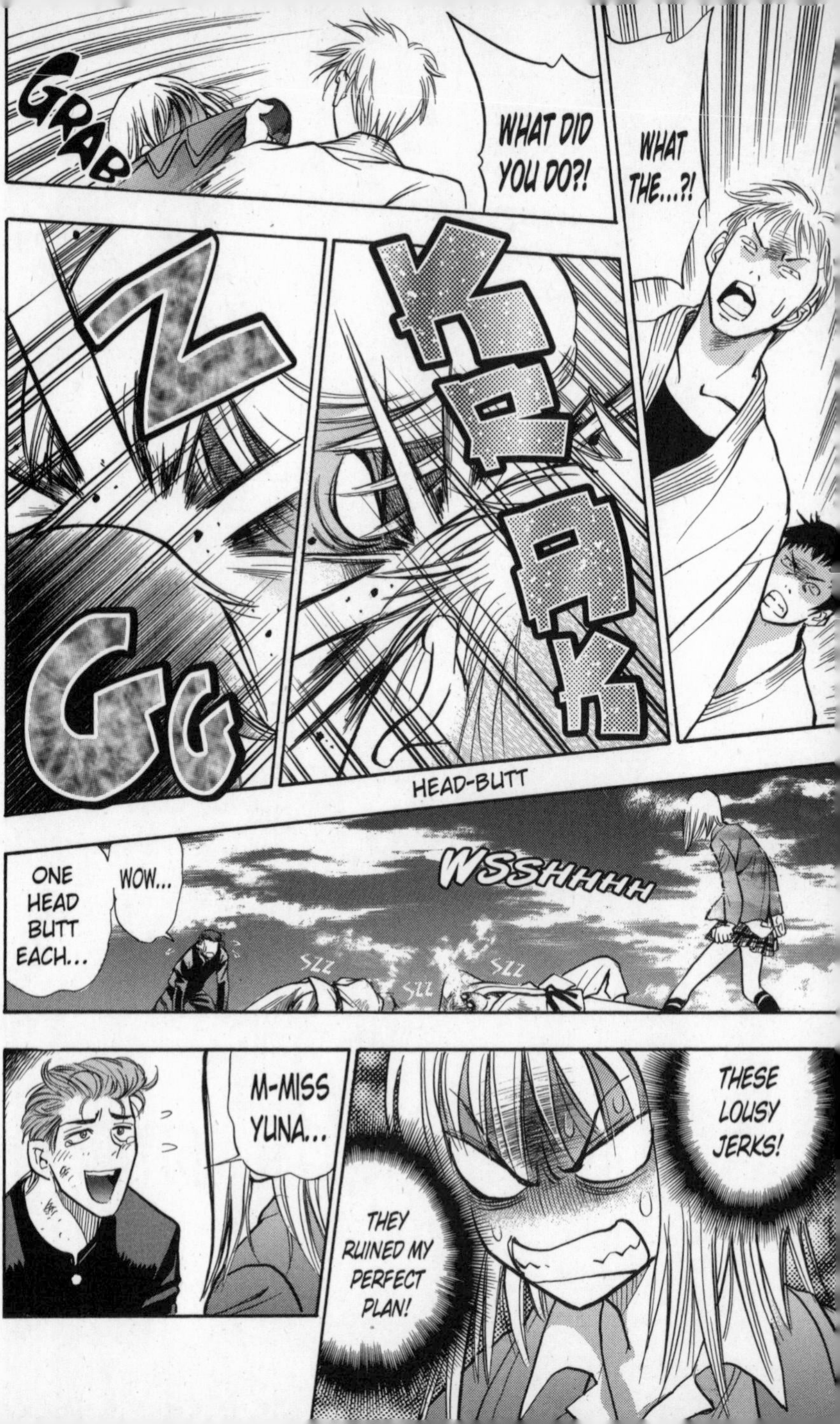
WHAT THE...?!
WHAT DID YOU DO?!
GRAB
KRAAK
HEAD-BUTT
WSSHHHHH
WOW...
ONE HEAD BUTT EACH...
THESE LOUSY JERKS!
THEY RUINED MY PERFECT PLAN!
M-MISS YUNA...

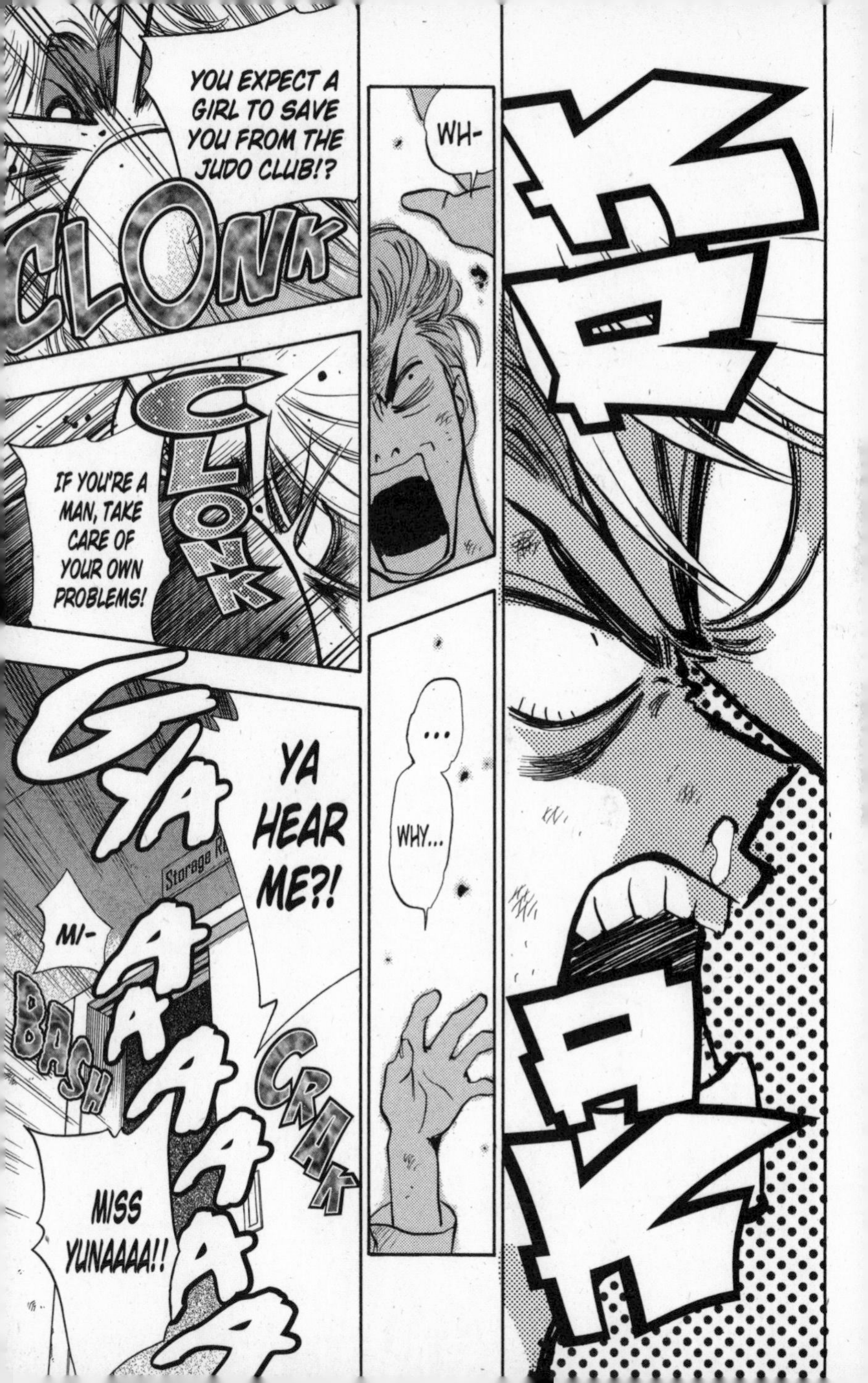
WH-
...
WHY...
YOU EXPECT A GIRL TO SAVE YOU FROM THE JUDO CLUB!?
CLONK
IF YOU'RE A MAN, TAKE CARE OF YOUR OWN PROBLEMS!
CLONK
YA HEAR ME?!
GYAAAAAAA
MI-
BASH
CRAK
MISS YUNAAAA!!

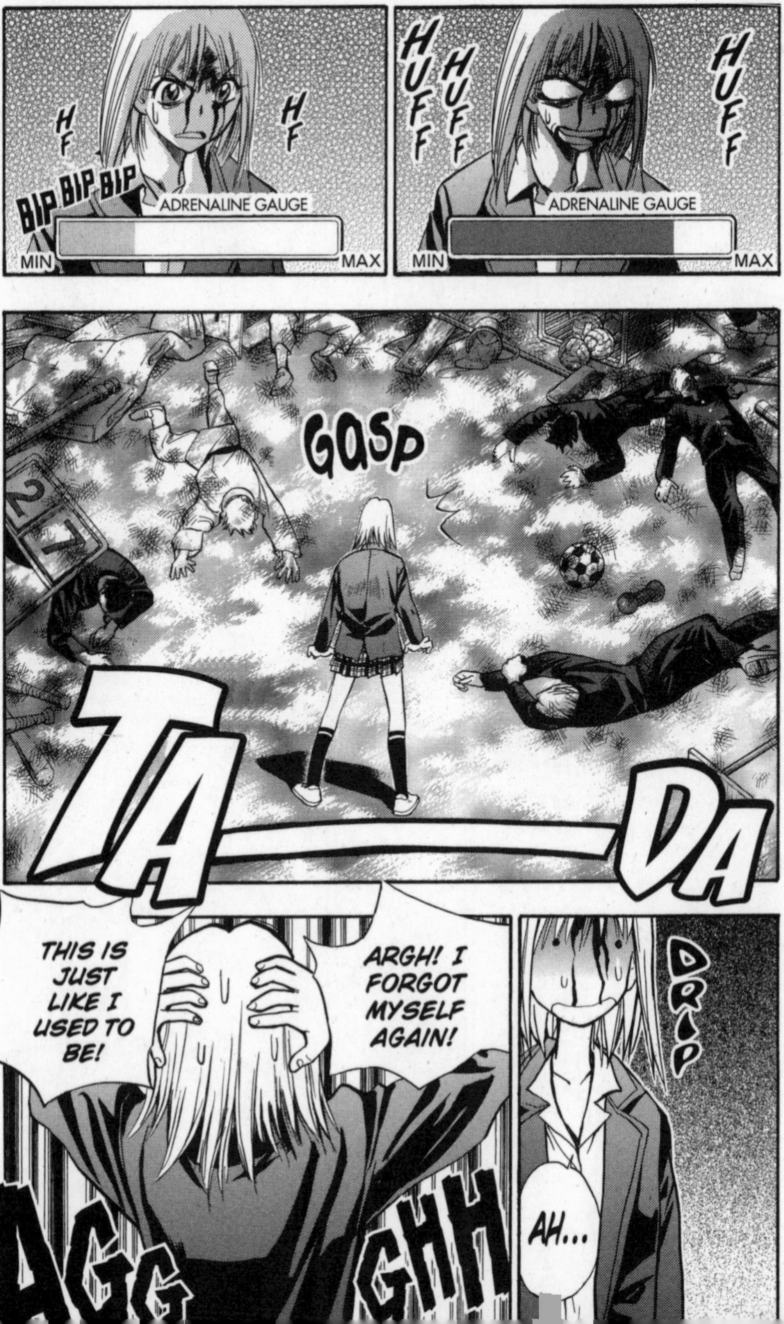
HUFF
HUFF
HUFF
ADRENALINE GAUGE
MIN
MAX
HF
HF
BIP BIP BIP
ADRENALINE GAUGE
MIN
MAX
GASP
TA—DA
DRIP
AH...
ARGH! I FORGOT MYSELF AGAIN!
THIS IS JUST LIKE I USED TO BE!
AGG GHH

READ THIS WAY

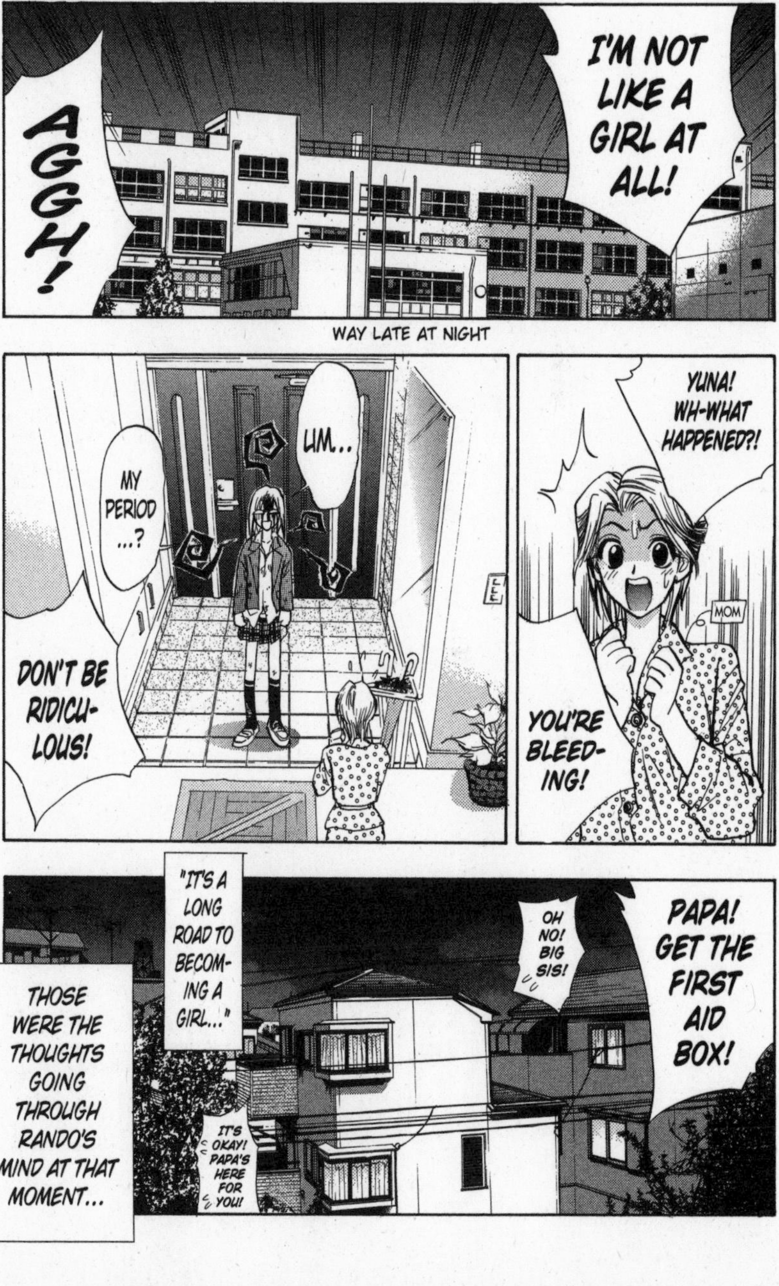
I'M NOT LIKE A GIRL AT ALL!
AGGH!
WAY LATE AT NIGHT
YUNA! WH-WHAT HAPPENED?!
MOM
YOU'RE BLEEDING!
UM...
MY PERIOD ...?
DON'T BE RIDICULOUS!
PAPA! GET THE FIRST AID BOX!
OH NO! BIG SIS!
"IT'S A LONG ROAD TO BECOMING A GIRL..."
IT'S OKAY! PAPA'S HERE FOR YOU!
THOSE WERE THE THOUGHTS GOING THROUGH RANDO'S MIND AT THAT MOMENT...

Pretty Face

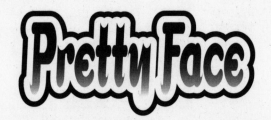

Chapter 3:
A Day in the Life of Sisters

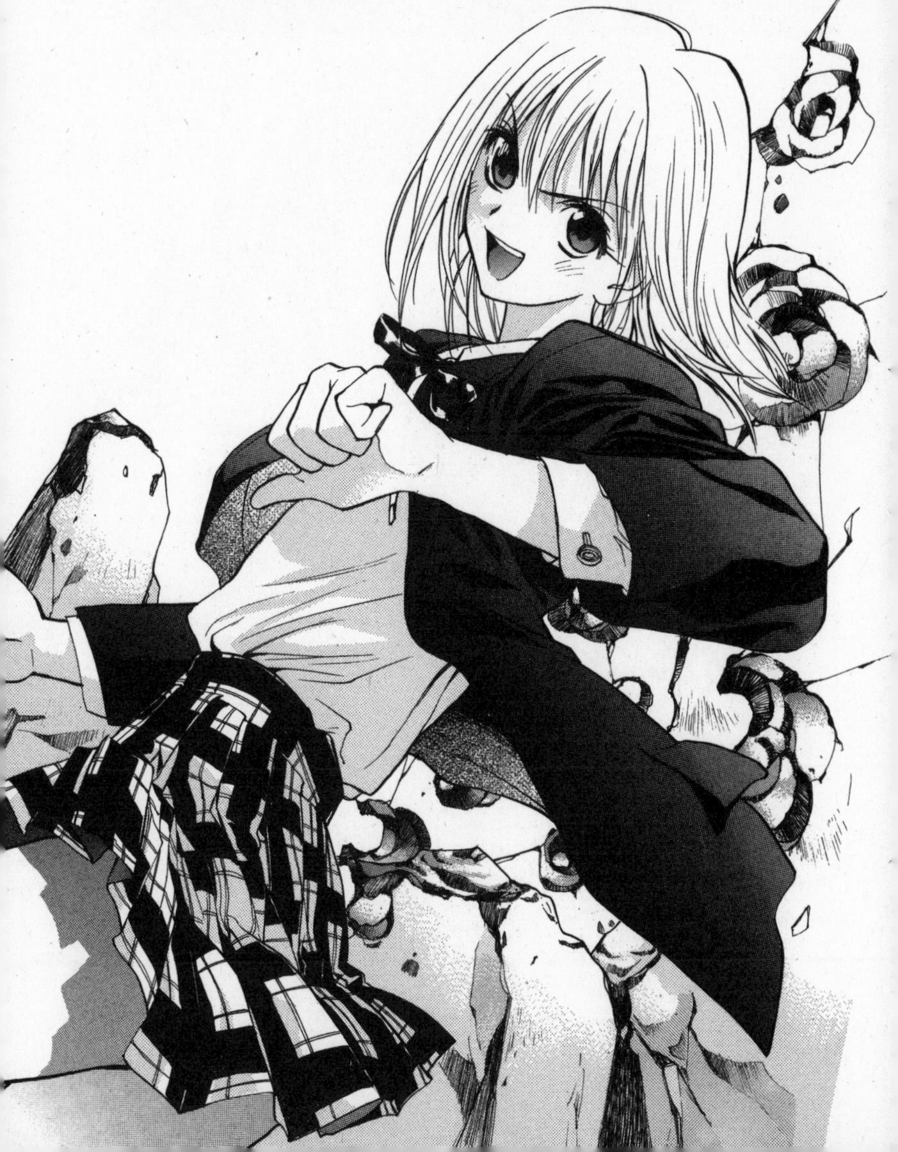

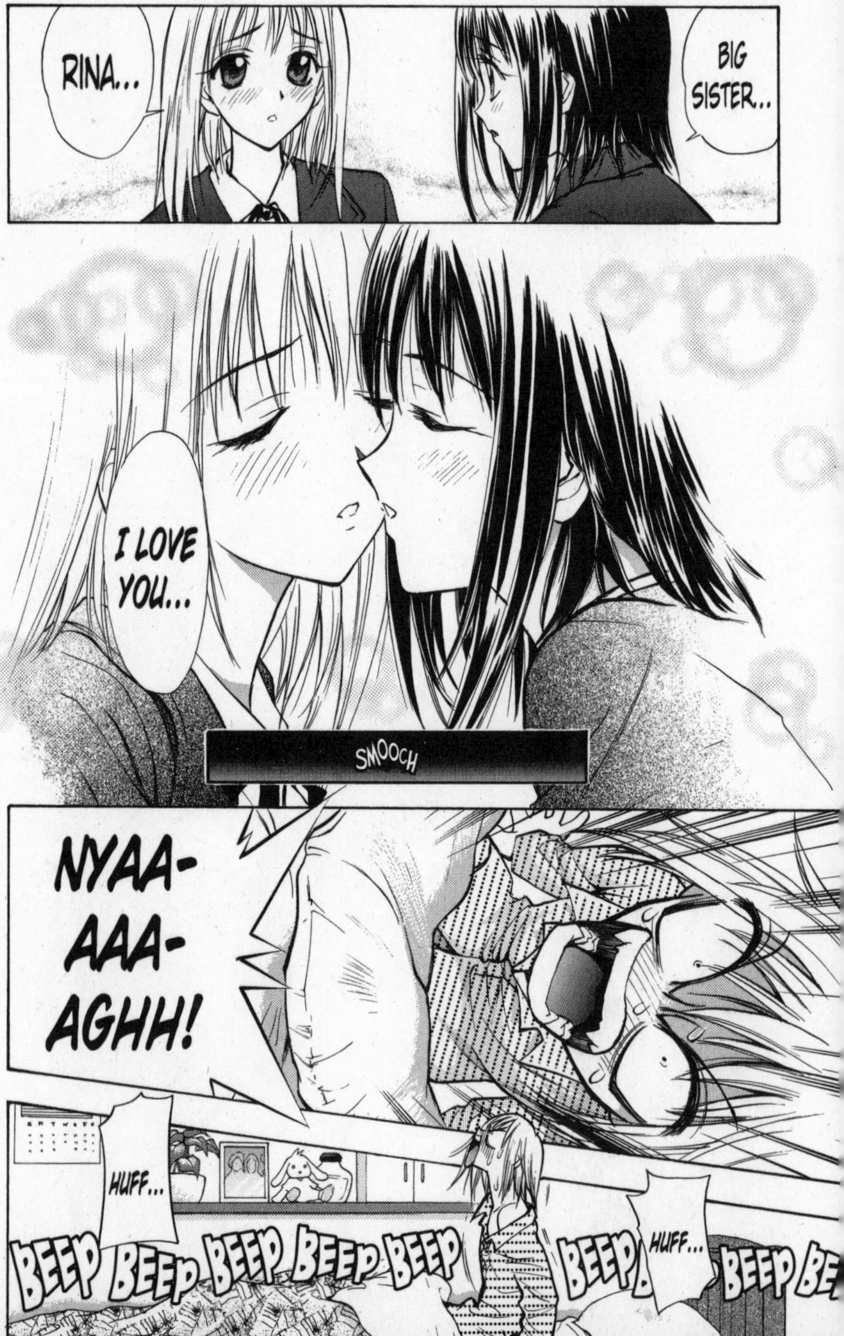
BIG SISTER...
RINA...
I LOVE YOU...
SMOOCH
NYAA-AAA-AGHH!
HUFF...
HUFF...
BEEP BEEP BEEP BEEP BEEP BEEP BEEP BEEP

READ THIS WAY

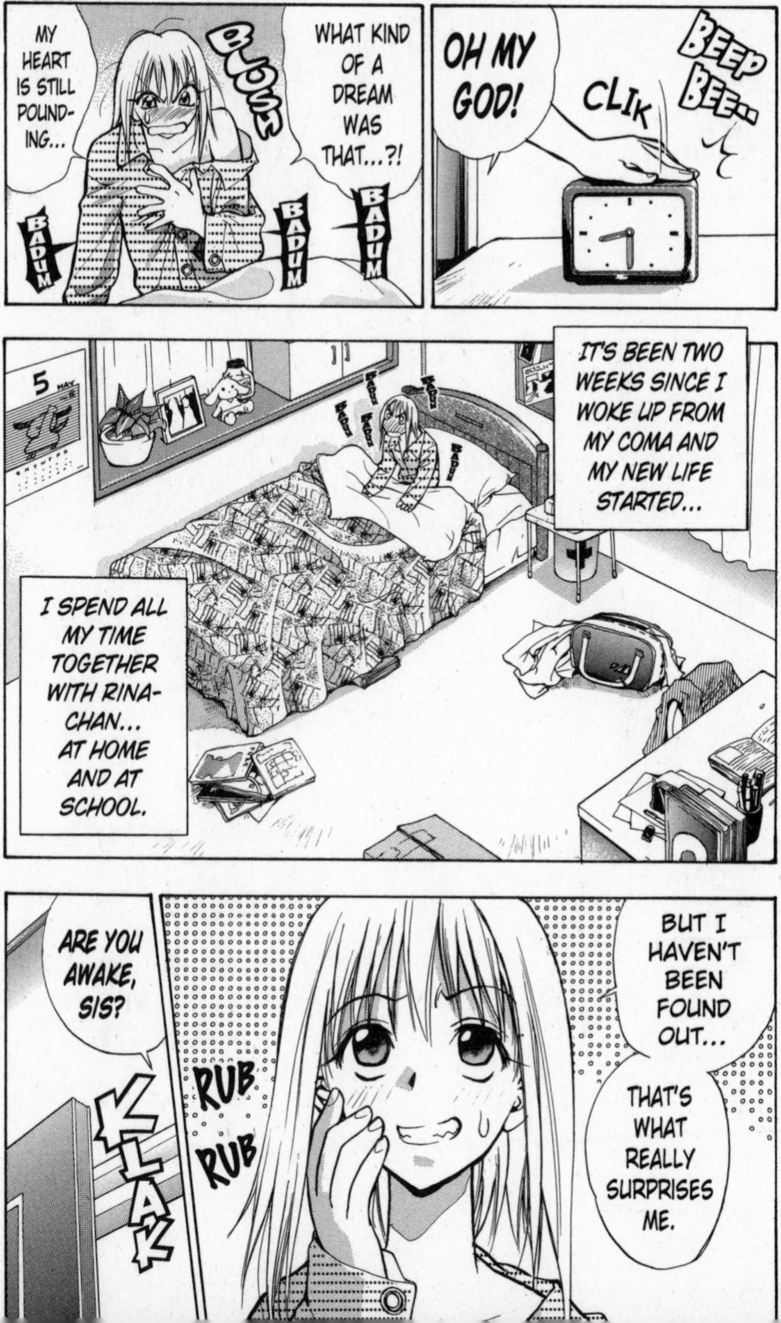

BEEP BEE..
CLIK
OH MY GOD!
WHAT KIND OF A DREAM WAS THAT...?!
BLUSH
MY HEART IS STILL POUND-ING...
BADUM
BADUM
BADUM
IT'S BEEN TWO WEEKS SINCE I WOKE UP FROM MY COMA AND MY NEW LIFE STARTED...
I SPEND ALL MY TIME TOGETHER WITH RINA-CHAN... AT HOME AND AT SCHOOL.
BUT I HAVEN'T BEEN FOUND OUT...
THAT'S WHAT REALLY SURPRISES ME.
RUB
RUB
ARE YOU AWAKE, SIS?
KLAK

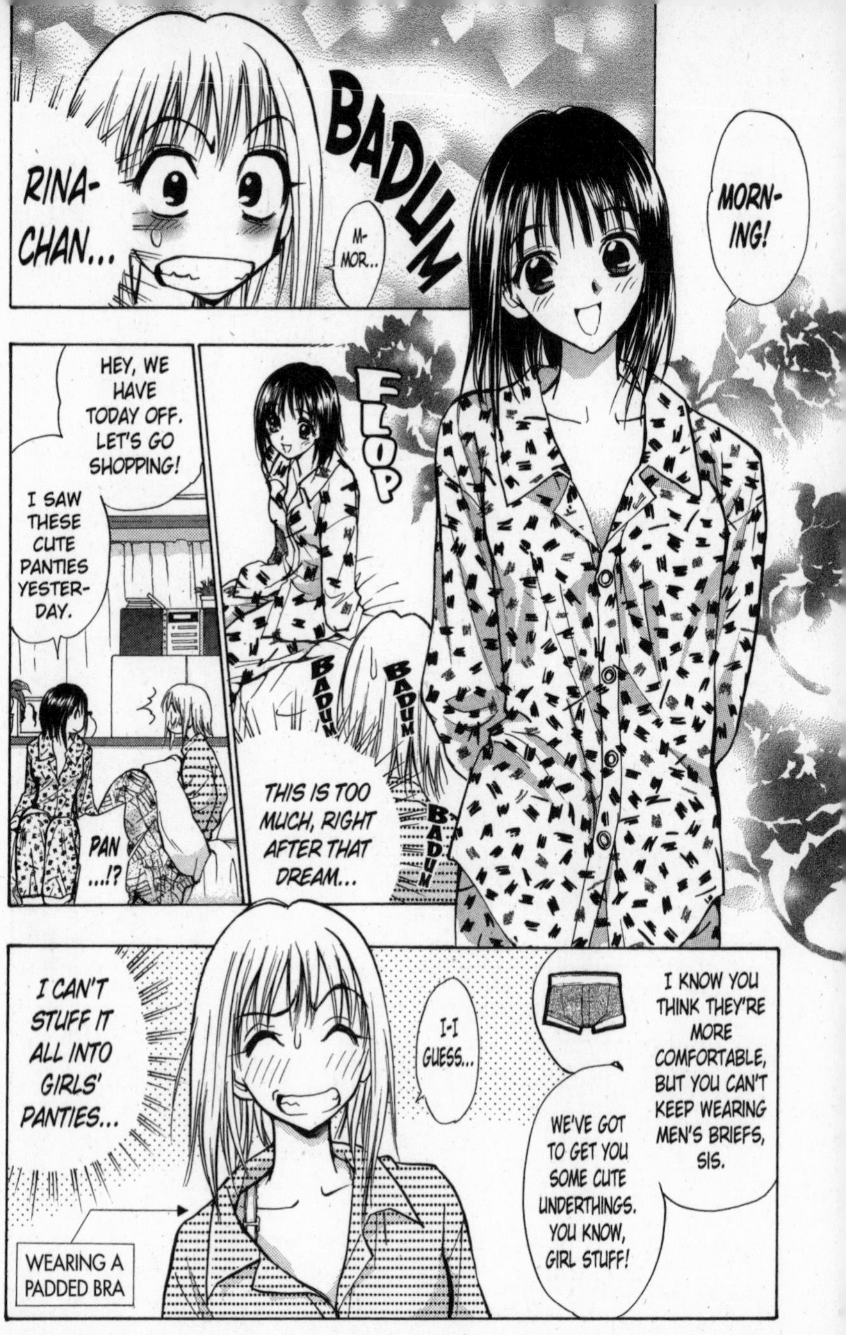
MORN-ING!
BADUM
M-MOR...
RINA-CHAN...
FLOP
BADUM
BADUM
BADUM
THIS IS TOO MUCH, RIGHT AFTER THAT DREAM...
HEY, WE HAVE TODAY OFF. LET'S GO SHOPPING!
I SAW THESE CUTE PANTIES YESTER-DAY.
PAN ...!?
I KNOW YOU THINK THEY'RE MORE COMFORTABLE, BUT YOU CAN'T KEEP WEARING MEN'S BRIEFS, SIS.
WE'VE GOT TO GET YOU SOME CUTE UNDERTHINGS. YOU KNOW, GIRL STUFF!
I-I GUESS...
I CAN'T STUFF IT ALL INTO GIRLS' PANTIES...
WEARING A PADDED BRA

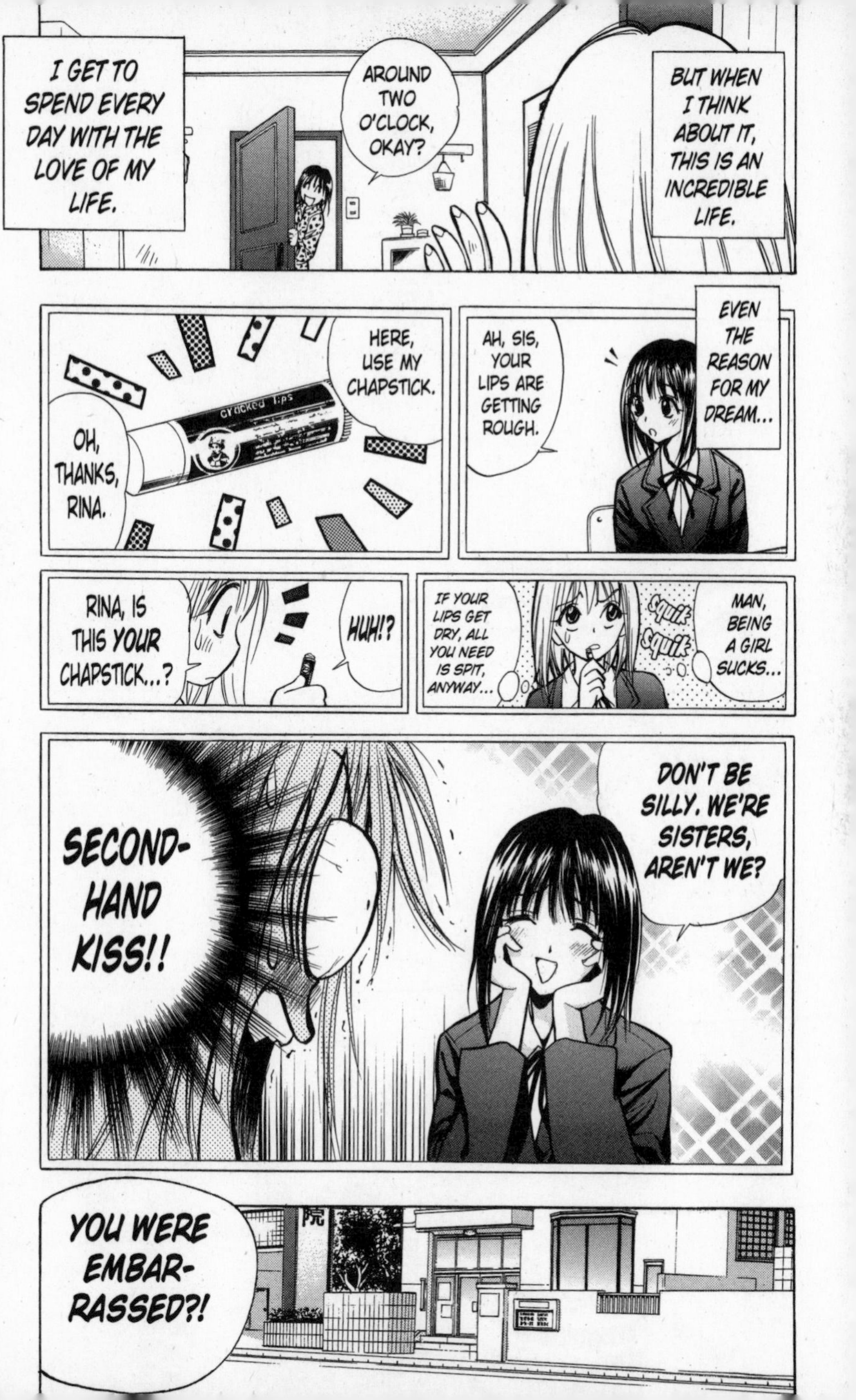
BUT WHEN I THINK ABOUT IT, THIS IS AN INCREDIBLE LIFE.
AROUND TWO O'CLOCK, OKAY?
I GET TO SPEND EVERY DAY WITH THE LOVE OF MY LIFE.
EVEN THE REASON FOR MY DREAM...
AH, SIS, YOUR LIPS ARE GETTING ROUGH.
HERE, USE MY CHAPSTICK.
Cracked Lips
OH, THANKS, RINA.
MAN, BEING A GIRL SUCKS...
squit
squit
IF YOUR LIPS GET DRY, ALL YOU NEED IS SPIT, ANYWAY...
HUH!?
RINA, IS THIS YOUR CHAPSTICK...?
DON'T BE SILLY. WE'RE SISTERS, AREN'T WE?
SECOND-HAND KISS!!
院
YOU WERE EMBARRASSED?!

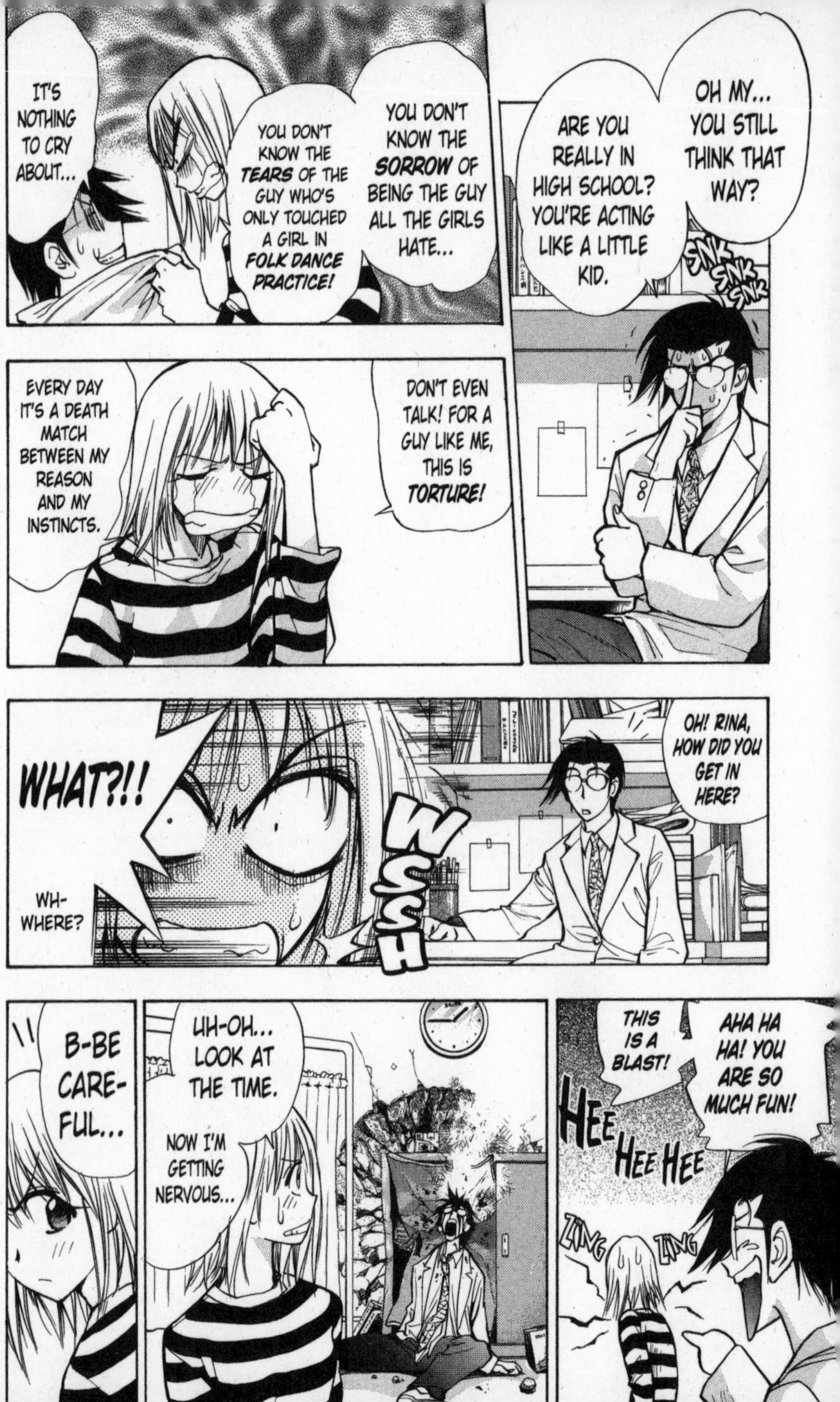
OH MY... YOU STILL THINK THAT WAY?
ARE YOU REALLY IN HIGH SCHOOL? YOU'RE ACTING LIKE A LITTLE KID.
SNK SNK SNK
YOU DON'T KNOW THE SORROW OF BEING THE GUY ALL THE GIRLS HATE...
YOU DON'T KNOW THE TEARS OF THE GUY WHO'S ONLY TOUCHED A GIRL IN FOLK DANCE PRACTICE!
IT'S NOTHING TO CRY ABOUT...
DON'T EVEN TALK! FOR A GUY LIKE ME, THIS IS TORTURE!
EVERY DAY IT'S A DEATH MATCH BETWEEN MY REASON AND MY INSTINCTS.
OH! RINA, HOW DID YOU GET IN HERE?
WSSH
WHAT?!!
WH- WHERE?
AHA HA HA! YOU ARE SO MUCH FUN!
THIS IS A BLAST!
HEE HEE HEE
ZING ZING
UH-OH... LOOK AT THE TIME.
NOW I'M GETTING NERVOUS...
B-BE CARE-FUL...

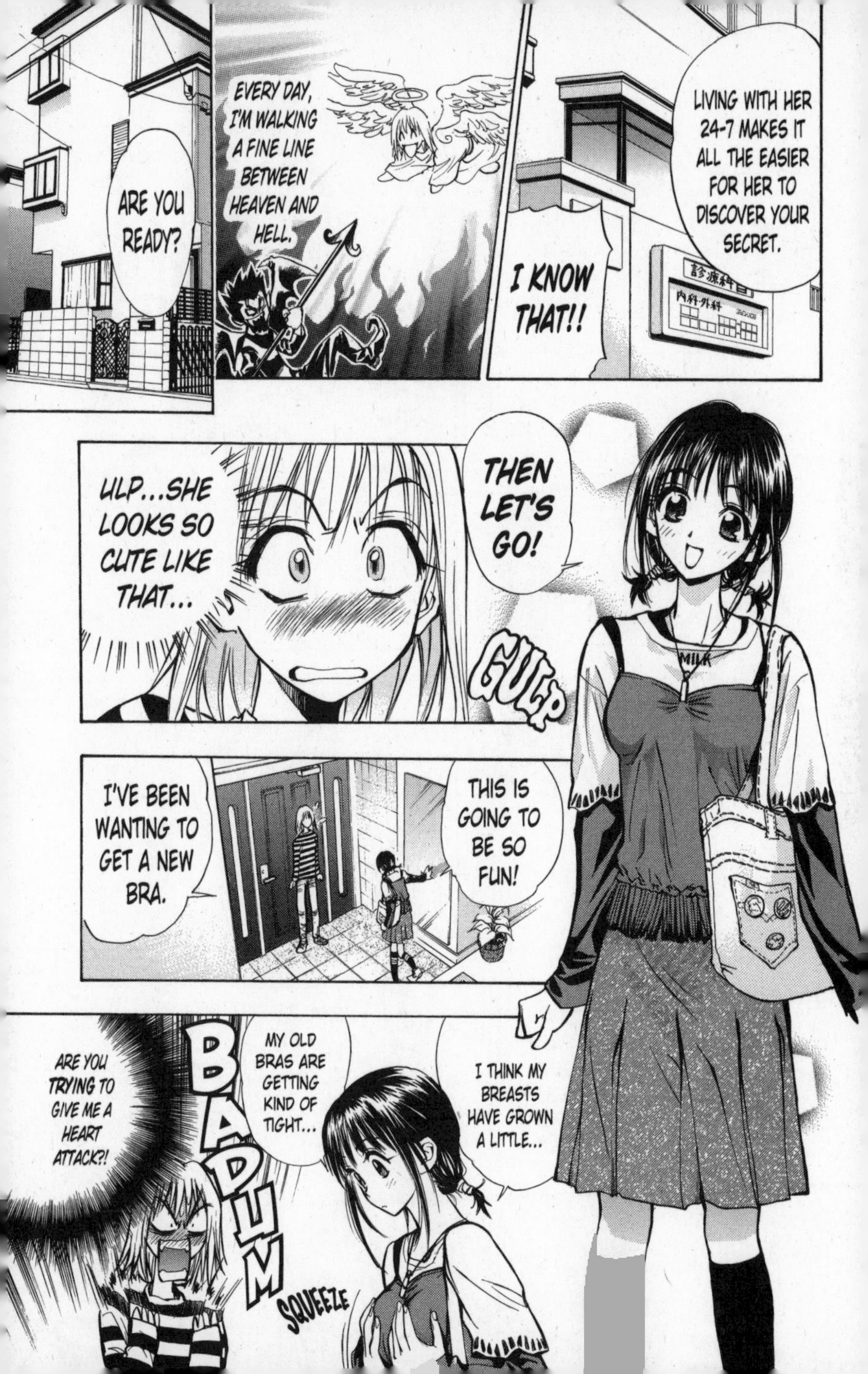

LIVING WITH HER 24-7 MAKES IT ALL THE EASIER FOR HER TO DISCOVER YOUR SECRET.
診療科目
内科・外科
I KNOW THAT!!
EVERY DAY, I'M WALKING A FINE LINE BETWEEN HEAVEN AND HELL.
ARE YOU READY?
THEN LET'S GO!
MILK
ULP...SHE LOOKS SO CUTE LIKE THAT...
GULP
THIS IS GOING TO BE SO FUN!
I'VE BEEN WANTING TO GET A NEW BRA.
I THINK MY BREASTS HAVE GROWN A LITTLE...
MY OLD BRAS ARE GETTING KIND OF TIGHT...
BADUM
SQUEEZE
ARE YOU TRYING TO GIVE ME A HEART ATTACK?!

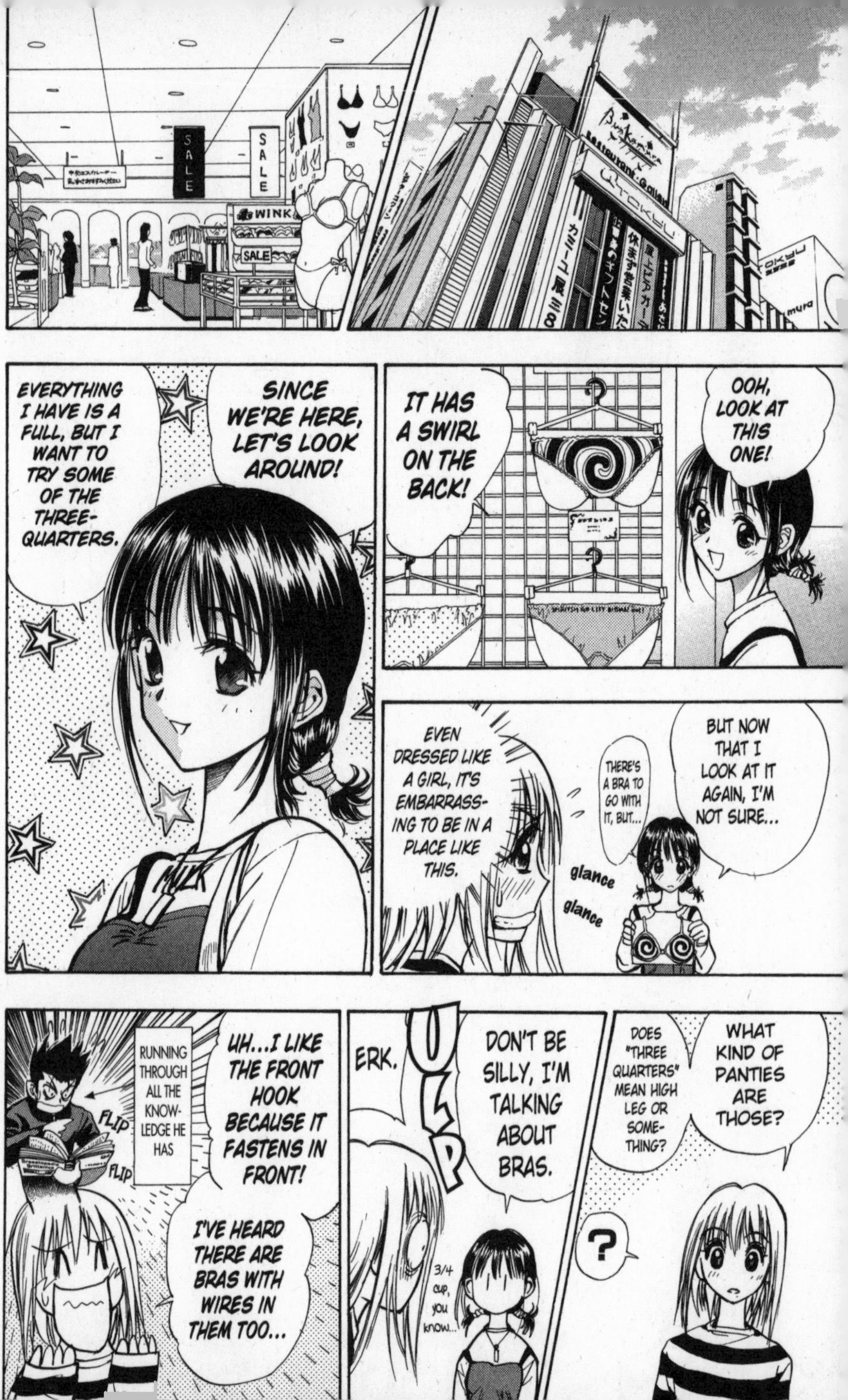
TOKYU
SALE
SALE
WINK
SALE
OOH, LOOK AT THIS ONE!
IT HAS A SWIRL ON THE BACK!
BUT NOW THAT I LOOK AT IT AGAIN, I'M NOT SURE...
THERE'S A BRA TO GO WITH IT, BUT...
EVEN DRESSED LIKE A GIRL, IT'S EMBARRASSING TO BE IN A PLACE LIKE THIS.
glance
glance
SINCE WE'RE HERE, LET'S LOOK AROUND!
EVERYTHING I HAVE IS A FULL, BUT I WANT TO TRY SOME OF THE THREE-QUARTERS.
MILK
WHAT KIND OF PANTIES ARE THOSE?
DOES "THREE QUARTERS" MEAN HIGH LEG OR SOMETHING?
?
DON'T BE SILLY, I'M TALKING ABOUT BRAS.
ERK.
ULP
3/4 cup, you know...
UH...I LIKE THE FRONT HOOK BECAUSE IT FASTENS IN FRONT!
RUNNING THROUGH ALL THE KNOW-LEDGE HE HAS
FLIP
FLIP
I'VE HEARD THERE ARE BRAS WITH WIRES IN THEM TOO...

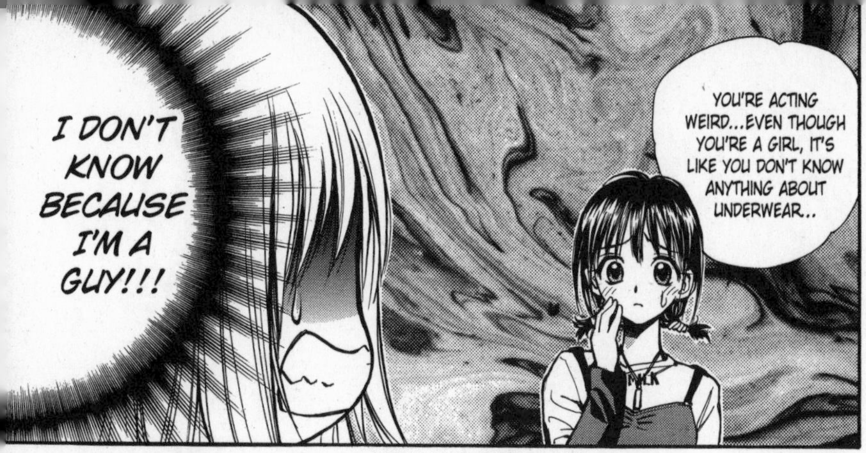
YOU'RE ACTING WEIRD...EVEN THOUGH YOU'RE A GIRL, IT'S LIKE YOU DON'T KNOW ANYTHING ABOUT UNDERWEAR..
I DON'T KNOW BECAUSE I'M A GUY!!!

I DON'T KNOW EITHER —KANO

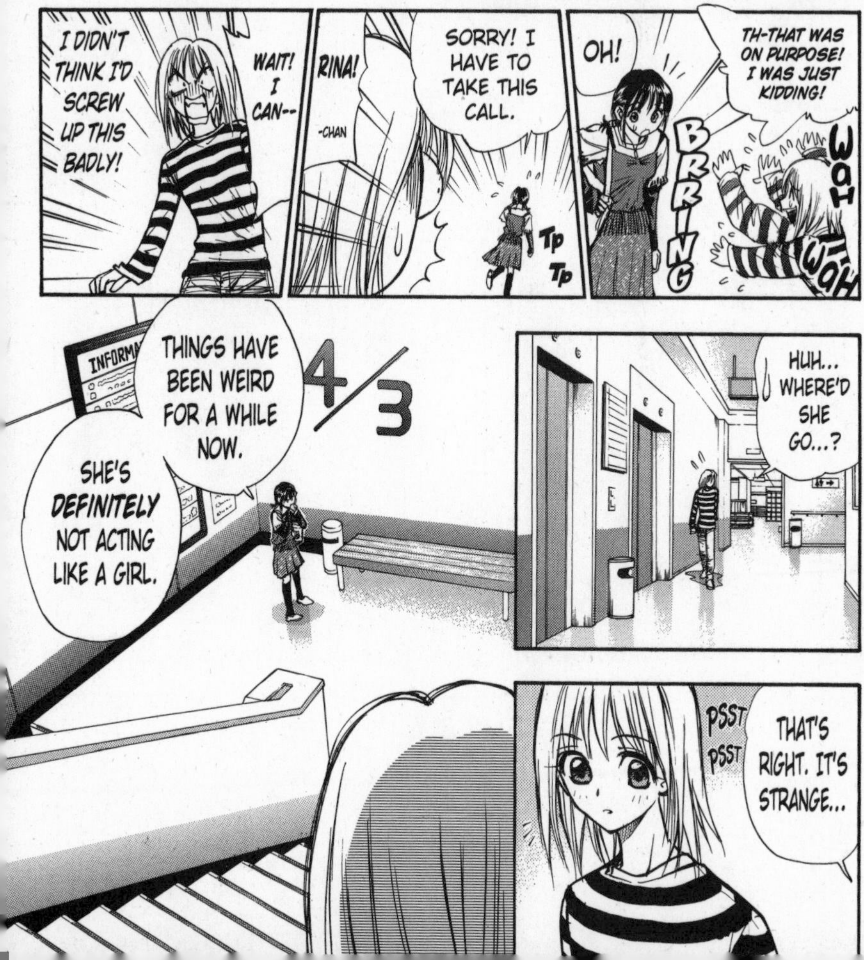
TH-THAT WAS ON PURPOSE! I WAS JUST KIDDING!
WAH
WAH
BRRING
OH!
SORRY! I HAVE TO TAKE THIS CALL.
RINA!
-CHAN
Tp
Tp
WAIT! I CAN--
I DIDN'T THINK I'D SCREW UP THIS BADLY!
HUH... WHERE'D SHE GO...?
4/3
INFORMA
THINGS HAVE BEEN WEIRD FOR A WHILE NOW.
SHE'S DEFINITELY NOT ACTING LIKE A GIRL.
PSST
PSST
THAT'S RIGHT. IT'S STRANGE...

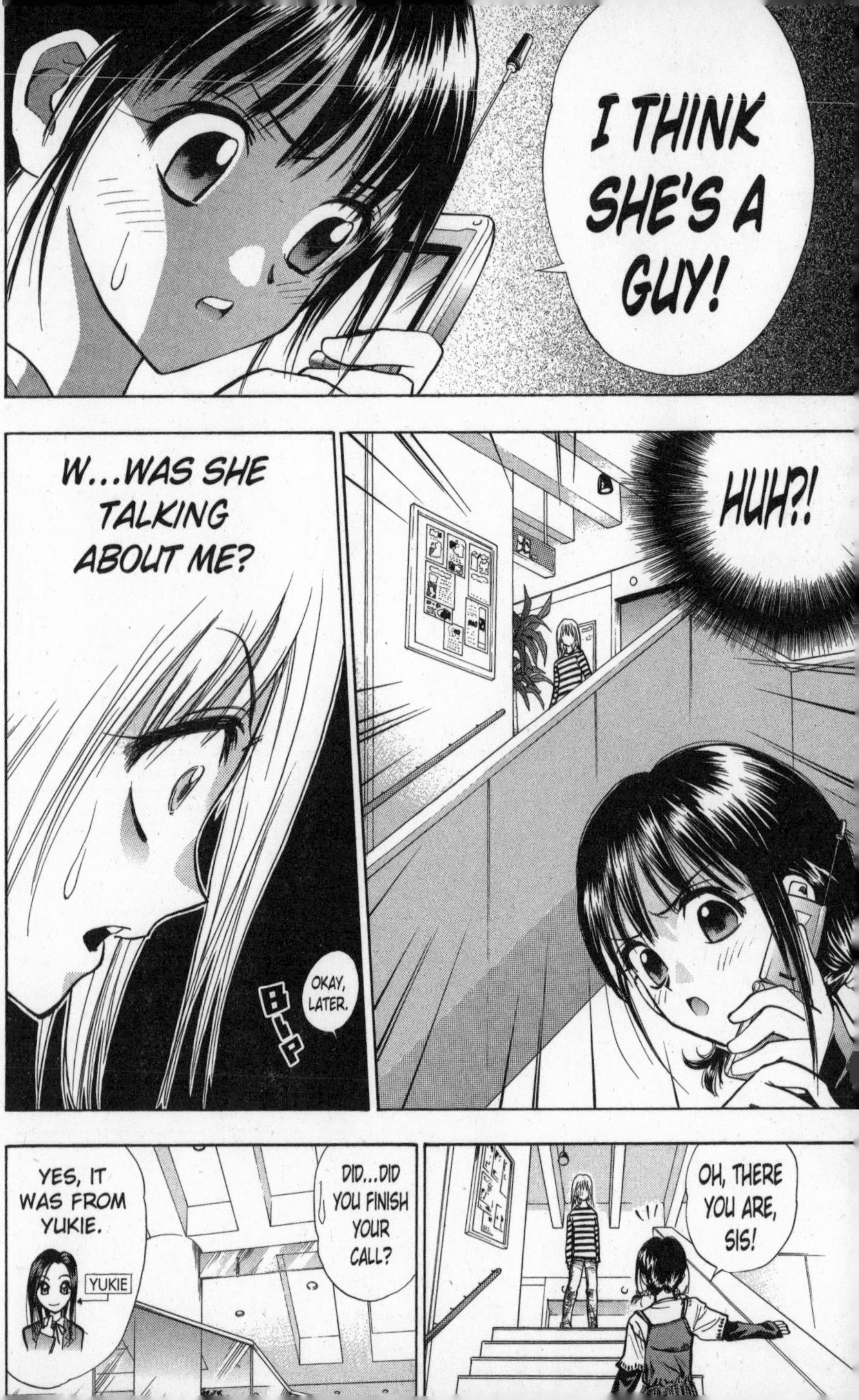
I THINK SHE'S A GUY!
HUH?!
W...WAS SHE TALKING ABOUT ME?
OKAY, LATER.
BLIP
OH, THERE YOU ARE, SIS!
DID...DID YOU FINISH YOUR CALL?
YES, IT WAS FROM YUKIE.
YUKIE

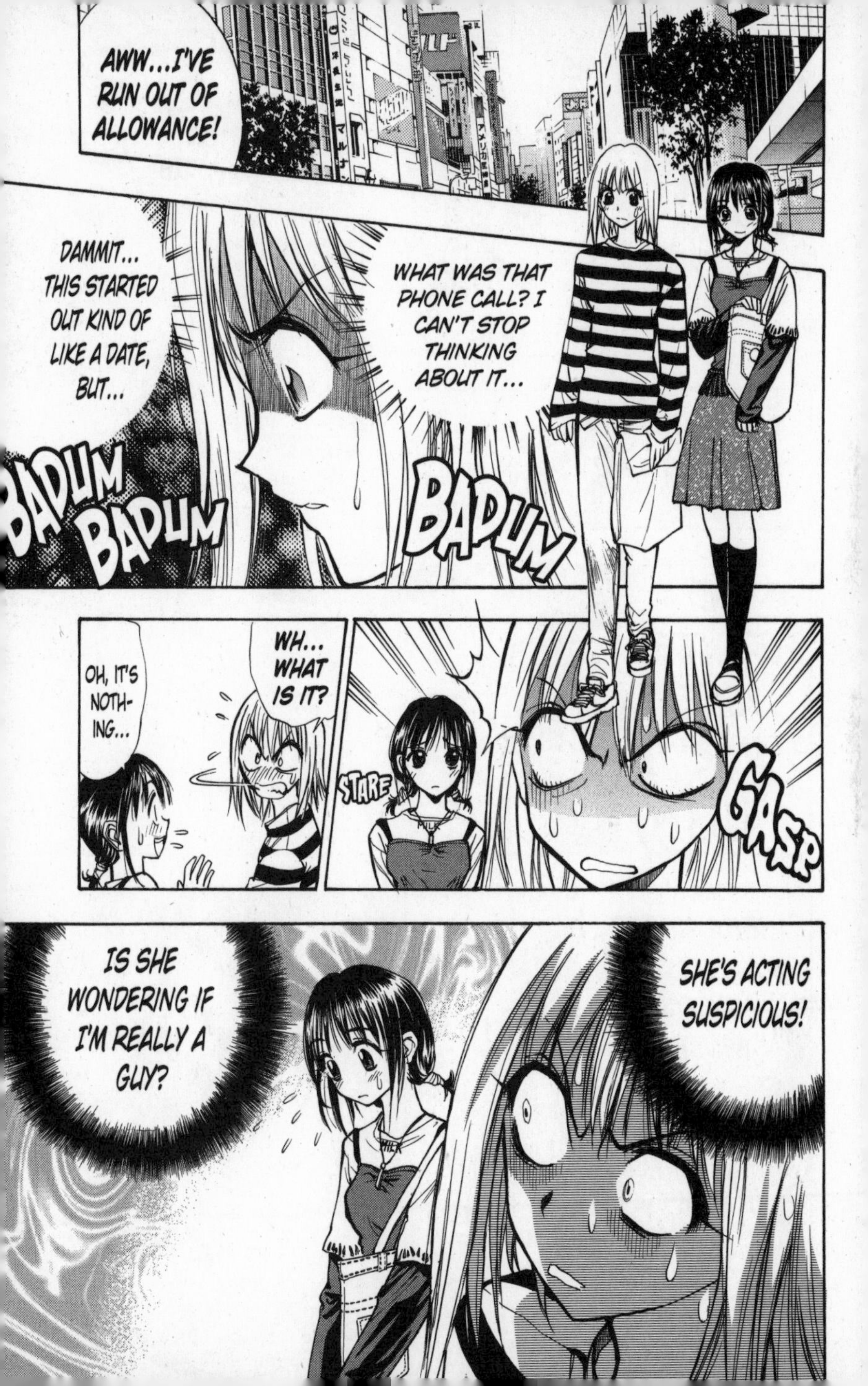
AWW...I'VE RUN OUT OF ALLOWANCE!
WHAT WAS THAT PHONE CALL? I CAN'T STOP THINKING ABOUT IT...
BADUM
DAMMIT... THIS STARTED OUT KIND OF LIKE A DATE, BUT...
BADUM BADUM
GASP
STARE
WH... WHAT IS IT?
OH, IT'S NOTH-ING...
SHE'S ACTING SUSPICIOUS!
IS SHE WONDERING IF I'M REALLY A GUY?

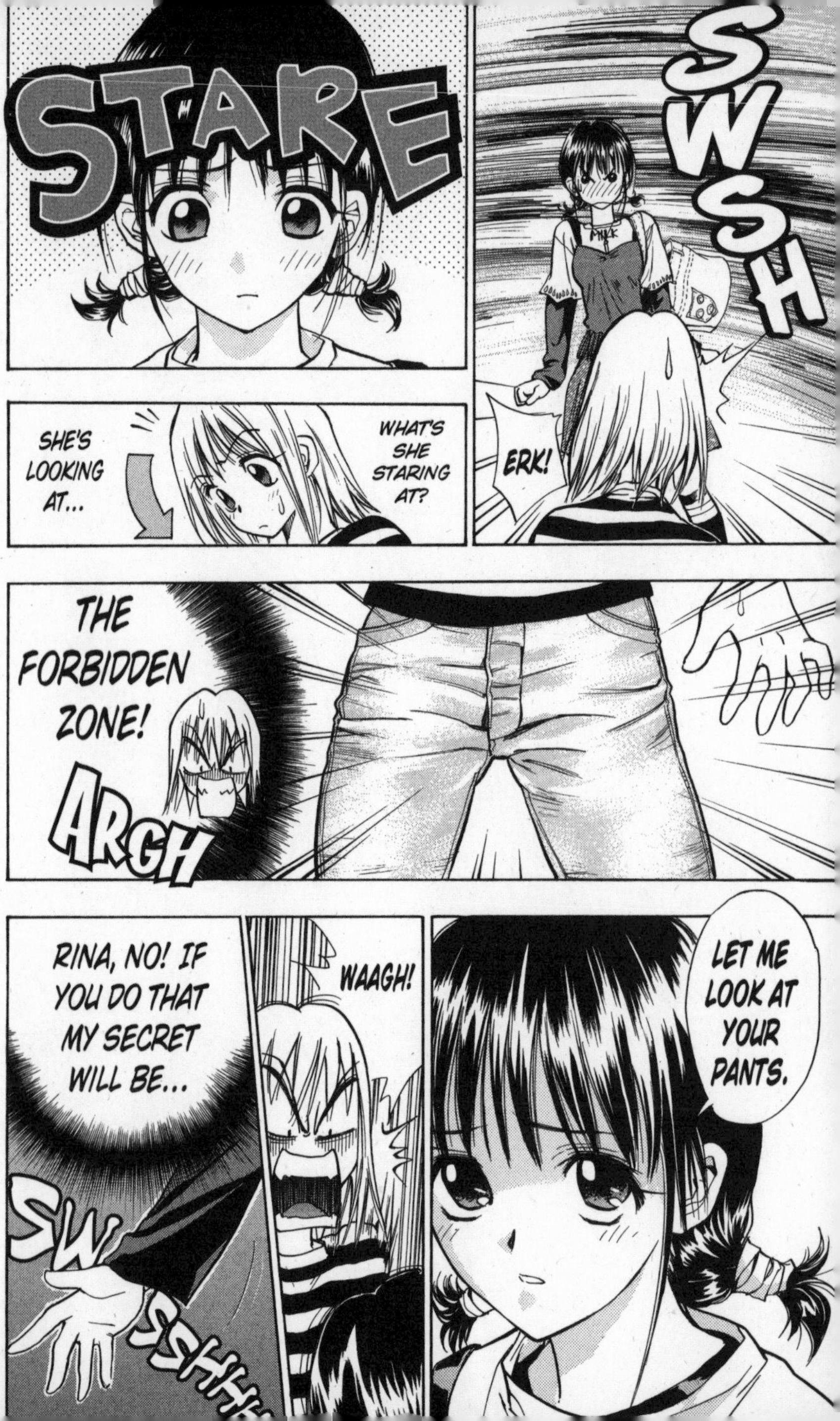
SWSH
ERK!
STARE
WHAT'S SHE STARING AT?
SHE'S LOOKING AT...
THE FORBIDDEN ZONE!
ARGH
LET ME LOOK AT YOUR PANTS.
WAAGH!
RINA, NO! IF YOU DO THAT MY SECRET WILL BE...
SWSSHH

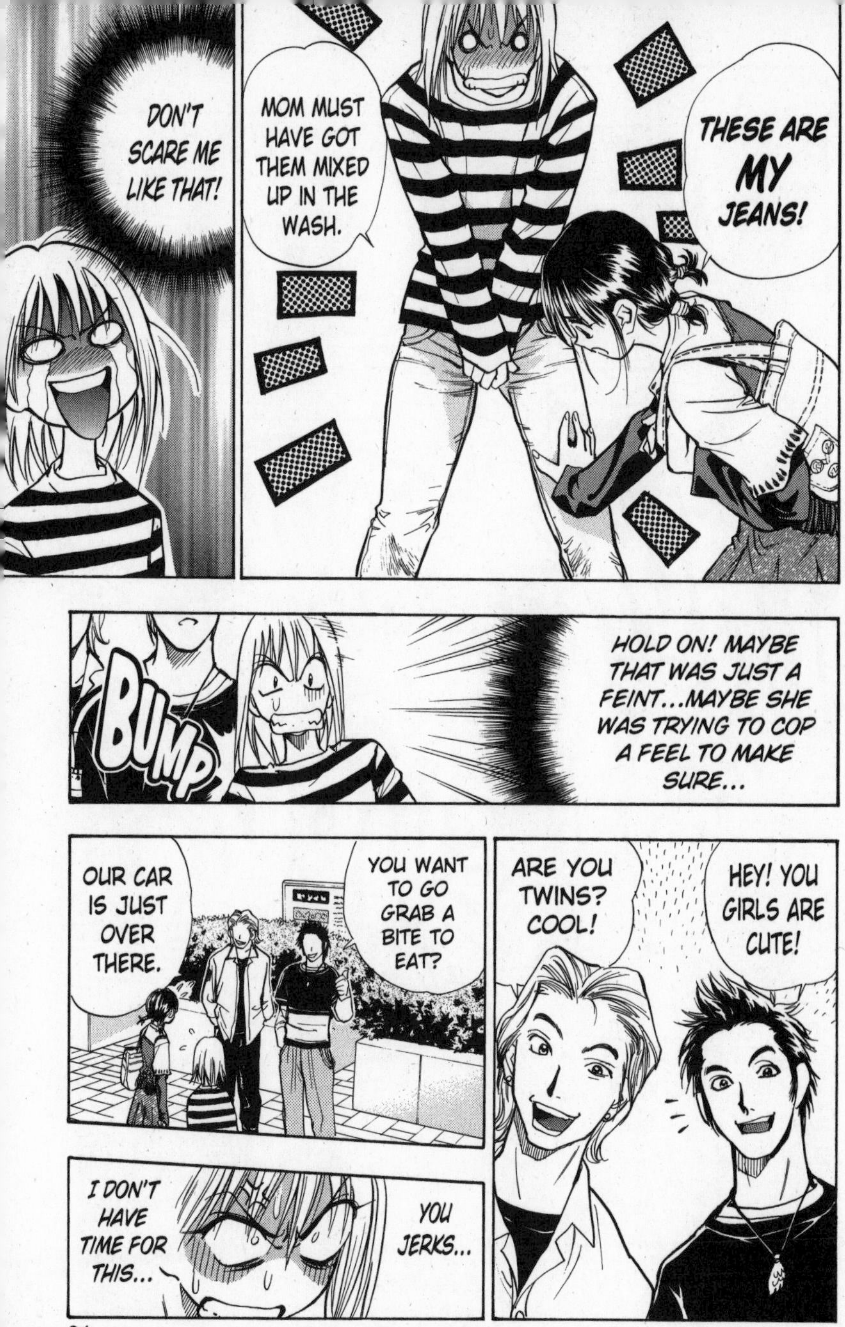
THESE ARE MY JEANS!
MOM MUST HAVE GOT THEM MIXED UP IN THE WASH.
DON'T SCARE ME LIKE THAT!
HOLD ON! MAYBE THAT WAS JUST A FEINT...MAYBE SHE WAS TRYING TO COP A FEEL TO MAKE SURE...
BUMP
HEY! YOU GIRLS ARE CUTE!
ARE YOU TWINS? COOL!
YOU WANT TO GO GRAB A BITE TO EAT?
OUR CAR IS JUST OVER THERE.
YOU JERKS...
I DON'T HAVE TIME FOR THIS...

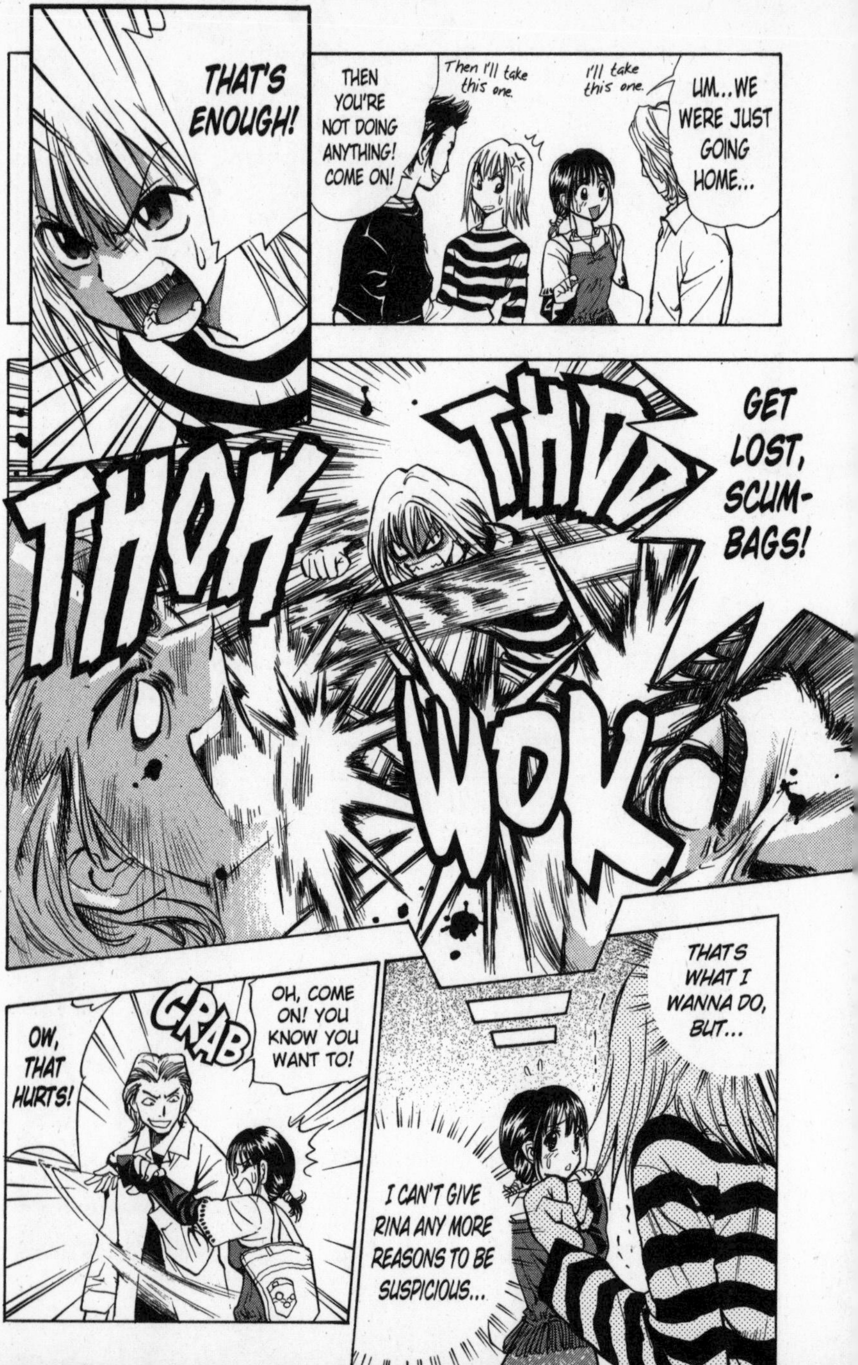

UM...WE WERE JUST GOING HOME...
I'll take this one.
Then I'll take this one.
THEN YOU'RE NOT DOING ANYTHING! COME ON!
THAT'S ENOUGH!
GET LOST, SCUM-BAGS!
THUD
THOK
WOK
THATS WHAT I WANNA DO, BUT...
I CAN'T GIVE RINA ANY MORE REASONS TO BE SUSPICIOUS...
OH, COME ON! YOU KNOW YOU WANT TO!
CRAB
OW, THAT HURTS!

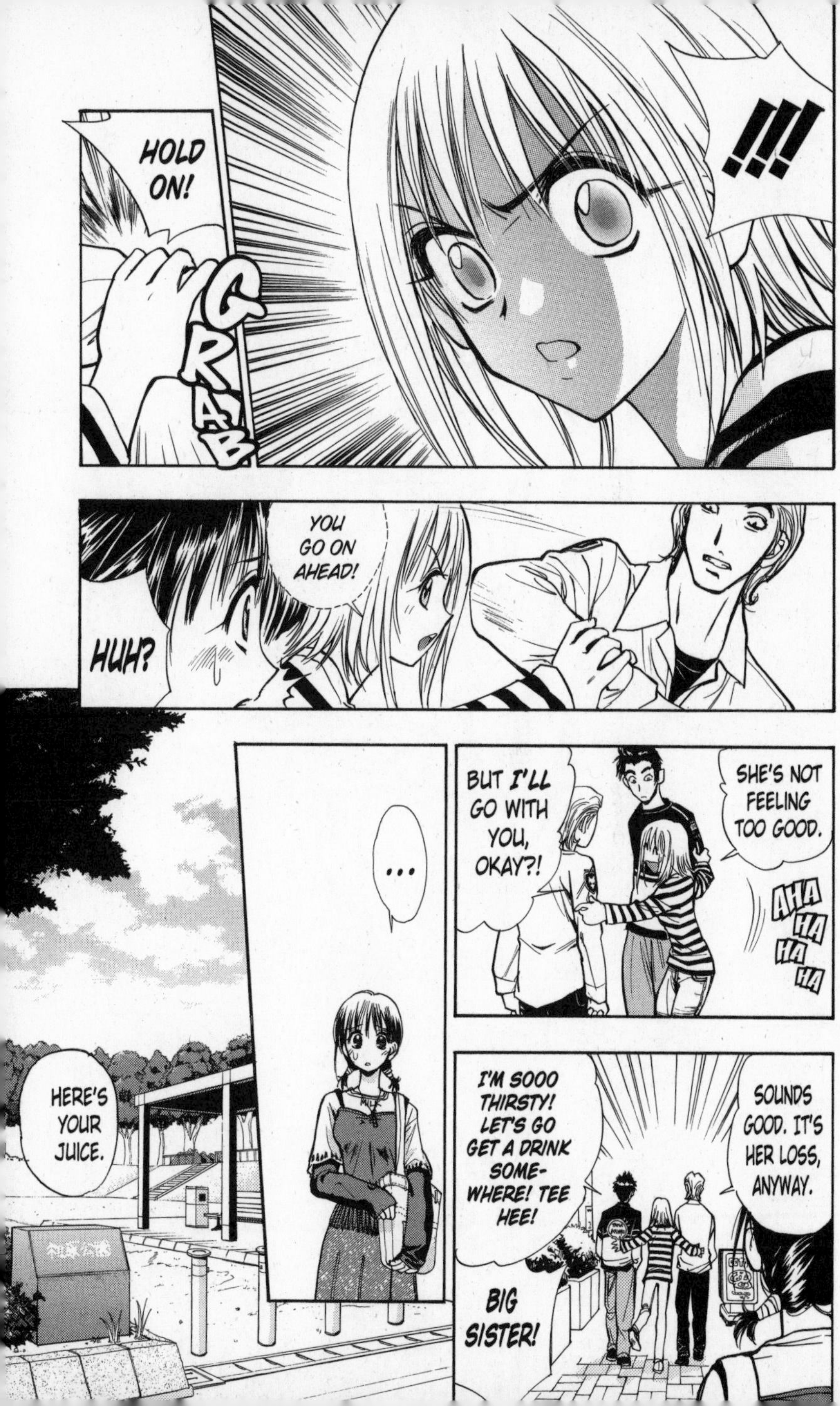
!!!
HOLD ON!
GRAB
YOU GO ON AHEAD!
HUH?
SHE'S NOT FEELING TOO GOOD.
AHA HA HA HA
BUT I'LL GO WITH YOU, OKAY?!
SOUNDS GOOD. IT'S HER LOSS, ANYWAY.
I'M SOOO THIRSTY! LET'S GO GET A DRINK SOME-WHERE! TEE HEE!
BIG SISTER!
...
HERE'S YOUR JUICE.

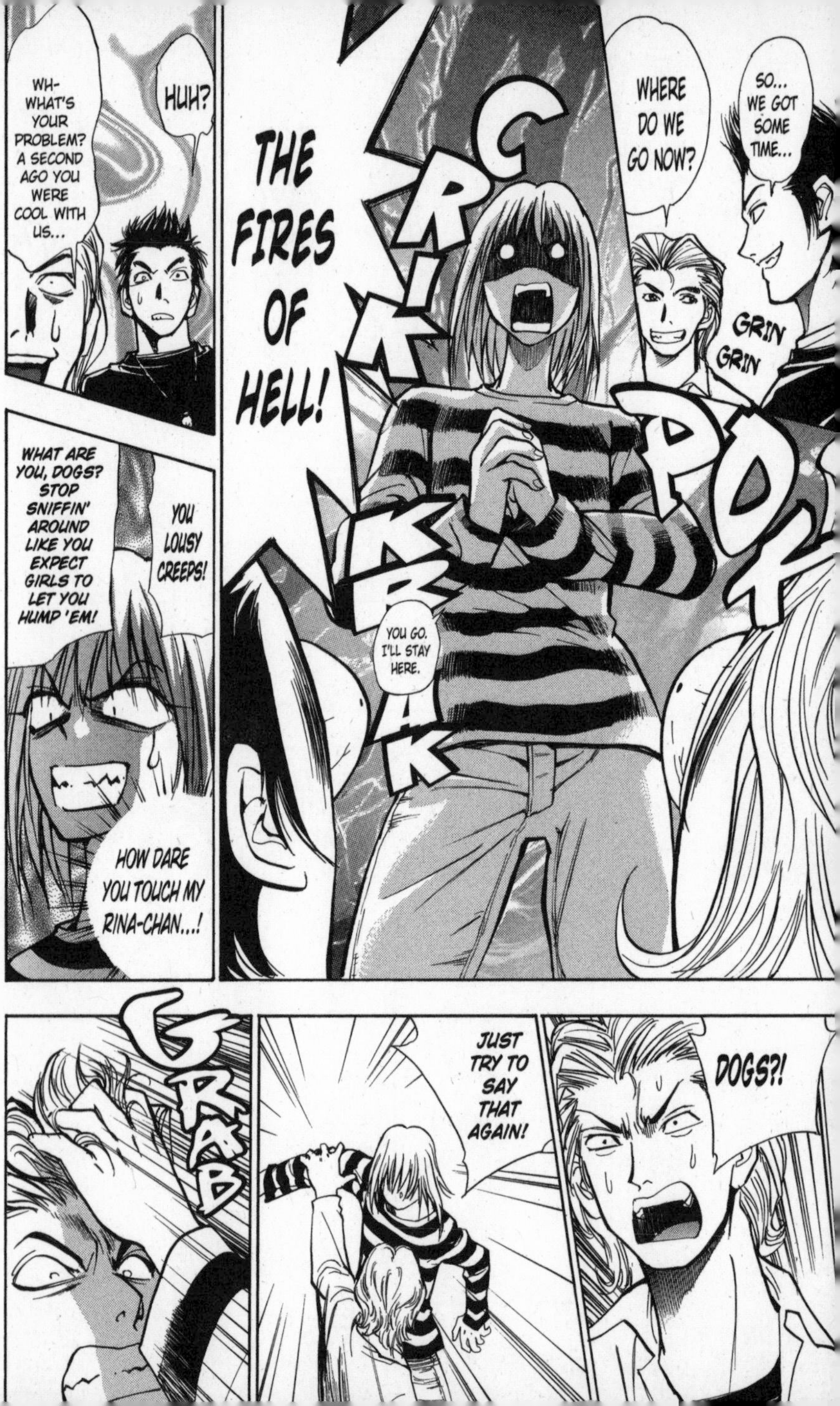
SO... WE GOT SOME TIME...
WHERE DO WE GO NOW?
GRIN GRIN
CRIK
THE FIRES OF HELL!
POK
KRAK
YOU GO. I'LL STAY HERE.
HUH?
WH- WHAT'S YOUR PROBLEM? A SECOND AGO YOU WERE COOL WITH US...
YOU LOUSY CREEPS!
WHAT ARE YOU, DOGS? STOP SNIFFIN' AROUND LIKE YOU EXPECT GIRLS TO LET YOU HUMP 'EM!
HOW DARE YOU TOUCH MY RINA-CHAN...!
DOGS?!
JUST TRY TO SAY THAT AGAIN!
GRAB

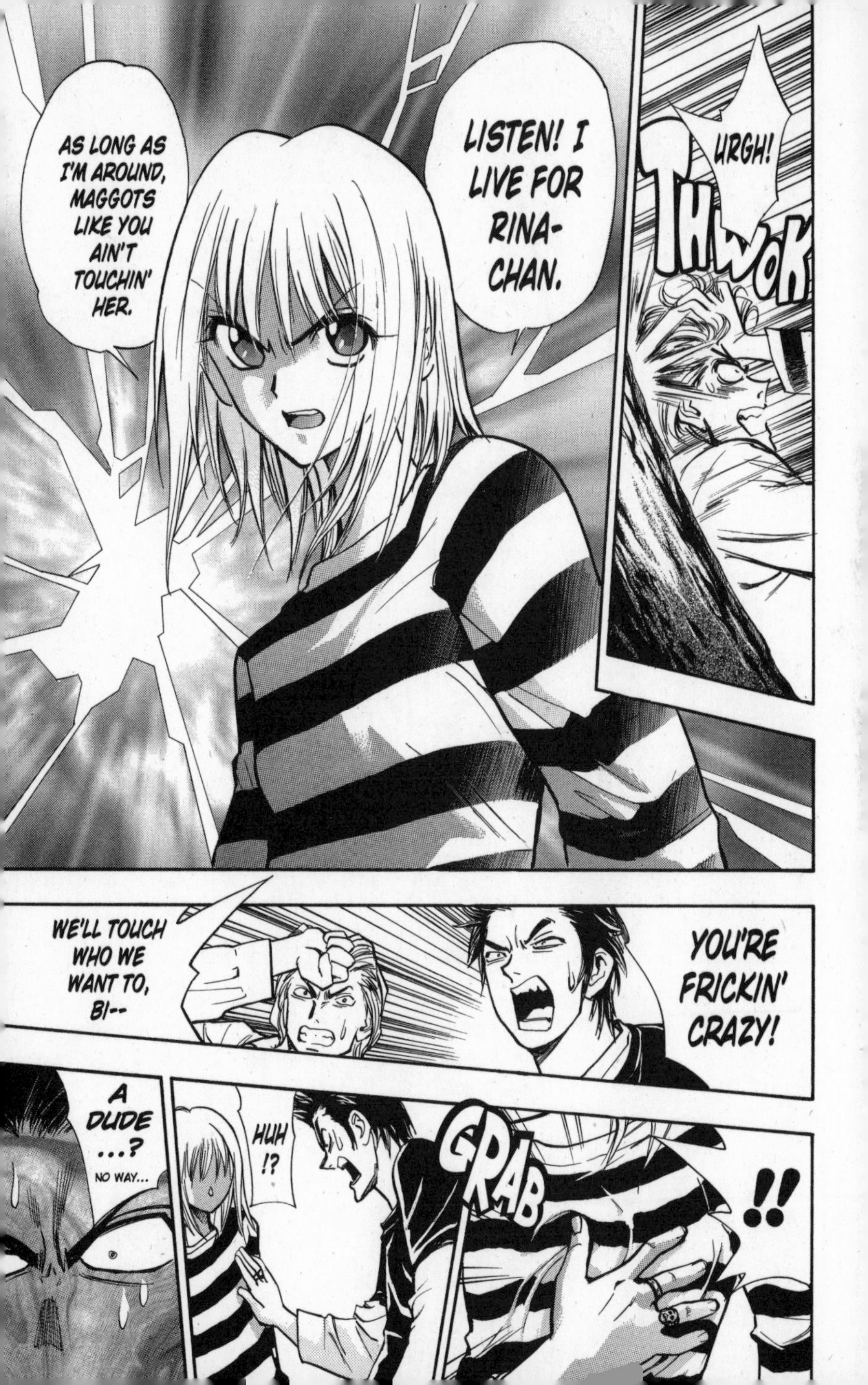
URGH!
THWOK
LISTEN! I LIVE FOR RINA-CHAN.
AS LONG AS I'M AROUND, MAGGOTS LIKE YOU AIN'T TOUCHIN' HER.
YOU'RE FRICKIN' CRAZY!
WE'LL TOUCH WHO WE WANT TO, BI--
!!
GRAB
HUH !?
A DUDE ...?
NO WAY...

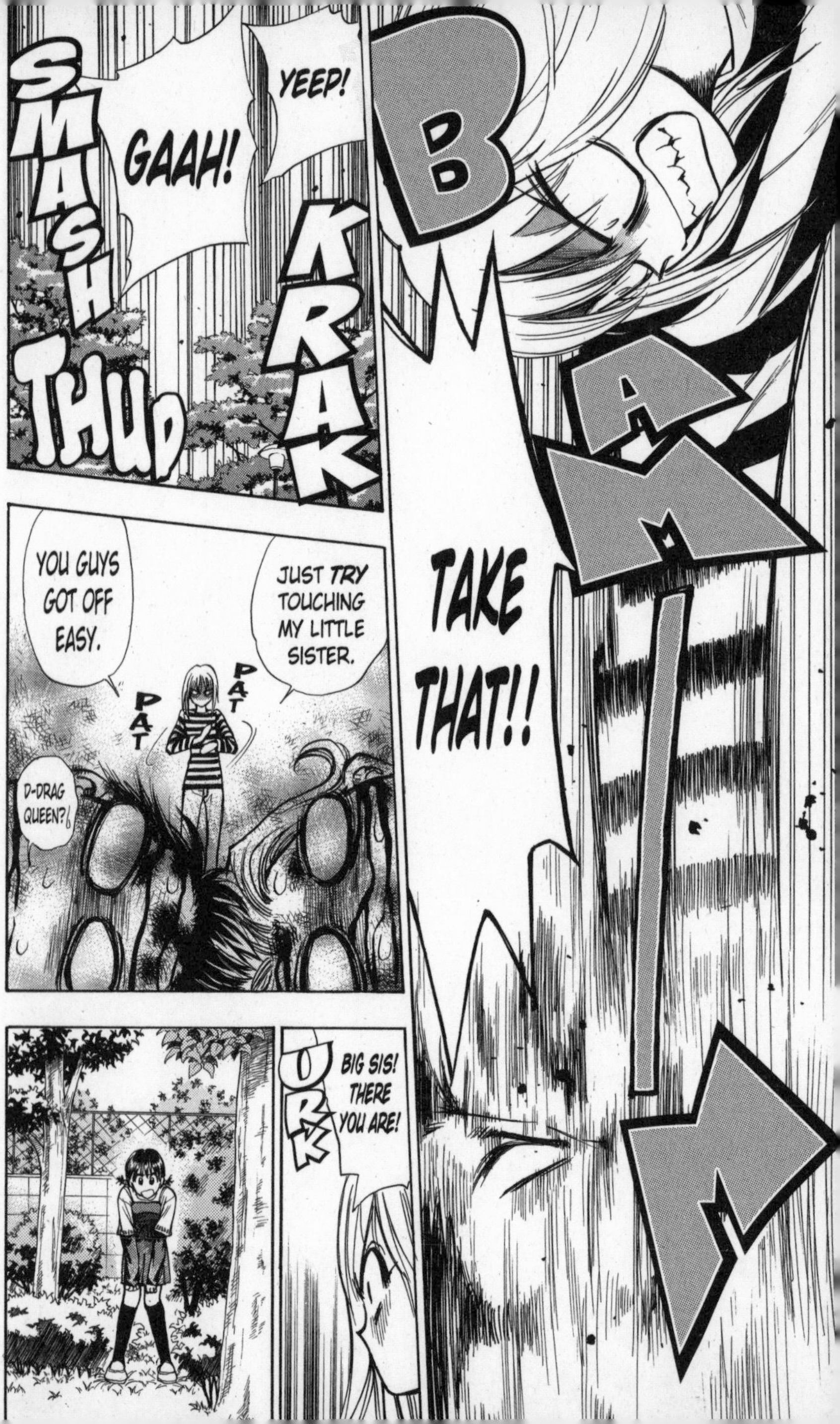
BAM
TAKE THAT!!
YEEP!
KRAK
GAAH!
SMASH
THUD
JUST TRY TOUCHING MY LITTLE SISTER.
PAT PAT
YOU GUYS GOT OFF EASY.
D-DRAG QUEEN?
BIG SIS! THERE YOU ARE!
URK

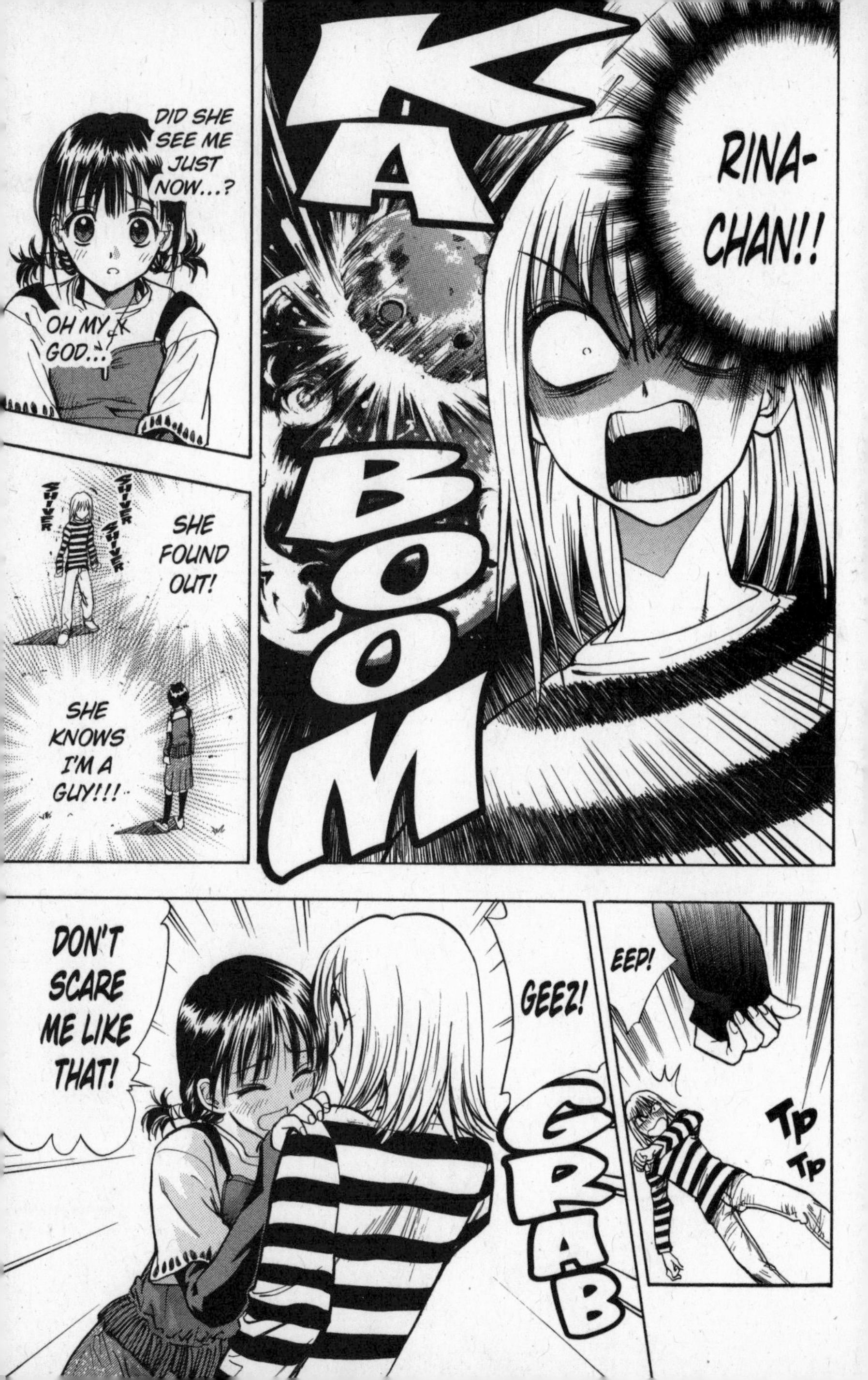
RINA-CHAN!!
KA
BOOM
DID SHE SEE ME JUST NOW...?
OH MY GOD...
SHIVER
SHIVER SHIVER
SHE FOUND OUT!
SHE KNOWS I'M A GUY!!!
EEP!
Tp Tp
GEEZ!
GRAB
DON'T SCARE ME LIKE THAT!

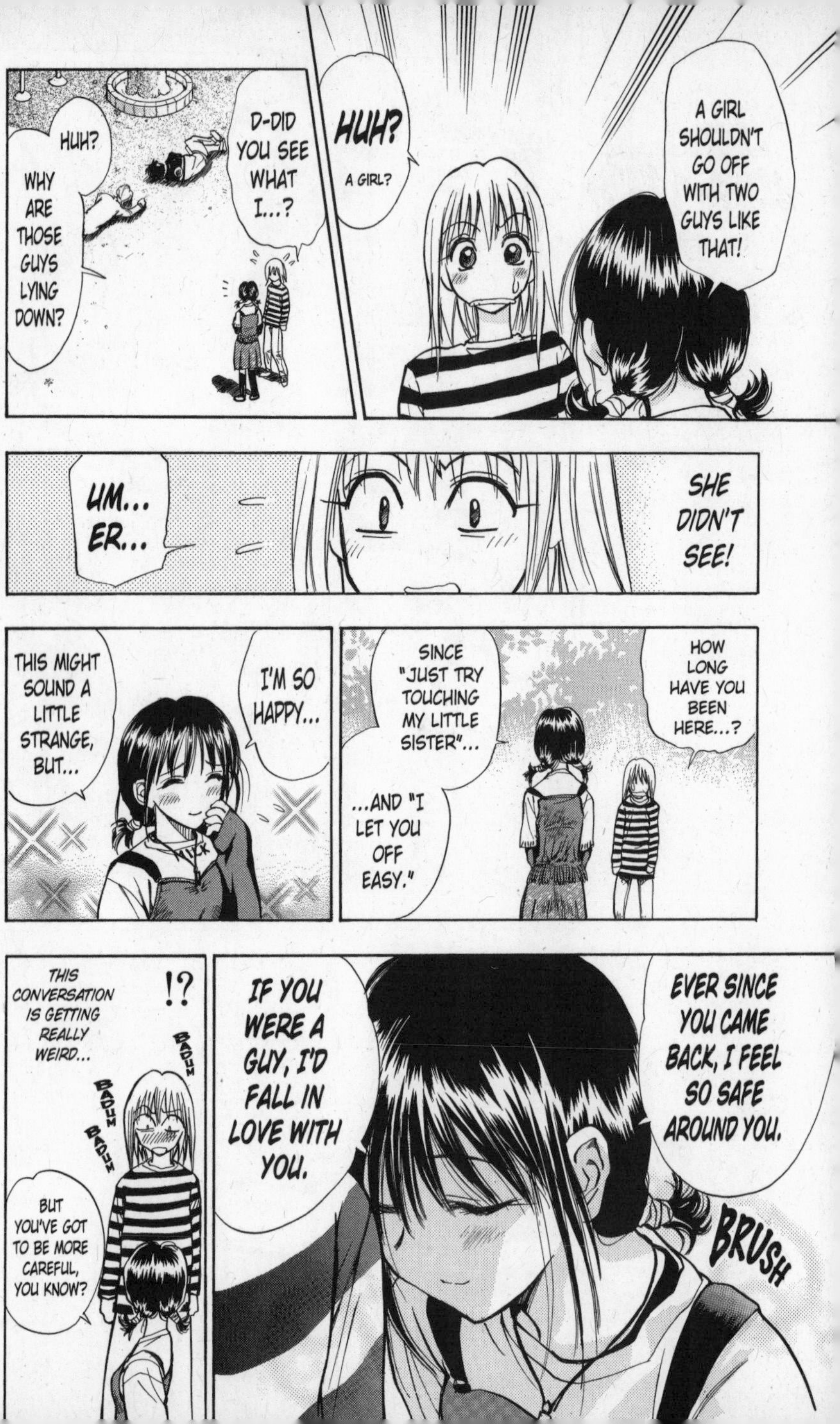
A GIRL SHOULDN'T GO OFF WITH TWO GUYS LIKE THAT!
HUH?
A GIRL?
D-DID YOU SEE WHAT I...?
HUH?
WHY ARE THOSE GUYS LYING DOWN?
SHE DIDN'T SEE!
UM... ER...
HOW LONG HAVE YOU BEEN HERE...?
SINCE "JUST TRY TOUCHING MY LITTLE SISTER"...
...AND "I LET YOU OFF EASY."
I'M SO HAPPY...
THIS MIGHT SOUND A LITTLE STRANGE, BUT...
EVER SINCE YOU CAME BACK, I FEEL SO SAFE AROUND YOU.
BRUSH
IF YOU WERE A GUY, I'D FALL IN LOVE WITH YOU.
!?
THIS CONVERSATION IS GETTING REALLY WEIRD...
BADUM
BADUM
BADUM
BUT YOU'VE GOT TO BE MORE CAREFUL, YOU KNOW?

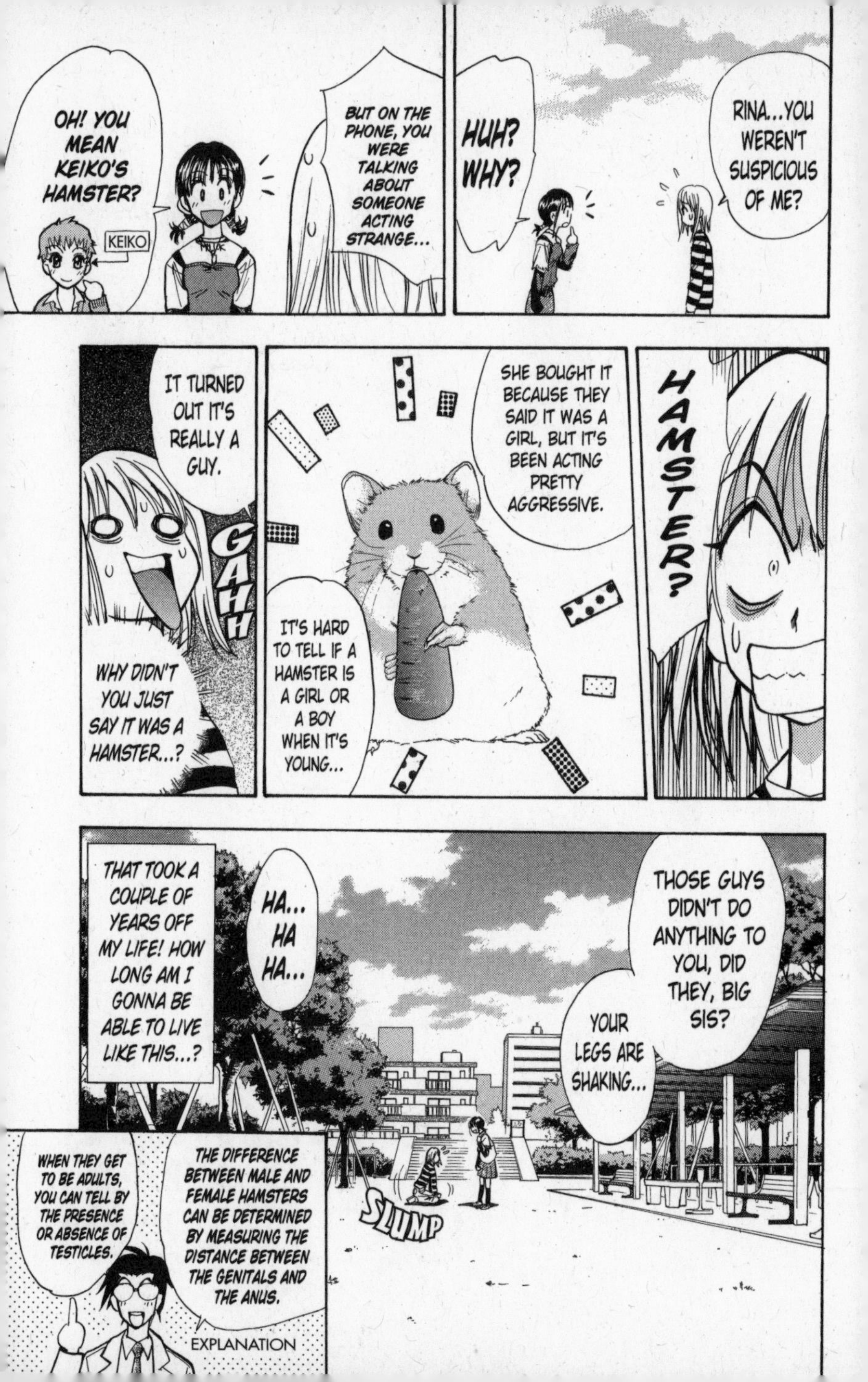

RINA...YOU WEREN'T SUSPICIOUS OF ME?
HUH? WHY?
BUT ON THE PHONE, YOU WERE TALKING ABOUT SOMEONE ACTING STRANGE...
OH! YOU MEAN KEIKO'S HAMSTER?
KEIKO
HAMSTER?
SHE BOUGHT IT BECAUSE THEY SAID IT WAS A GIRL, BUT IT'S BEEN ACTING PRETTY AGGRESSIVE.
IT'S HARD TO TELL IF A HAMSTER IS A GIRL OR A BOY WHEN IT'S YOUNG...
IT TURNED OUT IT'S REALLY A GUY.
GAHH
WHY DIDN'T YOU JUST SAY IT WAS A HAMSTER...?
THOSE GUYS DIDN'T DO ANYTHING TO YOU, DID THEY, BIG SIS?
YOUR LEGS ARE SHAKING...
HA... HA HA...
THAT TOOK A COUPLE OF YEARS OFF MY LIFE! HOW LONG AM I GONNA BE ABLE TO LIVE LIKE THIS...?
SLUMP
THE DIFFERENCE BETWEEN MALE AND FEMALE HAMSTERS CAN BE DETERMINED BY MEASURING THE DISTANCE BETWEEN THE GENITALS AND THE ANUS.
WHEN THEY GET TO BE ADULTS, YOU CAN TELL BY THE PRESENCE OR ABSENCE OF TESTICLES.
EXPLANATION

Pretty Face

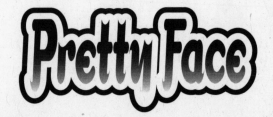

CHAPTER 4: THE PHYSICAL

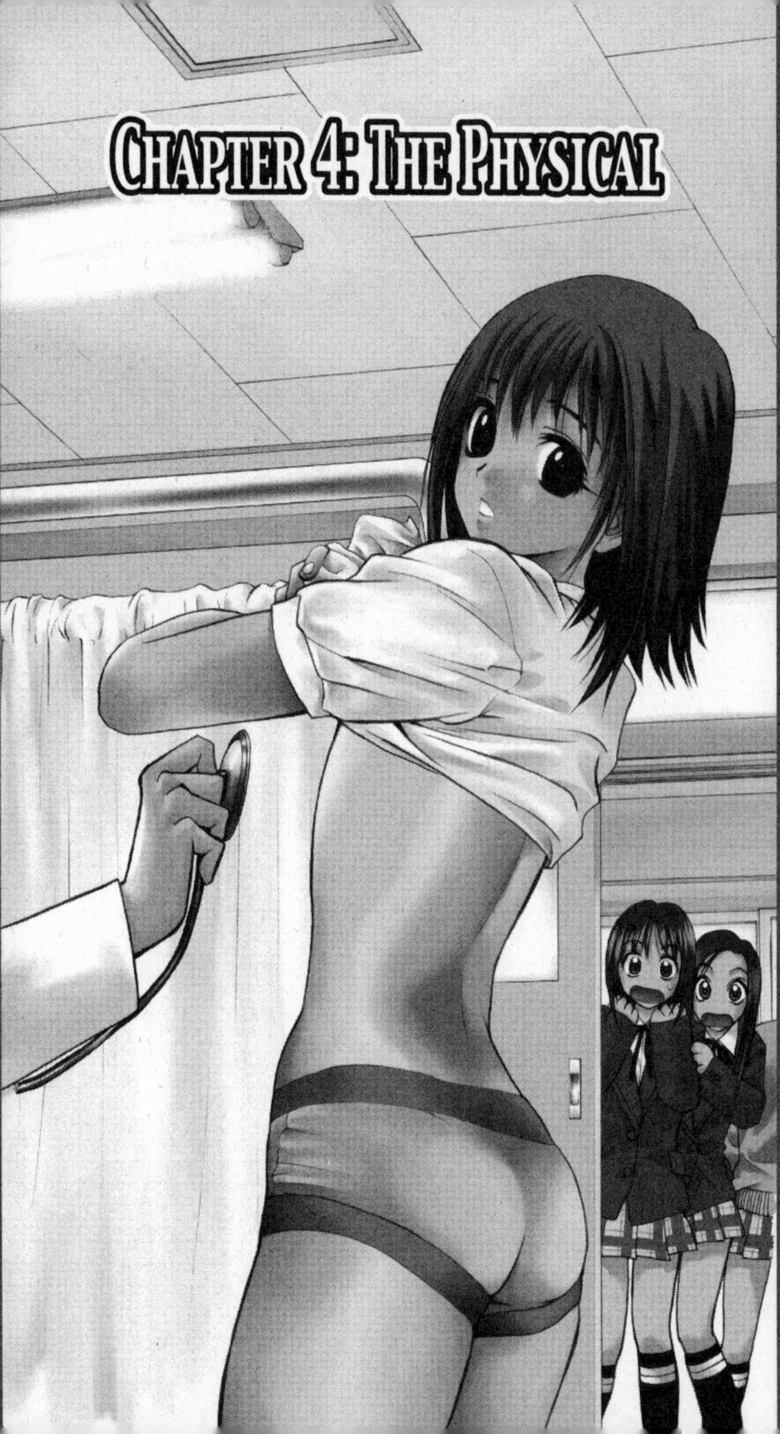

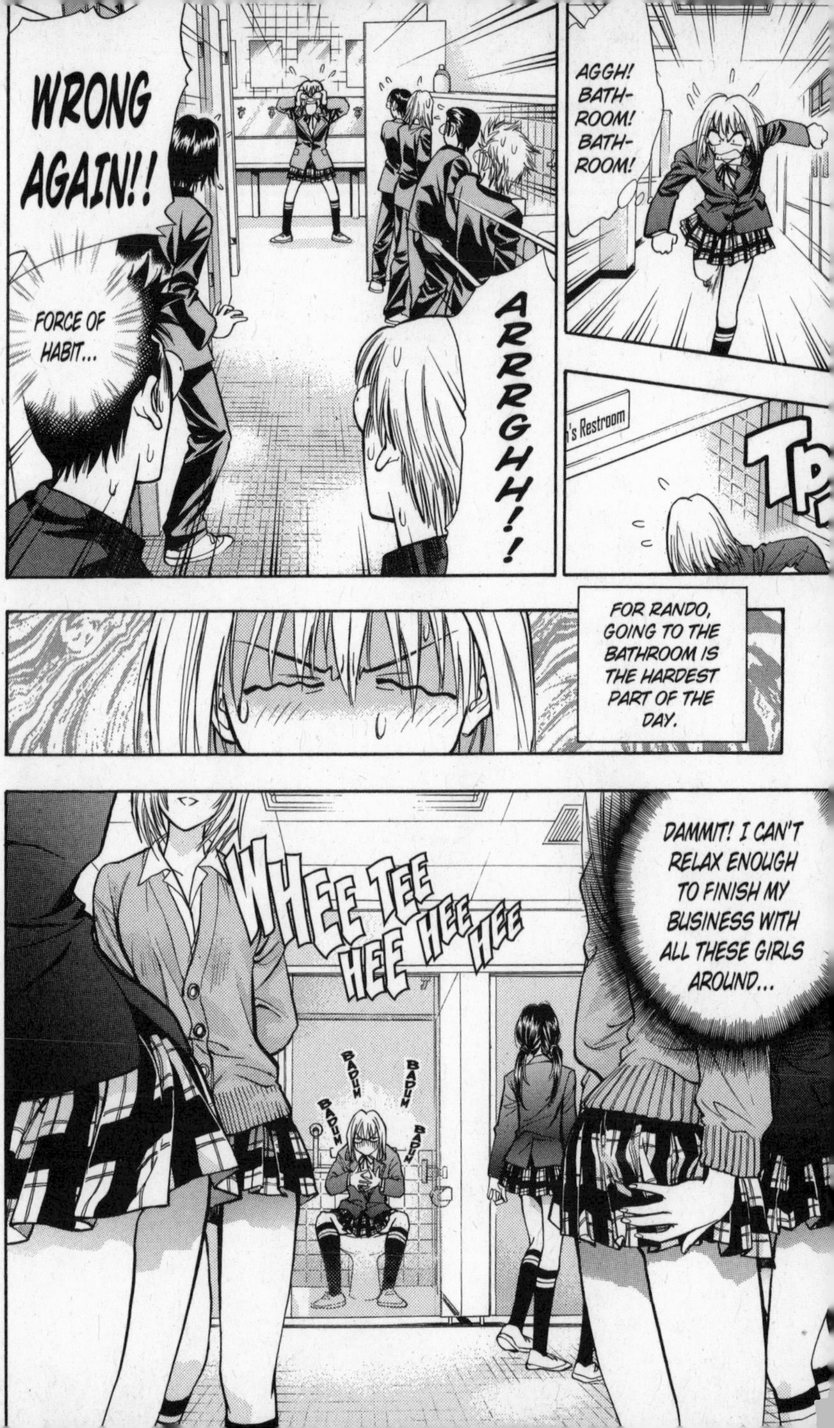
AGGH! BATHROOM! BATHROOM!
's Restroom
TP
WRONG AGAIN!!
ARRRGHH!!
FORCE OF HABIT...
FOR RANDO, GOING TO THE BATHROOM IS THE HARDEST PART OF THE DAY.
DAMMIT! I CAN'T RELAX ENOUGH TO FINISH MY BUSINESS WITH ALL THESE GIRLS AROUND...
WHEE TEE HEE HEE HEE
BADUM
BADUM
BADUM
BADUM

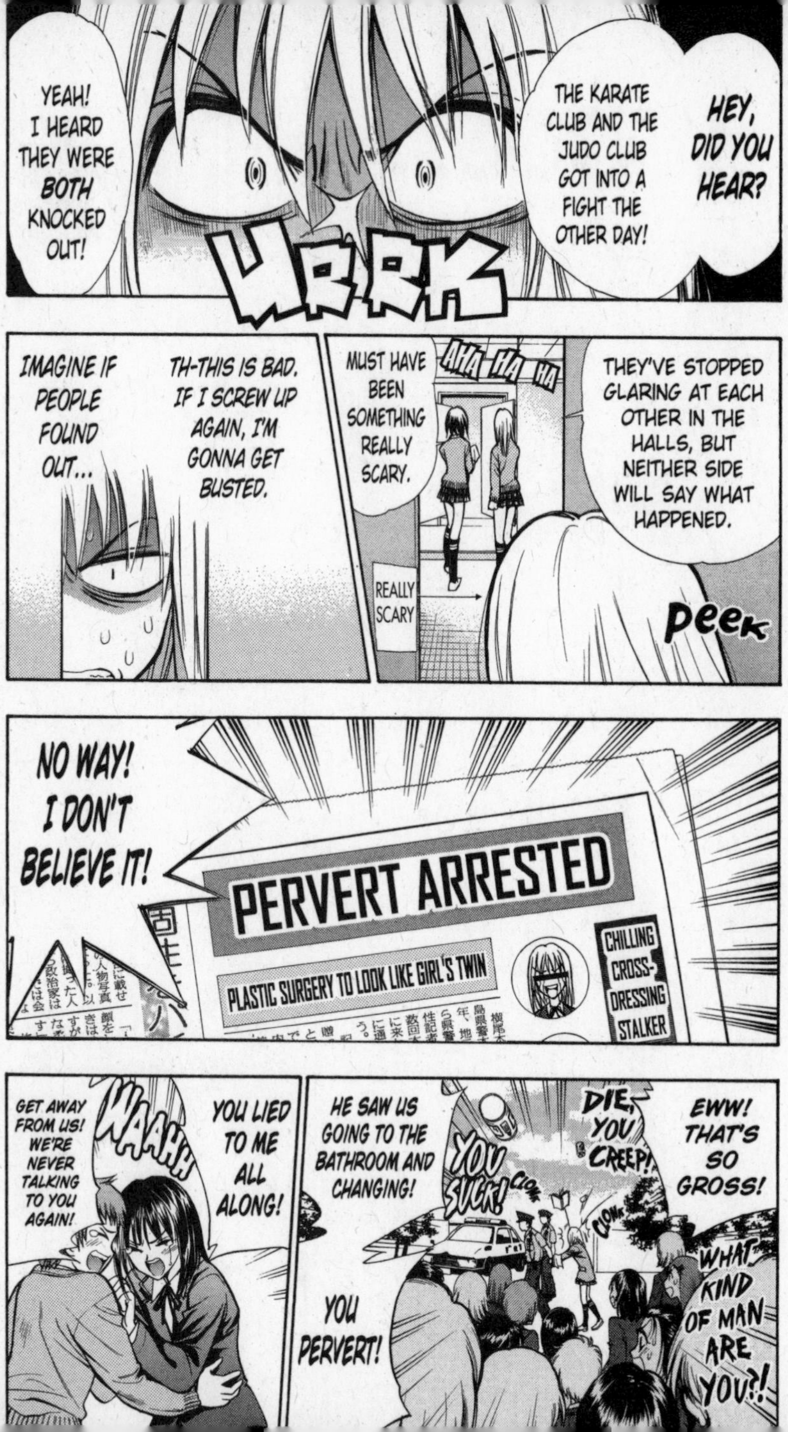
HEY, DID YOU HEAR?
THE KARATE CLUB AND THE JUDO CLUB GOT INTO A FIGHT THE OTHER DAY!
URRK
YEAH! I HEARD THEY WERE BOTH KNOCKED OUT!
THEY'VE STOPPED GLARING AT EACH OTHER IN THE HALLS, BUT NEITHER SIDE WILL SAY WHAT HAPPENED.
AHA HA HA
MUST HAVE BEEN SOMETHING REALLY SCARY.
REALLY SCARY
Peek
TH-THIS IS BAD. IF I SCREW UP AGAIN, I'M GONNA GET BUSTED.
IMAGINE IF PEOPLE FOUND OUT...
PERVERT ARRESTED
CHILLING CROSS-DRESSING STALKER
PLASTIC SURGERY TO LOOK LIKE GIRL'S TWIN
NO WAY! I DON'T BELIEVE IT!
EWW! THAT'S SO GROSS!
DIE, YOU CREEP!
WHAT KIND OF MAN ARE YOU?!
CLONK
CLONK
YOU SUCK!
HE SAW US GOING TO THE BATHROOM AND CHANGING!
YOU PERVERT!
YOU LIED TO ME ALL ALONG!
WAAHH
GET AWAY FROM US! WE'RE NEVER TALKING TO YOU AGAIN!

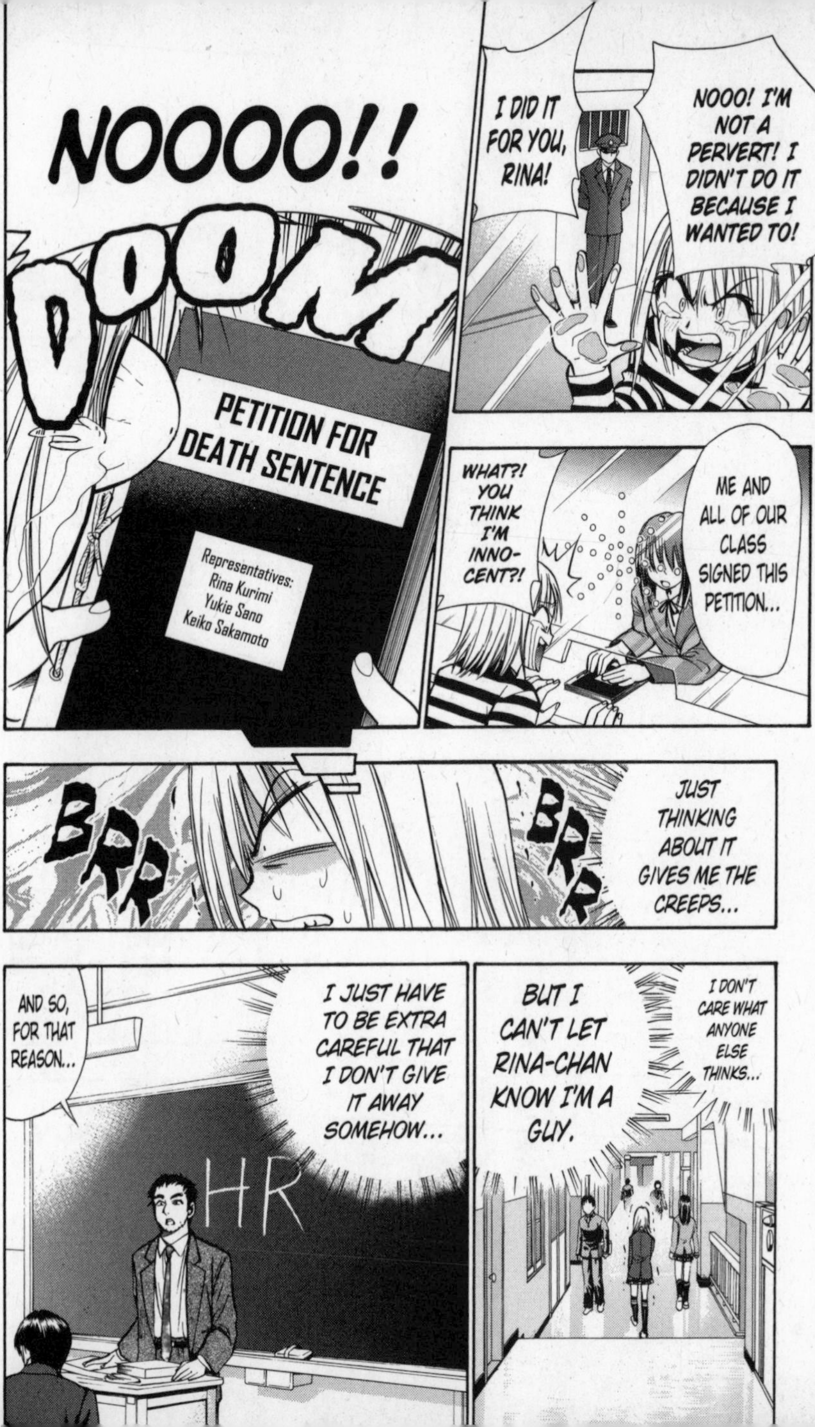
NOOO! I'M NOT A PERVERT! I DIDN'T DO IT BECAUSE I WANTED TO!
I DID IT FOR YOU, RINA!
ME AND ALL OF OUR CLASS SIGNED THIS PETITION...
WHAT?! YOU THINK I'M INNO-CENT?!
NOOOO!!
DOOM
PETITION FOR DEATH SENTENCE
Representatives: Rina Kurimi Yukie Sano Keiko Sakamoto
JUST THINKING ABOUT IT GIVES ME THE CREEPS...
BRRR
BRRR
I DON'T CARE WHAT ANYONE ELSE THINKS...
BUT I CAN'T LET RINA-CHAN KNOW I'M A GUY.
I JUST HAVE TO BE EXTRA CAREFUL THAT I DON'T GIVE IT AWAY SOMEHOW...
AND SO, FOR THAT REASON...
HR

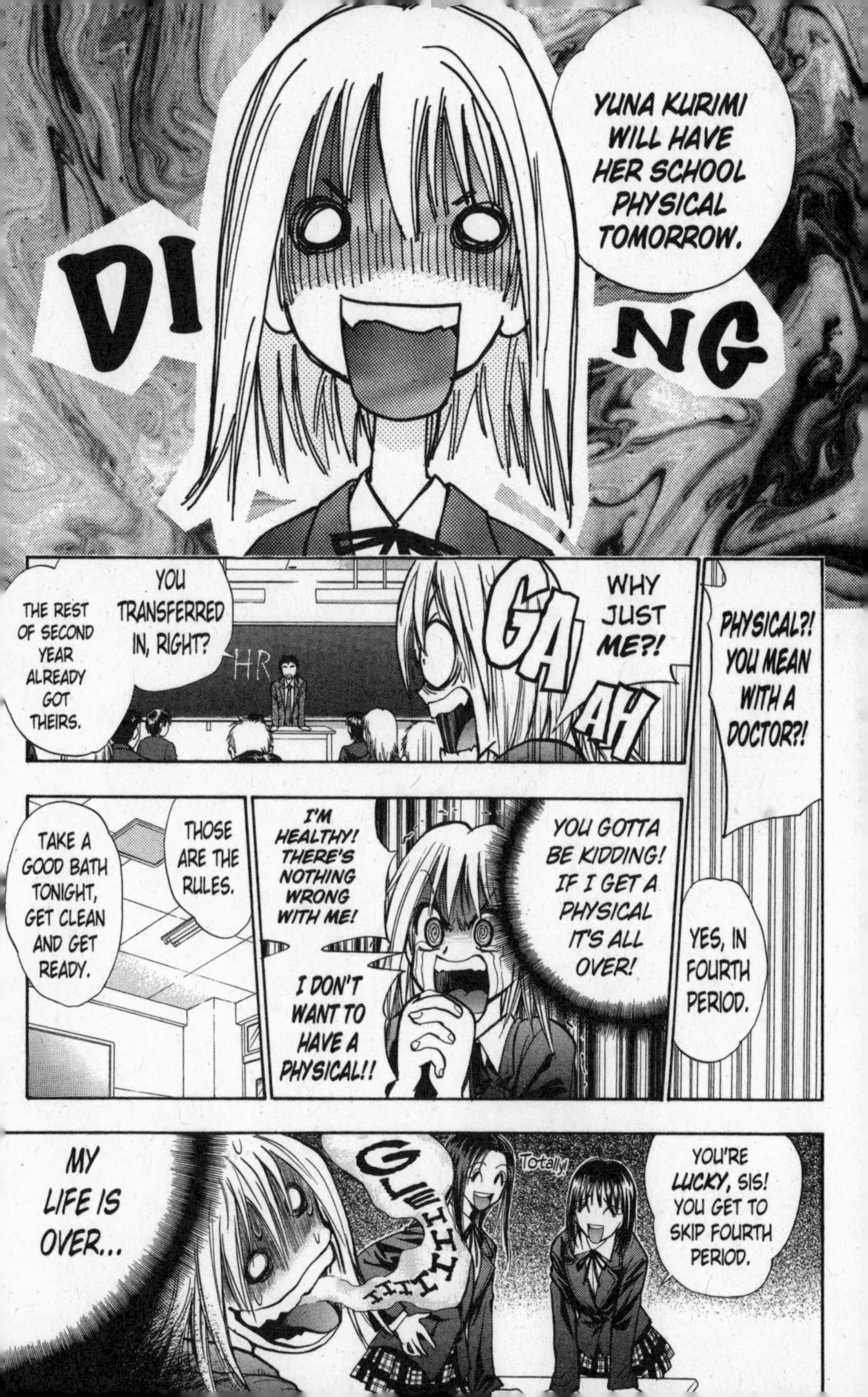
YUNA KURIMI WILL HAVE HER SCHOOL PHYSICAL TOMORROW.
DI NG
PHYSICAL?! YOU MEAN WITH A DOCTOR?!
YES, IN FOURTH PERIOD.
WHY JUST ME?!
GA AH
HR
YOU TRANSFERRED IN, RIGHT?
THE REST OF SECOND YEAR ALREADY GOT THEIRS.
YOU GOTTA BE KIDDING! IF I GET A PHYSICAL IT'S ALL OVER!
I'M HEALTHY! THERE'S NOTHING WRONG WITH ME!
I DON'T WANT TO HAVE A PHYSICAL!!
THOSE ARE THE RULES.
TAKE A GOOD BATH TONIGHT, GET CLEAN AND GET READY.
YOU'RE LUCKY, SIS! YOU GET TO SKIP FOURTH PERIOD.
Totally!
MY LIFE IS OVER...

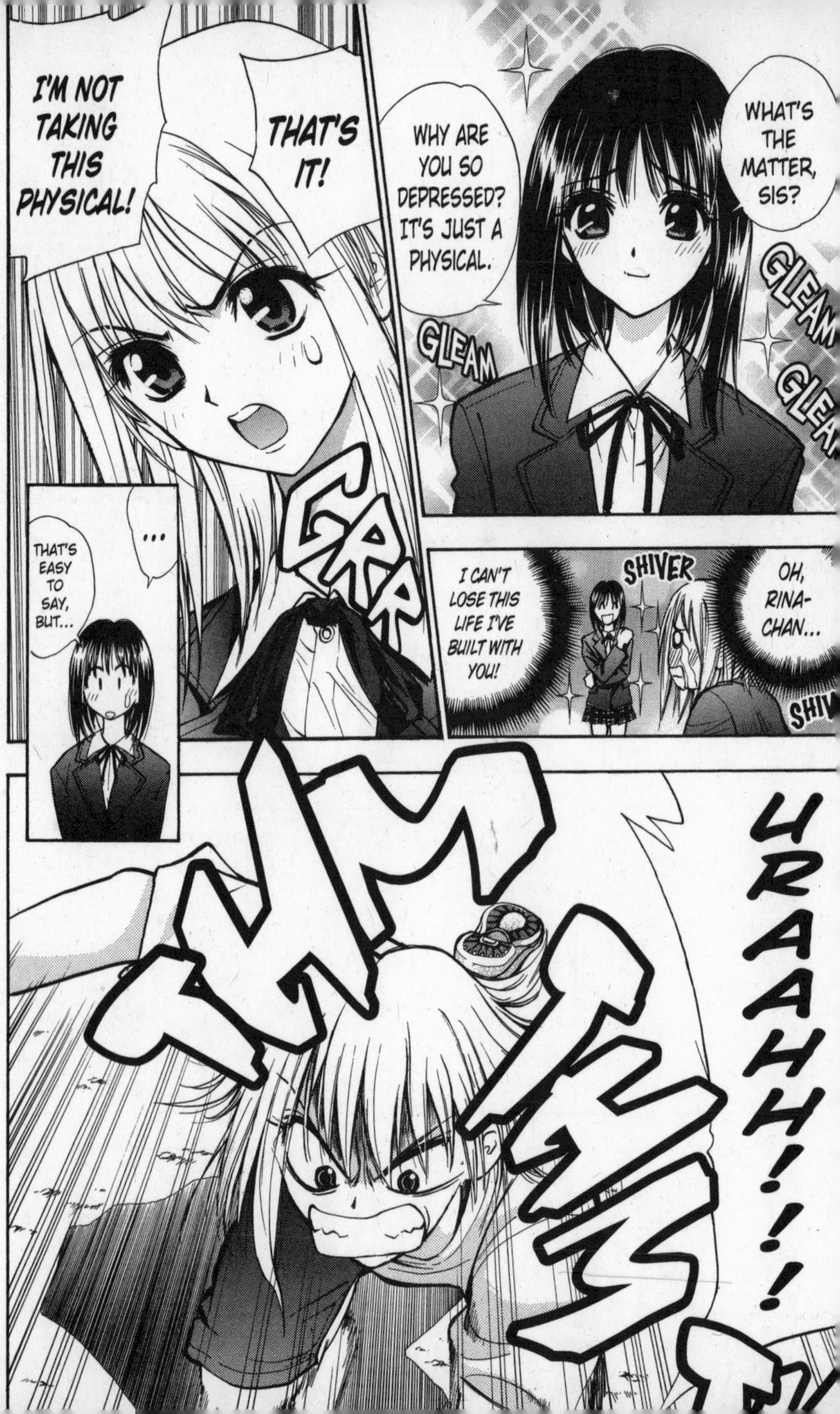

WHAT'S THE MATTER, SIS?
GLEAM
GLEAM
GLEAM
WHY ARE YOU SO DEPRESSED? IT'S JUST A PHYSICAL.
OH, RINA-CHAN...
SHIVER
SHIV
I CAN'T LOSE THIS LIFE I'VE BUILT WITH YOU!
THAT'S IT!
I'M NOT TAKING THIS PHYSICAL!
GRR
...
THAT'S EASY TO SAY, BUT...
URAAHH!!!

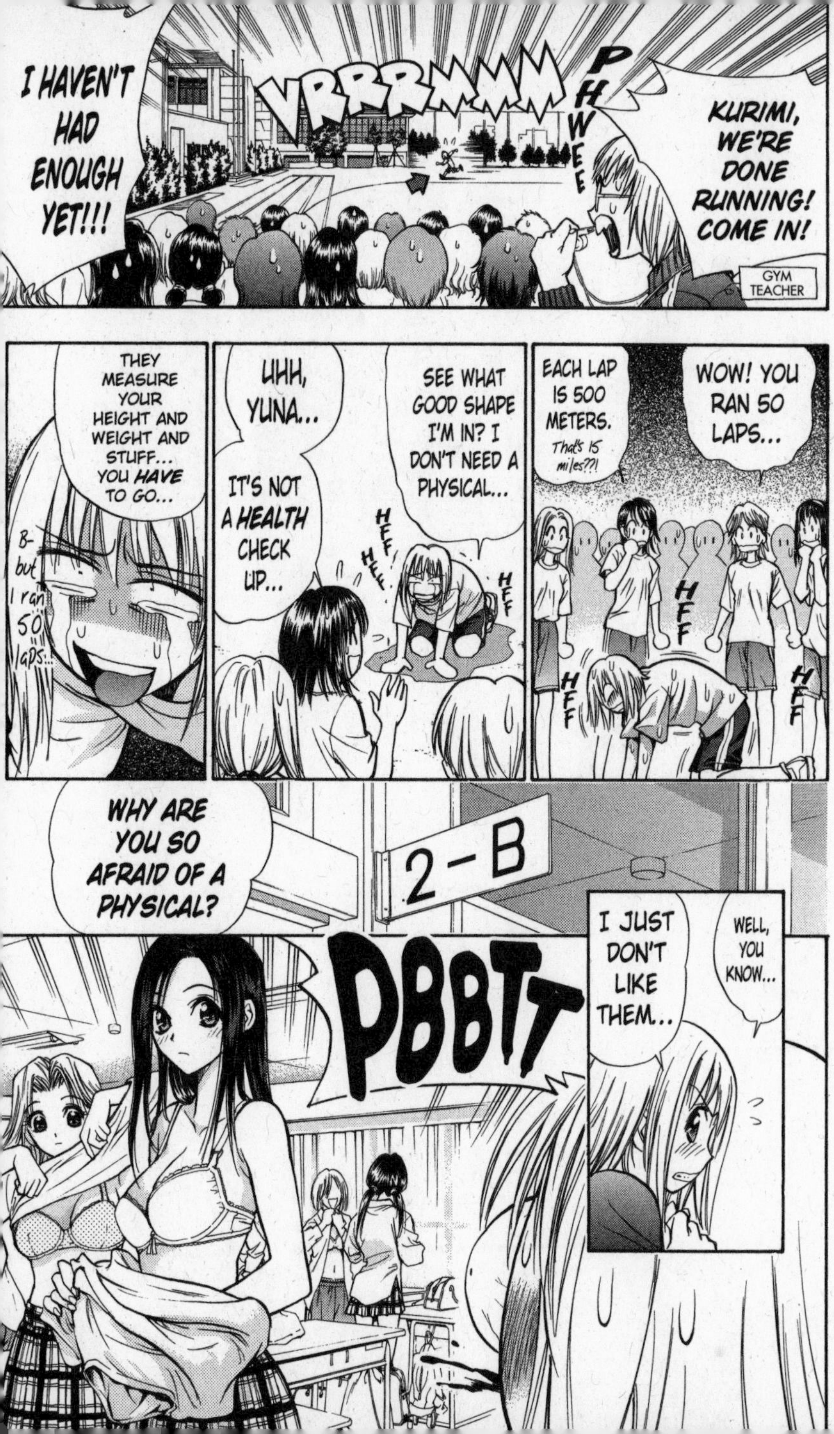
KURIMI, WE'RE DONE RUNNING! COME IN!
GYM TEACHER
PHWEE
VRRRMMMM
I HAVEN'T HAD ENOUGH YET!!!
WOW! YOU RAN 50 LAPS...
EACH LAP IS 500 METERS.
That's 15 miles??!
HFF
HFF
HFF
SEE WHAT GOOD SHAPE I'M IN? I DON'T NEED A PHYSICAL...
HFF
HFF
HFF
UHH, YUNA...
IT'S NOT A *HEALTH* CHECK UP...
THEY MEASURE YOUR HEIGHT AND WEIGHT AND STUFF... YOU *HAVE* TO GO...
B-but I ran 50 laps...
2-B
WHY ARE YOU SO AFRAID OF A PHYSICAL?
WELL, YOU KNOW...
I JUST DON'T LIKE THEM...
PBBT

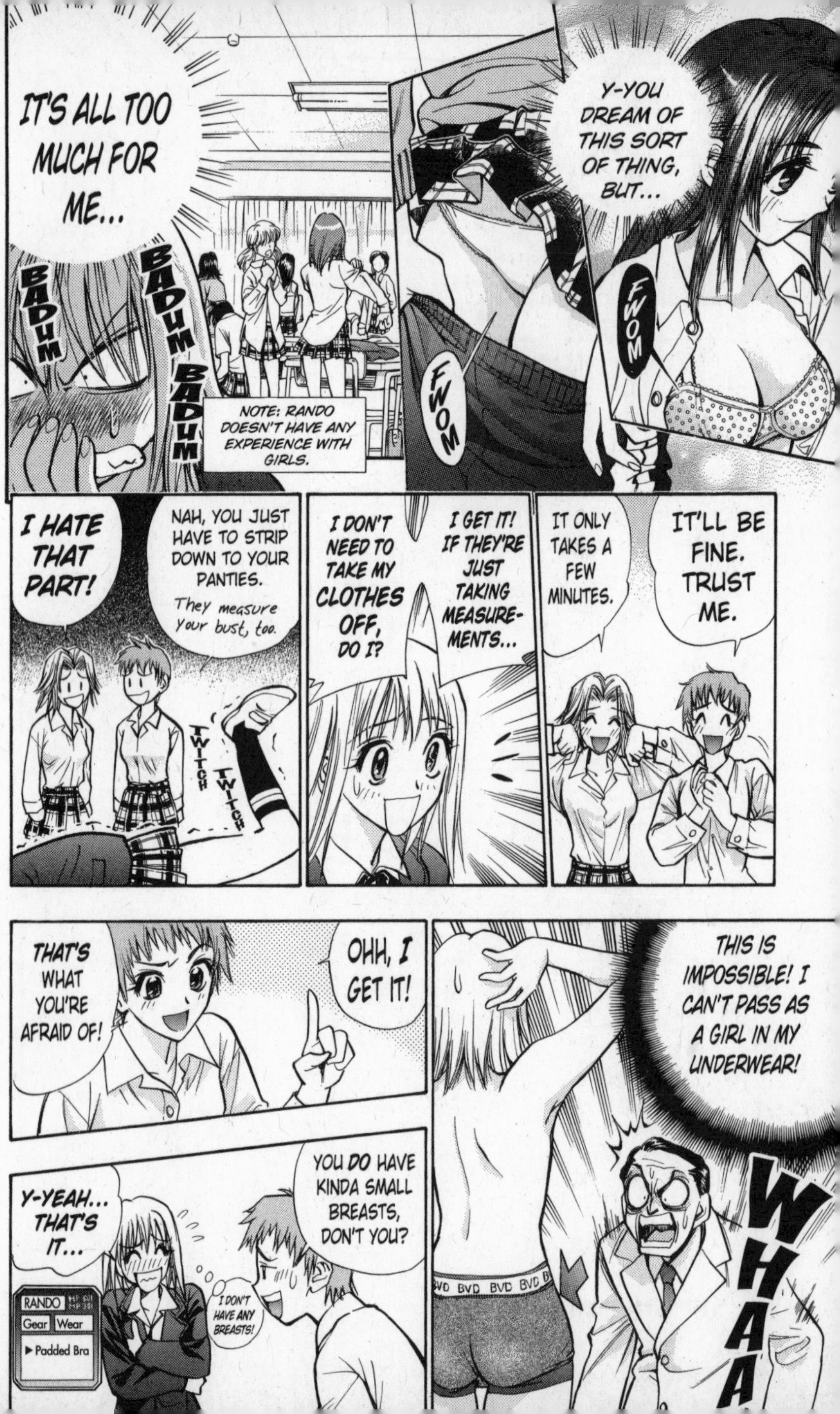
Y-YOU DREAM OF THIS SORT OF THING, BUT...
FWOM
FWOM
IT'S ALL TOO MUCH FOR ME...
BADUM BADUM BADUM
BADUM
NOTE: RANDO DOESN'T HAVE ANY EXPERIENCE WITH GIRLS.
IT'LL BE FINE. TRUST ME.
IT ONLY TAKES A FEW MINUTES.
I GET IT! IF THEY'RE JUST TAKING MEASUREMENTS...
I DON'T NEED TO TAKE MY CLOTHES OFF, DO I?
NAH, YOU JUST HAVE TO STRIP DOWN TO YOUR PANTIES. They measure your bust, too.
I HATE THAT PART!
TWITCH TWITCH
THIS IS IMPOSSIBLE! I CAN'T PASS AS A GIRL IN MY UNDERWEAR!
BVD BVD BVD BVD
WHAA
OHH, I GET IT!
THAT'S WHAT YOU'RE AFRAID OF!
YOU DO HAVE KINDA SMALL BREASTS, DON'T YOU?
Y-YEAH... THAT'S IT...
I DON'T HAVE ANY BREASTS!
RANDO
Gear Wear
▶ Padded Bra

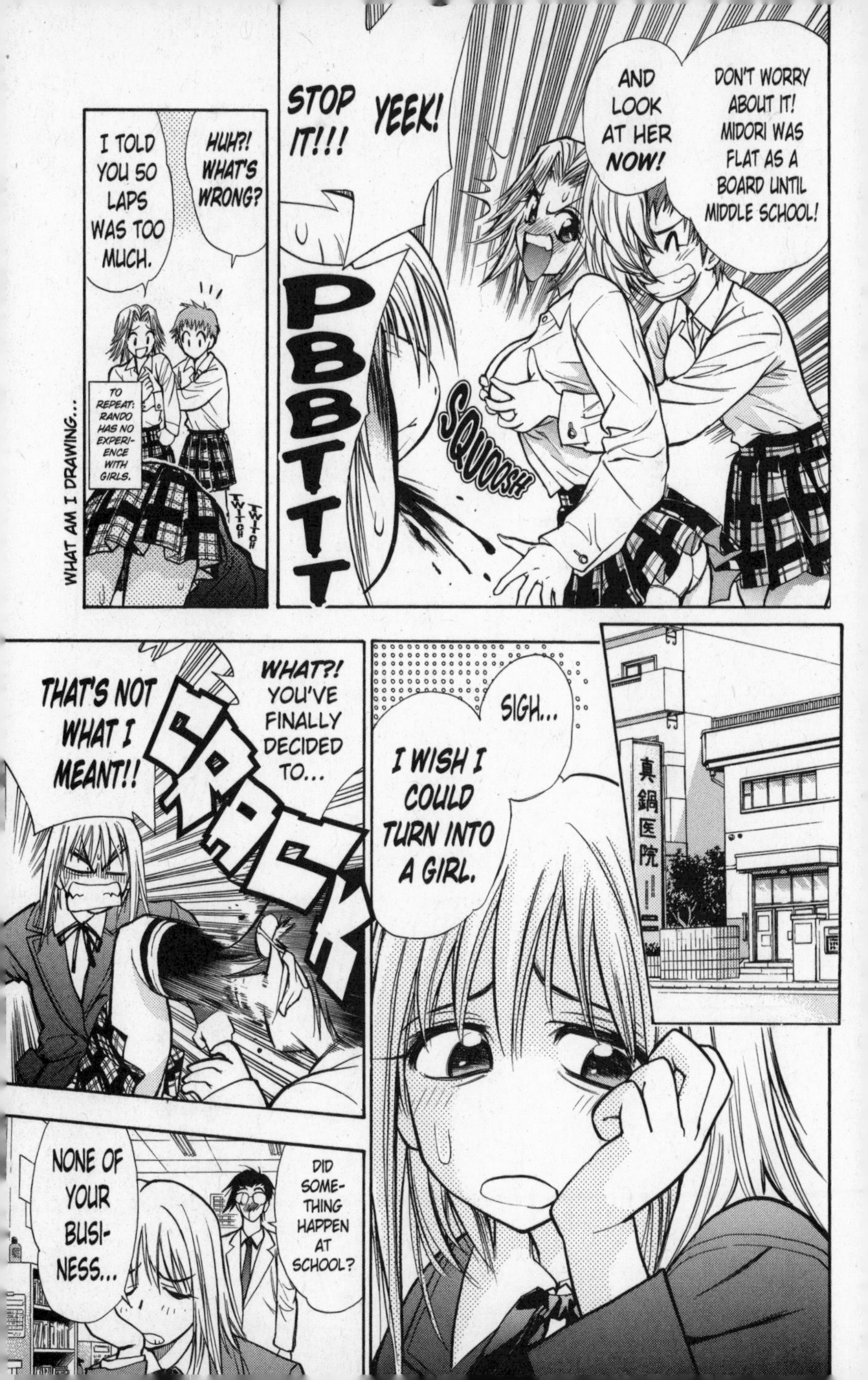
DON'T WORRY ABOUT IT! MIDORI WAS FLAT AS A BOARD UNTIL MIDDLE SCHOOL!
AND LOOK AT HER NOW!
YEEK!
STOP IT!!!
SQUOOSH
PBBTTT
HUH?! WHAT'S WRONG?
I TOLD YOU 50 LAPS WAS TOO MUCH.
TO REPEAT: RANDO HAS NO EXPERIENCE WITH GIRLS.
TWITCH TWITCH
WHAT AM I DRAWING...
真鍋医院
SIGH...
I WISH I COULD TURN INTO A GIRL.
WHAT?! YOU'VE FINALLY DECIDED TO...
THAT'S NOT WHAT I MEANT!!
DID SOMETHING HAPPEN AT SCHOOL?
NONE OF YOUR BUSINESS...

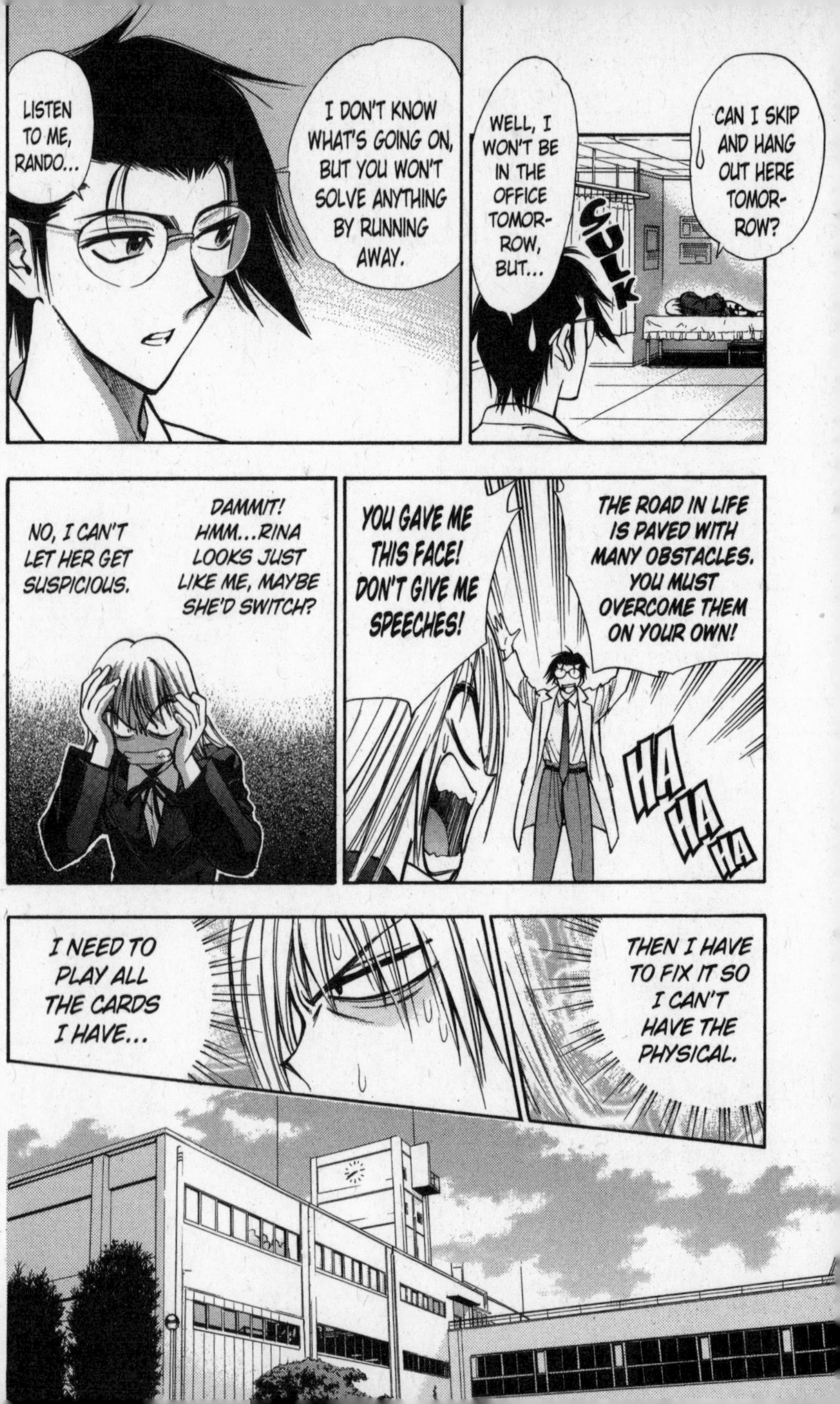
CAN I SKIP AND HANG OUT HERE TOMORROW?
WELL, I WON'T BE IN THE OFFICE TOMORROW, BUT...
SULK
I DON'T KNOW WHAT'S GOING ON, BUT YOU WON'T SOLVE ANYTHING BY RUNNING AWAY.
LISTEN TO ME, RANDO...
THE ROAD IN LIFE IS PAVED WITH MANY OBSTACLES. YOU MUST OVERCOME THEM ON YOUR OWN!
YOU GAVE ME THIS FACE! DON'T GIVE ME SPEECHES!
HA HA HA
DAMMIT! HMM...RINA LOOKS JUST LIKE ME, MAYBE SHE'D SWITCH?
NO, I CAN'T LET HER GET SUSPICIOUS.
THEN I HAVE TO FIX IT SO I CAN'T HAVE THE PHYSICAL.
I NEED TO PLAY ALL THE CARDS I HAVE...

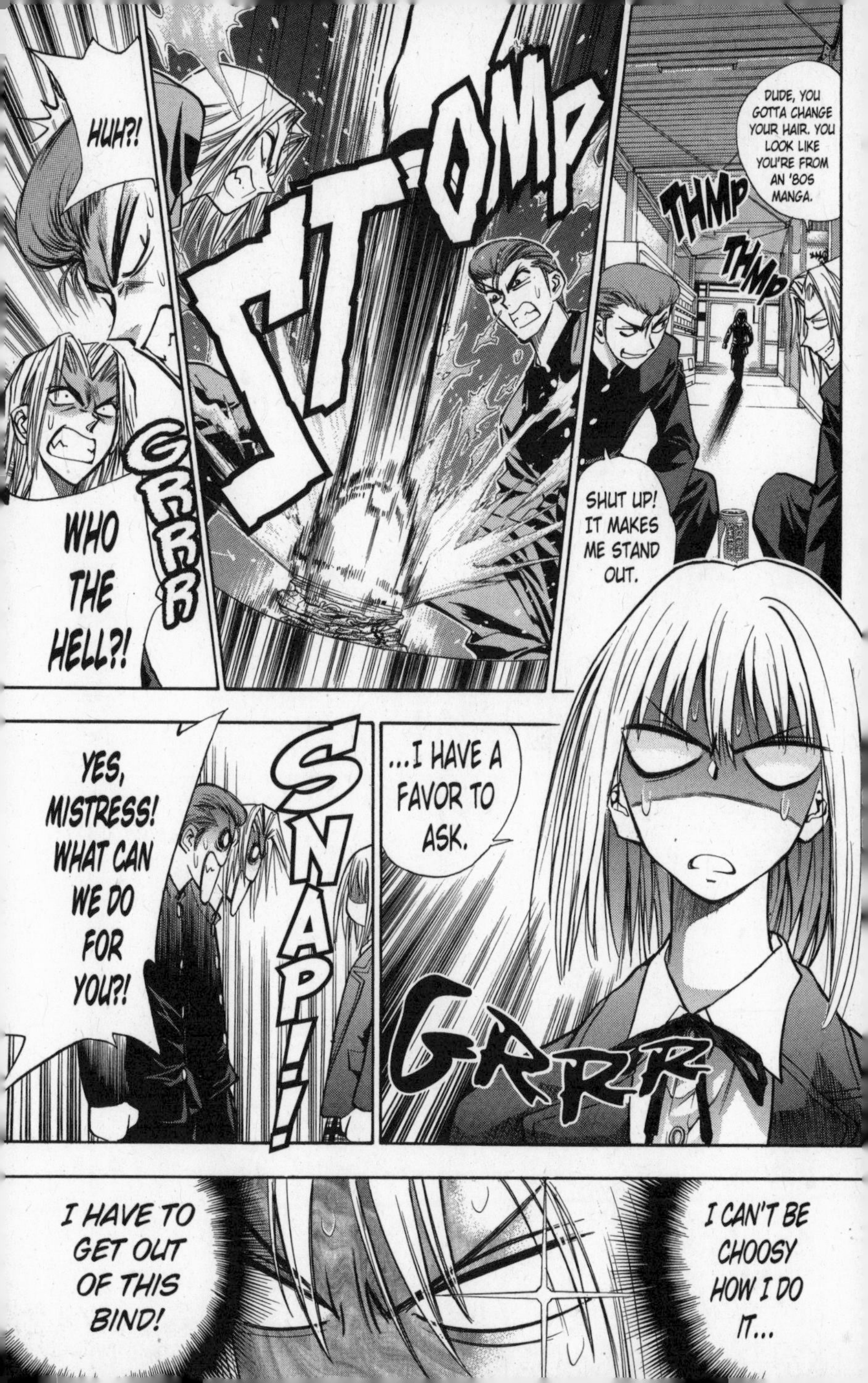
DUDE, YOU GOTTA CHANGE YOUR HAIR. YOU LOOK LIKE YOU'RE FROM AN '80S MANGA.
THMP
THMP
SHUT UP! IT MAKES ME STAND OUT.
STOMP
HUH?!
GRRR
WHO THE HELL?!
...I HAVE A FAVOR TO ASK.
GRRR
SNAP!!
YES, MISTRESS! WHAT CAN WE DO FOR YOU?!
I CAN'T BE CHOOSY HOW I DO IT...
I HAVE TO GET OUT OF THIS BIND!

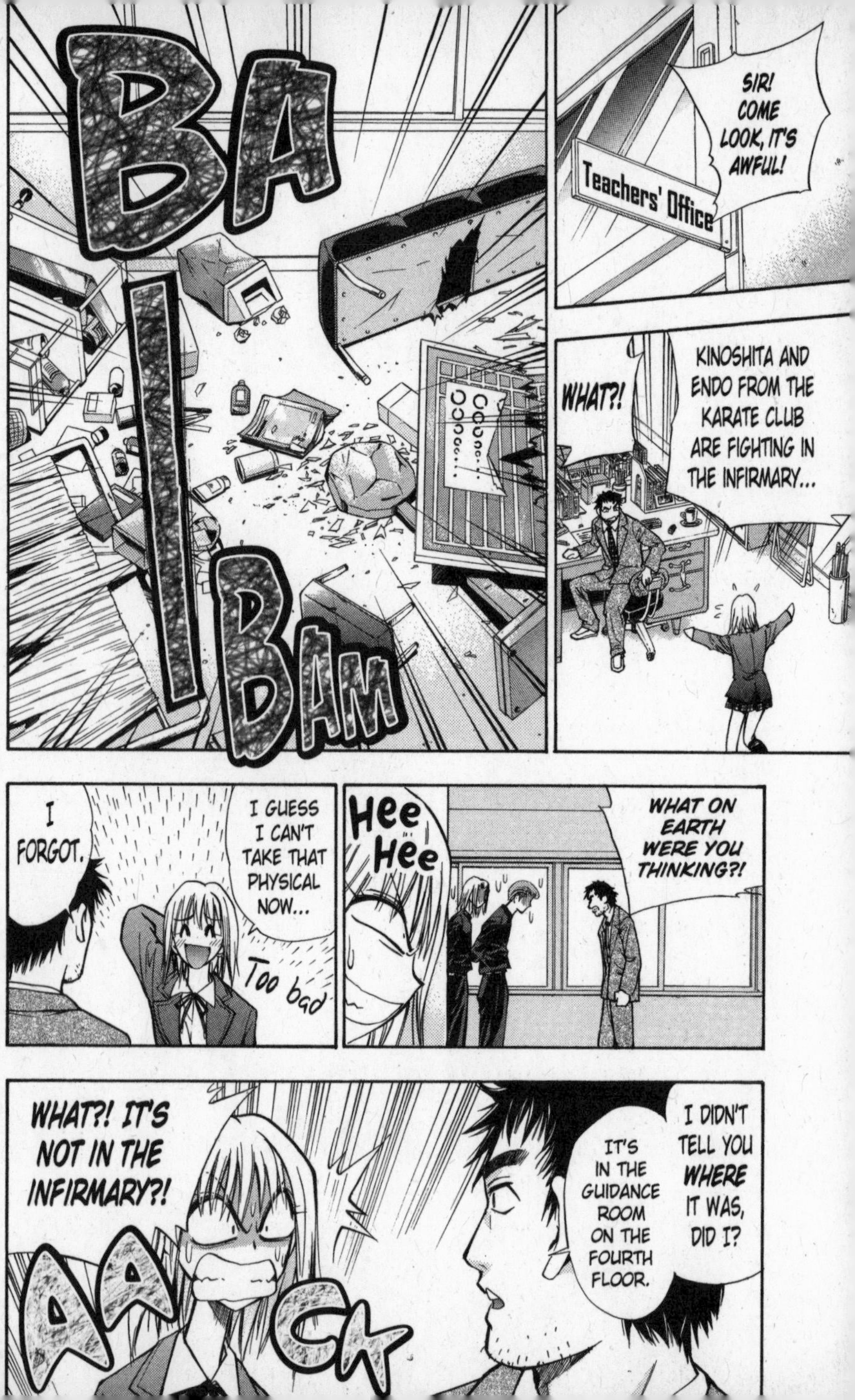
SIR! COME LOOK, IT'S AWFUL!
Teachers' Office
KINOSHITA AND ENDO FROM THE KARATE CLUB ARE FIGHTING IN THE INFIRMARY...
WHAT?!
BA I BAM
WHAT ON EARTH WERE YOU THINKING?!
Hee Hee
I GUESS I CAN'T TAKE THAT PHYSICAL NOW...
I FORGOT.
Too bad
I DIDN'T TELL YOU WHERE IT WAS, DID I?
IT'S IN THE GUIDANCE ROOM ON THE FOURTH FLOOR.
WHAT?! IT'S NOT IN THE INFIRMARY?!
AAACK

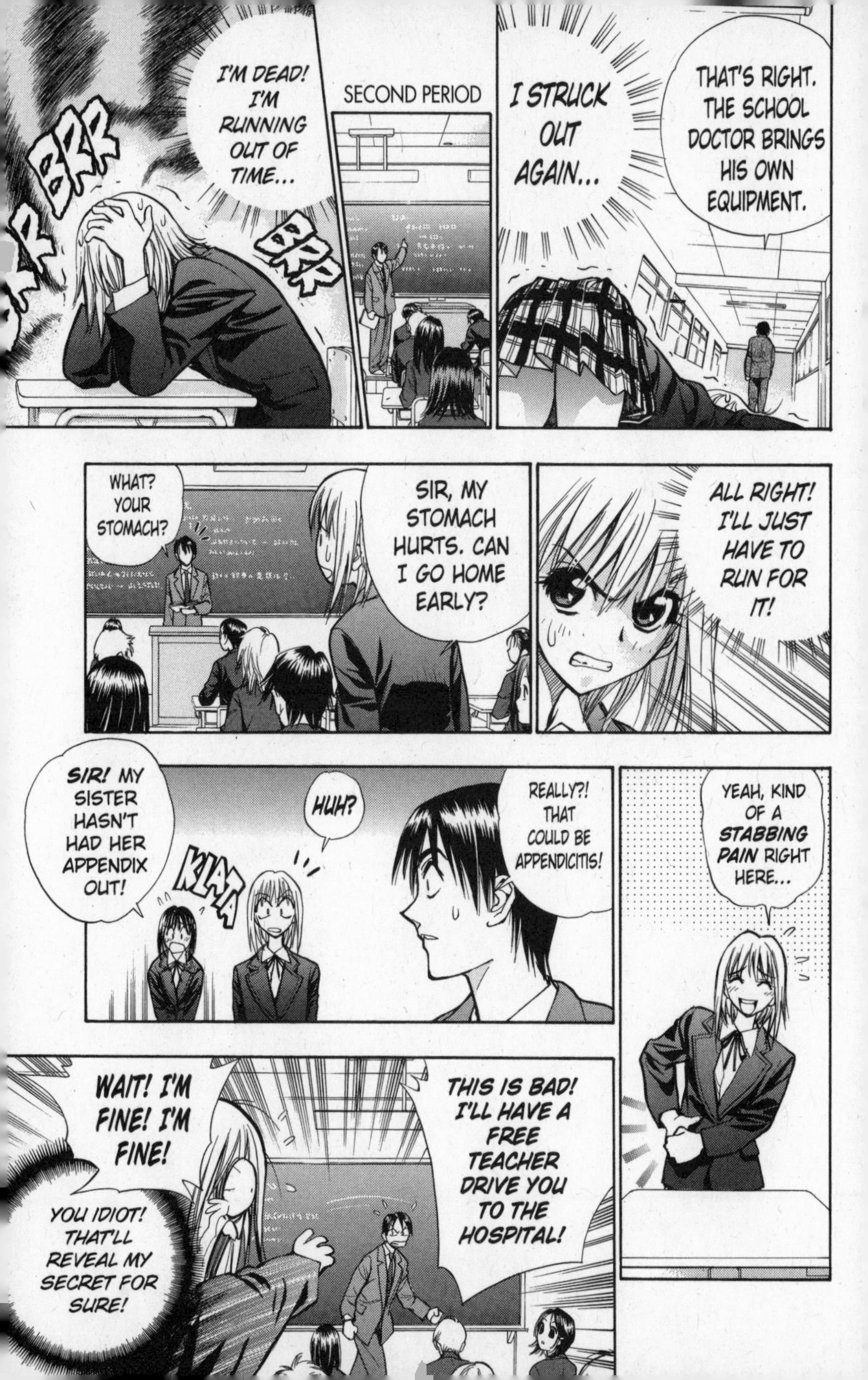
THAT'S RIGHT. THE SCHOOL DOCTOR BRINGS HIS OWN EQUIPMENT.
I STRUCK OUT AGAIN...
SECOND PERIOD
I'M DEAD! I'M RUNNING OUT OF TIME...
BRR
BRRR
ALL RIGHT! I'LL JUST HAVE TO RUN FOR IT!
SIR, MY STOMACH HURTS. CAN I GO HOME EARLY?
WHAT? YOUR STOMACH?
YEAH, KIND OF A STABBING PAIN RIGHT HERE...
REALLY?! THAT COULD BE APPENDICITIS!
HUH?
SIR! MY SISTER HASN'T HAD HER APPENDIX OUT!
KLATA
THIS IS BAD! I'LL HAVE A FREE TEACHER DRIVE YOU TO THE HOSPITAL!
WAIT! I'M FINE! I'M FINE!
YOU IDIOT! THAT'LL REVEAL MY SECRET FOR SURE!

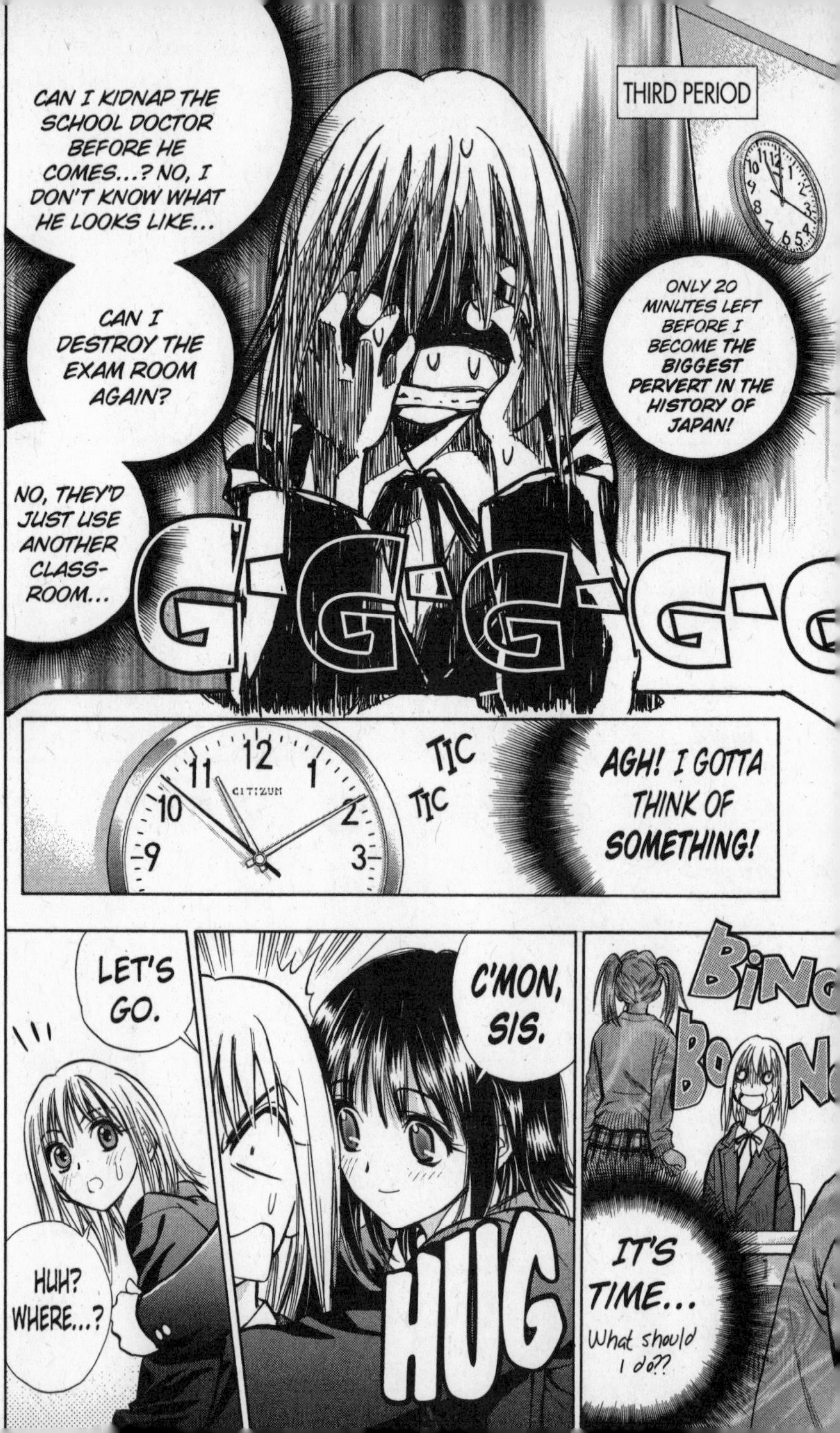
THIRD PERIOD
ONLY 20 MINUTES LEFT BEFORE I BECOME THE BIGGEST PERVERT IN THE HISTORY OF JAPAN!
CAN I KIDNAP THE SCHOOL DOCTOR BEFORE HE COMES...? NO, I DON'T KNOW WHAT HE LOOKS LIKE...
CAN I DESTROY THE EXAM ROOM AGAIN?
NO, THEY'D JUST USE ANOTHER CLASS-ROOM...
AGH! I GOTTA THINK OF SOMETHING!
TIC
TIC
CITIZUN
IT'S TIME...
What should I do??
C'MON, SIS.
HUG
LET'S GO.
HUH? WHERE...?

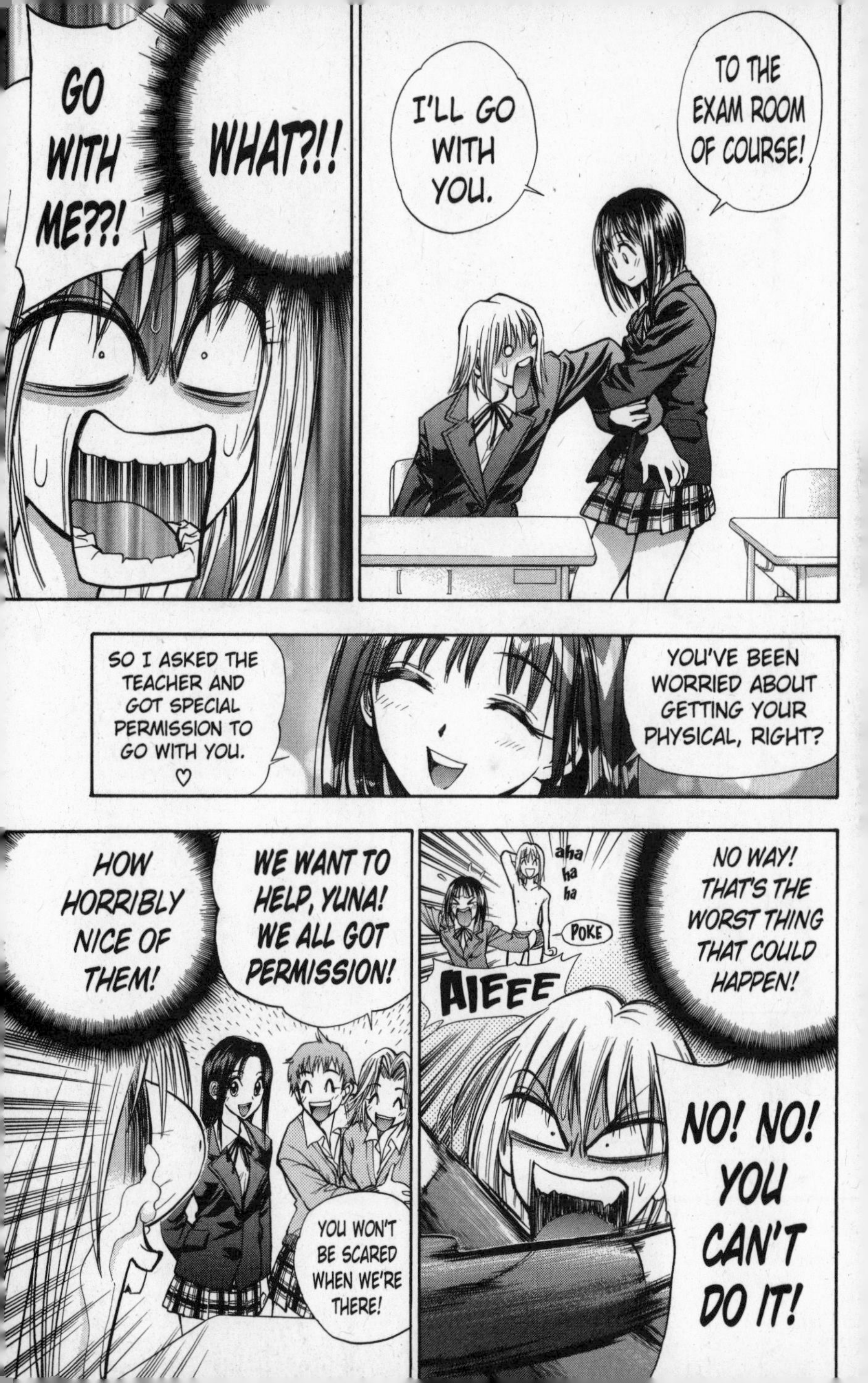
TO THE EXAM ROOM OF COURSE!
I'LL GO WITH YOU.
WHAT?!!
GO WITH ME??!
YOU'VE BEEN WORRIED ABOUT GETTING YOUR PHYSICAL, RIGHT?
SO I ASKED THE TEACHER AND GOT SPECIAL PERMISSION TO GO WITH YOU. ♡
NO WAY! THAT'S THE WORST THING THAT COULD HAPPEN!
aha ha ha
POKE
AIEEE
NO! NO! YOU CAN'T DO IT!
WE WANT TO HELP, YUNA! WE ALL GOT PERMISSION!
HOW HORRIBLY NICE OF THEM!
YOU WON'T BE SCARED WHEN WE'RE THERE!

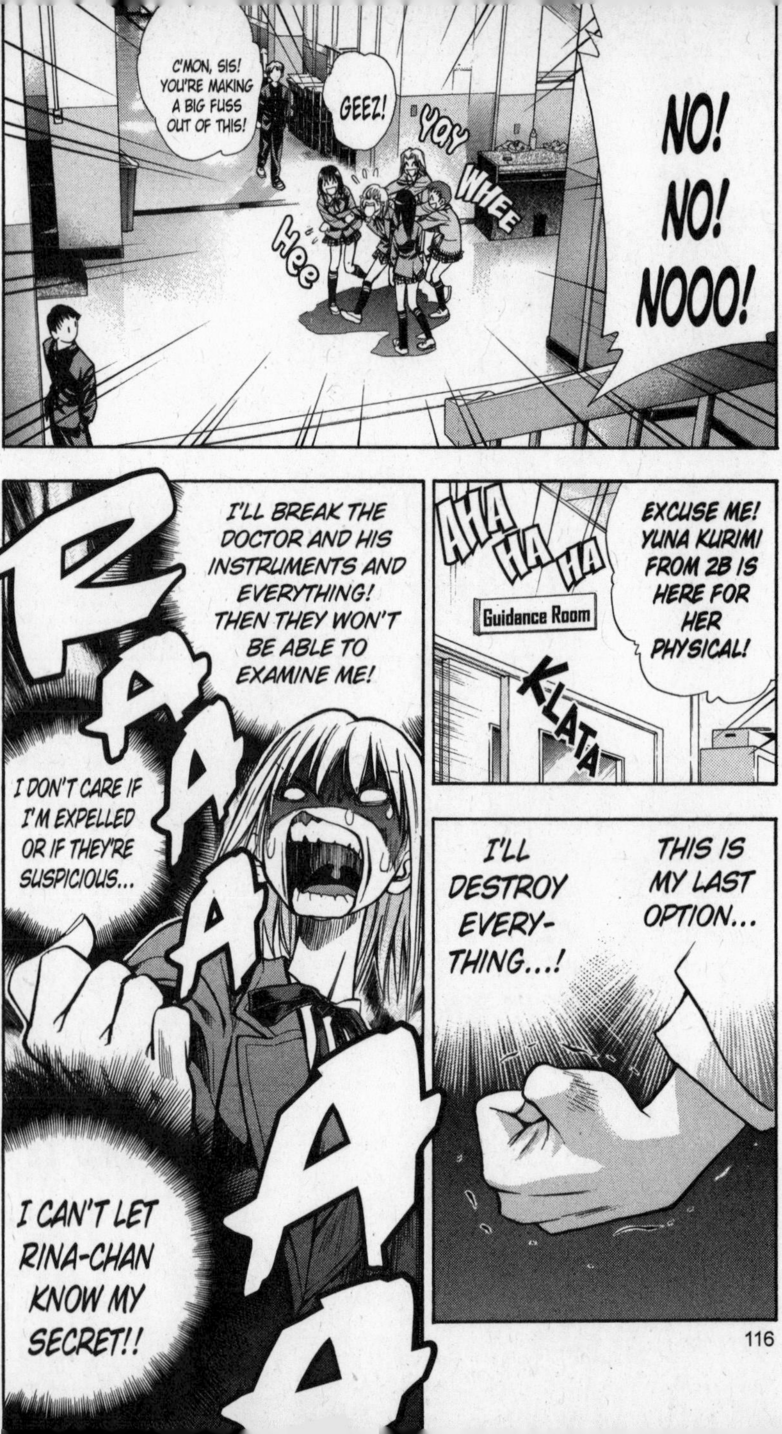
NO! NO! NOOO!
YAY
WHEE
GEEZ!
C'MON, SIS! YOU'RE MAKING A BIG FUSS OUT OF THIS!
HEE
AHA HA HA
Guidance Room
EXCUSE ME! YUNA KURIMI FROM 2B IS HERE FOR HER PHYSICAL!
KLATATA
THIS IS MY LAST OPTION...
I'LL DESTROY EVERY-THING...!
RAAAAA
I'LL BREAK THE DOCTOR AND HIS INSTRUMENTS AND EVERYTHING! THEN THEY WON'T BE ABLE TO EXAMINE ME!
I DON'T CARE IF I'M EXPELLED OR IF THEY'RE SUSPICIOUS...
I CAN'T LET RINA-CHAN KNOW MY SECRET!!

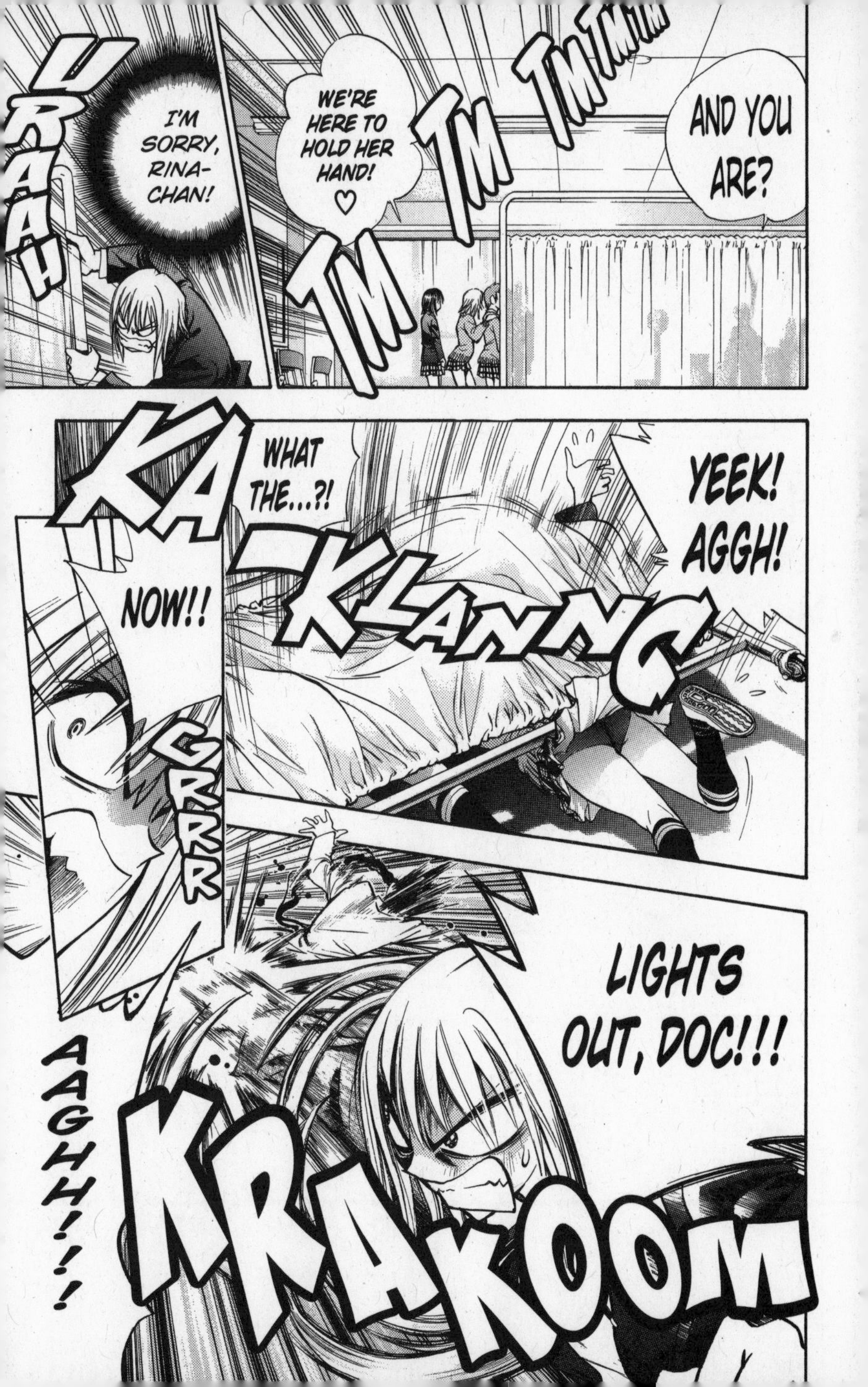
AND YOU ARE?
TM TM TM TM TM TM
WE'RE HERE TO HOLD HER HAND! ♡
I'M SORRY, RINA-CHAN!
URAAAH
YEEK! AGGH!
WHAT THE...?!
KLANNG
KA
NOW!!
GRRR
LIGHTS OUT, DOC!!!
KRAKOOM
AAGHH!!!

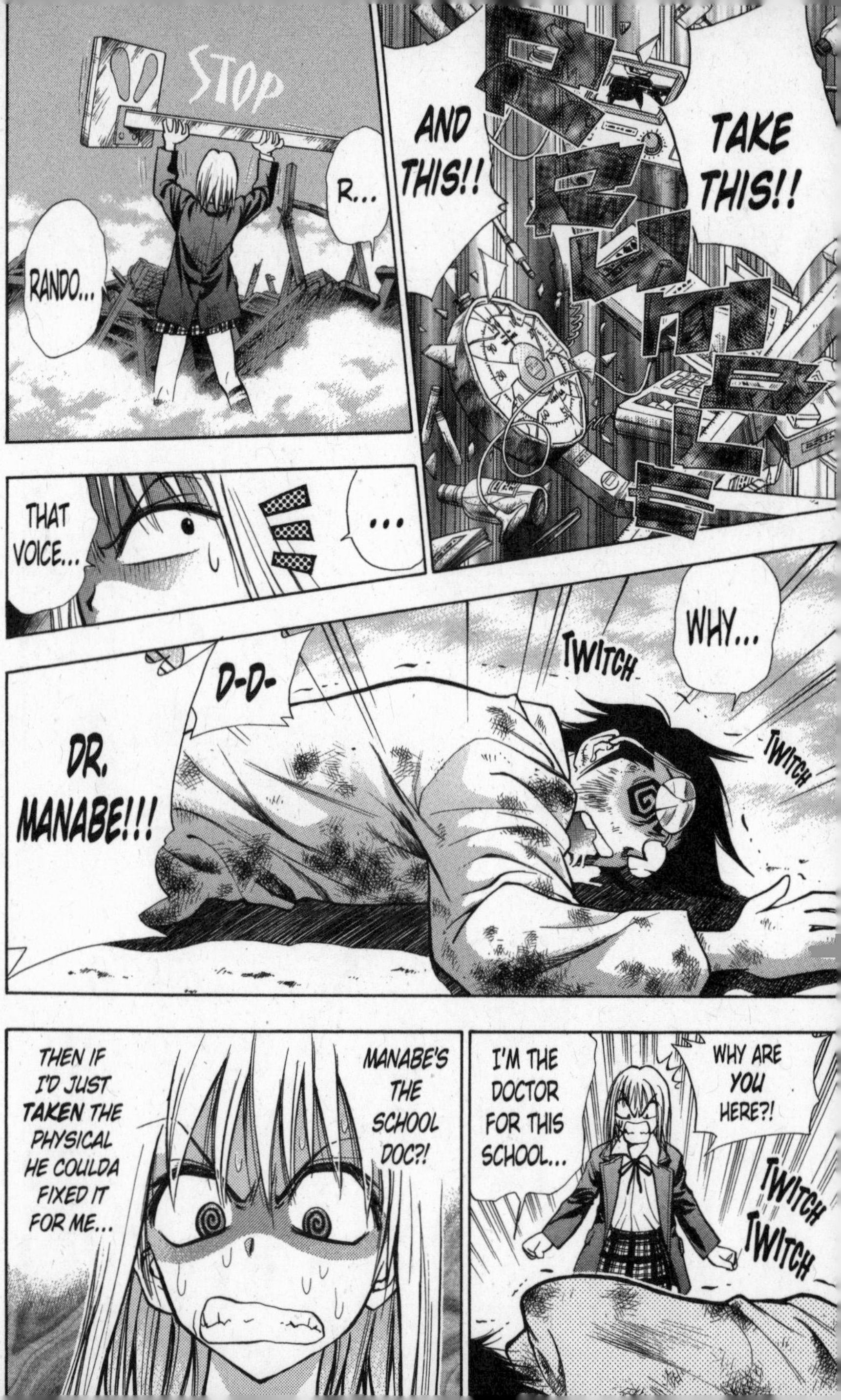
TAKE THIS!!
AND THIS!!
STOP
R...
RANDO...
...
THAT VOICE...
WHY...
TWITCH
TWITCH
D-D-
DR. MANABE!!!
WHY ARE YOU HERE?!
I'M THE DOCTOR FOR THIS SCHOOL...
TWITCH
TWITCH
MANABE'S THE SCHOOL DOC?!
THEN IF I'D JUST TAKEN THE PHYSICAL HE COULDA FIXED IT FOR ME...

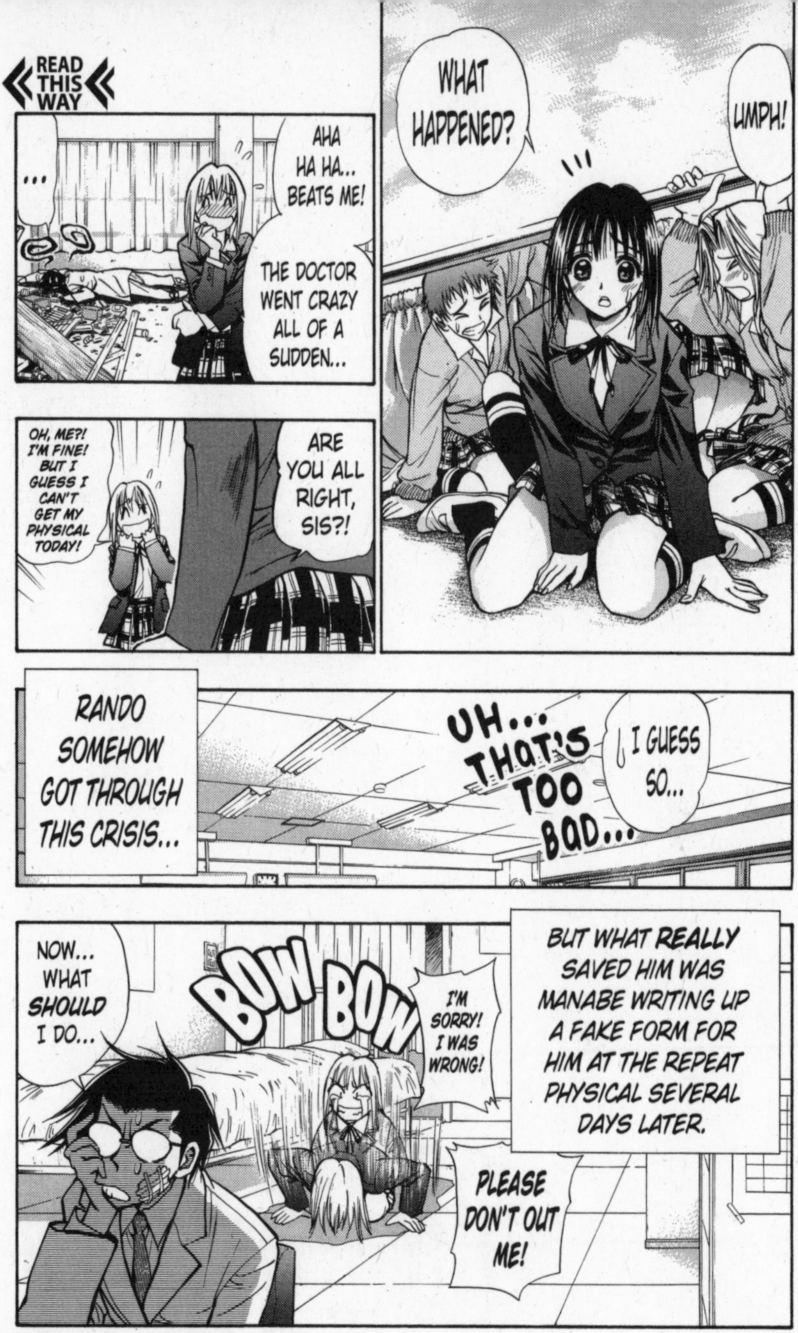
READ THIS WAY
UMPH!
WHAT HAPPENED?
AHA HA HA... BEATS ME!
THE DOCTOR WENT CRAZY ALL OF A SUDDEN...
...
ARE YOU ALL RIGHT, SIS?!
OH, ME?! I'M FINE! BUT I GUESS I CAN'T GET MY PHYSICAL TODAY!
I GUESS SO...
UH... THAT'S TOO BAD...
RANDO SOMEHOW GOT THROUGH THIS CRISIS...
BUT WHAT REALLY SAVED HIM WAS MANABE WRITING UP A FAKE FORM FOR HIM AT THE REPEAT PHYSICAL SEVERAL DAYS LATER.
I'M SORRY! I WAS WRONG!
BOW BOW
NOW... WHAT SHOULD I DO...
PLEASE DON'T OUT ME!

Pretty Face

Chapter 5: Midterm Wars, Part 1

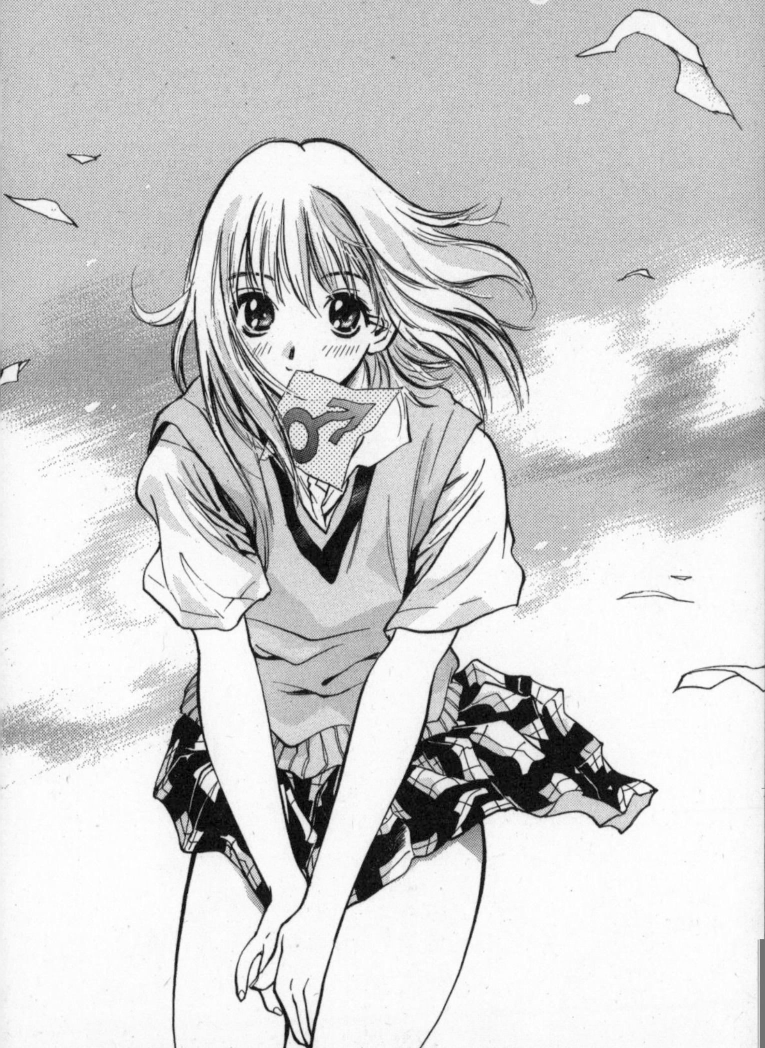

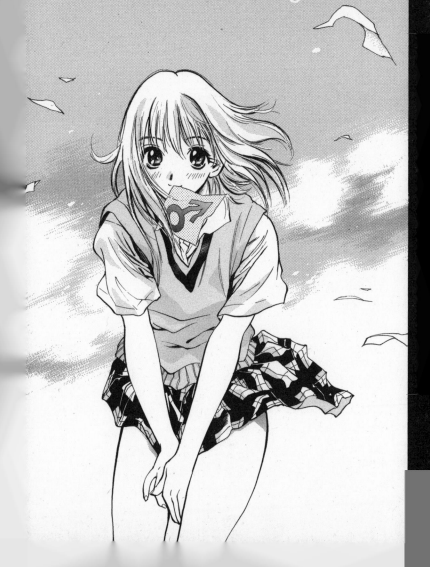

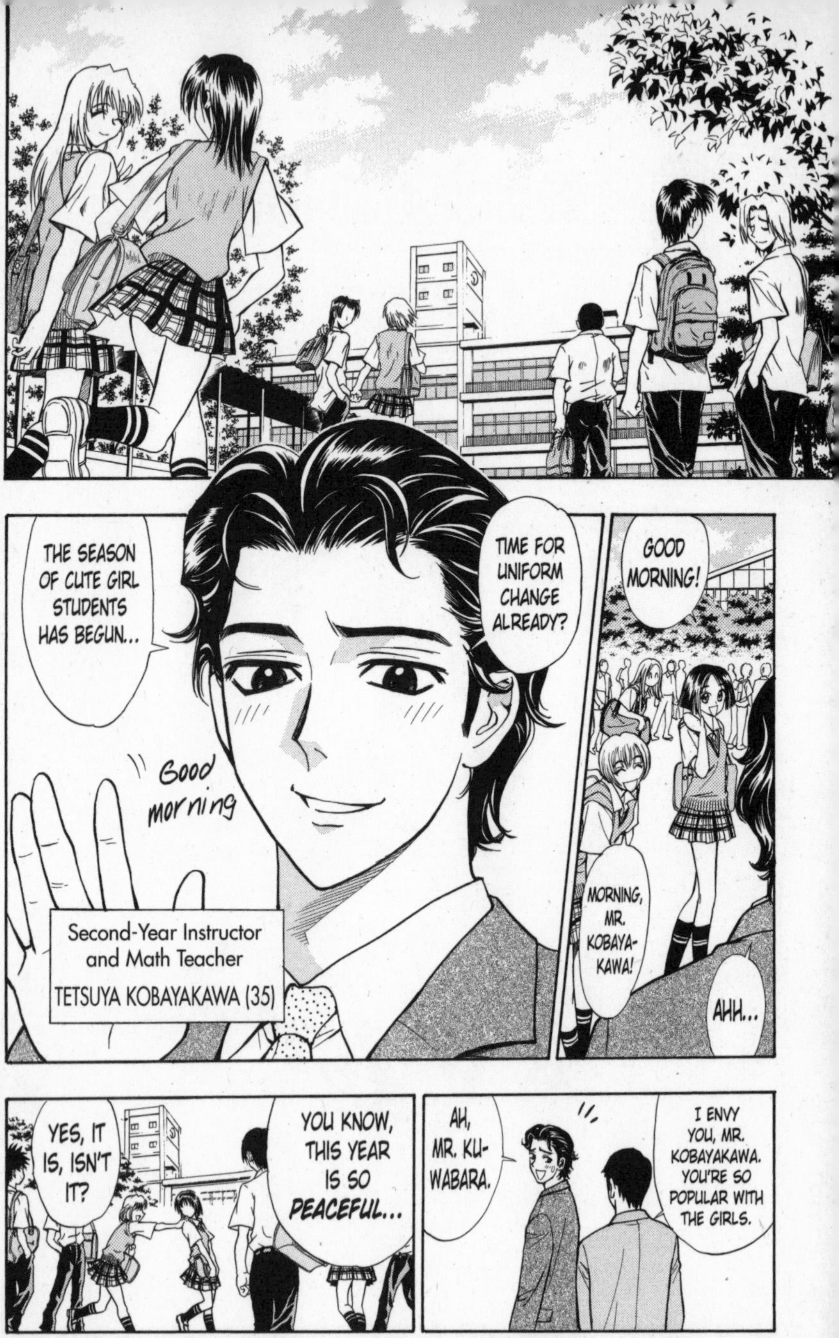
GOOD MORNING!
MORNING, MR. KOBAYA-KAWA!
AHH...
TIME FOR UNIFORM CHANGE ALREADY?
THE SEASON OF CUTE GIRL STUDENTS HAS BEGUN...
Good morning
Second-Year Instructor and Math Teacher
TETSUYA KOBAYAKAWA (35)
I ENVY YOU, MR. KOBAYAKAWA. YOU'RE SO POPULAR WITH THE GIRLS.
AH, MR. KU-WABARA.
YOU KNOW, THIS YEAR IS SO PEACEFUL...
YES, IT IS, ISN'T IT?

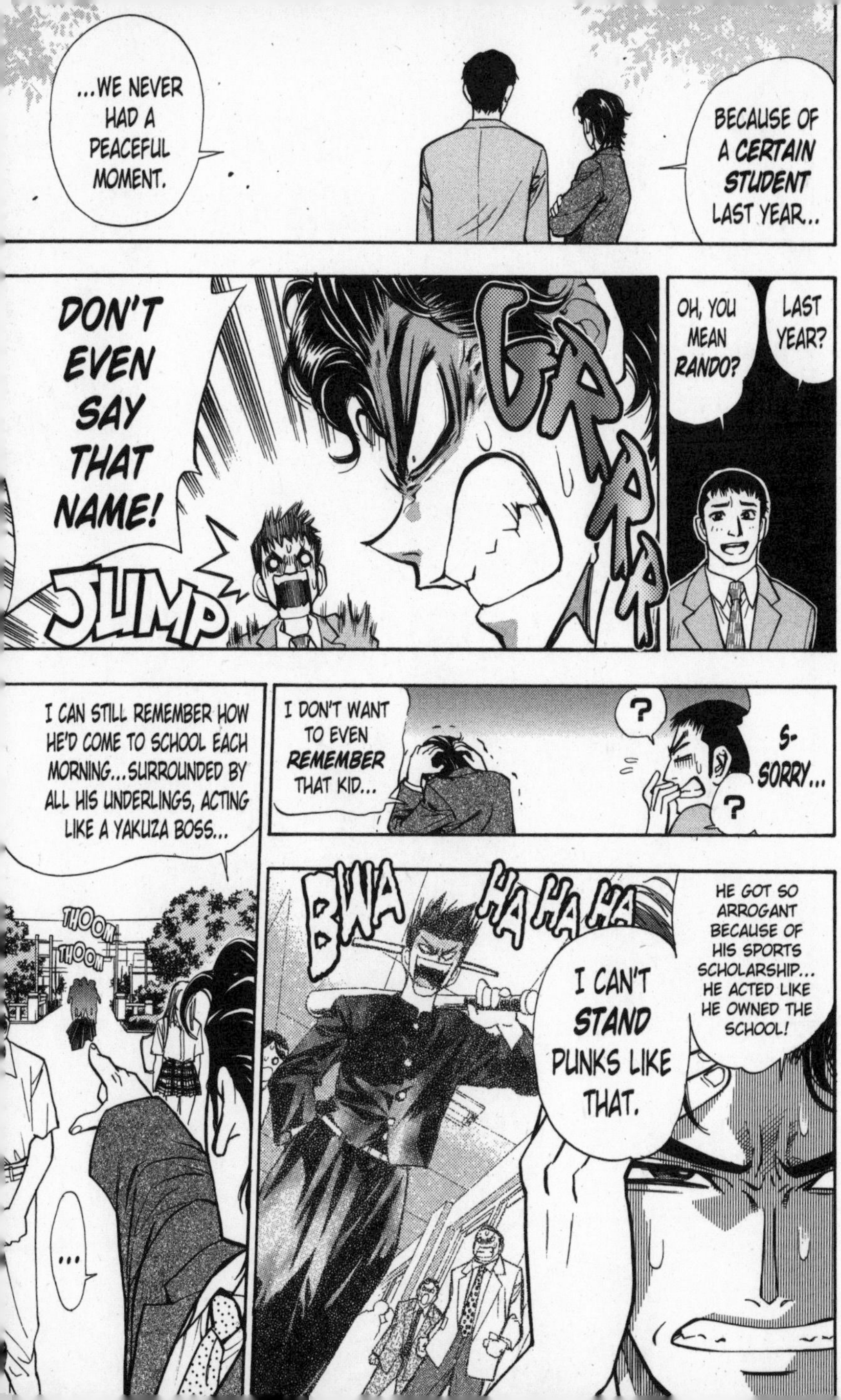
BECAUSE OF A CERTAIN STUDENT LAST YEAR...
...WE NEVER HAD A PEACEFUL MOMENT.
LAST YEAR?
OH, YOU MEAN RANDO?
GRRRR
DON'T EVEN SAY THAT NAME!
JUMP
S-SORRY...
?
?
I DON'T WANT TO EVEN REMEMBER THAT KID...
HE GOT SO ARROGANT BECAUSE OF HIS SPORTS SCHOLARSHIP... HE ACTED LIKE HE OWNED THE SCHOOL!
I CAN'T STAND PUNKS LIKE THAT.
BWA HA HA HA
I CAN STILL REMEMBER HOW HE'D COME TO SCHOOL EACH MORNING...SURROUNDED BY ALL HIS UNDERLINGS, ACTING LIKE A YAKUZA BOSS...
THOOM
THOOM
...

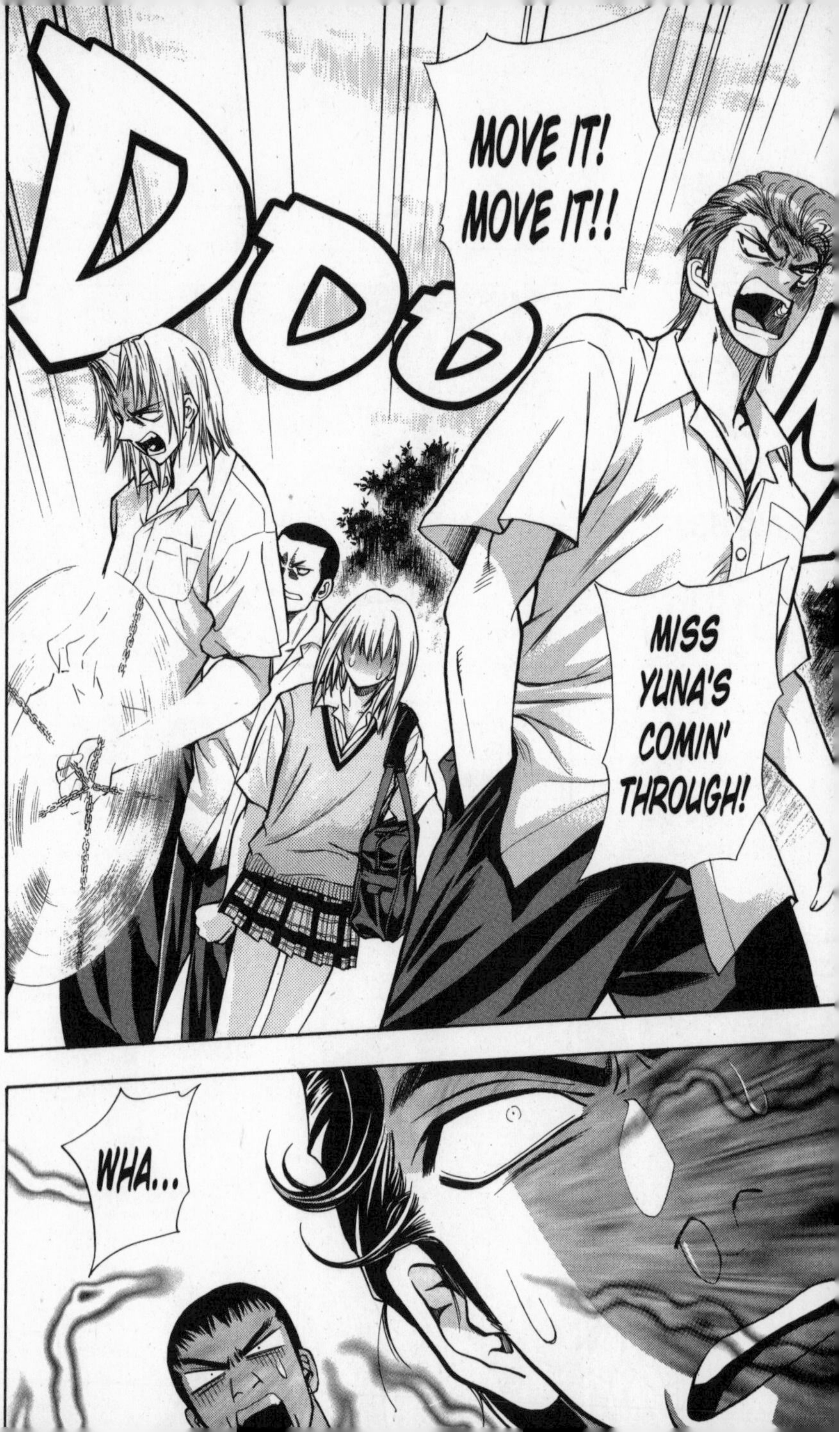
MOVE IT! MOVE IT!!
MISS YUNA'S COMIN' THROUGH!
WHA...

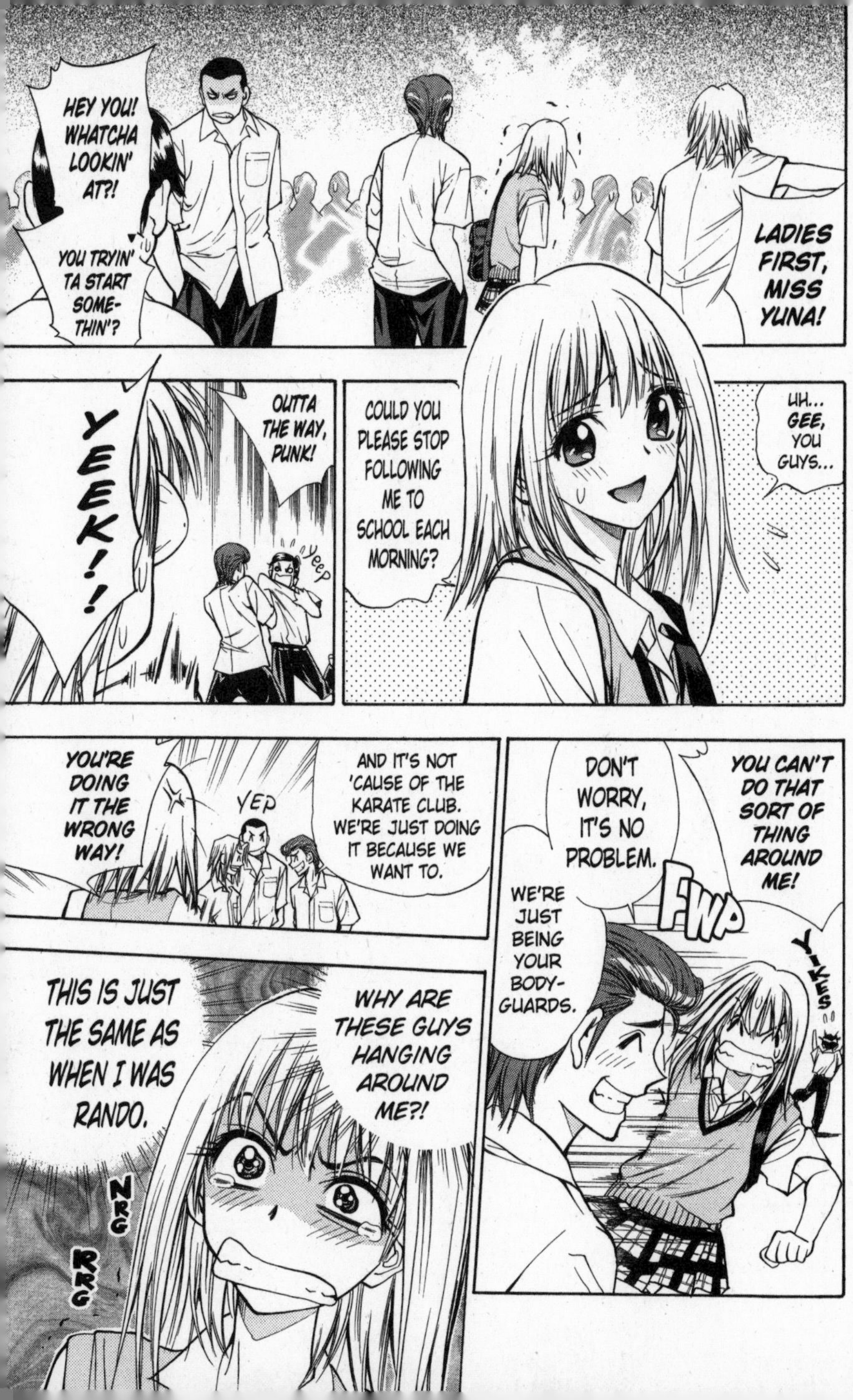
LADIES FIRST, MISS YUNA!
HEY YOU! WHATCHA LOOKIN' AT?!
YOU TRYIN' TA START SOME-THIN'?
UH... GEE, YOU GUYS...
COULD YOU PLEASE STOP FOLLOWING ME TO SCHOOL EACH MORNING?
OUTTA THE WAY, PUNK!
YEEP
YEEK!!
YOU CAN'T DO THAT SORT OF THING AROUND ME!
DON'T WORRY, IT'S NO PROBLEM.
FWP
WE'RE JUST BEING YOUR BODY-GUARDS.
YIKES
AND IT'S NOT 'CAUSE OF THE KARATE CLUB. WE'RE JUST DOING IT BECAUSE WE WANT TO.
YEP
YOU'RE DOING IT THE WRONG WAY!
WHY ARE THESE GUYS HANGING AROUND ME?!
THIS IS JUST THE SAME AS WHEN I WAS RANDO.
NRG
RRG

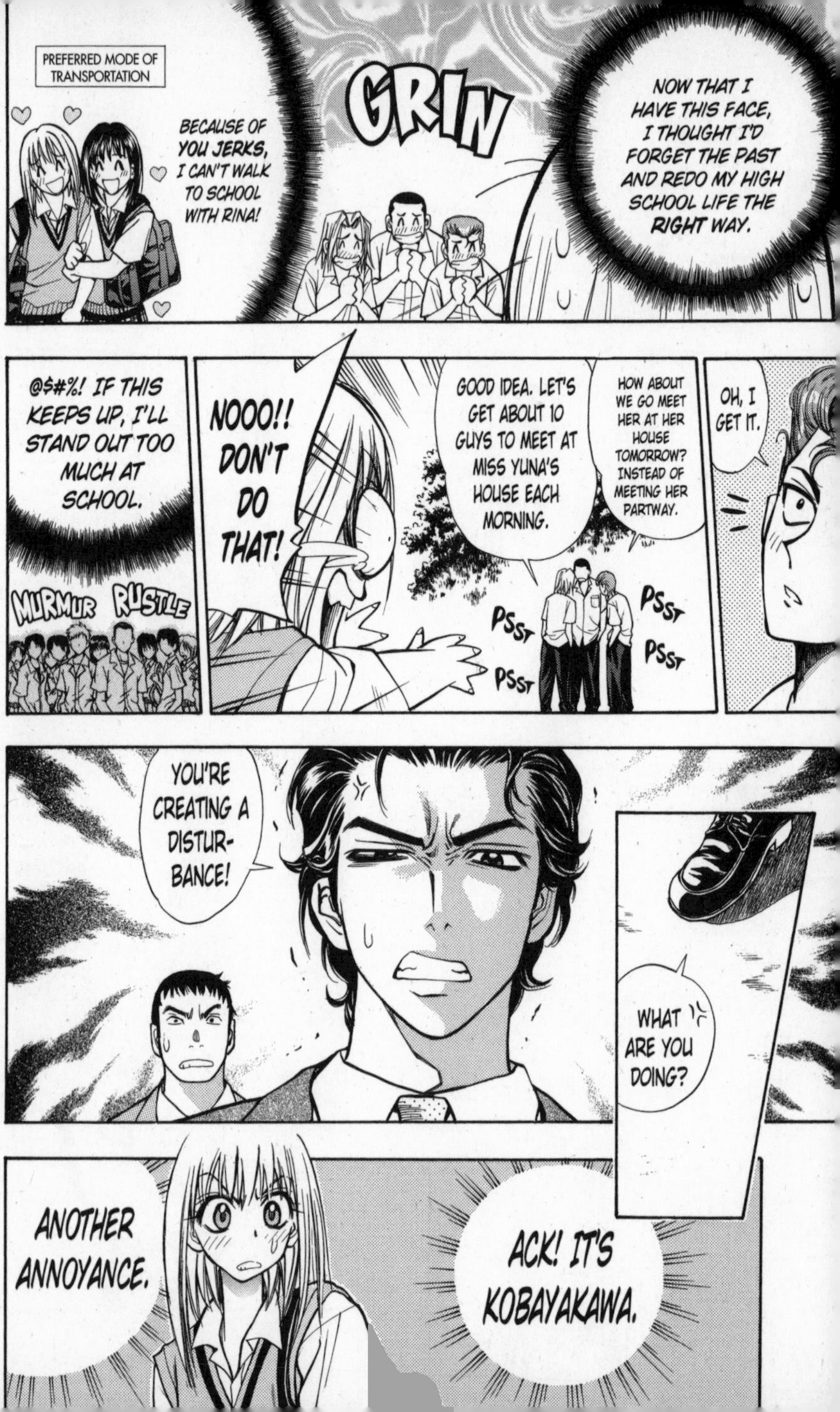

NOW THAT I HAVE THIS FACE, I THOUGHT I'D FORGET THE PAST AND REDO MY HIGH SCHOOL LIFE THE RIGHT WAY.
GRIN
PREFERRED MODE OF TRANSPORTATION
BECAUSE OF YOU JERKS, I CAN'T WALK TO SCHOOL WITH RINA!
OH, I GET IT.
HOW ABOUT WE GO MEET HER AT HER HOUSE TOMORROW? INSTEAD OF MEETING HER PARTWAY.
GOOD IDEA. LET'S GET ABOUT 10 GUYS TO MEET AT MISS YUNA'S HOUSE EACH MORNING.
PSST
PSST
PSST
PSST
NOOO!! DON'T DO THAT!
@$#%! IF THIS KEEPS UP, I'LL STAND OUT TOO MUCH AT SCHOOL.
MURMUR
RUSTLE
WHAT ARE YOU DOING?
YOU'RE CREATING A DISTUR-BANCE!
ACK! IT'S KOBAYAKAWA.
ANOTHER ANNOYANCE.

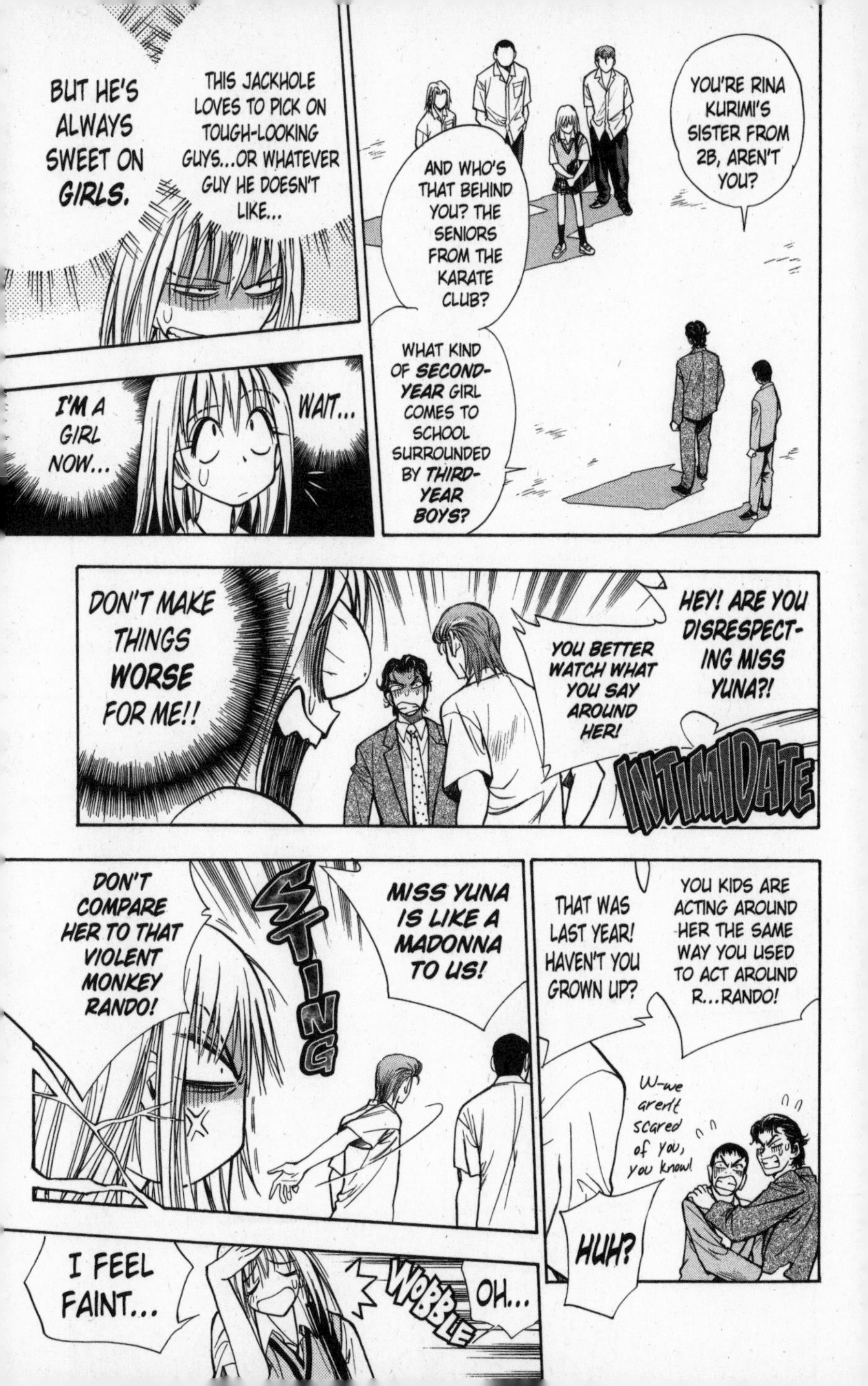
YOU'RE RINA KURIMI'S SISTER FROM 2B, AREN'T YOU?
AND WHO'S THAT BEHIND YOU? THE SENIORS FROM THE KARATE CLUB?
WHAT KIND OF SECOND-YEAR GIRL COMES TO SCHOOL SURROUNDED BY THIRD-YEAR BOYS?
THIS JACKHOLE LOVES TO PICK ON TOUGH-LOOKING GUYS...OR WHATEVER GUY HE DOESN'T LIKE...
BUT HE'S ALWAYS SWEET ON GIRLS.
WAIT...
I'M A GIRL NOW...
HEY! ARE YOU DISRESPECTING MISS YUNA?!
YOU BETTER WATCH WHAT YOU SAY AROUND HER!
INTIMIDATE
DON'T MAKE THINGS WORSE FOR ME!!
YOU KIDS ARE ACTING AROUND HER THE SAME WAY YOU USED TO ACT AROUND R...RANDO!
THAT WAS LAST YEAR! HAVEN'T YOU GROWN UP?
W-we aren't scared of you, you know!
HUH?
MISS YUNA IS LIKE A MADONNA TO US!
STING
DON'T COMPARE HER TO THAT VIOLENT MONKEY RANDO!
OH...
WOBBLE
I FEEL FAINT...

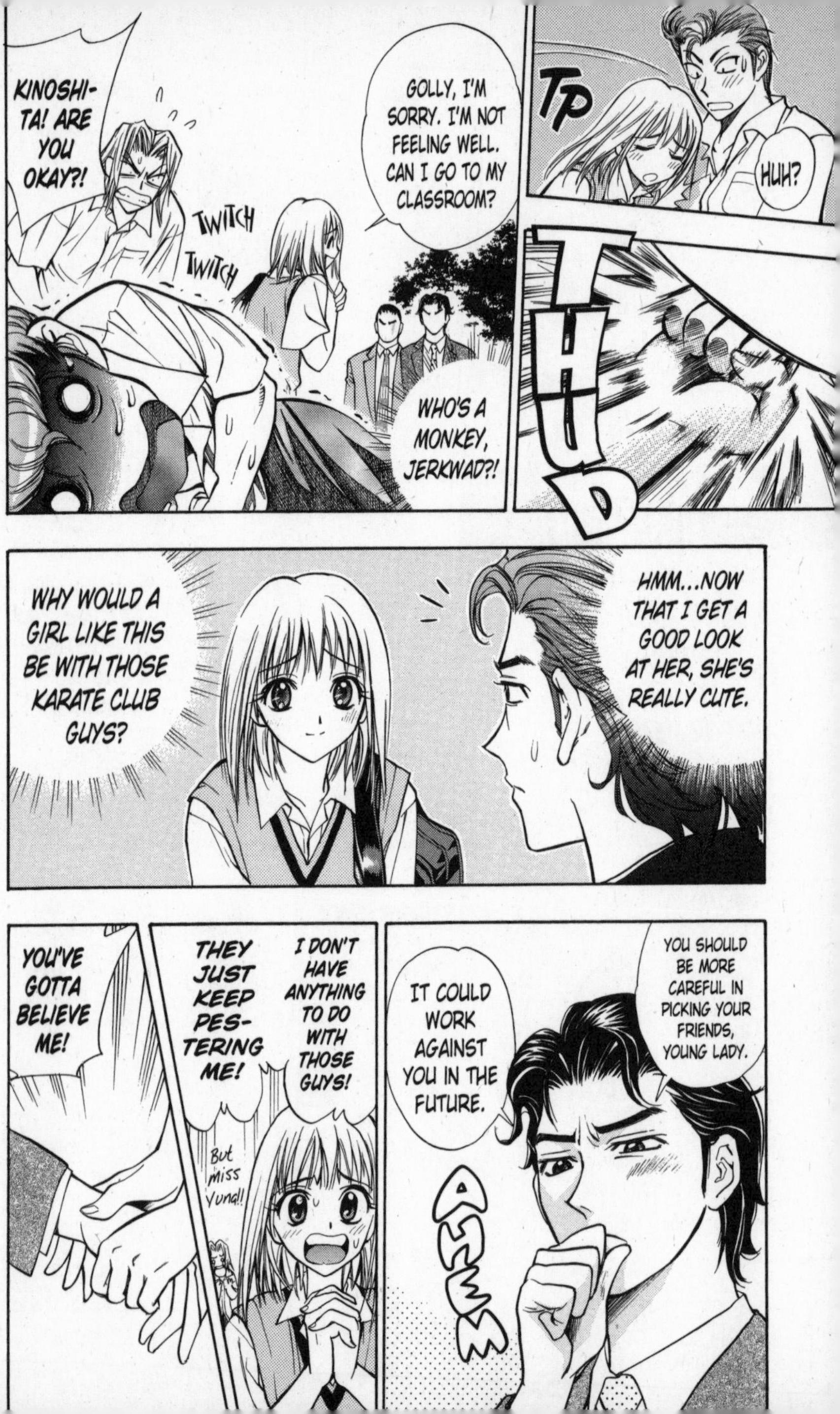
TP
HUH?
THUD
GOLLY, I'M SORRY. I'M NOT FEELING WELL. CAN I GO TO MY CLASSROOM?
KINOSHI-TA! ARE YOU OKAY?!
TWITCH
TWITCH
WHO'S A MONKEY, JERKWAD?!
HMM...NOW THAT I GET A GOOD LOOK AT HER, SHE'S REALLY CUTE.
WHY WOULD A GIRL LIKE THIS BE WITH THOSE KARATE CLUB GUYS?
YOU SHOULD BE MORE CAREFUL IN PICKING YOUR FRIENDS, YOUNG LADY.
IT COULD WORK AGAINST YOU IN THE FUTURE.
AHEM
I DON'T HAVE ANYTHING TO DO WITH THOSE GUYS!
THEY JUST KEEP PES-TERING ME!
But miss Yung!!
YOU'VE GOTTA BELIEVE ME!

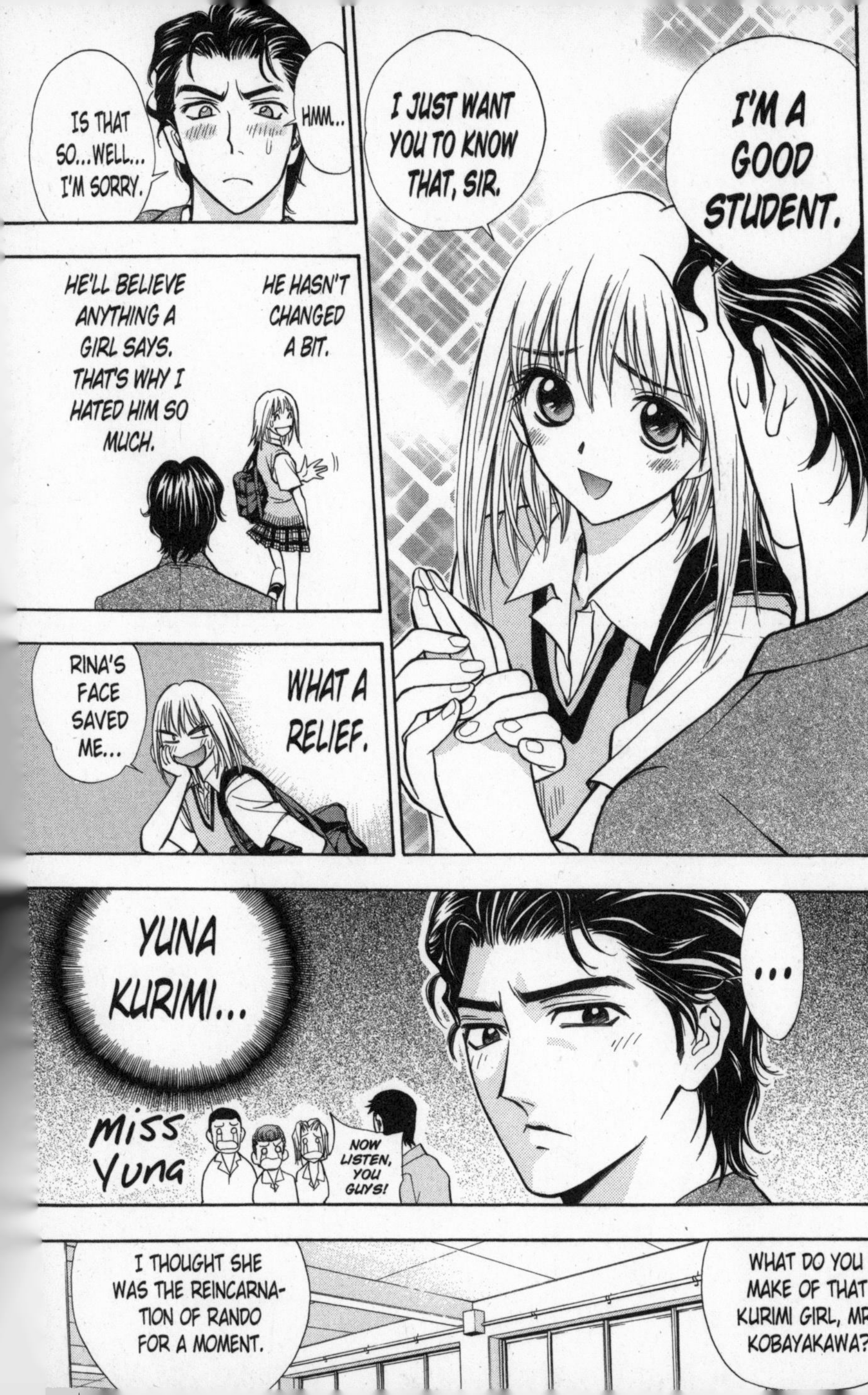
I'M A GOOD STUDENT.
I JUST WANT YOU TO KNOW THAT, SIR.
HMM...
IS THAT SO...WELL... I'M SORRY.
HE HASN'T CHANGED A BIT.
HE'LL BELIEVE ANYTHING A GIRL SAYS. THAT'S WHY I HATED HIM SO MUCH.
WHAT A RELIEF.
RINA'S FACE SAVED ME...
...
YUNA KURIMI...
NOW LISTEN, YOU GUYS!
miss Yuna
WHAT DO YOU MAKE OF THAT KURIMI GIRL, MR. KOBAYAKAWA?
I THOUGHT SHE WAS THE REINCARNATION OF RANDO FOR A MOMENT.

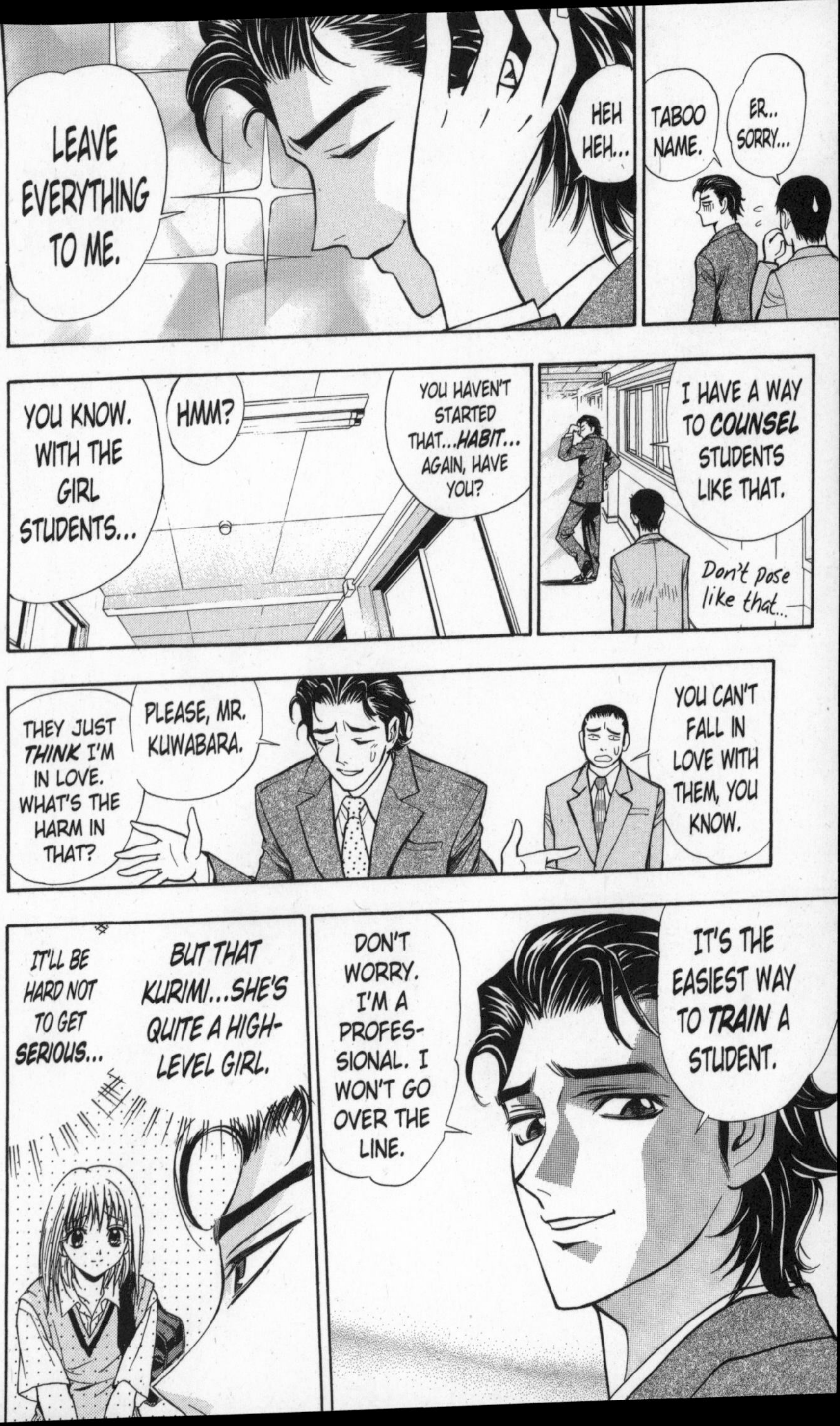
ER.. SORRY...
TABOO NAME.
HEH HEH...
LEAVE EVERYTHING TO ME.
I HAVE A WAY TO *COUNSEL* STUDENTS LIKE THAT.
Don't pose like that...
YOU HAVEN'T STARTED THAT...*HABIT*... AGAIN, HAVE YOU?
HMM?
YOU KNOW. WITH THE GIRL STUDENTS...
YOU CAN'T FALL IN LOVE WITH THEM, YOU KNOW.
PLEASE, MR. KUWABARA.
THEY JUST *THINK* I'M IN LOVE. WHAT'S THE HARM IN THAT?
IT'S THE EASIEST WAY TO *TRAIN* A STUDENT.
DON'T WORRY. I'M A PROFESSIONAL. I WON'T GO OVER THE LINE.
BUT THAT KURIMI...SHE'S QUITE A HIGH-LEVEL GIRL.
IT'LL BE HARD NOT TO GET SERIOUS...

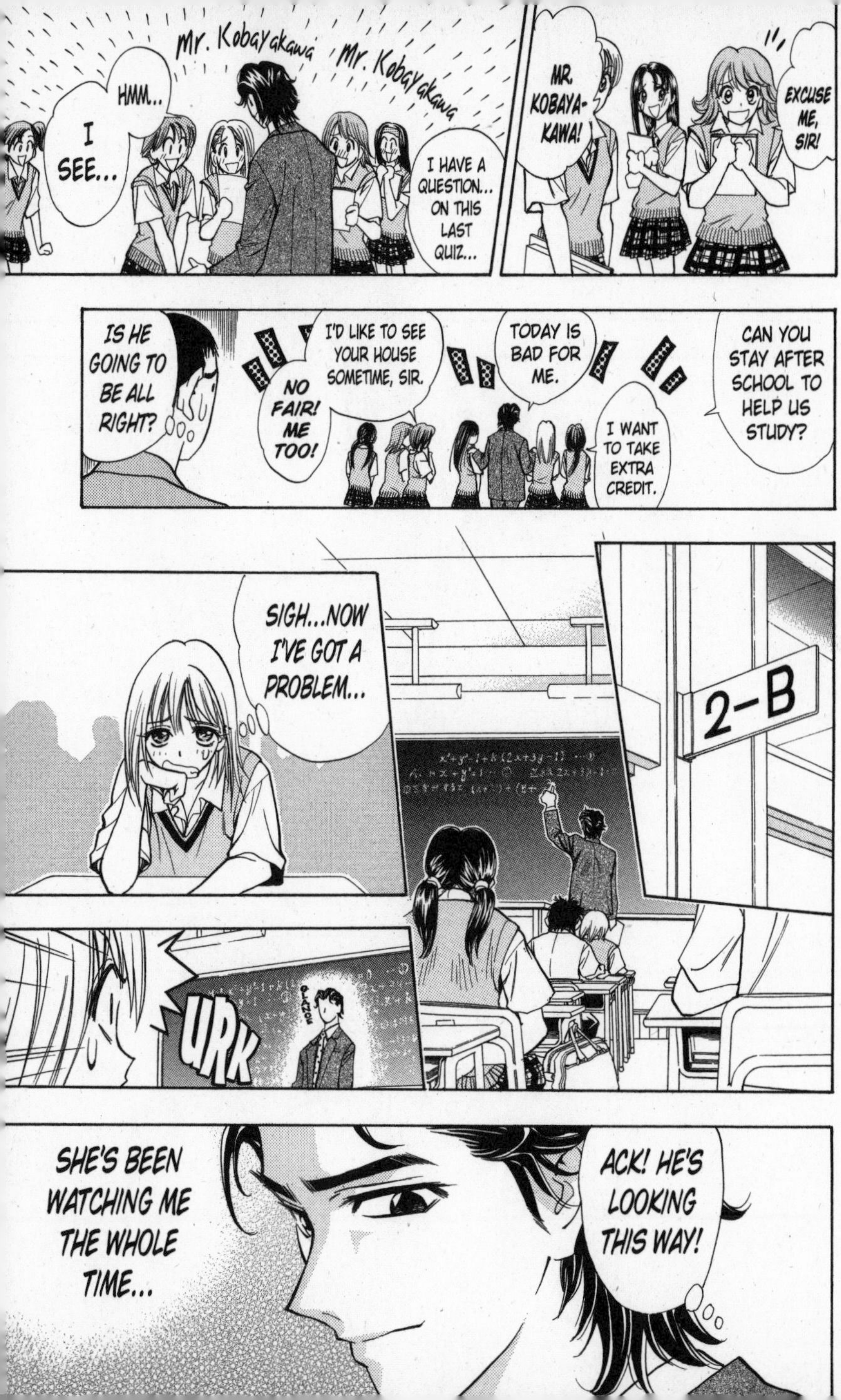
EXCUSE ME, SIR!
MR. KOBAYA-KAWA!
Mr. Kobayakawa
Mr. Kobayakawa
I HAVE A QUESTION... ON THIS LAST QUIZ...
HMM... I SEE...
CAN YOU STAY AFTER SCHOOL TO HELP US STUDY?
TODAY IS BAD FOR ME.
I WANT TO TAKE EXTRA CREDIT.
I'D LIKE TO SEE YOUR HOUSE SOMETIME, SIR.
NO FAIR! ME TOO!
IS HE GOING TO BE ALL RIGHT?
2-B
SIGH...NOW I'VE GOT A PROBLEM...
GLANCE
URK
ACK! HE'S LOOKING THIS WAY!
SHE'S BEEN WATCHING ME THE WHOLE TIME...

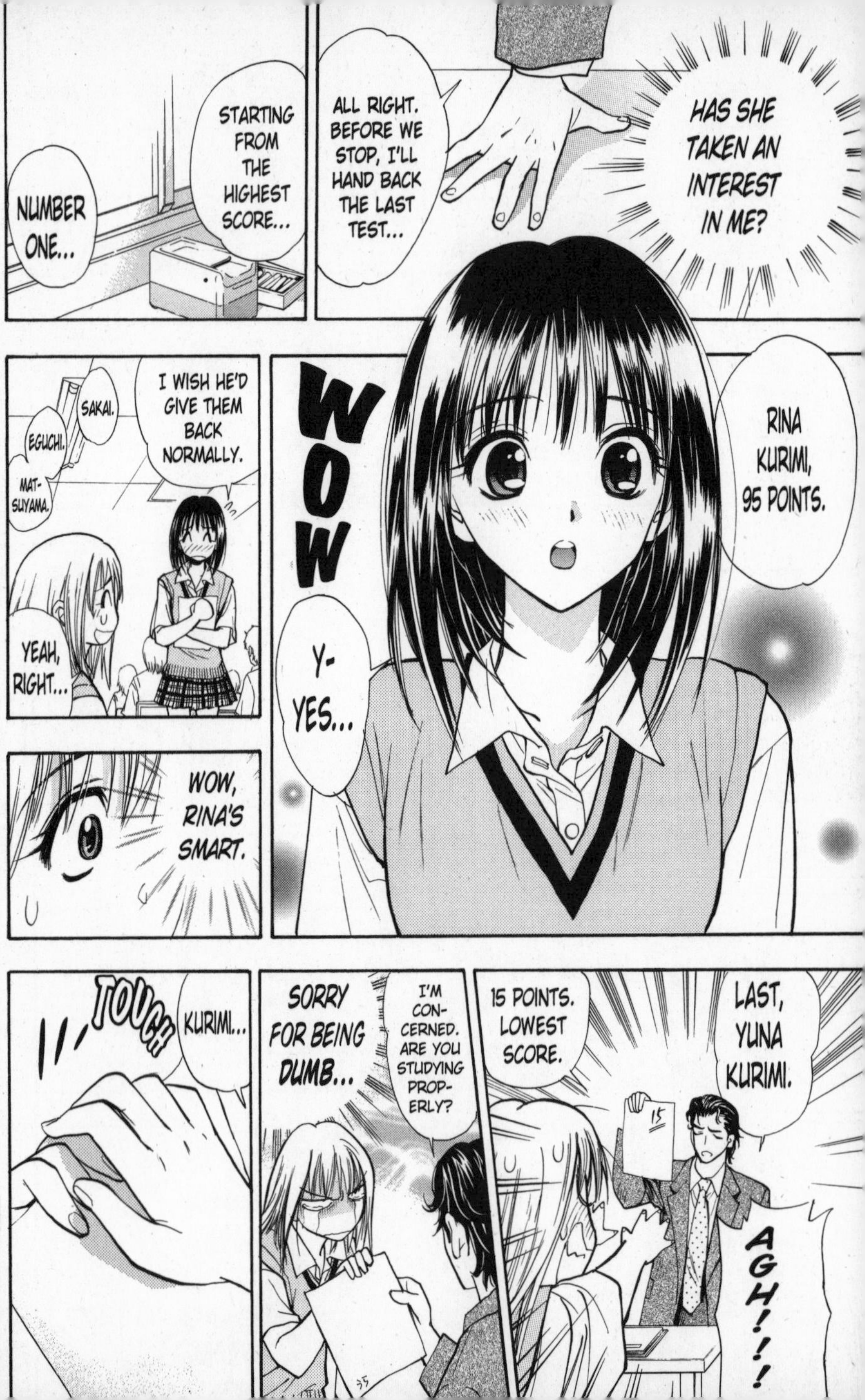
HAS SHE TAKEN AN INTEREST IN ME?
ALL RIGHT. BEFORE WE STOP, I'LL HAND BACK THE LAST TEST...
STARTING FROM THE HIGHEST SCORE...
NUMBER ONE...
RINA KURIMI, 95 POINTS.
WOW
Y-YES...
I WISH HE'D GIVE THEM BACK NORMALLY.
SAKAI.
EGUCHI.
MAT-SUYAMA.
YEAH, RIGHT...
WOW, RINA'S SMART.
LAST, YUNA KURIMI.
15 POINTS. LOWEST SCORE.
AGH!!!
I'M CON-CERNED. ARE YOU STUDYING PROP-ERLY?
SORRY FOR BEING DUMB...
KURIMI...
TOUCH

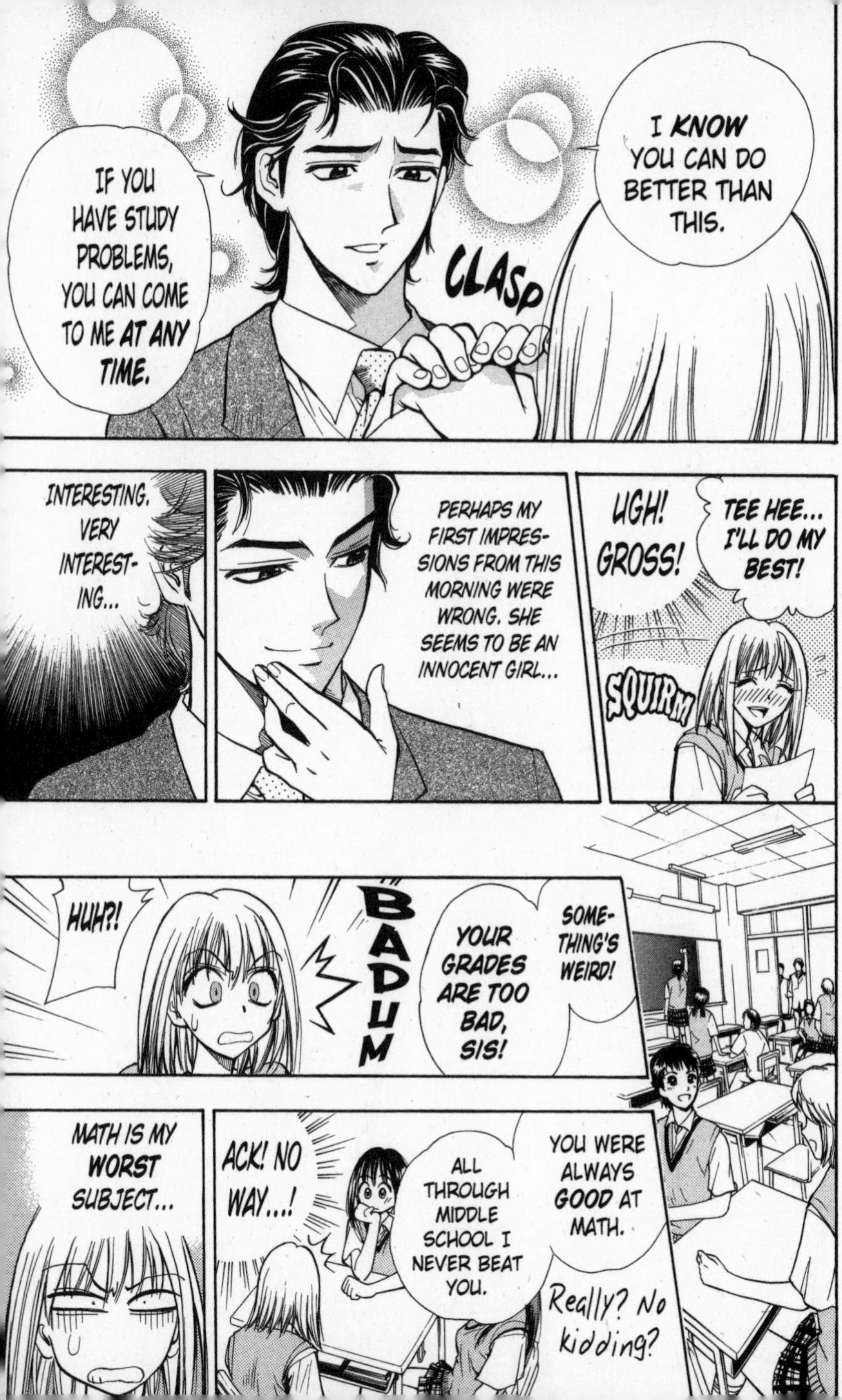
I KNOW YOU CAN DO BETTER THAN THIS.
CLASP
IF YOU HAVE STUDY PROBLEMS, YOU CAN COME TO ME AT ANY TIME.
TEE HEE... I'LL DO MY BEST!
UGH! GROSS!
SQUIRM
PERHAPS MY FIRST IMPRESSIONS FROM THIS MORNING WERE WRONG. SHE SEEMS TO BE AN INNOCENT GIRL...
INTERESTING. VERY INTERESTING...
SOME-THING'S WEIRD!
YOUR GRADES ARE TOO BAD, SIS!
BADUM
HUH?!
YOU WERE ALWAYS GOOD AT MATH.
Really? No kidding?
ALL THROUGH MIDDLE SCHOOL I NEVER BEAT YOU.
ACK! NO WAY...!
MATH IS MY WORST SUBJECT...

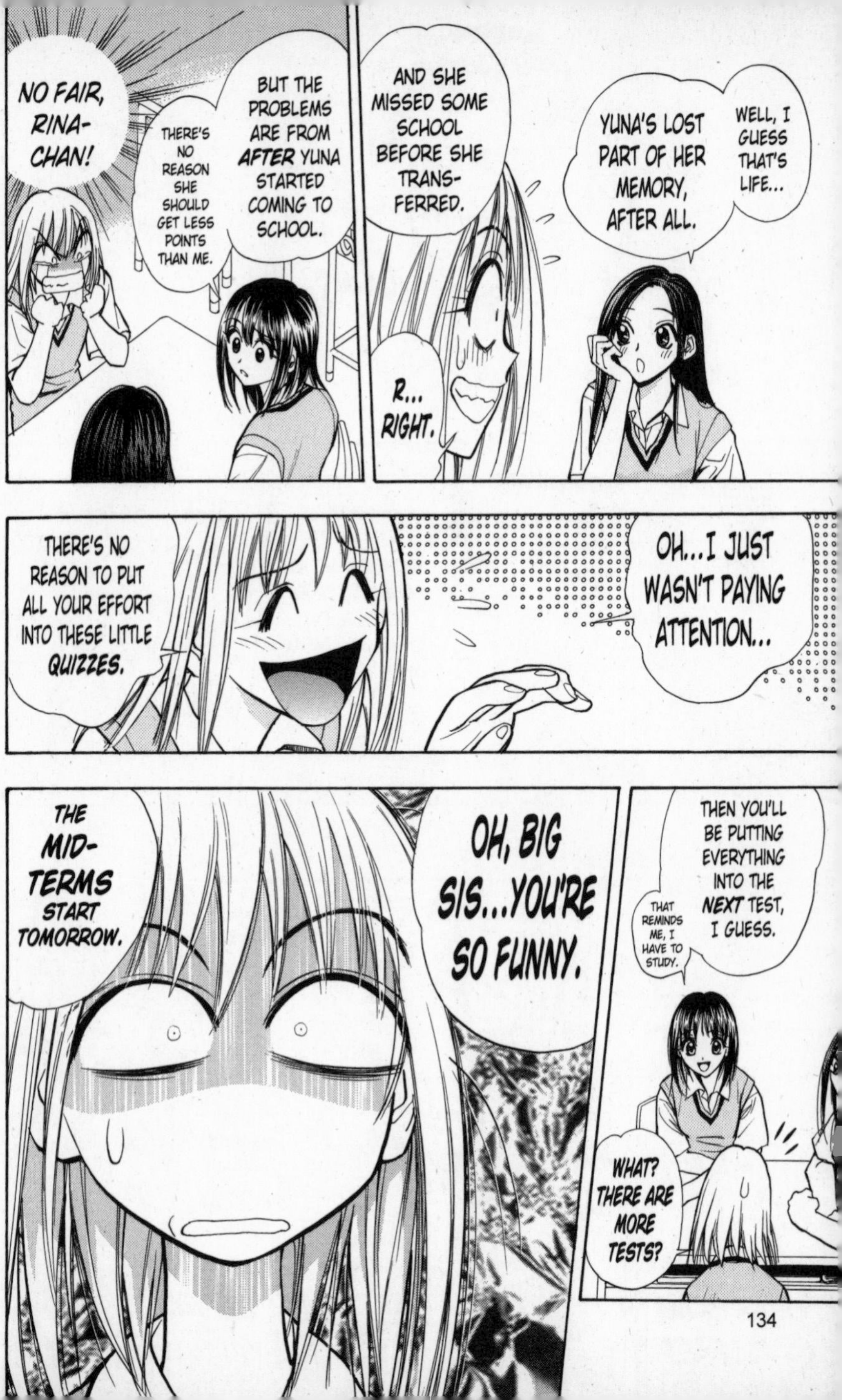

WELL, I GUESS THAT'S LIFE...
YUNA'S LOST PART OF HER MEMORY, AFTER ALL.
AND SHE MISSED SOME SCHOOL BEFORE SHE TRANS-FERRED.
R... RIGHT.
BUT THE PROBLEMS ARE FROM AFTER YUNA STARTED COMING TO SCHOOL.
THERE'S NO REASON SHE SHOULD GET LESS POINTS THAN ME.
NO FAIR, RINA-CHAN!
OH...I JUST WASN'T PAYING ATTENTION...
THERE'S NO REASON TO PUT ALL YOUR EFFORT INTO THESE LITTLE QUIZZES.
THEN YOU'LL BE PUTTING EVERYTHING INTO THE NEXT TEST, I GUESS.
THAT REMINDS ME, I HAVE TO STUDY.
WHAT? THERE ARE MORE TESTS?
OH, BIG SIS...YOU'RE SO FUNNY.
THE MID-TERMS START TOMORROW.

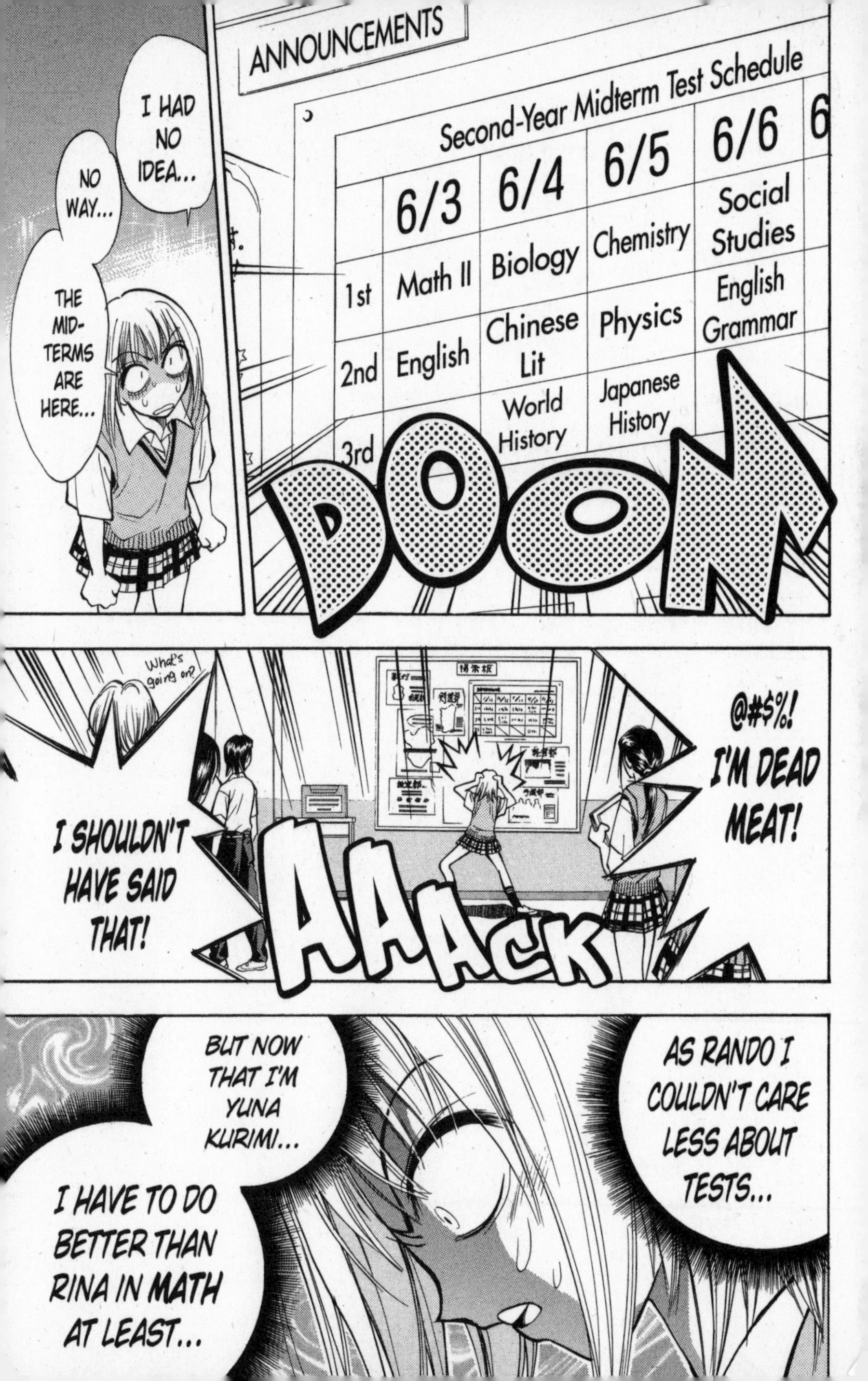
ANNOUNCEMENTS
Second-Year Midterm Test Schedule
6/3
6/4
6/5
6/6
1st
Math II
Biology
Chemistry
Social Studies
2nd
English
Chinese Lit
Physics
English Grammar
3rd
World History
Japanese History
DOOM
I HAD NO IDEA...
NO WAY...
THE MID-TERMS ARE HERE...
@#$%! I'M DEAD MEAT!
What's going on?
I SHOULDN'T HAVE SAID THAT!
AAACK
AS RANDO I COULDN'T CARE LESS ABOUT TESTS...
BUT NOW THAT I'M YUNA KURIMI...
I HAVE TO DO BETTER THAN RINA IN MATH AT LEAST...

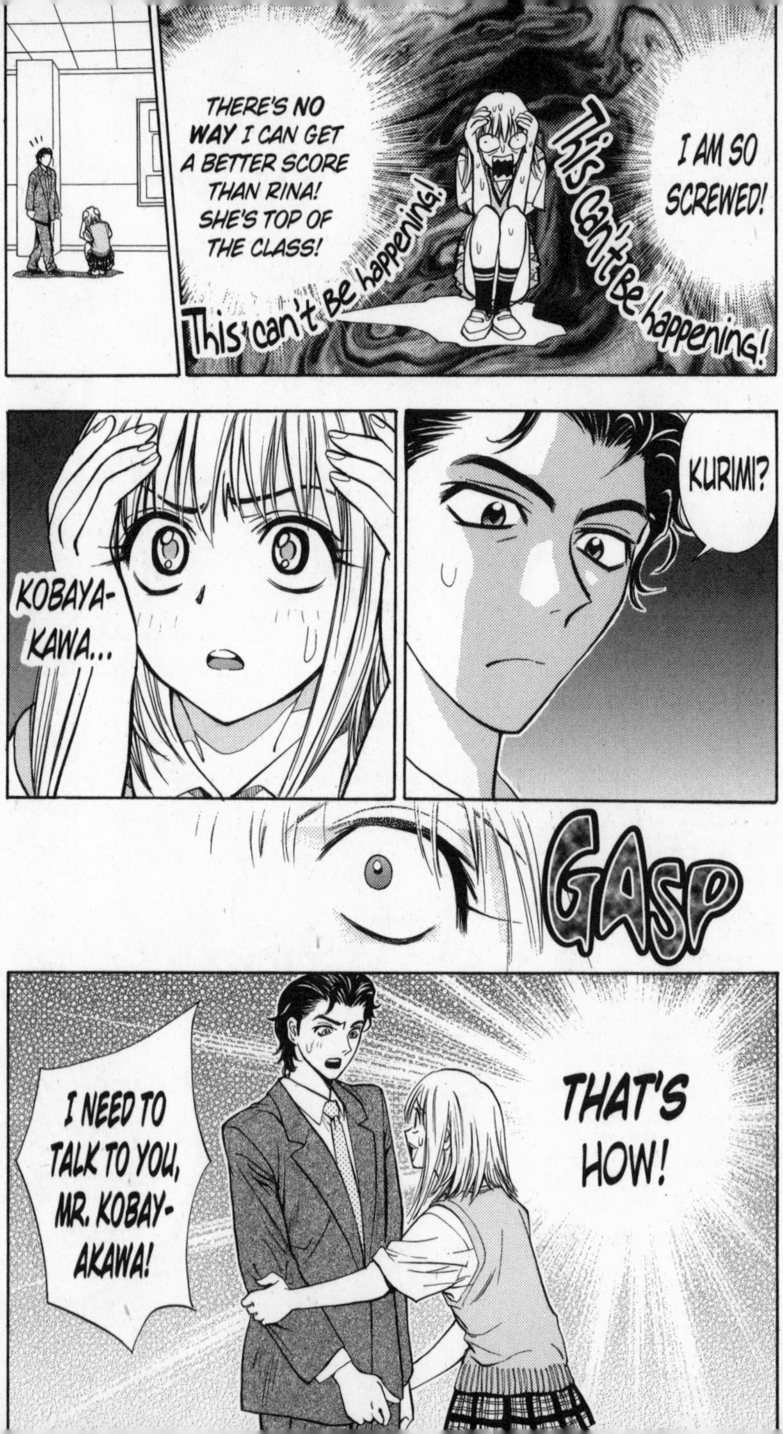
I AM SO SCREWED!
This can't be happening!
THERE'S NO WAY I CAN GET A BETTER SCORE THAN RINA! SHE'S TOP OF THE CLASS!
This can't be happening!
This can't be happening!
KURIMI?
KOBAYA-KAWA...
GASP
THAT'S HOW!
I NEED TO TALK TO YOU, MR. KOBAY-AKAWA!

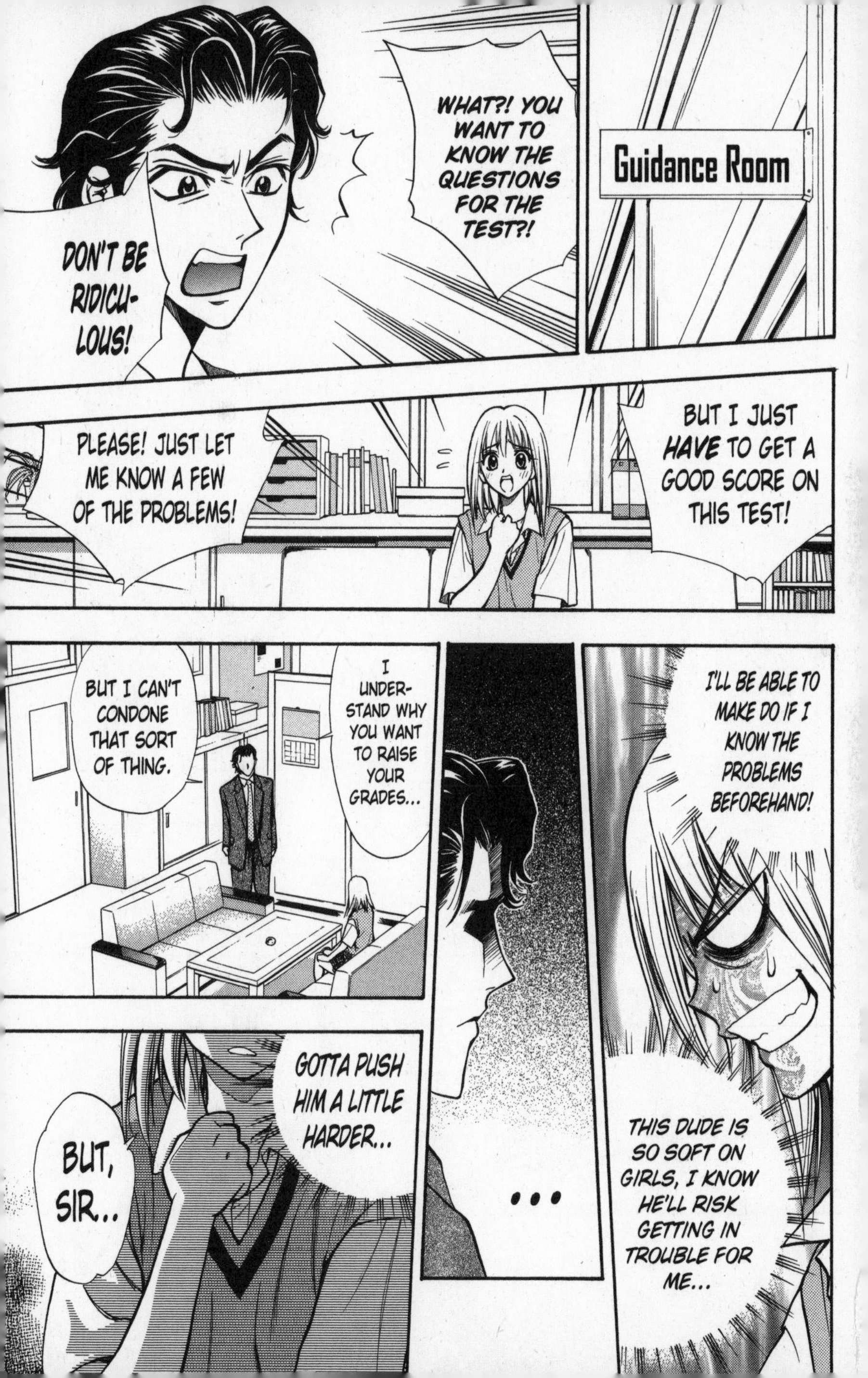
Guidance Room
WHAT?! YOU WANT TO KNOW THE QUESTIONS FOR THE TEST?!
DON'T BE RIDICULOUS!
BUT I JUST HAVE TO GET A GOOD SCORE ON THIS TEST!
PLEASE! JUST LET ME KNOW A FEW OF THE PROBLEMS!
I'LL BE ABLE TO MAKE DO IF I KNOW THE PROBLEMS BEFOREHAND!
THIS DUDE IS SO SOFT ON GIRLS, I KNOW HE'LL RISK GETTING IN TROUBLE FOR ME...
...
I UNDERSTAND WHY YOU WANT TO RAISE YOUR GRADES...
BUT I CAN'T CONDONE THAT SORT OF THING.
GOTTA PUSH HIM A LITTLE HARDER...
BUT, SIR...

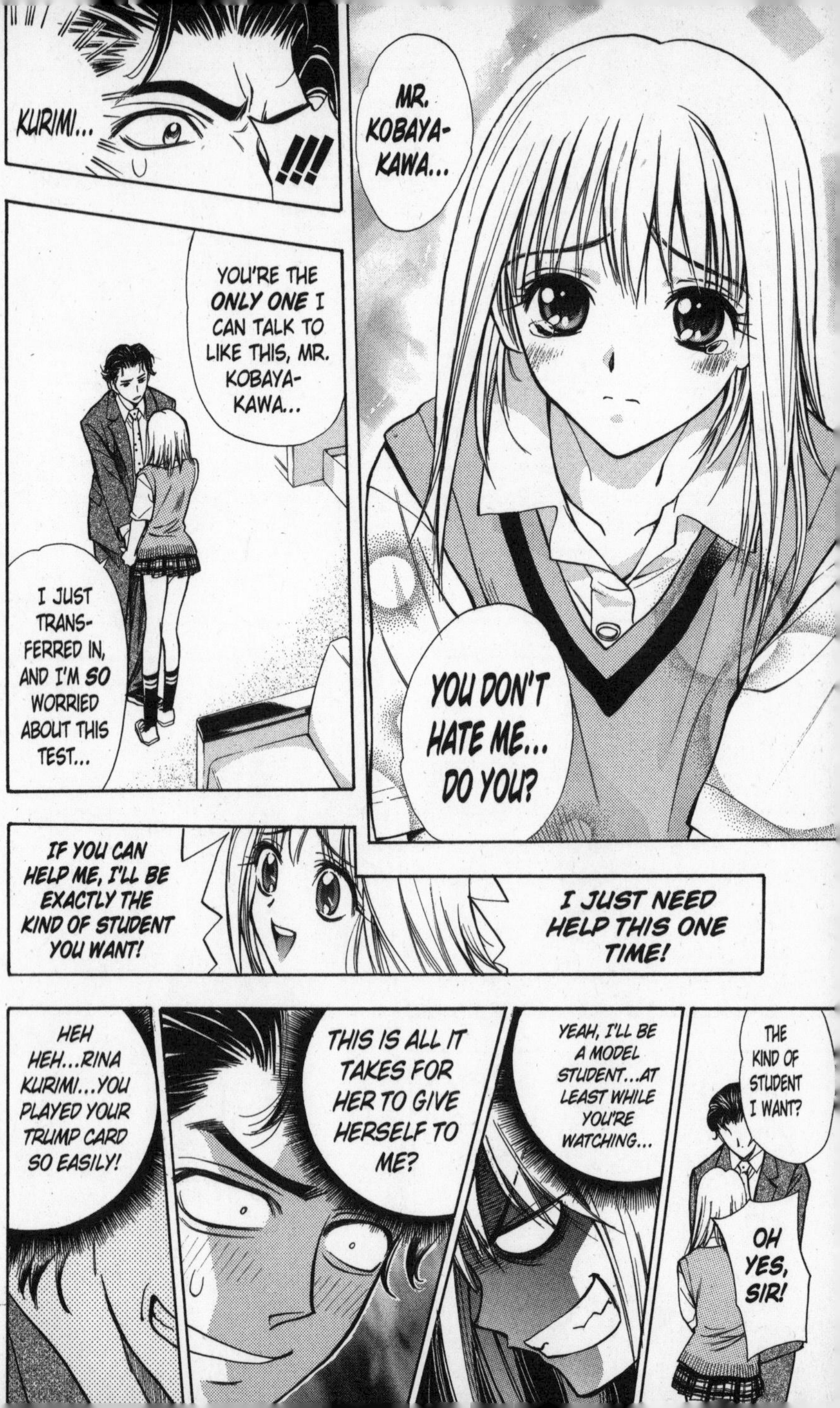
MR. KOBAYA-KAWA...
YOU DON'T HATE ME... DO YOU?
KURIMI...
!!!
YOU'RE THE ONLY ONE I CAN TALK TO LIKE THIS, MR. KOBAYA-KAWA...
I JUST TRANS-FERRED IN, AND I'M SO WORRIED ABOUT THIS TEST...
I JUST NEED HELP THIS ONE TIME!
IF YOU CAN HELP ME, I'LL BE EXACTLY THE KIND OF STUDENT YOU WANT!
THE KIND OF STUDENT I WANT?
OH YES, SIR!
YEAH, I'LL BE A MODEL STUDENT...AT LEAST WHILE YOU'RE WATCHING...
THIS IS ALL IT TAKES FOR HER TO GIVE HERSELF TO ME?
HEH HEH...RINA KURIMI...YOU PLAYED YOUR TRUMP CARD SO EASILY!

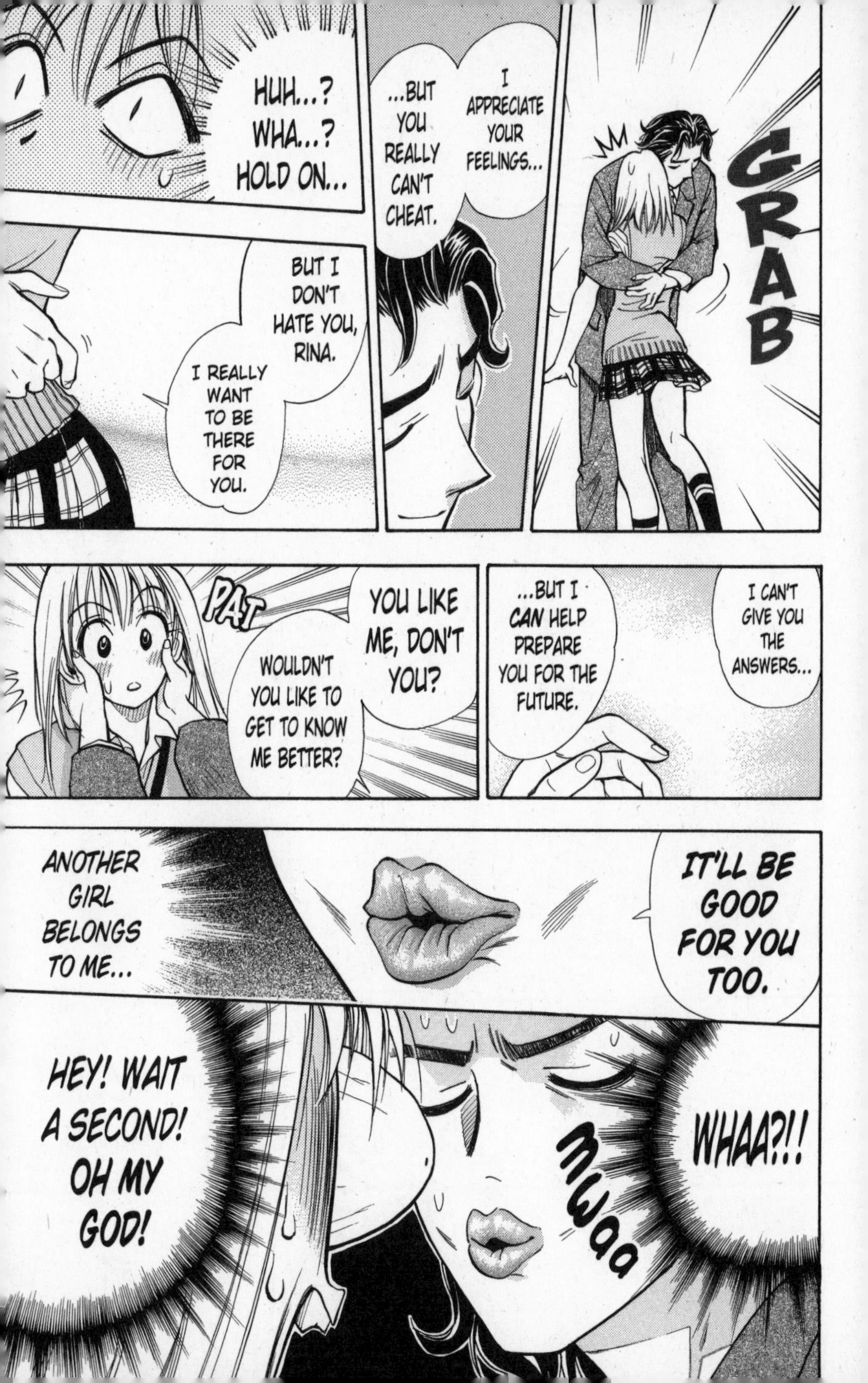
GRAB
I APPRECIATE YOUR FEELINGS...
...BUT YOU REALLY CAN'T CHEAT.
HUH...? WHA...? HOLD ON...
BUT I DON'T HATE YOU, RINA.
I REALLY WANT TO BE THERE FOR YOU.
I CAN'T GIVE YOU THE ANSWERS...
...BUT I CAN HELP PREPARE YOU FOR THE FUTURE.
YOU LIKE ME, DON'T YOU?
WOULDN'T YOU LIKE TO GET TO KNOW ME BETTER?
PAT
IT'LL BE GOOD FOR YOU TOO.
ANOTHER GIRL BELONGS TO ME...
WHAA?!!
MWAA
HEY! WAIT A SECOND! OH MY GOD!

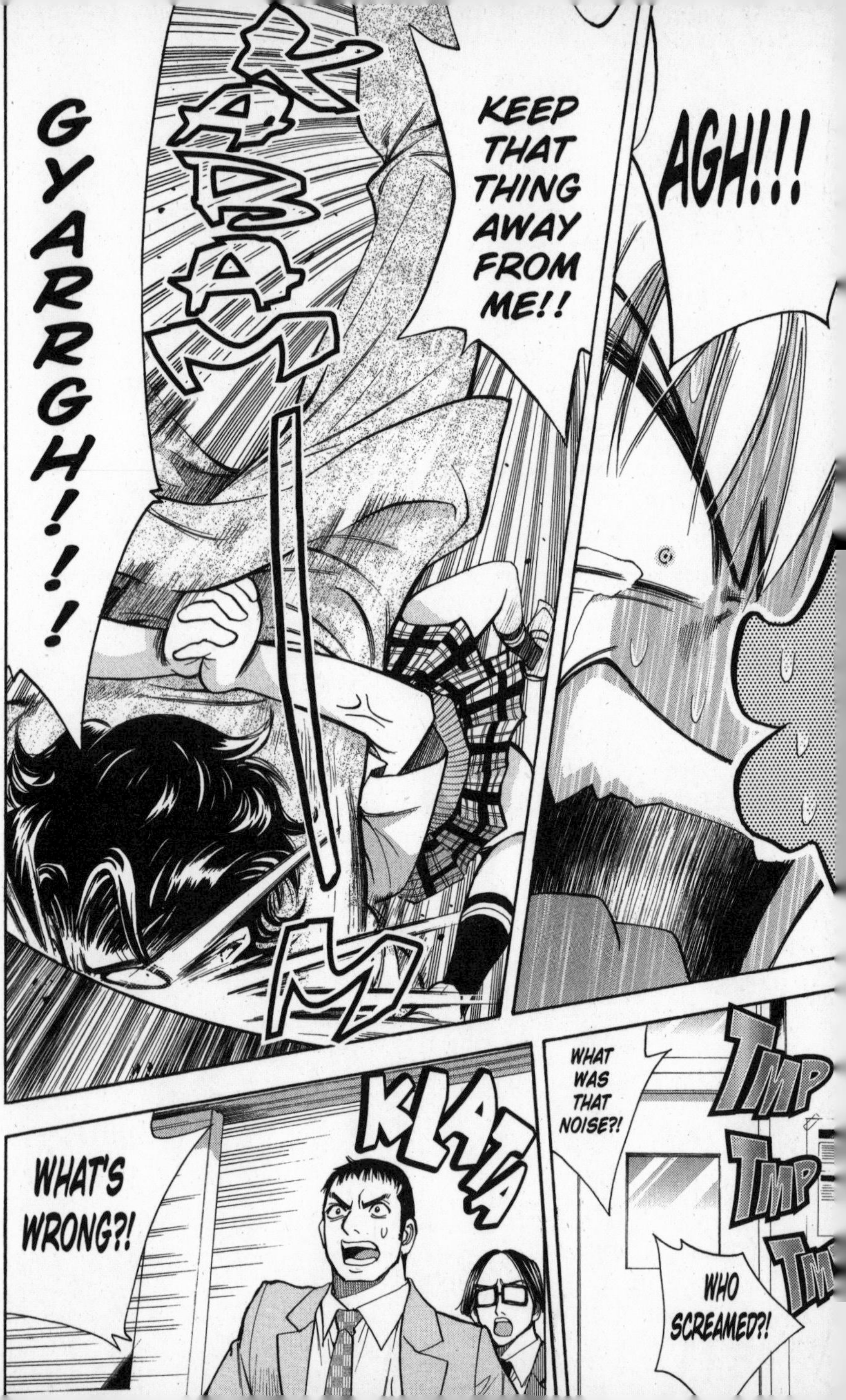
AGH!!!
KEEP THAT THING AWAY FROM ME!!
KABAM
GYARRGH!!!
WHAT WAS THAT NOISE?!
TMP
TMP
WHO SCREAMED?!
KLATA
WHAT'S WRONG?!

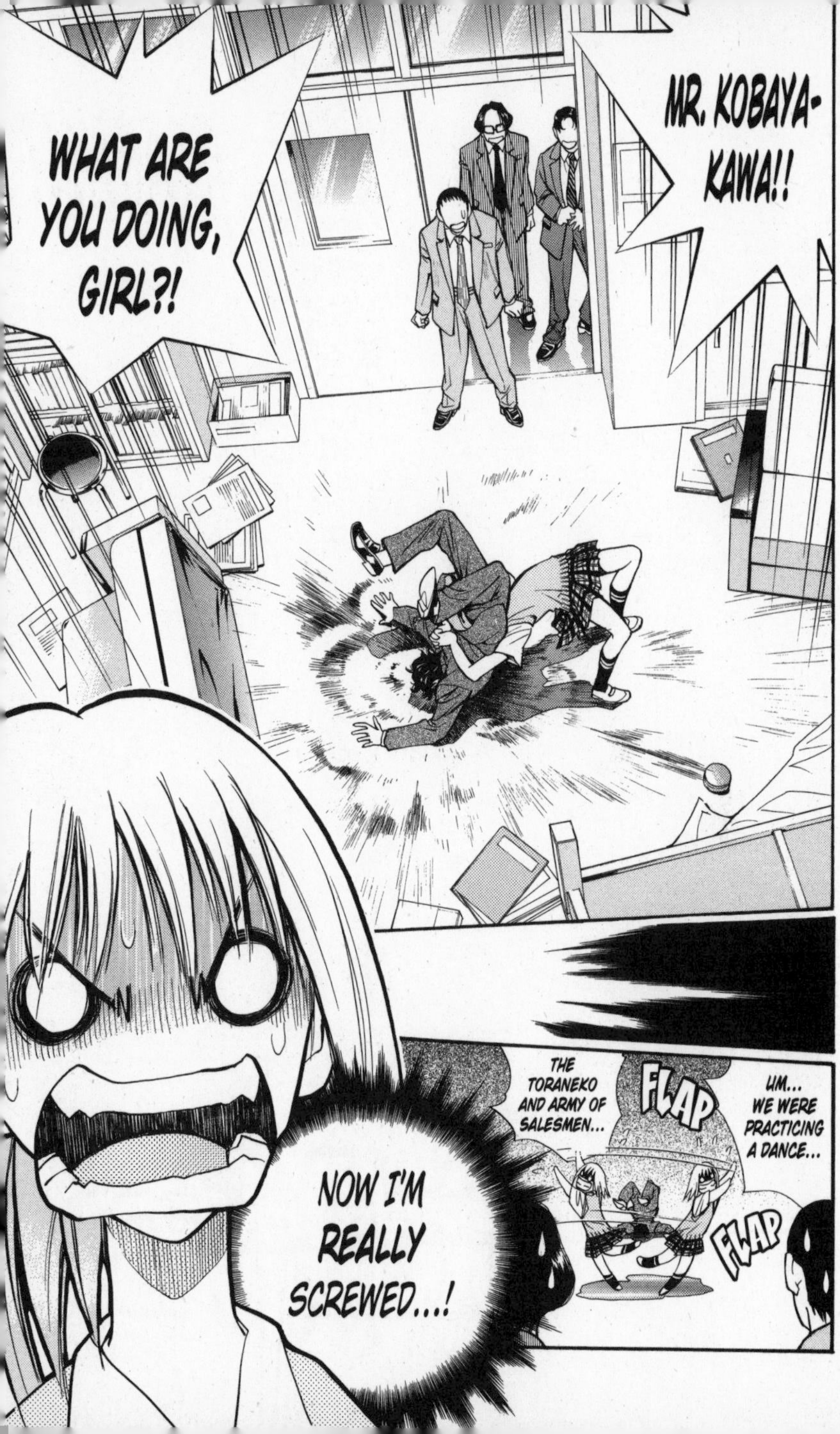
MR. KOBAYA-KAWA!!
WHAT ARE YOU DOING, GIRL?!
UM... WE WERE PRACTICING A DANCE...
FLAP
THE TORANEKO AND ARMY OF SALESMEN...
FLAP
NOW I'M REALLY SCREWED...!

Pretty Face

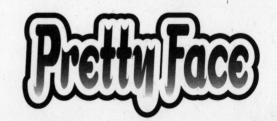

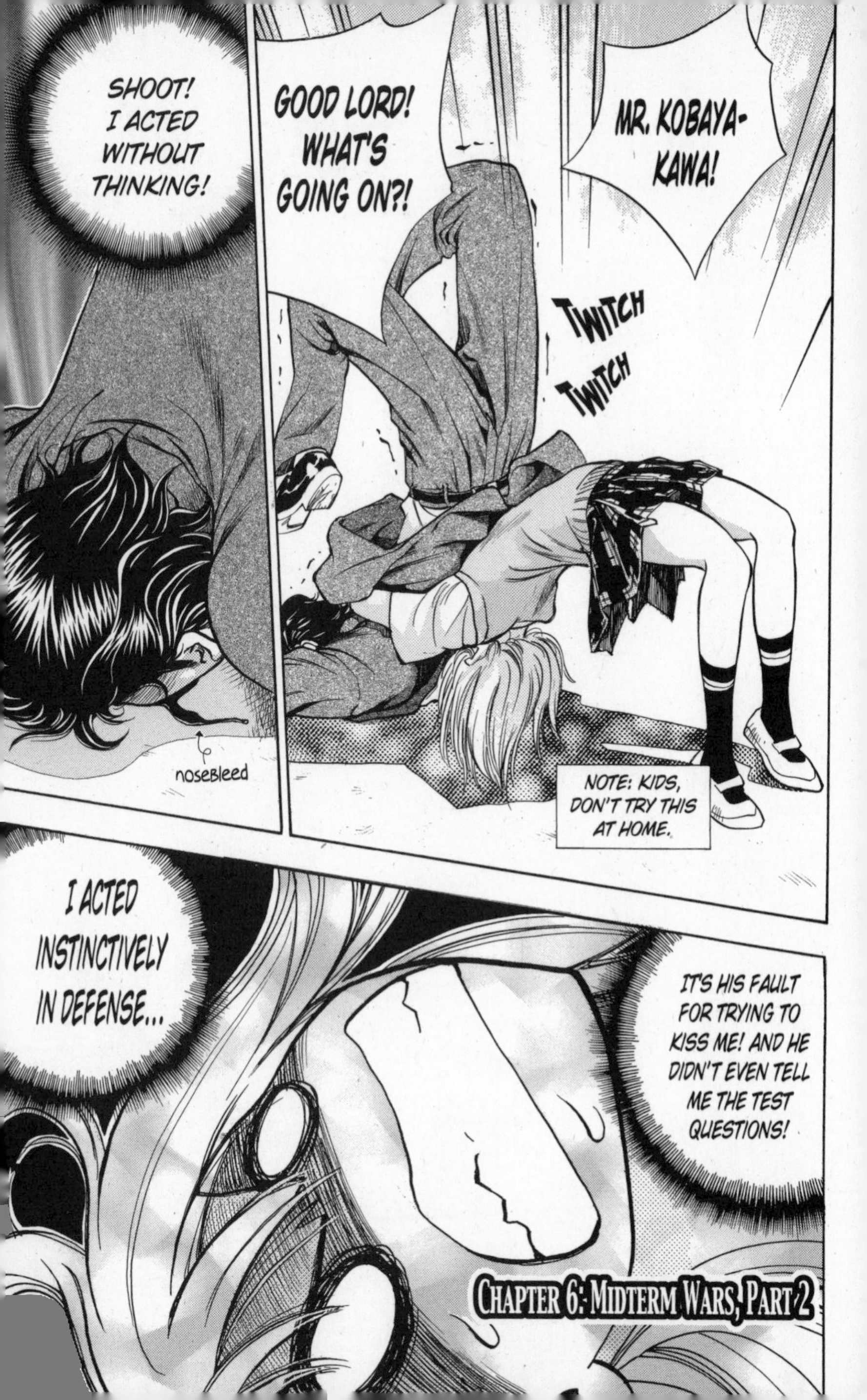
MR. KOBAYA-KAWA!
GOOD LORD! WHAT'S GOING ON?!
TWITCH
TWITCH
NOTE: KIDS, DON'T TRY THIS AT HOME.
SHOOT! I ACTED WITHOUT THINKING!
nosebleed
IT'S HIS FAULT FOR TRYING TO KISS ME! AND HE DIDN'T EVEN TELL ME THE TEST QUESTIONS!
I ACTED INSTINCTIVELY IN DEFENSE...
CHAPTER 6: MIDTERM WARS, PART 2

Chapter 6: Midterm Wars, Part 2

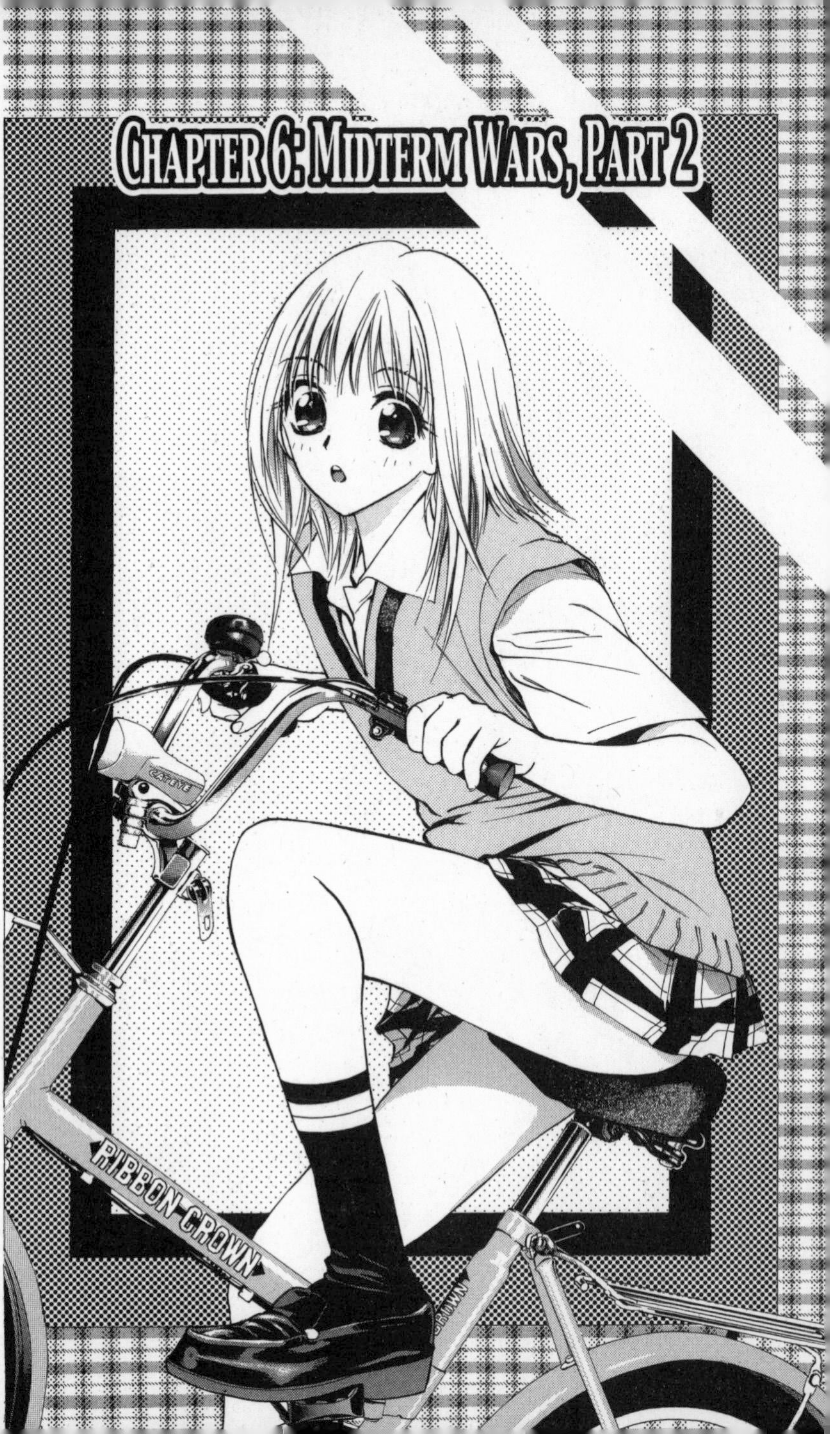
RIBBON CROWN

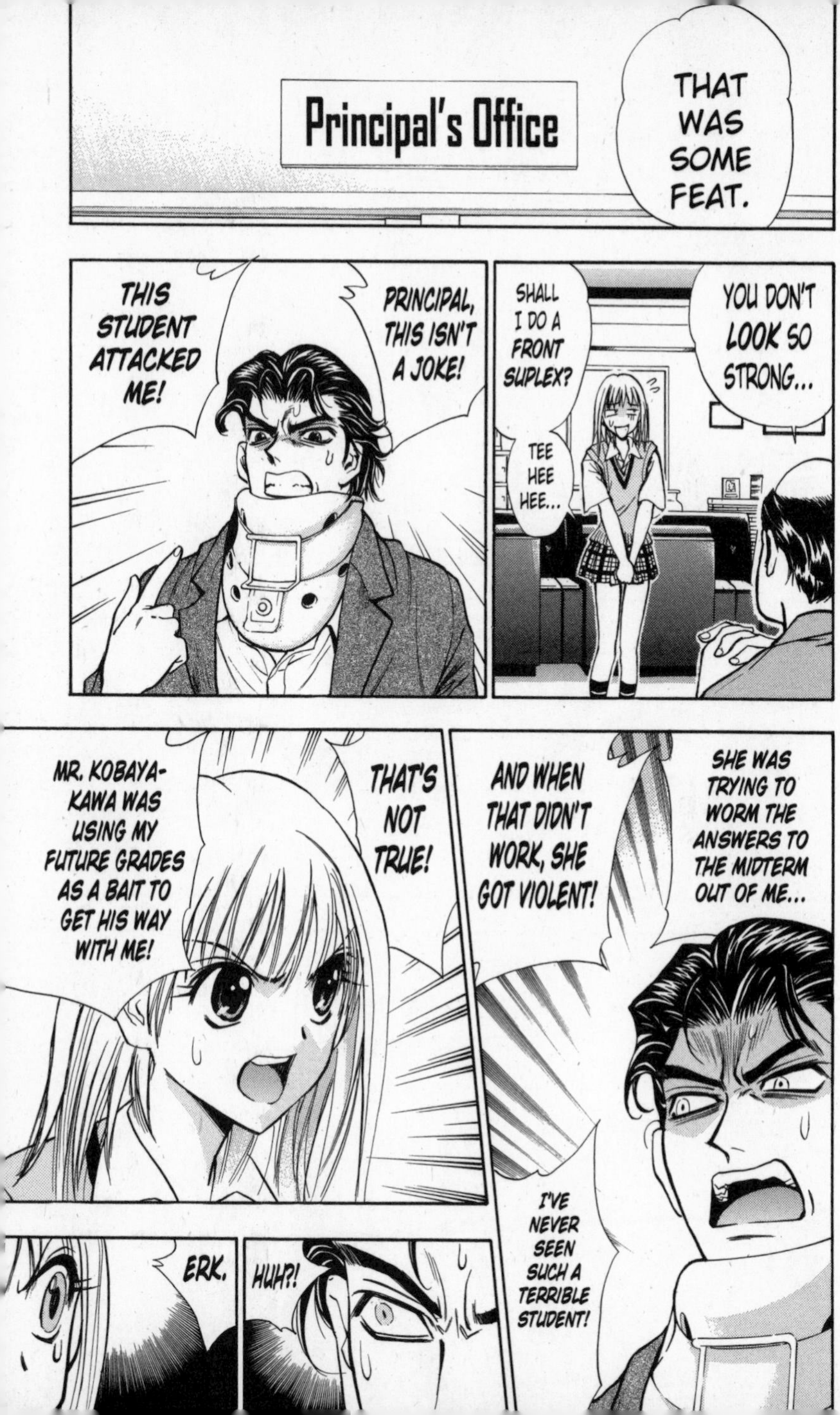
THAT WAS SOME FEAT.
Principal's Office
YOU DON'T LOOK SO STRONG...
SHALL I DO A FRONT SUPLEX?
TEE HEE HEE...
PRINCIPAL, THIS ISN'T A JOKE!
THIS STUDENT ATTACKED ME!
SHE WAS TRYING TO WORM THE ANSWERS TO THE MIDTERM OUT OF ME...
AND WHEN THAT DIDN'T WORK, SHE GOT VIOLENT!
I'VE NEVER SEEN SUCH A TERRIBLE STUDENT!
THAT'S NOT TRUE!
MR. KOBAYA-KAWA WAS USING MY FUTURE GRADES AS A BAIT TO GET HIS WAY WITH ME!
HUH?!
ERK.

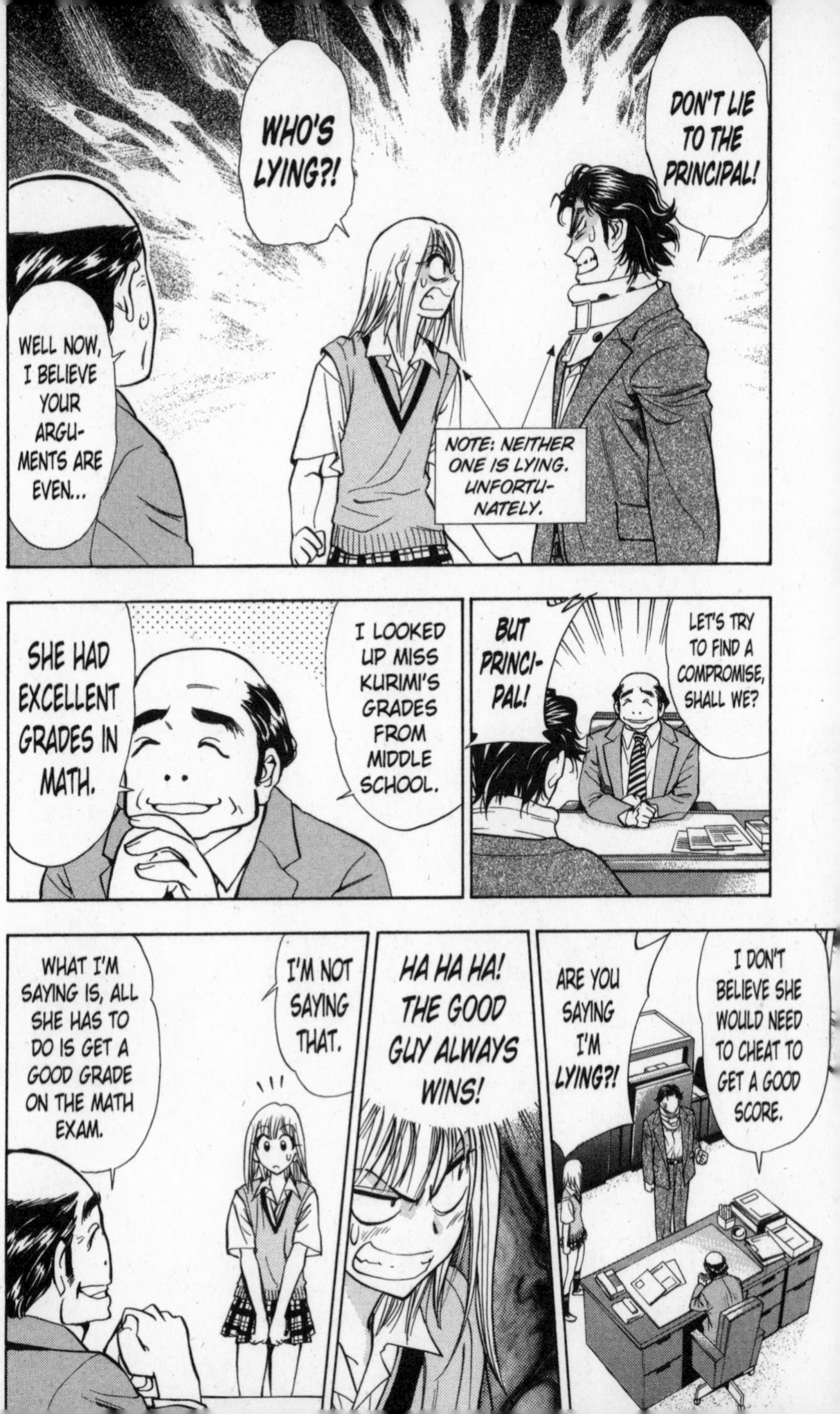
DON'T LIE TO THE PRINCIPAL!
WHO'S LYING?!
NOTE: NEITHER ONE IS LYING. UNFORTUNATELY.
WELL NOW, I BELIEVE YOUR ARGUMENTS ARE EVEN...
LET'S TRY TO FIND A COMPROMISE, SHALL WE?
BUT PRINCIPAL!
I LOOKED UP MISS KURIMI'S GRADES FROM MIDDLE SCHOOL.
SHE HAD EXCELLENT GRADES IN MATH.
I DON'T BELIEVE SHE WOULD NEED TO CHEAT TO GET A GOOD SCORE.
ARE YOU SAYING I'M LYING?!
HA HA HA! THE GOOD GUY ALWAYS WINS!
I'M NOT SAYING THAT.
WHAT I'M SAYING IS, ALL SHE HAS TO DO IS GET A GOOD GRADE ON THE MATH EXAM.

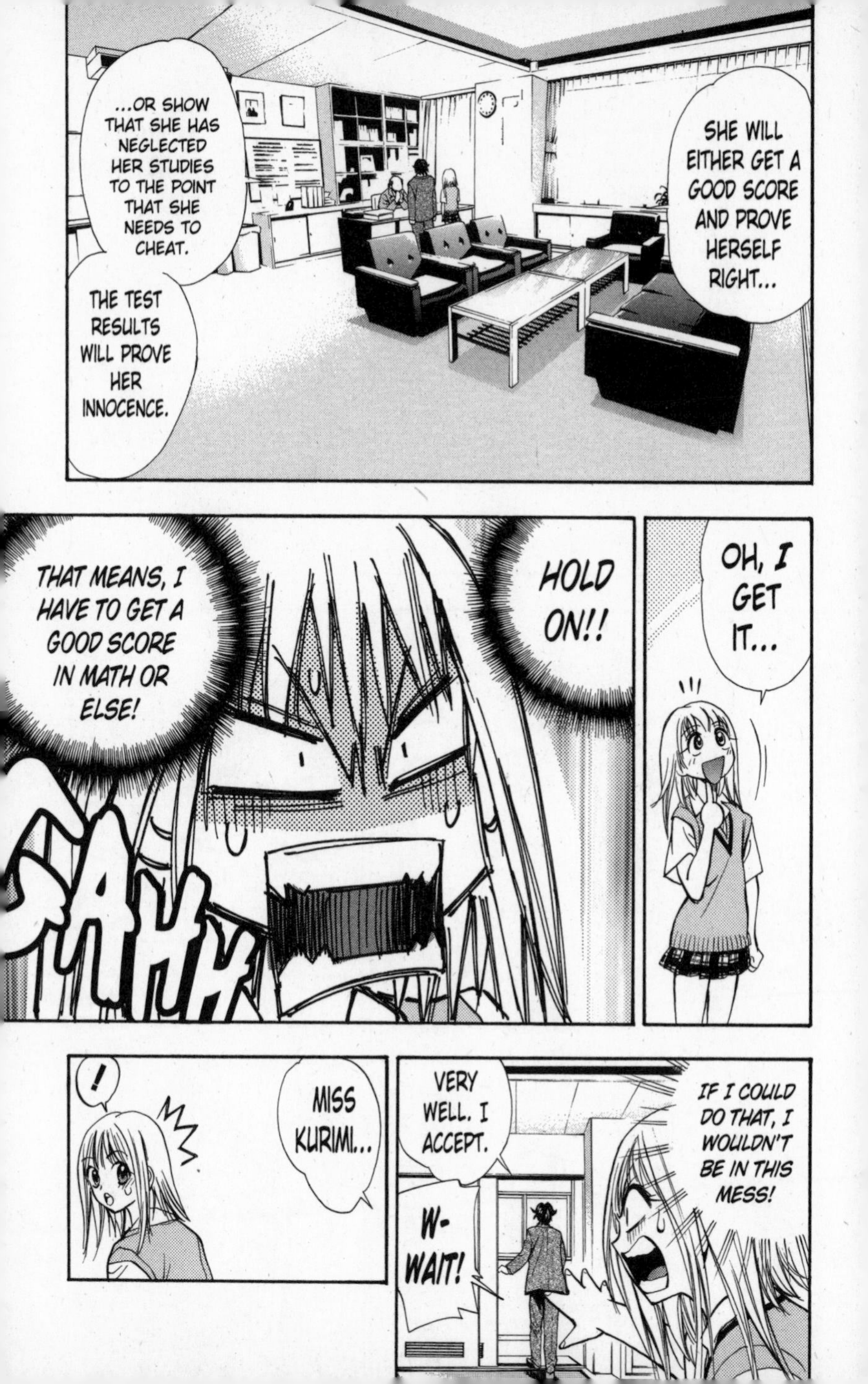
SHE WILL EITHER GET A GOOD SCORE AND PROVE HERSELF RIGHT...
...OR SHOW THAT SHE HAS NEGLECTED HER STUDIES TO THE POINT THAT SHE NEEDS TO CHEAT.
THE TEST RESULTS WILL PROVE HER INNOCENCE.
OH, I GET IT...
HOLD ON!!
THAT MEANS, I HAVE TO GET A GOOD SCORE IN MATH OR ELSE!
IF I COULD DO THAT, I WOULDN'T BE IN THIS MESS!
VERY WELL. I ACCEPT.
W-WAIT!
MISS KURIMI...
!

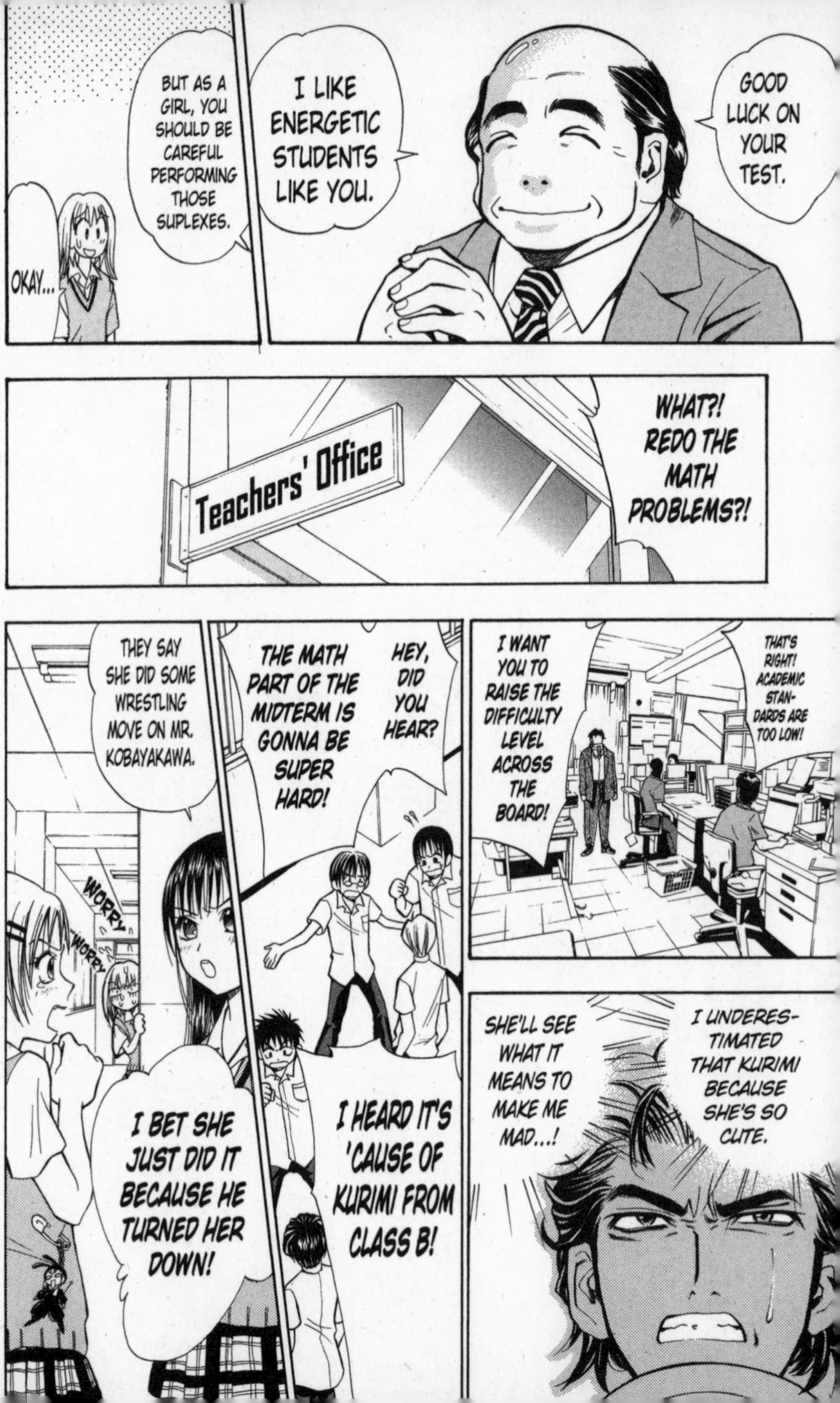
GOOD LUCK ON YOUR TEST.
I LIKE ENERGETIC STUDENTS LIKE YOU.
BUT AS A GIRL, YOU SHOULD BE CAREFUL PERFORMING THOSE SUPLEXES.
OKAY...
WHAT?! REDO THE MATH PROBLEMS?!
Teachers' Office
THAT'S RIGHT! ACADEMIC STAN-DARDS ARE TOO LOW!
I WANT YOU TO RAISE THE DIFFICULTY LEVEL ACROSS THE BOARD!
I UNDERES-TIMATED THAT KURIMI BECAUSE SHE'S SO CUTE.
SHE'LL SEE WHAT IT MEANS TO MAKE ME MAD...!
HEY, DID YOU HEAR?
THE MATH PART OF THE MIDTERM IS GONNA BE SUPER HARD!
I HEARD IT'S 'CAUSE OF KURIMI FROM CLASS B!
THEY SAY SHE DID SOME WRESTLING MOVE ON MR. KOBAYAKAWA.
WORRY
WORRY
I BET SHE JUST DID IT BECAUSE HE TURNED HER DOWN!

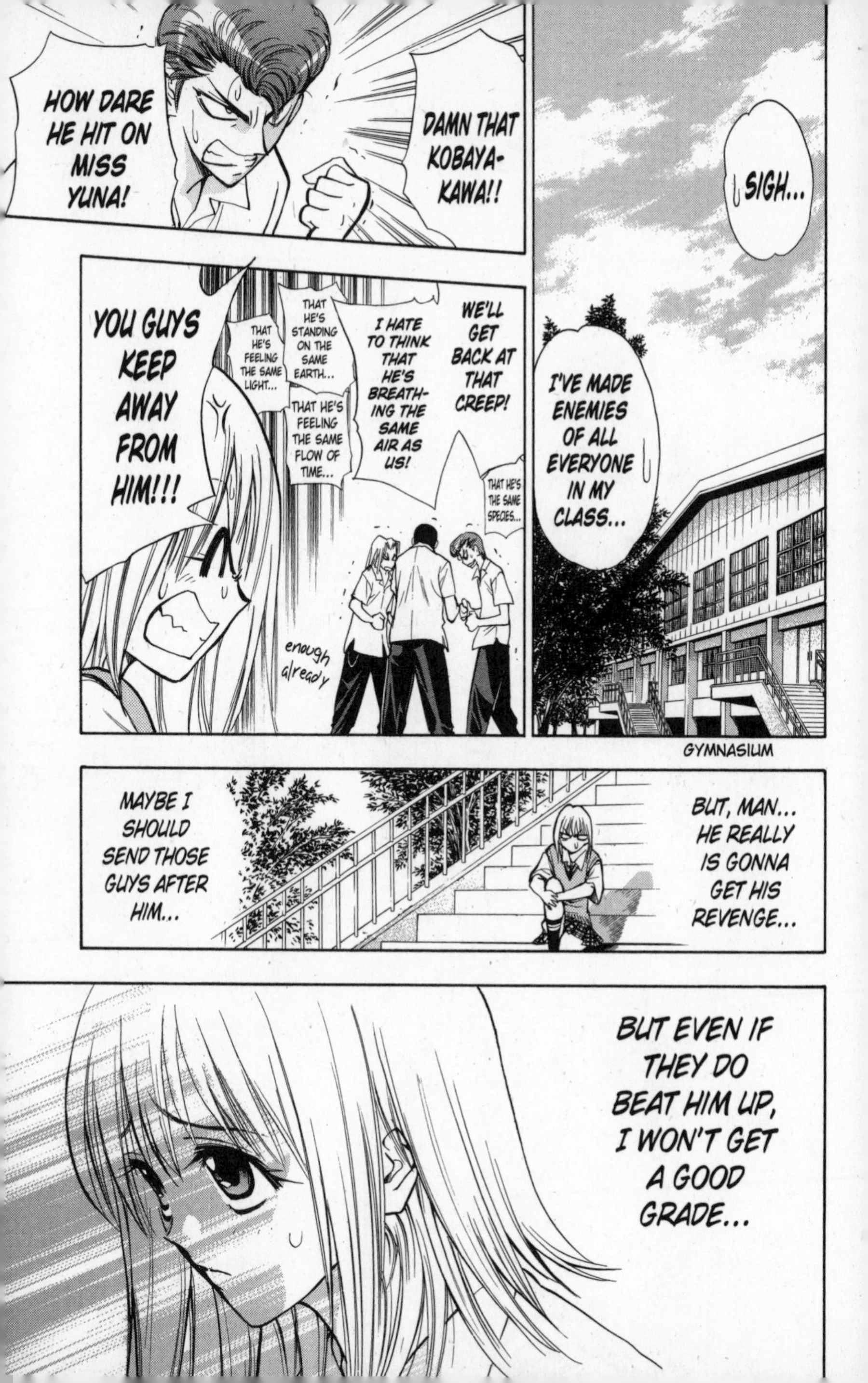
SIGH...
I'VE MADE ENEMIES OF ALL EVERYONE IN MY CLASS...
GYMNASIUM
DAMN THAT KOBAYA-KAWA!!
HOW DARE HE HIT ON MISS YUNA!
WE'LL GET BACK AT THAT CREEP!
THAT HE'S THE SAME SPECIES...
I HATE TO THINK THAT HE'S BREATH-ING THE SAME AIR AS US!
THAT HE'S STANDING ON THE SAME EARTH...
THAT HE'S FEELING THE SAME FLOW OF TIME...
THAT HE'S FEELING THE SAME LIGHT...
YOU GUYS KEEP AWAY FROM HIM!!!
enough already
BUT, MAN... HE REALLY IS GONNA GET HIS REVENGE...
MAYBE I SHOULD SEND THOSE GUYS AFTER HIM...
BUT EVEN IF THEY DO BEAT HIM UP, I WON'T GET A GOOD GRADE...

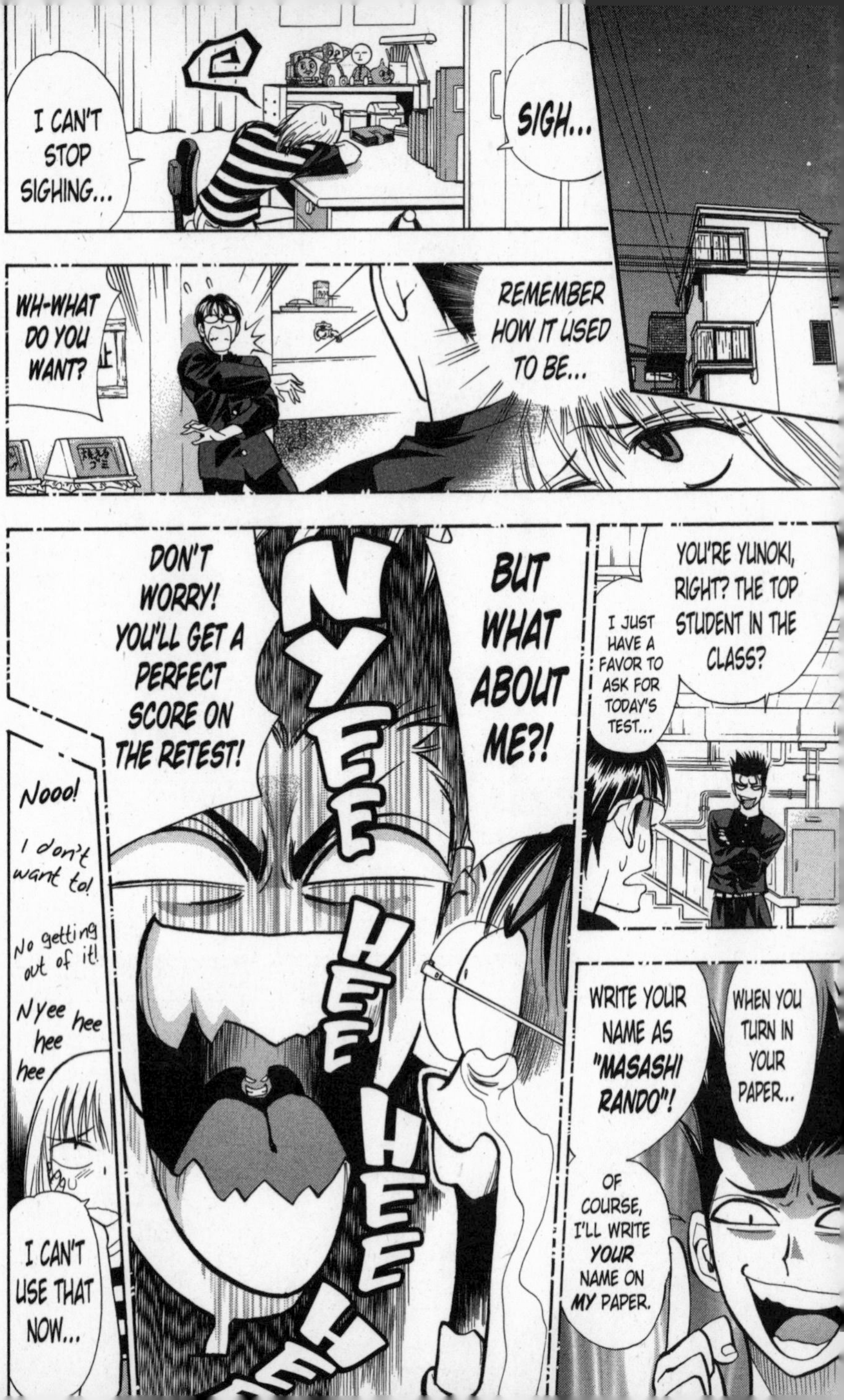
SIGH...
I CAN'T STOP SIGHING...
REMEMBER HOW IT USED TO BE...
WH-WHAT DO YOU WANT?
YOU'RE YUNOKI, RIGHT? THE TOP STUDENT IN THE CLASS?
I JUST HAVE A FAVOR TO ASK FOR TODAY'S TEST...
WHEN YOU TURN IN YOUR PAPER...
WRITE YOUR NAME AS "MASASHI RANDO"!
OF COURSE, I'LL WRITE YOUR NAME ON MY PAPER.
BUT WHAT ABOUT ME?!
DON'T WORRY! YOU'LL GET A PERFECT SCORE ON THE RETEST!
NYEE HEE HEE HEE
Nooo!
I don't want to!
No getting out of it!
Nyee hee hee hee
I CAN'T USE THAT NOW...

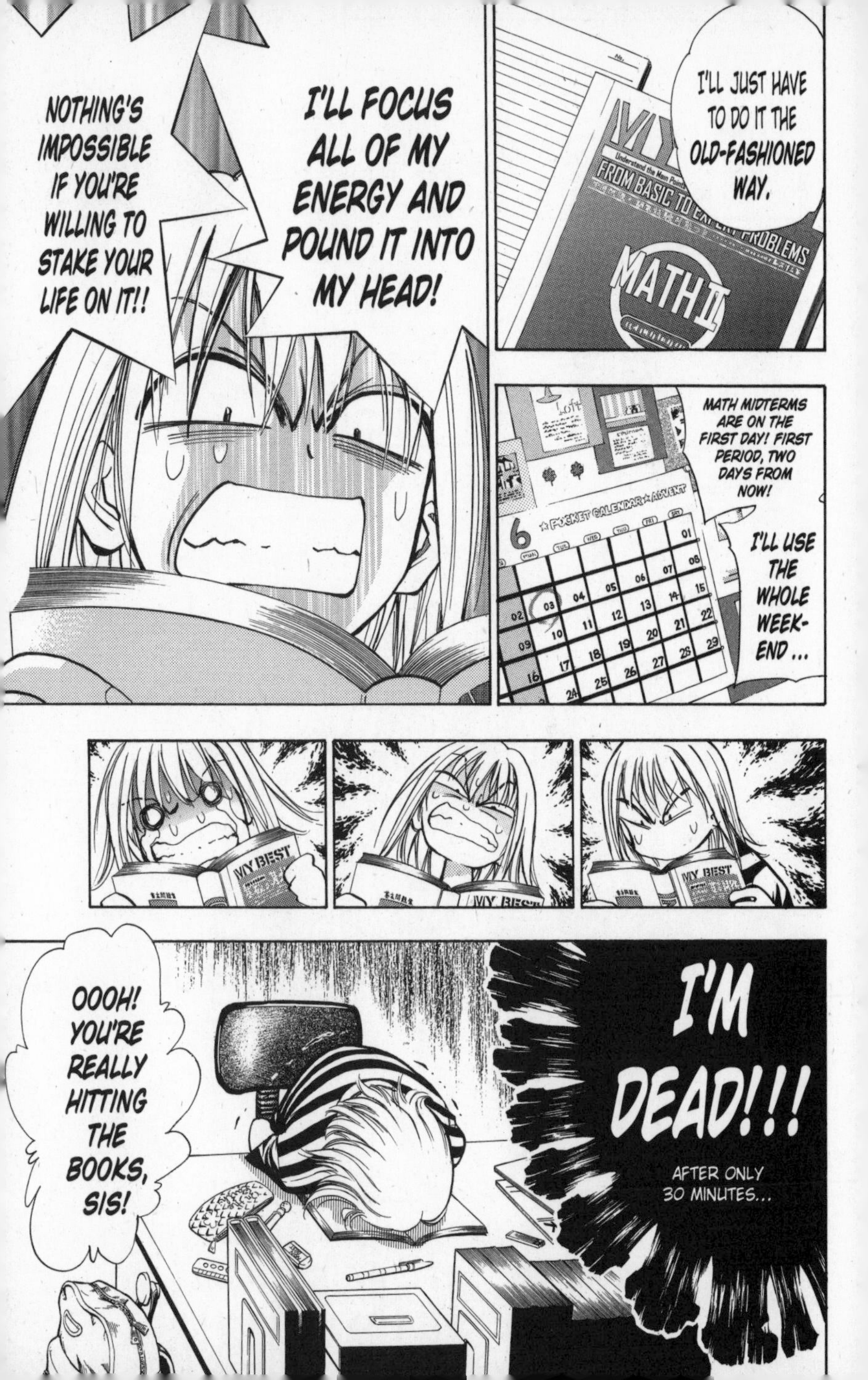
I'LL JUST HAVE TO DO IT THE OLD-FASHIONED WAY.
FROM BASIC TO EXPERT PROBLEMS
MATH II
MATH MIDTERMS ARE ON THE FIRST DAY! FIRST PERIOD, TWO DAYS FROM NOW!
I'LL USE THE WHOLE WEEK-END ...
POCKET CALENDAR★ADVENT
I'LL FOCUS ALL OF MY ENERGY AND POUND IT INTO MY HEAD!
NOTHING'S IMPOSSIBLE IF YOU'RE WILLING TO STAKE YOUR LIFE ON IT!!
MY BEST
MY BEST
MY BEST
I'M DEAD!!!
AFTER ONLY 30 MINUTES...
OOOH! YOU'RE REALLY HITTING THE BOOKS, SIS!

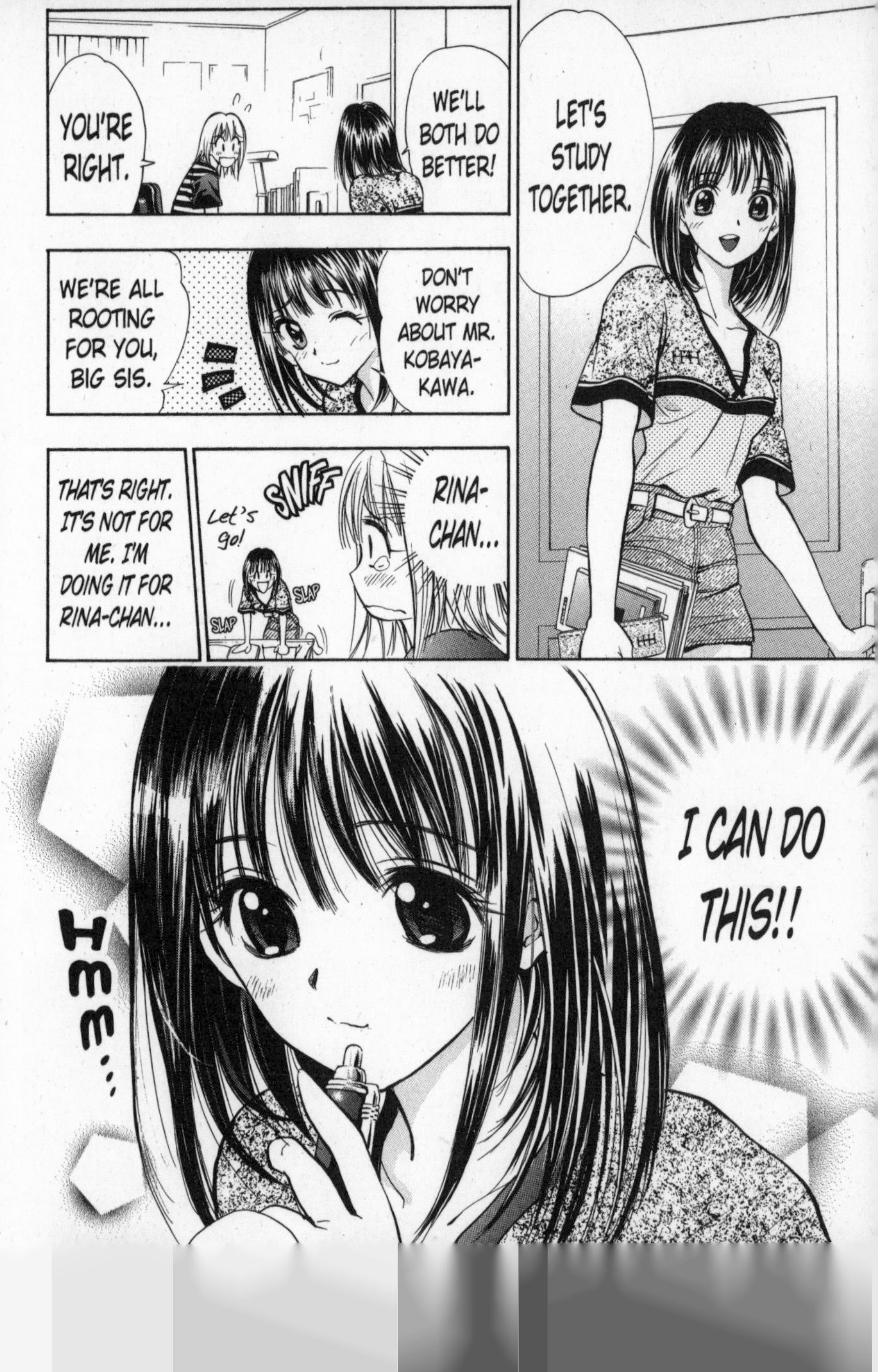
LET'S STUDY TOGETHER.
WE'LL BOTH DO BETTER!
YOU'RE RIGHT.
DON'T WORRY ABOUT MR. KOBAYA-KAWA.
WE'RE ALL ROOTING FOR YOU, BIG SIS.
RINA-CHAN...
SNIFF
Let's go!
SLAP
SLAP
THAT'S RIGHT. IT'S NOT FOR ME. I'M DOING IT FOR RINA-CHAN...
I CAN DO THIS!!
HMM...

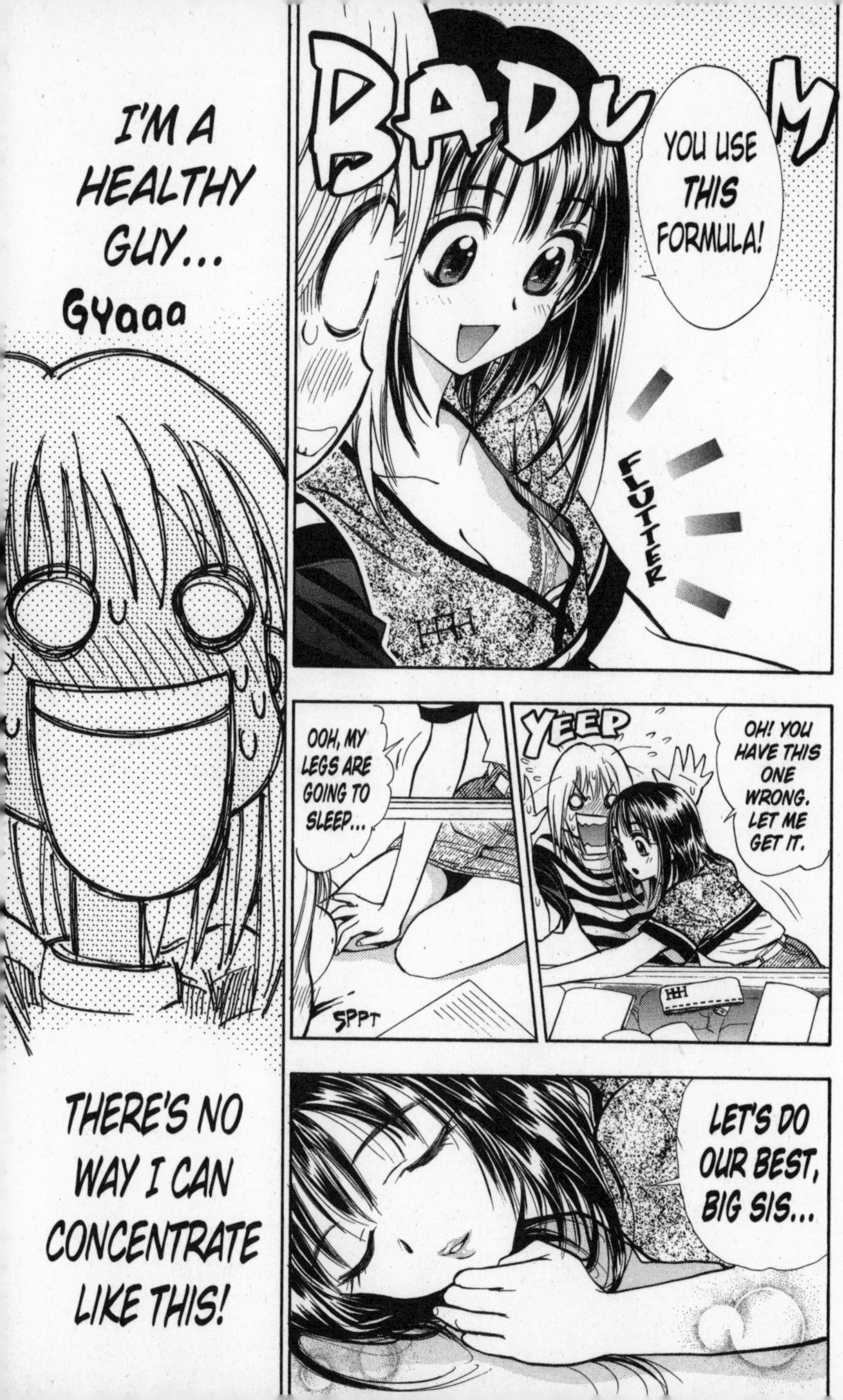
BADUM
YOU USE THIS FORMULA!
FLUTTER
YEEP
OH! YOU HAVE THIS ONE WRONG. LET ME GET IT.
OOH, MY LEGS ARE GOING TO SLEEP...
SPPT
LET'S DO OUR BEST, BIG SIS...
I'M A HEALTHY GUY...
Gyaaa
THERE'S NO WAY I CAN CONCENTRATE LIKE THIS!

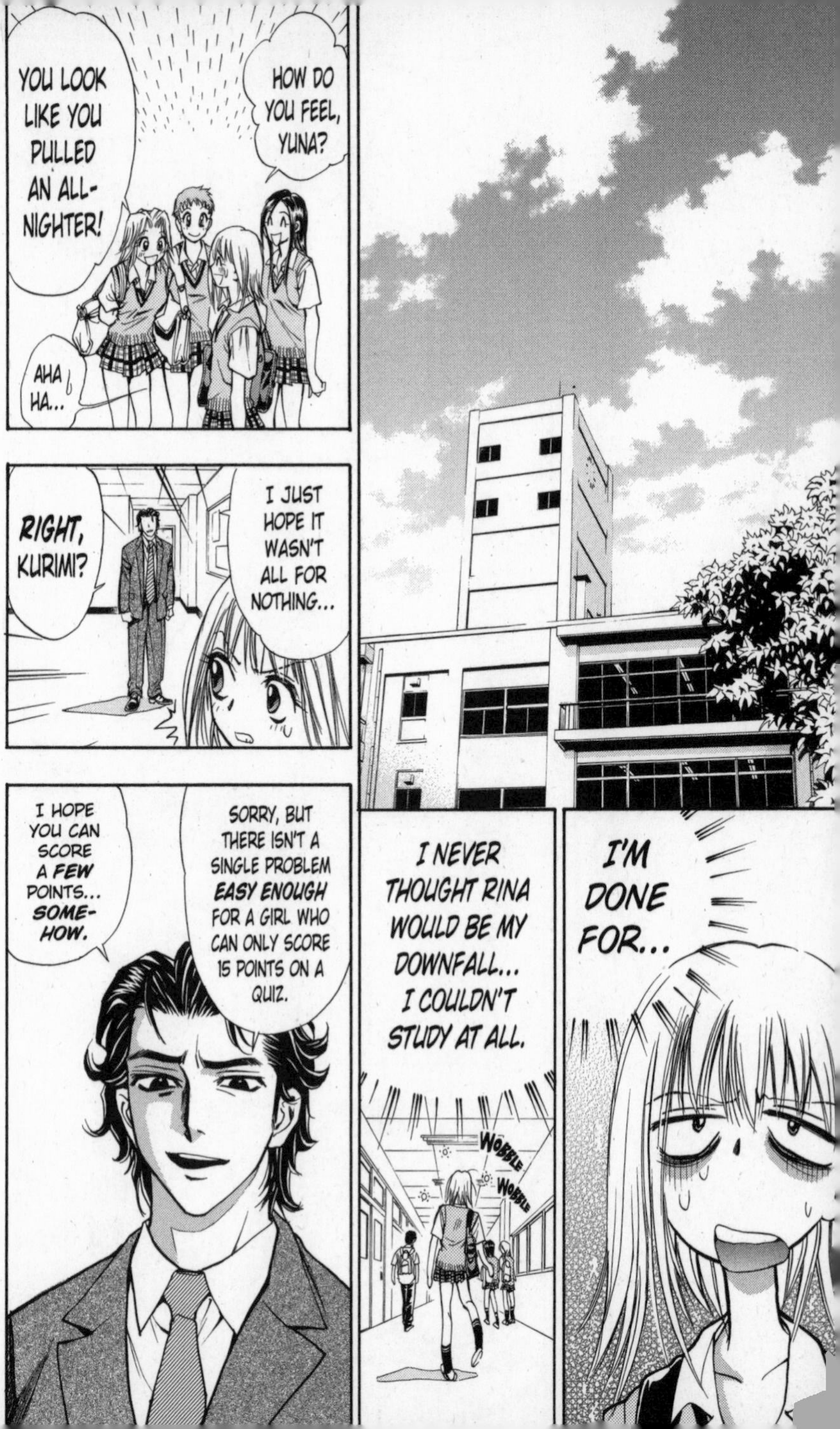
HOW DO YOU FEEL, YUNA?
YOU LOOK LIKE YOU PULLED AN ALL-NIGHTER!
AHA HA...
I JUST HOPE IT WASN'T ALL FOR NOTHING...
RIGHT, KURIMI?
I'M DONE FOR...
I NEVER THOUGHT RINA WOULD BE MY DOWNFALL... I COULDN'T STUDY AT ALL.
WOBBLE
WOBBLE
SORRY, BUT THERE ISN'T A SINGLE PROBLEM EASY ENOUGH FOR A GIRL WHO CAN ONLY SCORE 15 POINTS ON A QUIZ.
I HOPE YOU CAN SCORE A FEW POINTS... SOME-HOW.

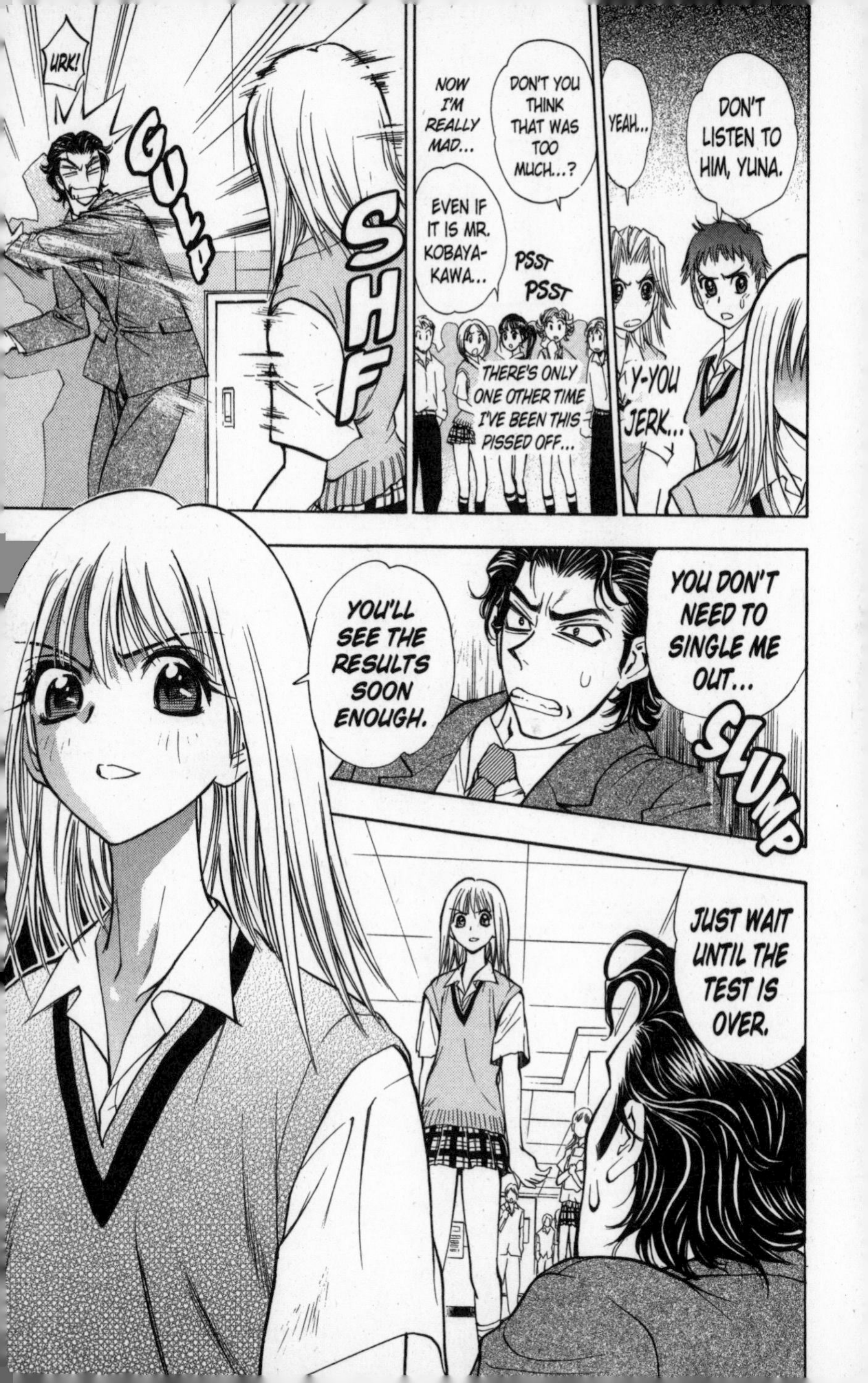
DON'T LISTEN TO HIM, YUNA.
YEAH...
Y-YOU JERK...
DON'T YOU THINK THAT WAS TOO MUCH...?
NOW I'M REALLY MAD...
EVEN IF IT IS MR. KOBAYA-KAWA...
PSST PSST
THERE'S ONLY ONE OTHER TIME I'VE BEEN THIS PISSED OFF...
URK!
GULP
SHF
YOU DON'T NEED TO SINGLE ME OUT...
YOU'LL SEE THE RESULTS SOON ENOUGH.
SLUMP
JUST WAIT UNTIL THE TEST IS OVER.

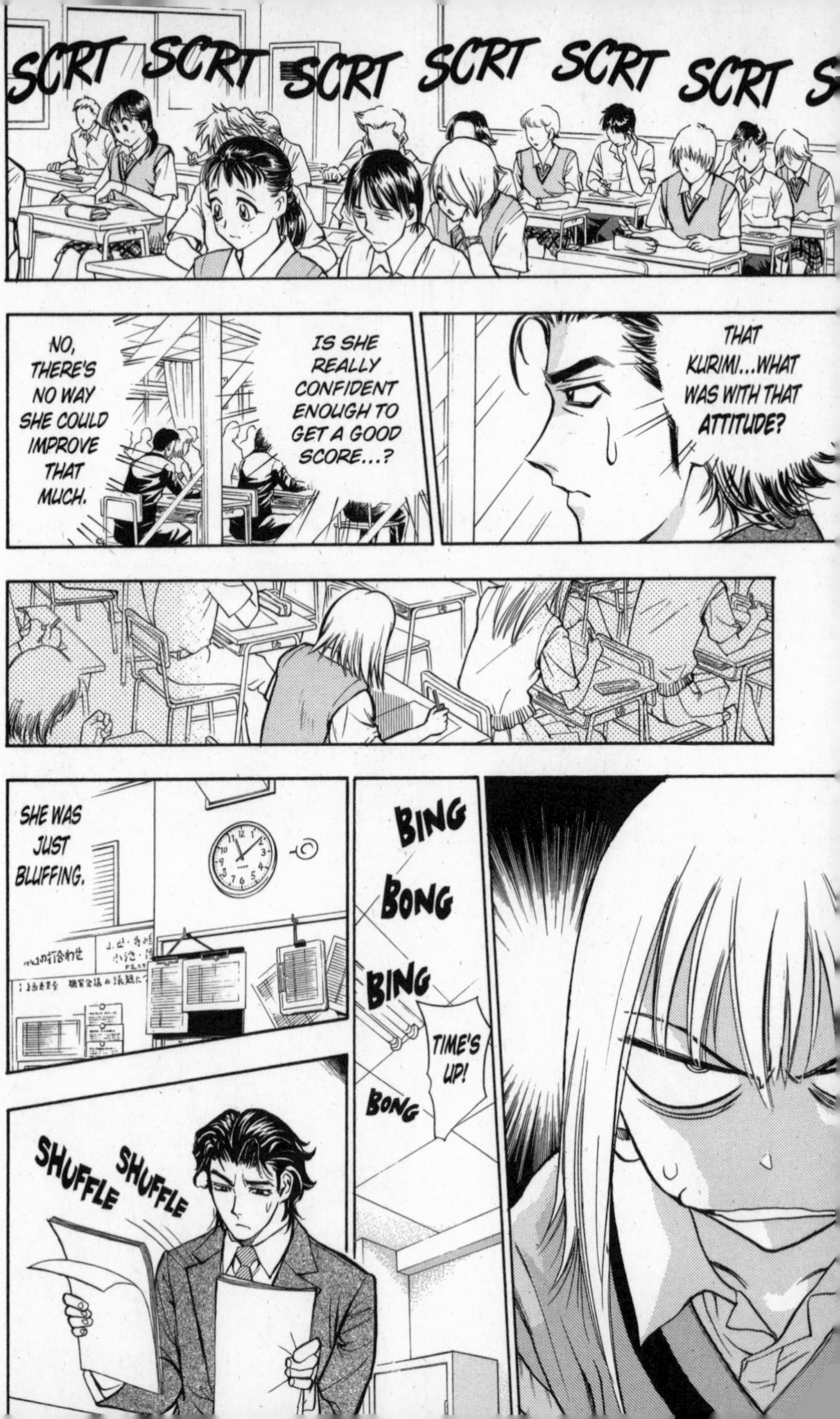
SCRT SCRT SCRT SCRT SCRT SCRT S
THAT KURIMI...WHAT WAS WITH THAT ATTITUDE?
IS SHE REALLY CONFIDENT ENOUGH TO GET A GOOD SCORE...?
NO, THERE'S NO WAY SHE COULD IMPROVE THAT MUCH.
BING
BONG
BING
TIME'S UP!
BONG
SHE WAS JUST BLUFFING.
SHUFFLE
SHUFFLE

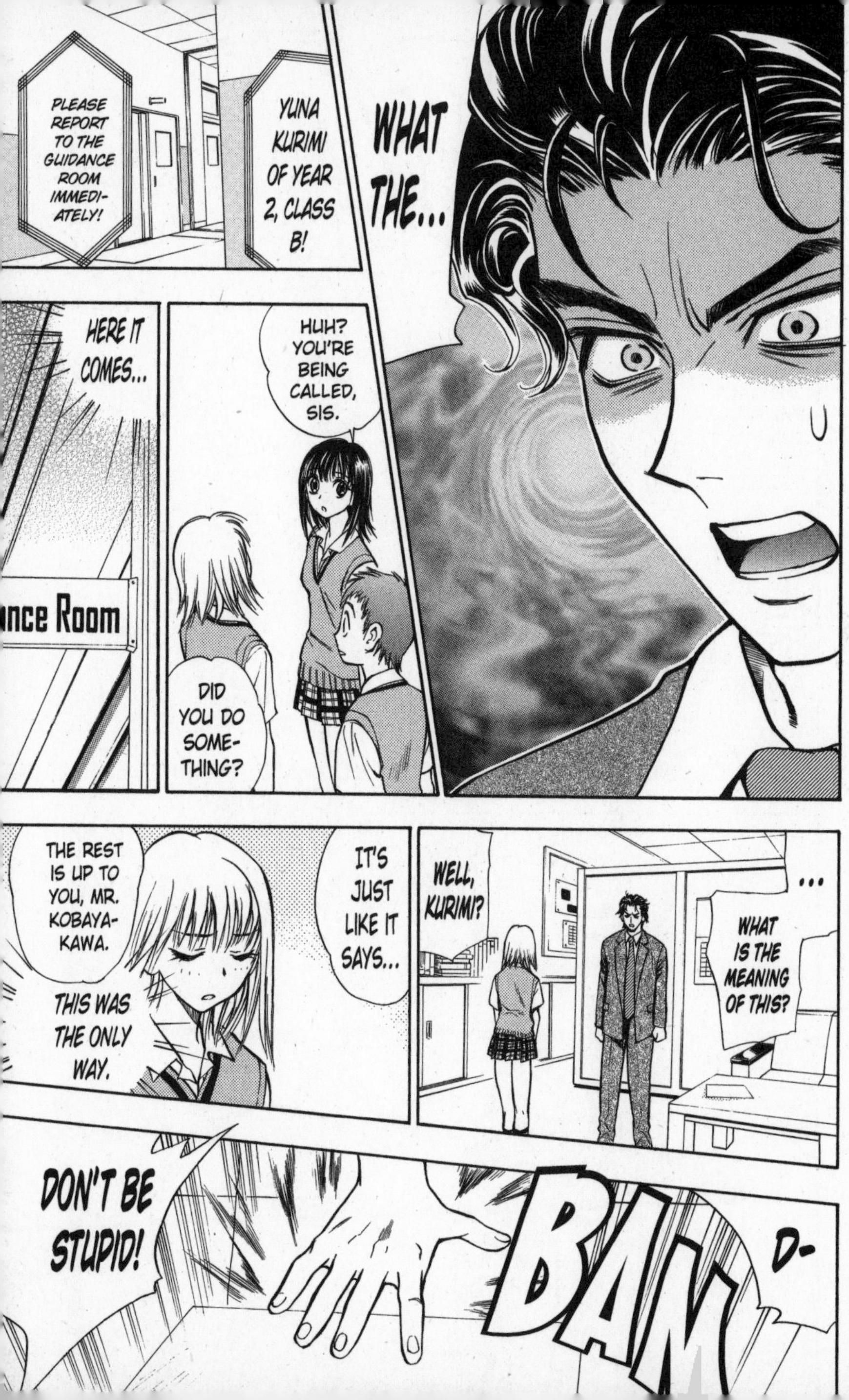
WHAT THE...
YUNA KURIMI OF YEAR 2, CLASS B!
PLEASE REPORT TO THE GUIDANCE ROOM IMMEDI-ATELY!
HUH? YOU'RE BEING CALLED, SIS.
DID YOU DO SOME-THING?
HERE IT COMES...
ance Room
...
WHAT IS THE MEANING OF THIS?
WELL, KURIMI?
IT'S JUST LIKE IT SAYS...
THE REST IS UP TO YOU, MR. KOBAYA-KAWA.
THIS WAS THE ONLY WAY.
D-
BAM
DON'T BE STUPID!

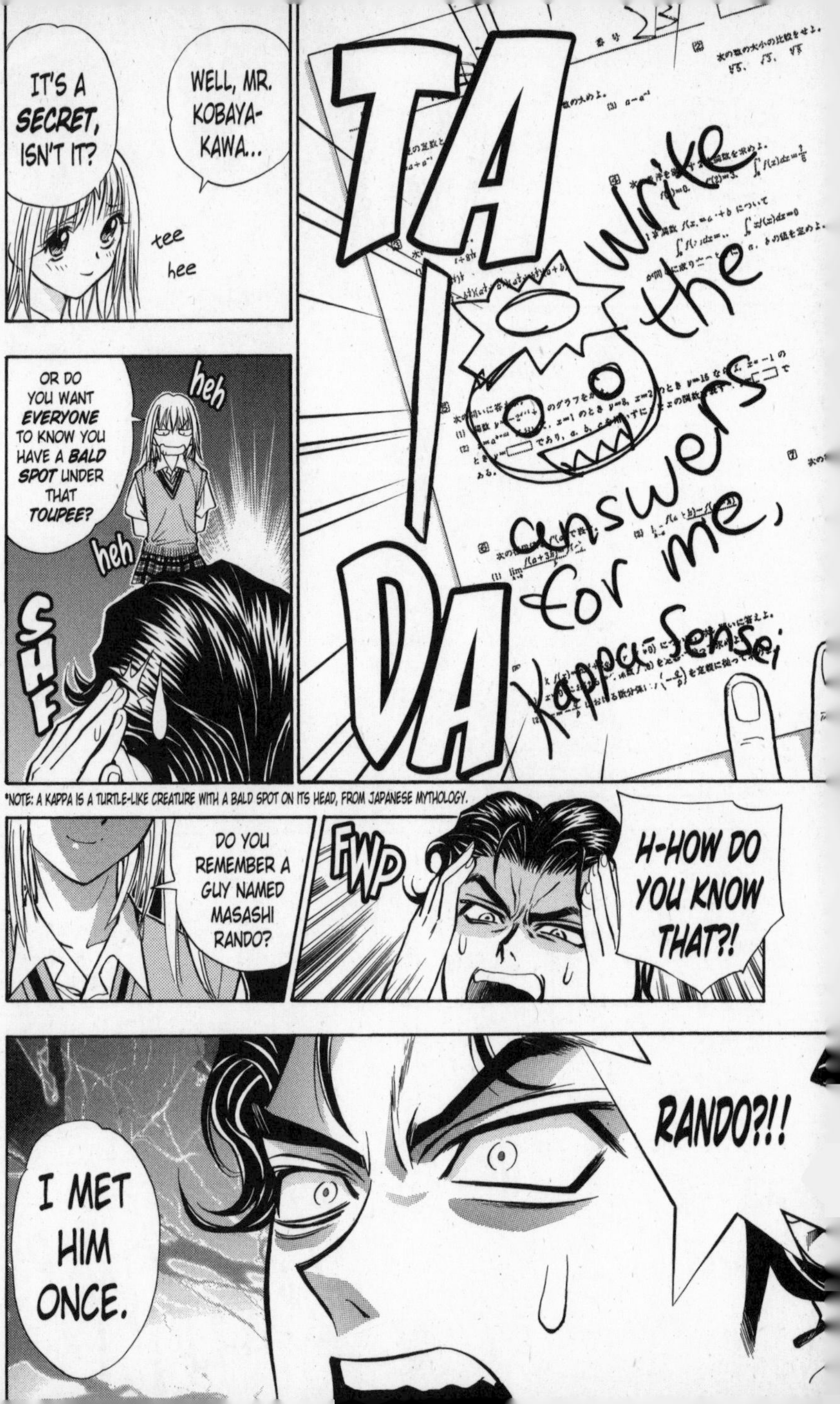
TA
I
DA
write the answers for me, Kappa-sensei
WELL, MR. KOBAYA-KAWA...
IT'S A SECRET, ISN'T IT?
tee hee
heh
OR DO YOU WANT EVERYONE TO KNOW YOU HAVE A BALD SPOT UNDER THAT TOUPEE?
heh
SHF
*NOTE: A KAPPA IS A TURTLE-LIKE CREATURE WITH A BALD SPOT ON ITS HEAD, FROM JAPANESE MYTHOLOGY.
H-HOW DO YOU KNOW THAT?!
FWP
DO YOU REMEMBER A GUY NAMED MASASHI RANDO?
RANDO?!!
I MET HIM ONCE.

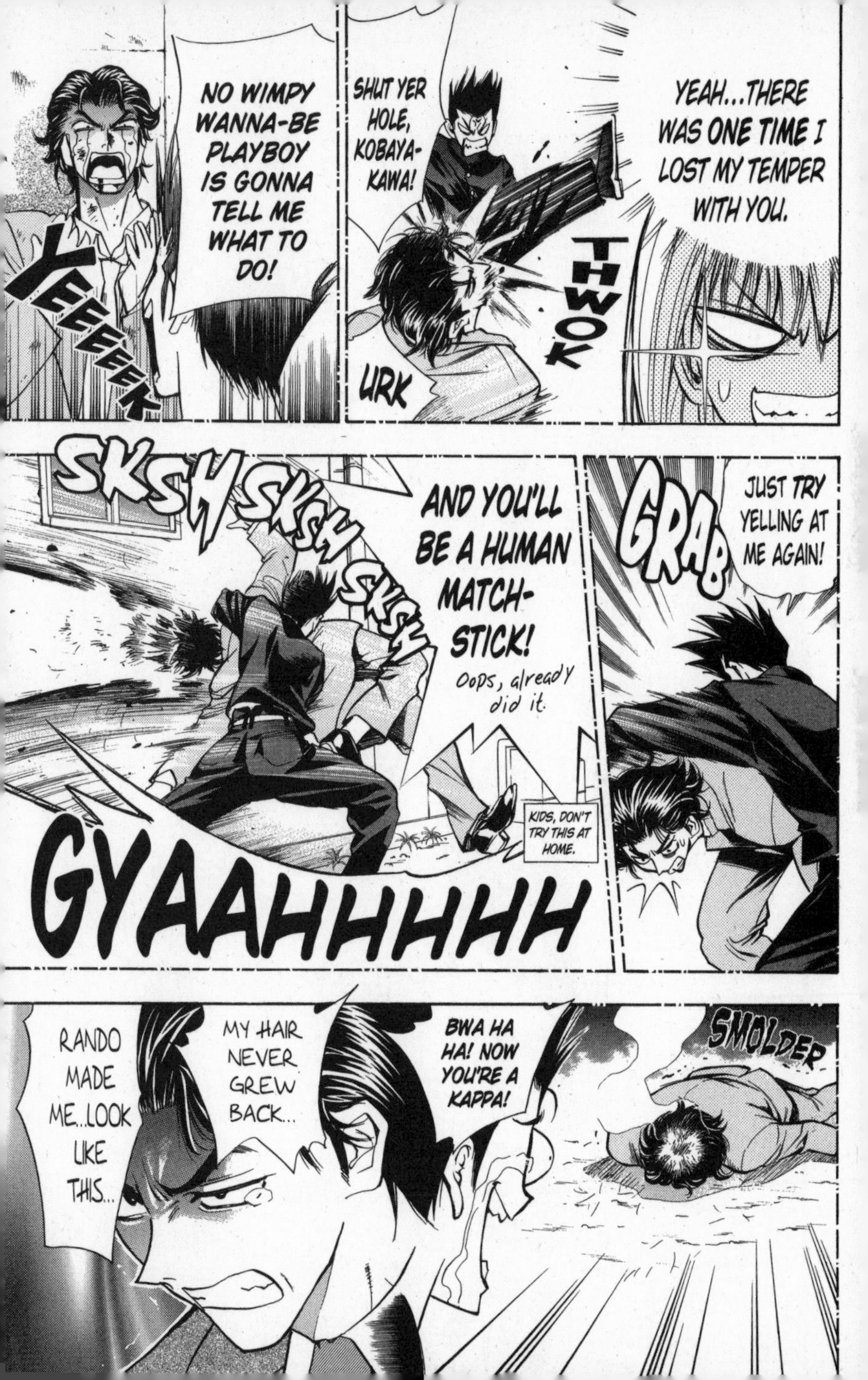
YEAH...THERE WAS ONE TIME I LOST MY TEMPER WITH YOU.
SHUT YER HOLE, KOBAYA-KAWA!
THWOK
URK
NO WIMPY WANNA-BE PLAYBOY IS GONNA TELL ME WHAT TO DO!
YEEEEEEK
GRAB
JUST TRY YELLING AT ME AGAIN!
AND YOU'LL BE A HUMAN MATCH-STICK!
Oops, already did it.
SKSH SKSH SKSH
KIDS, DON'T TRY THIS AT HOME.
GYAAHHHHHH
SMOLDER
BWA HA HA! NOW YOU'RE A KAPPA!
MY HAIR NEVER GREW BACK...
RANDO MADE ME...LOOK LIKE THIS...

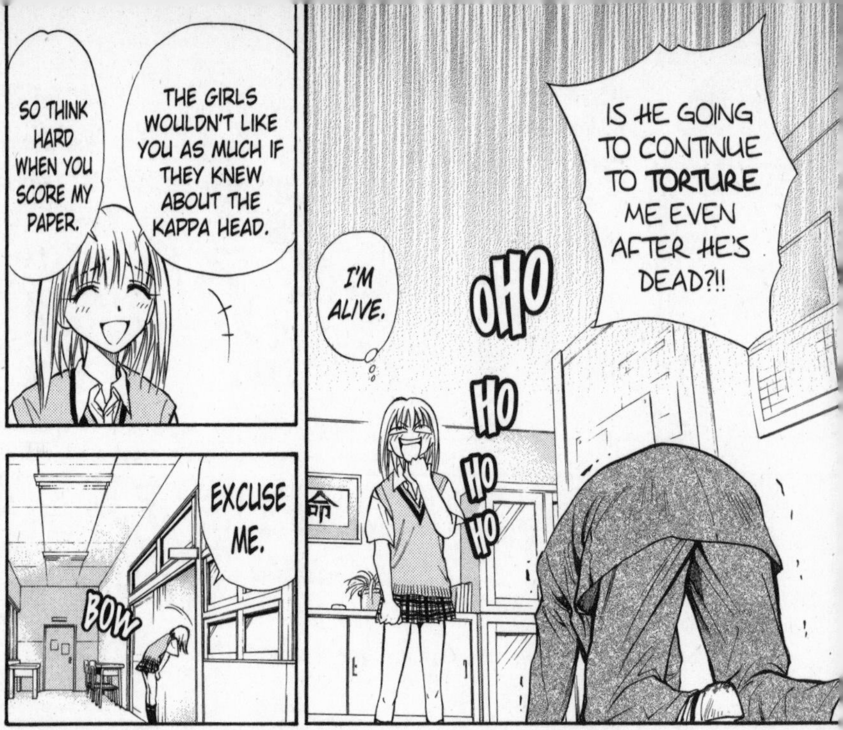
IS HE GOING TO CONTINUE TO **TORTURE** ME EVEN AFTER HE'S DEAD?!!
OHO
HO
HO
HO
I'M ALIVE.
THE GIRLS WOULDN'T LIKE YOU AS MUCH IF THEY KNEW ABOUT THE KAPPA HEAD.
SO THINK HARD WHEN YOU SCORE MY PAPER.
EXCUSE ME.
BOW

SEVERAL DAYS LATER…

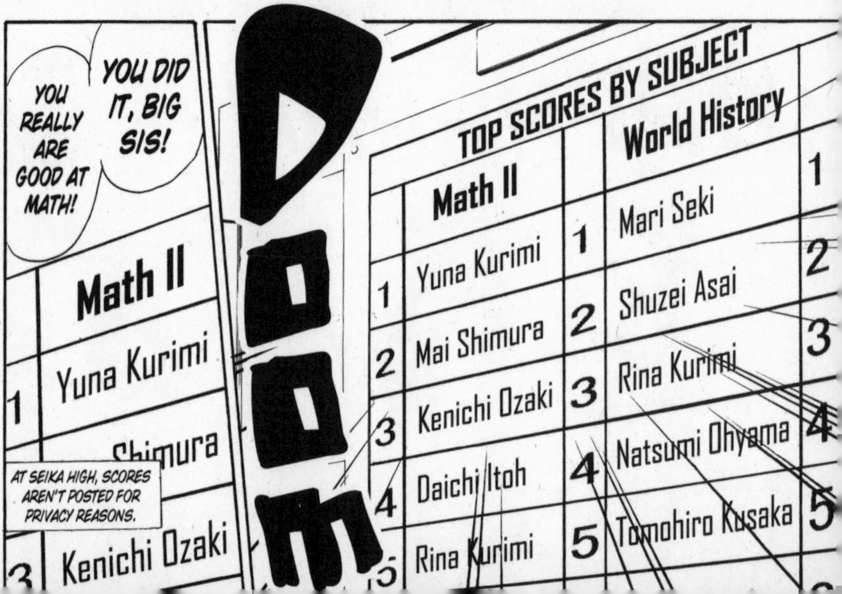
DOOM
TOP SCORES BY SUBJECT
World History
1 Mari Seki
2 Shuzei Asai
3 Rina Kurimi
4 Natsumi Ohyama
5 Tomohiro Kusaka
Math II
1 Yuna Kurimi
2 Mai Shimura
3 Kenichi Ozaki
4 Daichi Itoh
5 Rina Kurimi
YOU DID IT, BIG SIS!
YOU REALLY ARE GOOD AT MATH!
Math II
1 Yuna Kurimi
Shimura
3 Kenichi Ozaki
AT SEIKA HIGH, SCORES AREN'T POSTED FOR PRIVACY REASONS.

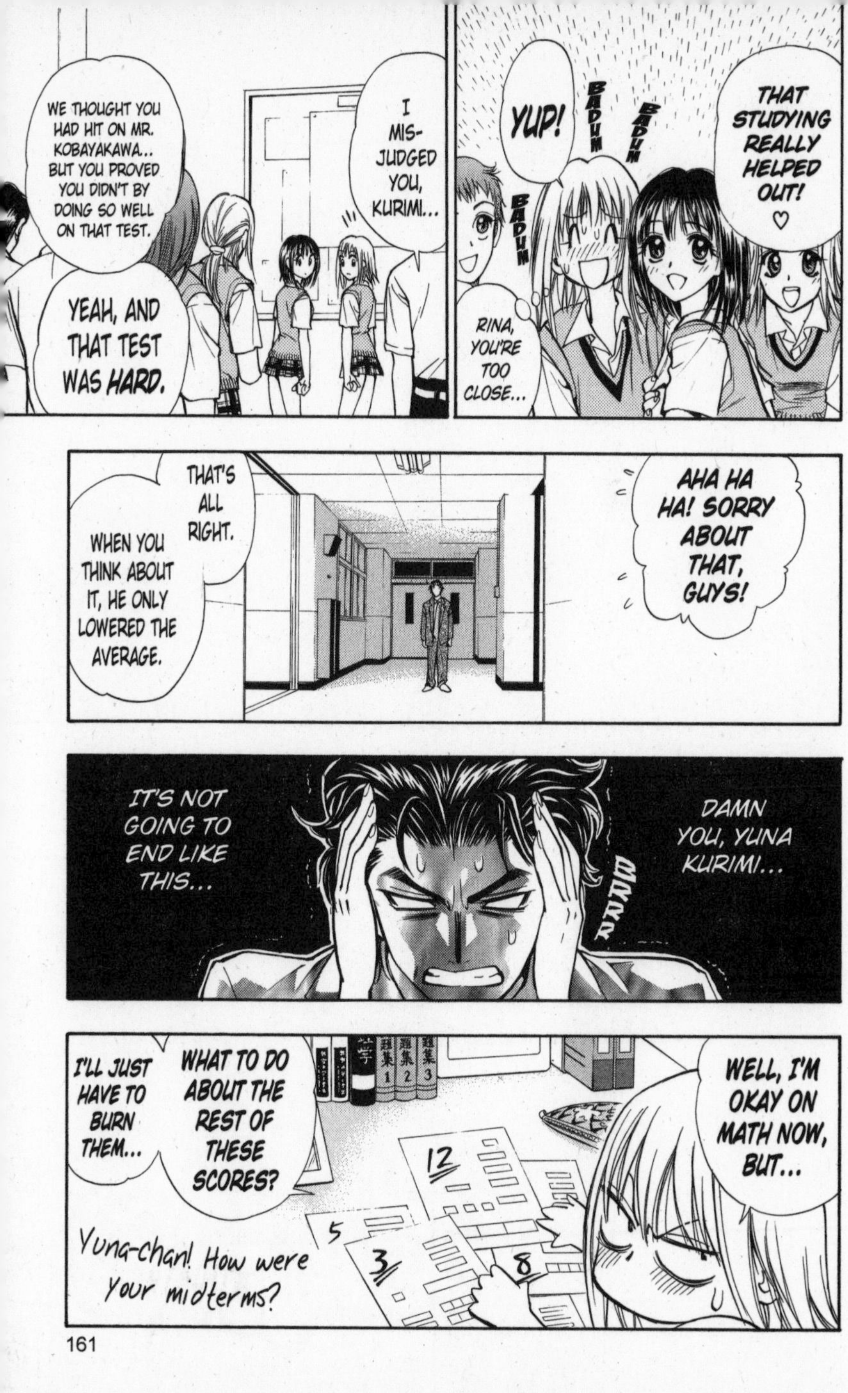
THAT STUDYING REALLY HELPED OUT! ♡
YUP!
RINA, YOU'RE TOO CLOSE...
I MIS-JUDGED YOU, KURIMI...
WE THOUGHT YOU HAD HIT ON MR. KOBAYAKAWA... BUT YOU PROVED YOU DIDN'T BY DOING SO WELL ON THAT TEST.
YEAH, AND THAT TEST WAS HARD.
AHA HA HA! SORRY ABOUT THAT, GUYS!
THAT'S ALL RIGHT.
WHEN YOU THINK ABOUT IT, HE ONLY LOWERED THE AVERAGE.
DAMN YOU, YUNA KURIMI...
IT'S NOT GOING TO END LIKE THIS...
WELL, I'M OKAY ON MATH NOW, BUT...
WHAT TO DO ABOUT THE REST OF THESE SCORES?
I'LL JUST HAVE TO BURN THEM...
Yuna-chan! How were your midterms?

Pretty Face

Chapter 7: Manabe (Rando+2π)= πR2

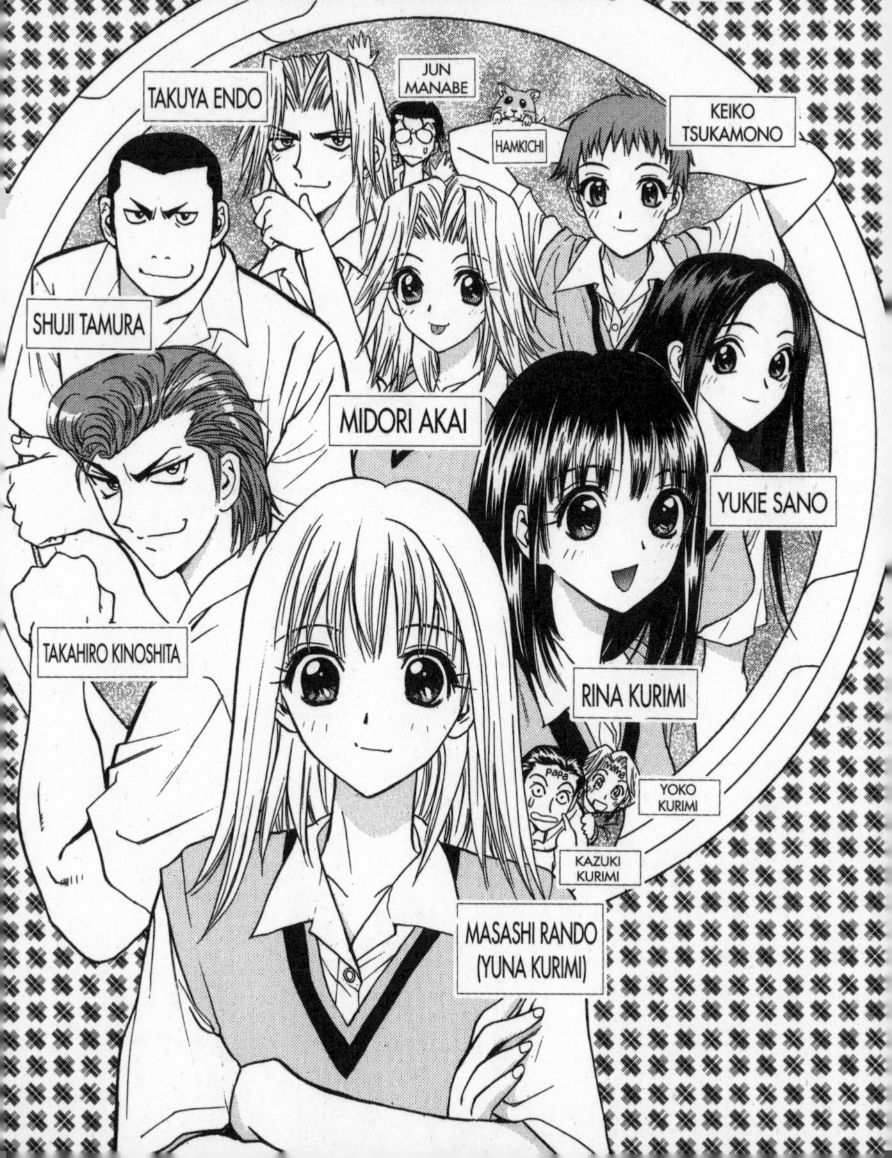
KEIKO TSUKAMONO
HAMKICHI
JUN MANABE
TAKUYA ENDO
SHUJI TAMURA
MIDORI AKAI
YUKIE SANO
TAKAHIRO KINOSHITA
RINA KURIMI
YOKO KURIMI
Mama
Papa
KAZUKI KURIMI
MASASHI RANDO (YUNA KURIMI)

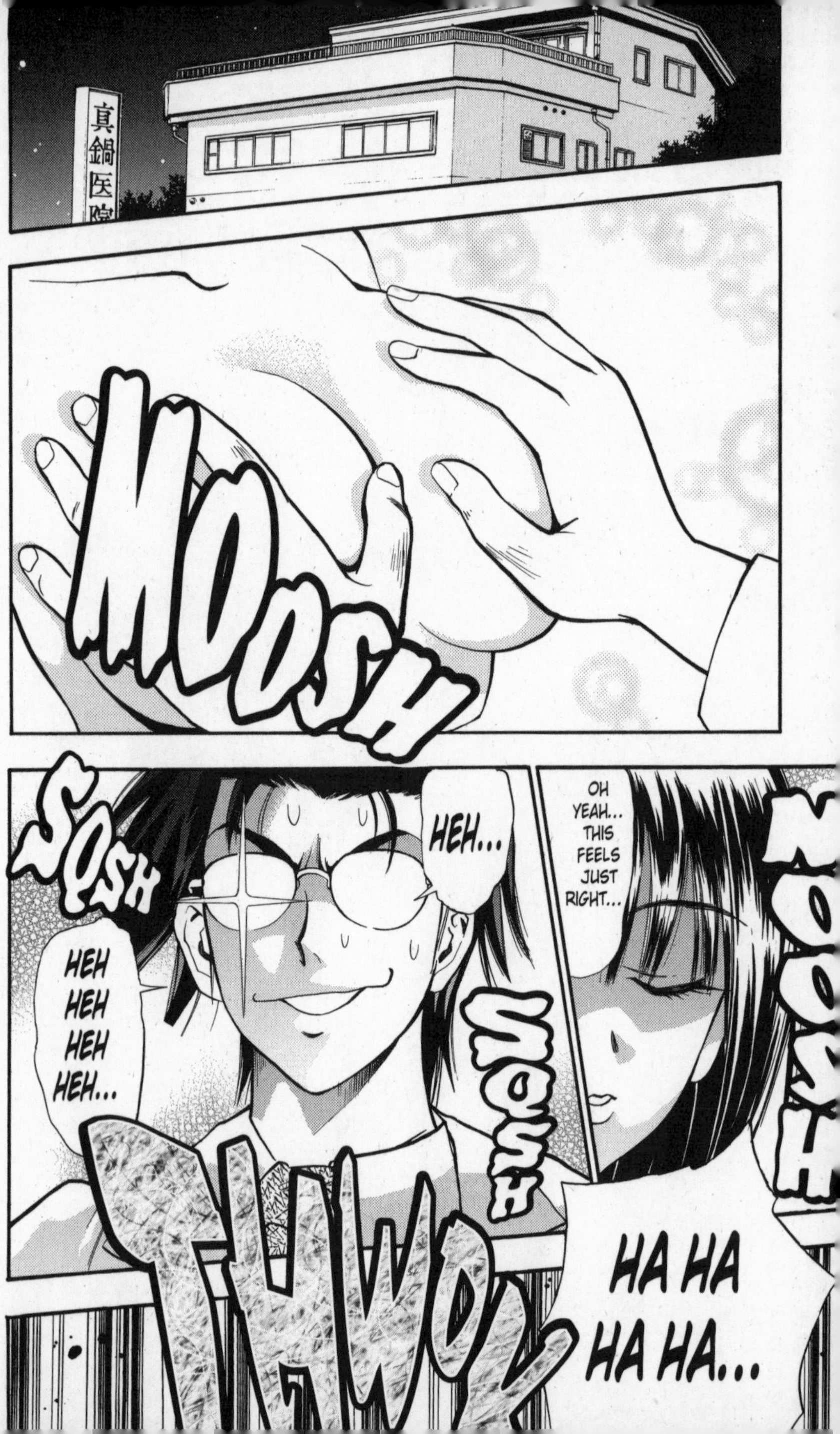
真鍋医院
MOOSH
OH YEAH... THIS FEELS JUST RIGHT...
MOOSH
HEH...
SQSH
HEH HEH HEH HEH...
SQSH
THWOK
HA HA HA HA...

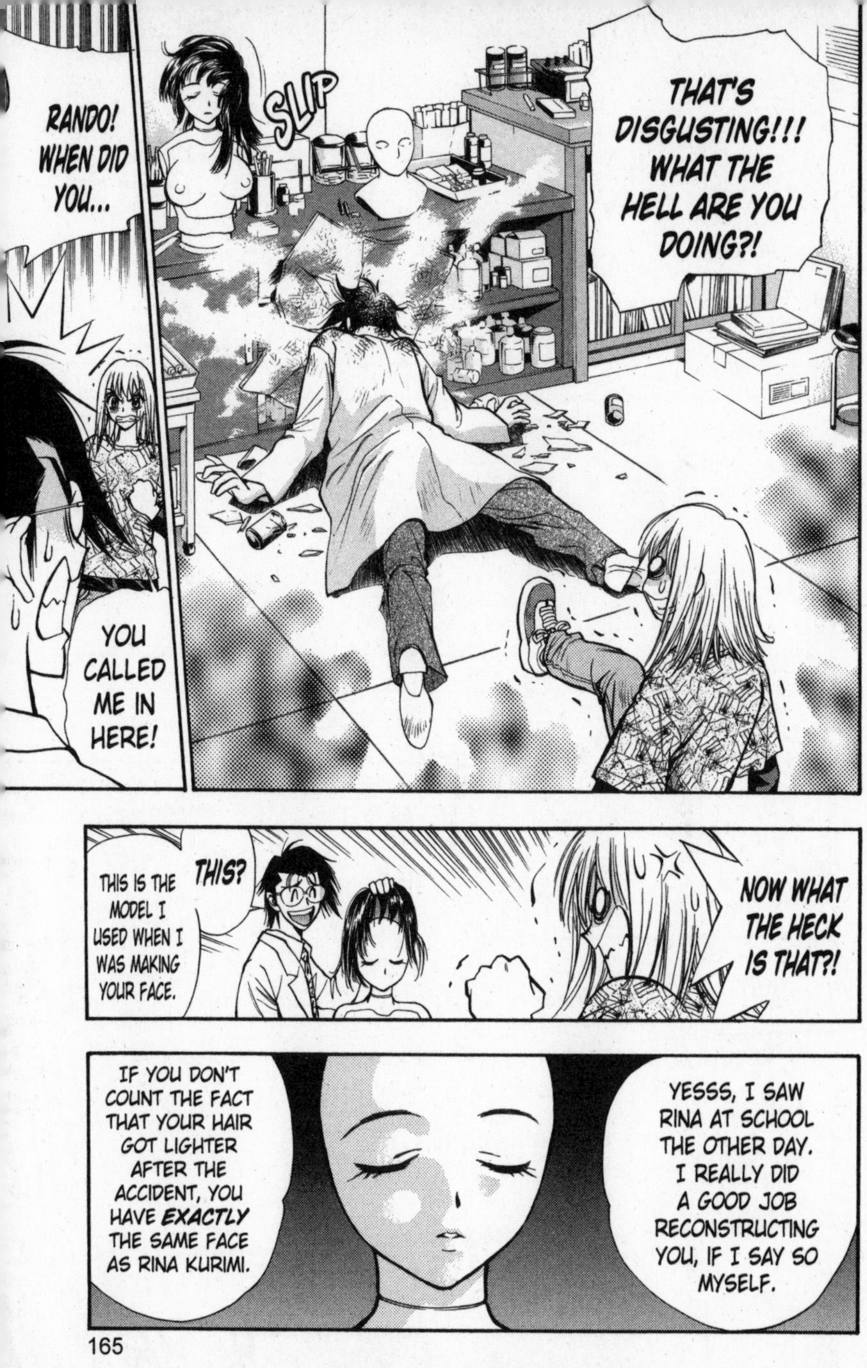
THAT'S DISGUSTING!!! WHAT THE HELL ARE YOU DOING?!
SLIP
RANDO! WHEN DID YOU...
YOU CALLED ME IN HERE!
NOW WHAT THE HECK IS THAT?!
THIS?
THIS IS THE MODEL I USED WHEN I WAS MAKING YOUR FACE.
YESSS, I SAW RINA AT SCHOOL THE OTHER DAY. I REALLY DID A GOOD JOB RECONSTRUCTING YOU, IF I SAY SO MYSELF.
IF YOU DON'T COUNT THE FACT THAT YOUR HAIR GOT LIGHTER AFTER THE ACCIDENT, YOU HAVE *EXACTLY* THE SAME FACE AS RINA KURIMI.

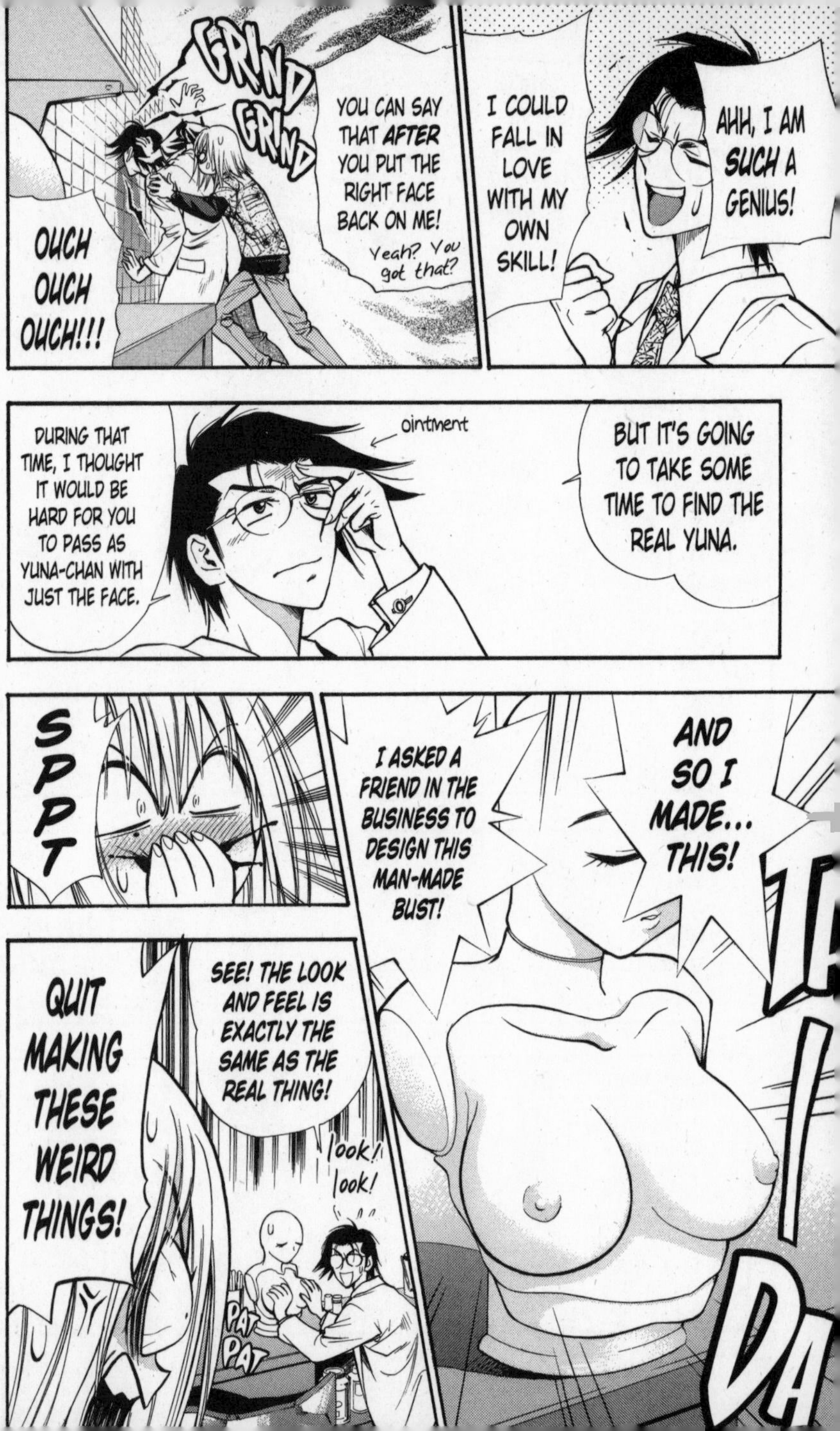
AHH, I AM SUCH A GENIUS!
I COULD FALL IN LOVE WITH MY OWN SKILL!
GRIND GRIND
YOU CAN SAY THAT AFTER YOU PUT THE RIGHT FACE BACK ON ME!
Yeah? You got that?
OUCH OUCH OUCH!!!
BUT IT'S GOING TO TAKE SOME TIME TO FIND THE REAL YUNA.
ointment
DURING THAT TIME, I THOUGHT IT WOULD BE HARD FOR YOU TO PASS AS YUNA-CHAN WITH JUST THE FACE.
AND SO I MADE... THIS!
I ASKED A FRIEND IN THE BUSINESS TO DESIGN THIS MAN-MADE BUST!
SPPT
SEE! THE LOOK AND FEEL IS EXACTLY THE SAME AS THE REAL THING!
look! look!
PAT PAT
QUIT MAKING THESE WEIRD THINGS!

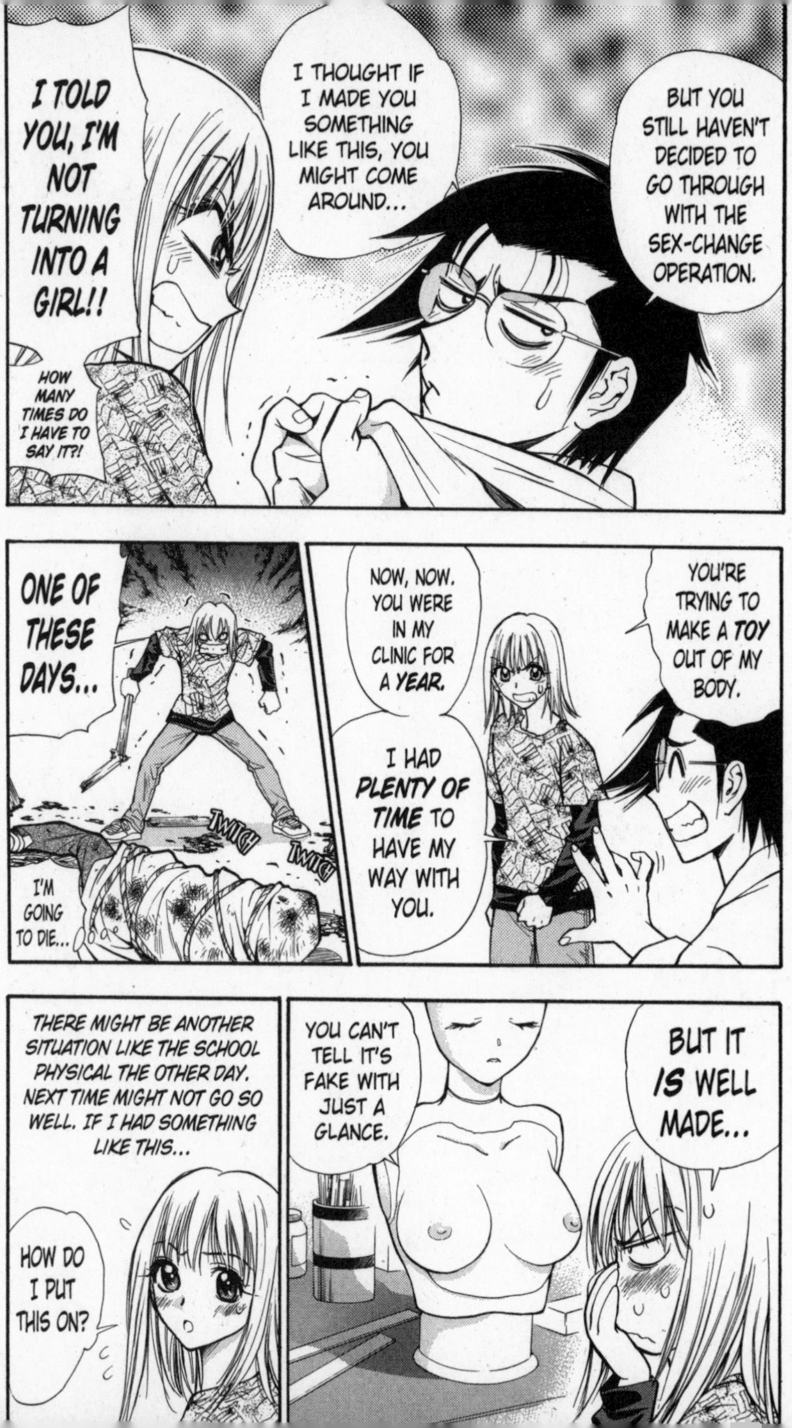
BUT YOU STILL HAVEN'T DECIDED TO GO THROUGH WITH THE SEX-CHANGE OPERATION.
I THOUGHT IF I MADE YOU SOMETHING LIKE THIS, YOU MIGHT COME AROUND...
I TOLD YOU, I'M NOT TURNING INTO A GIRL!!
HOW MANY TIMES DO I HAVE TO SAY IT?!
YOU'RE TRYING TO MAKE A TOY OUT OF MY BODY.
NOW, NOW. YOU WERE IN MY CLINIC FOR A YEAR.
I HAD PLENTY OF TIME TO HAVE MY WAY WITH YOU.
ONE OF THESE DAYS...
TWITCH
TWITCH
I'M GOING TO DIE...
BUT IT IS WELL MADE...
YOU CAN'T TELL IT'S FAKE WITH JUST A GLANCE.
THERE MIGHT BE ANOTHER SITUATION LIKE THE SCHOOL PHYSICAL THE OTHER DAY. NEXT TIME MIGHT NOT GO SO WELL. IF I HAD SOMETHING LIKE THIS...
HOW DO I PUT THIS ON?

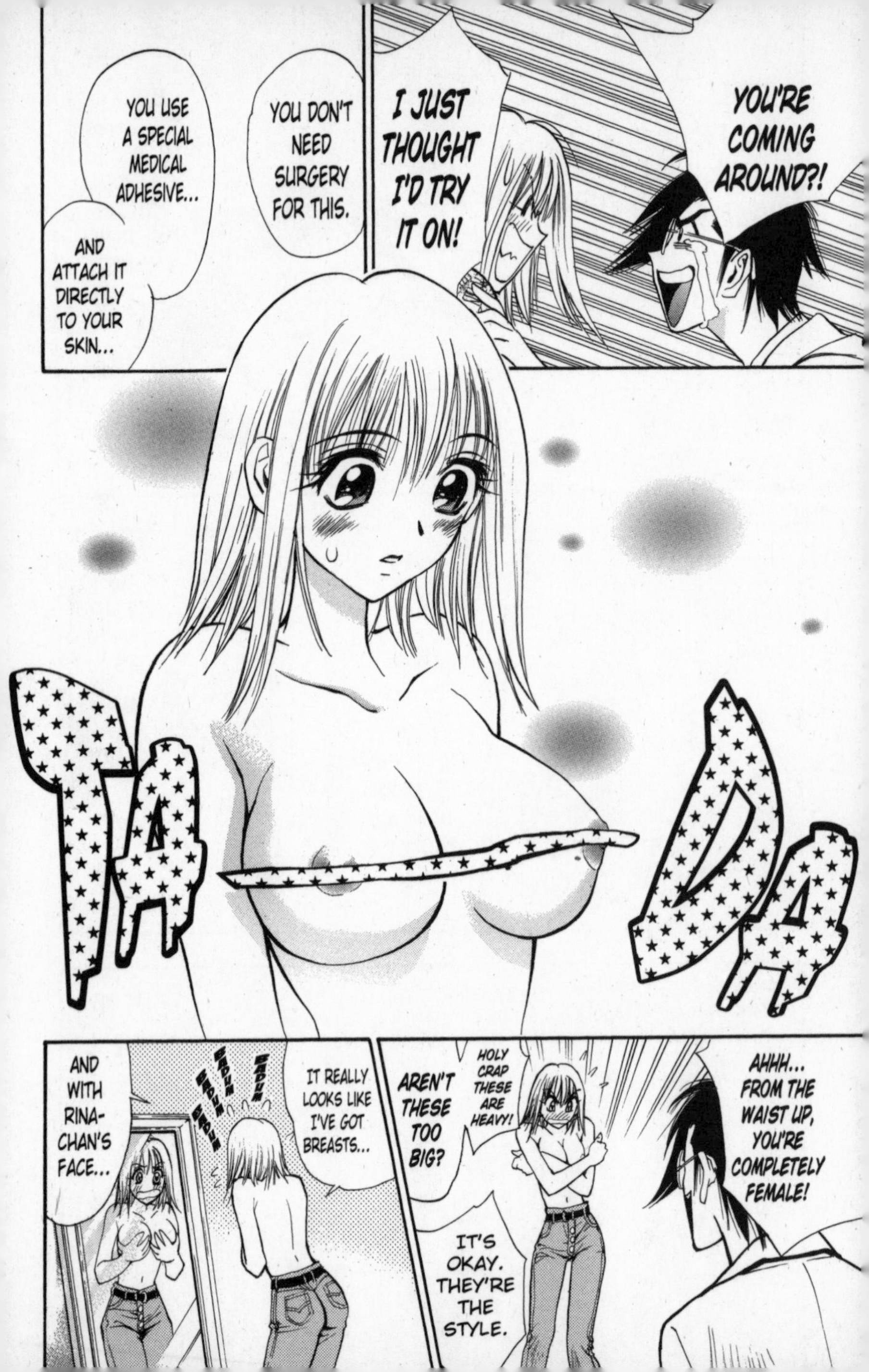
YOU'RE COMING AROUND?!
I JUST THOUGHT I'D TRY IT ON!
YOU DON'T NEED SURGERY FOR THIS.
YOU USE A SPECIAL MEDICAL ADHESIVE...
AND ATTACH IT DIRECTLY TO YOUR SKIN...
TA DA
AHHH... FROM THE WAIST UP, YOU'RE COMPLETELY FEMALE!
HOLY CRAP THESE ARE HEAVY!
AREN'T THESE TOO BIG?
IT'S OKAY. THEY'RE THE STYLE.
IT REALLY LOOKS LIKE I'VE GOT BREASTS...
AND WITH RINA-CHAN'S FACE...

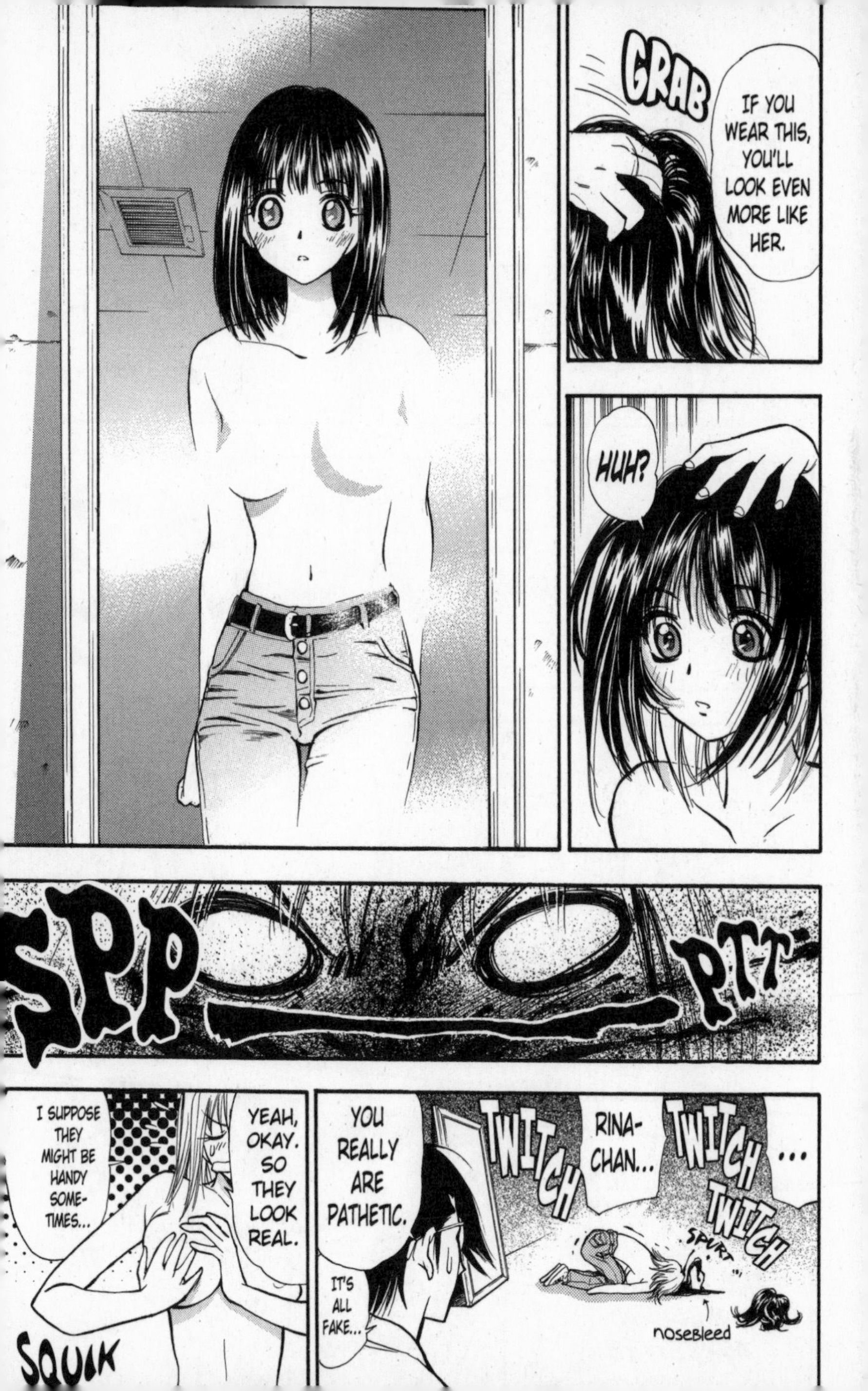
GRAB
IF YOU WEAR THIS, YOU'LL LOOK EVEN MORE LIKE HER.
HUH?
SPP
PTT
...
TWITCH TWITCH
RINA-CHAN...
TWITCH
SPURT
nosebleed
YOU REALLY ARE PATHETIC.
IT'S ALL FAKE...
YEAH, OKAY. SO THEY LOOK REAL.
I SUPPOSE THEY MIGHT BE HANDY SOME-TIMES...
SQUIK

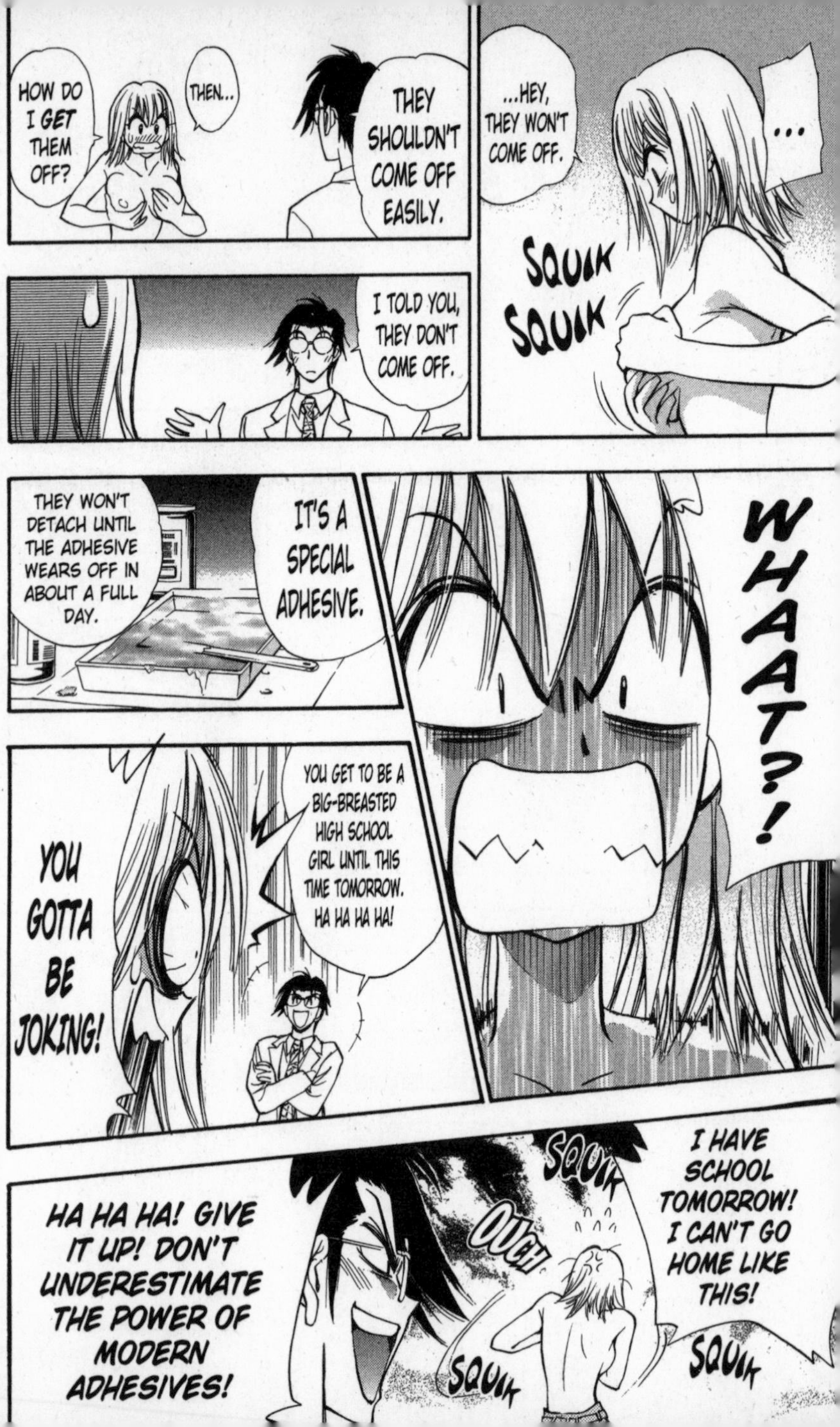
...HEY, THEY WON'T COME OFF.
...
SQUIK SQUIK
THEY SHOULDN'T COME OFF EASILY.
THEN...
HOW DO I GET THEM OFF?
I TOLD YOU, THEY DON'T COME OFF.
WHAAT?!
IT'S A SPECIAL ADHESIVE.
THEY WON'T DETACH UNTIL THE ADHESIVE WEARS OFF IN ABOUT A FULL DAY.
YOU GET TO BE A BIG-BREASTED HIGH SCHOOL GIRL UNTIL THIS TIME TOMORROW. HA HA HA HA!
YOU GOTTA BE JOKING!
I HAVE SCHOOL TOMORROW! I CAN'T GO HOME LIKE THIS!
SQUIK
OUCH
SQUIK
SQUIK
HA HA HA! GIVE IT UP! DON'T UNDERESTIMATE THE POWER OF MODERN ADHESIVES!

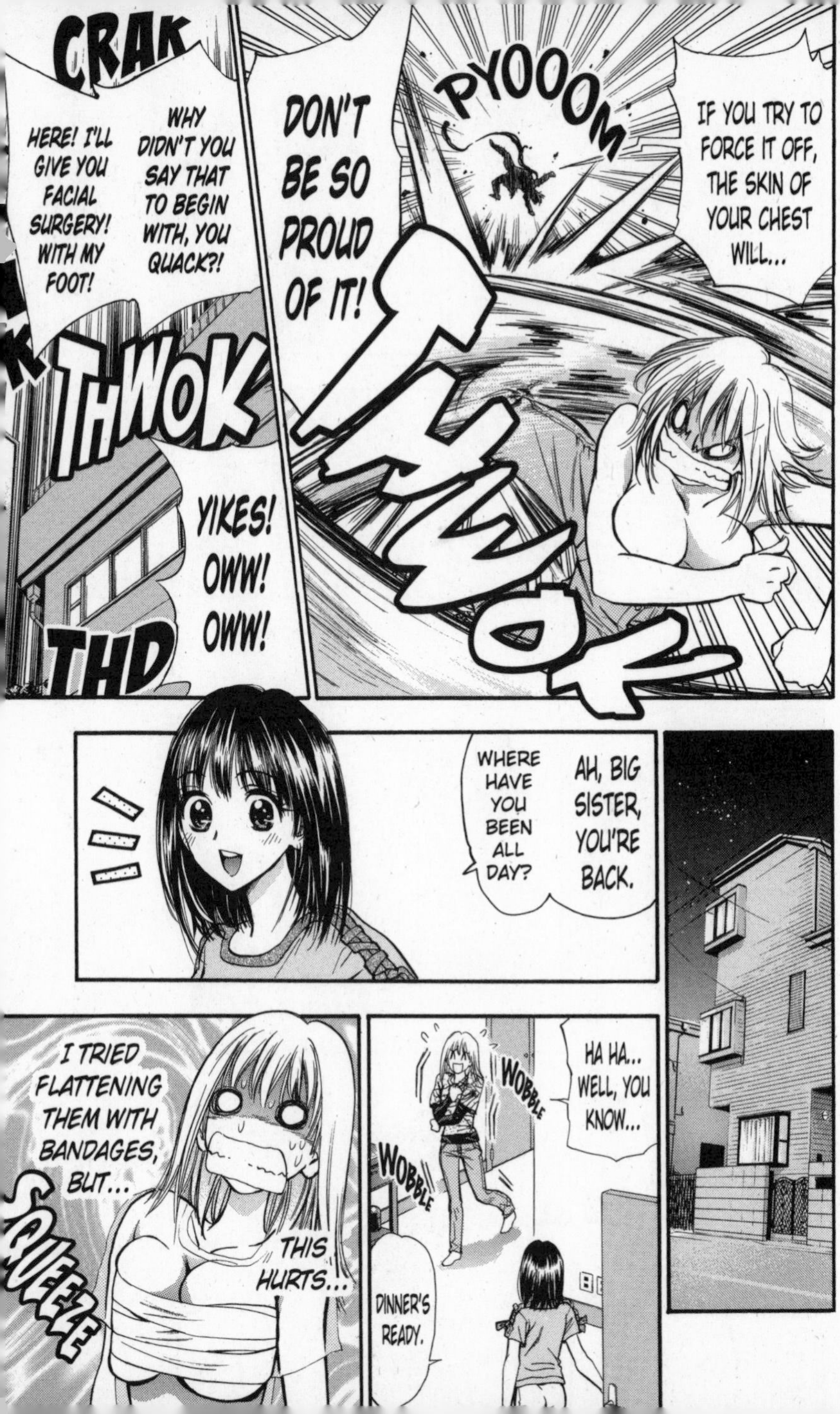
IF YOU TRY TO FORCE IT OFF, THE SKIN OF YOUR CHEST WILL...
PYOOOM
DON'T BE SO PROUD OF IT!
THWOK
WHY DIDN'T YOU SAY THAT TO BEGIN WITH, YOU QUACK?!
HERE! I'LL GIVE YOU FACIAL SURGERY! WITH MY FOOT!
CRAK
THWOK
YIKES! OWW! OWW!
THD
AH, BIG SISTER, YOU'RE BACK.
WHERE HAVE YOU BEEN ALL DAY?
HA HA... WELL, YOU KNOW...
WOBBLE
WOBBLE
DINNER'S READY.
I TRIED FLATTENING THEM WITH BANDAGES, BUT...
THIS HURTS...
SQUEEZE

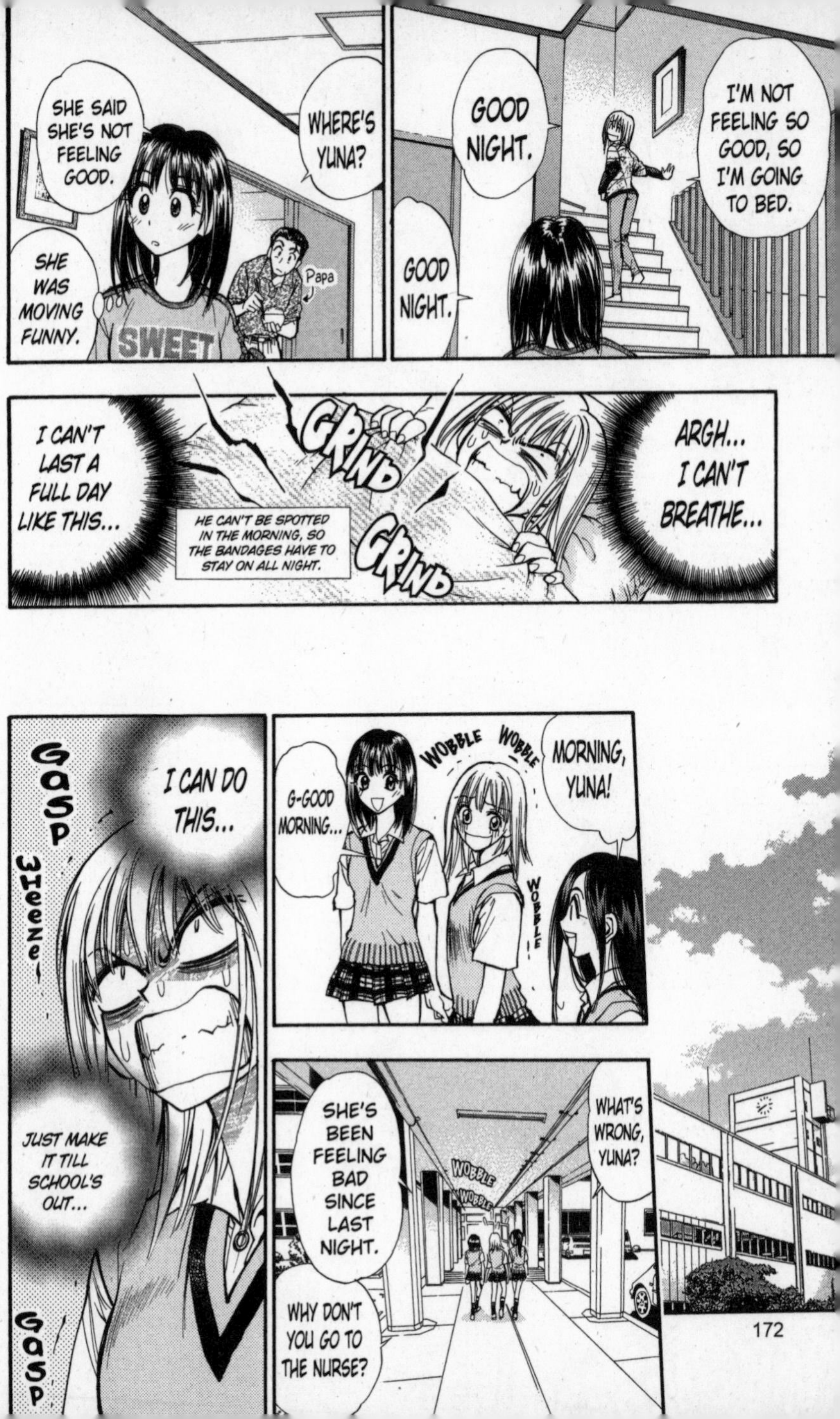
I'M NOT FEELING SO GOOD, SO I'M GOING TO BED.
GOOD NIGHT.
GOOD NIGHT.
WHERE'S YUNA?
SHE SAID SHE'S NOT FEELING GOOD.
Papa
SHE WAS MOVING FUNNY.
SWEET
ARGH... I CAN'T BREATHE...
GRIND
GRIND
HE CAN'T BE SPOTTED IN THE MORNING, SO THE BANDAGES HAVE TO STAY ON ALL NIGHT.
I CAN'T LAST A FULL DAY LIKE THIS...
MORNING, YUNA!
WOBBLE WOBBLE
G-GOOD MORNING...
WOBBLE
WHAT'S WRONG, YUNA?
SHE'S BEEN FEELING BAD SINCE LAST NIGHT.
WHY DON'T YOU GO TO THE NURSE?
WOBBLE
WOBBLE
I CAN DO THIS...
GASP
WHEEZE
JUST MAKE IT TILL SCHOOL'S OUT...
GASP

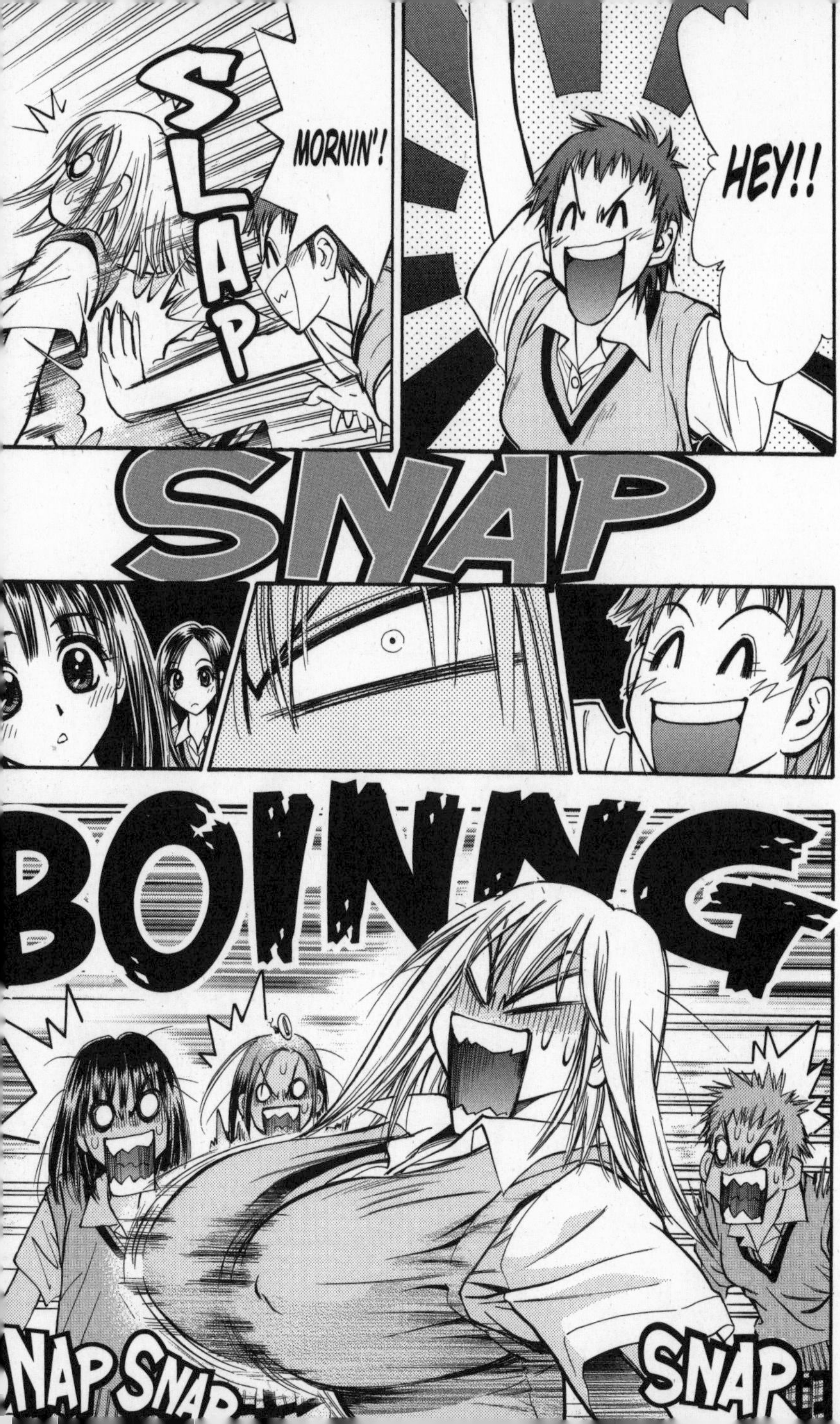
HEY!!
SLAP
MORNIN'!
SNAP
BOINNG
SNAP
NAP SNAP

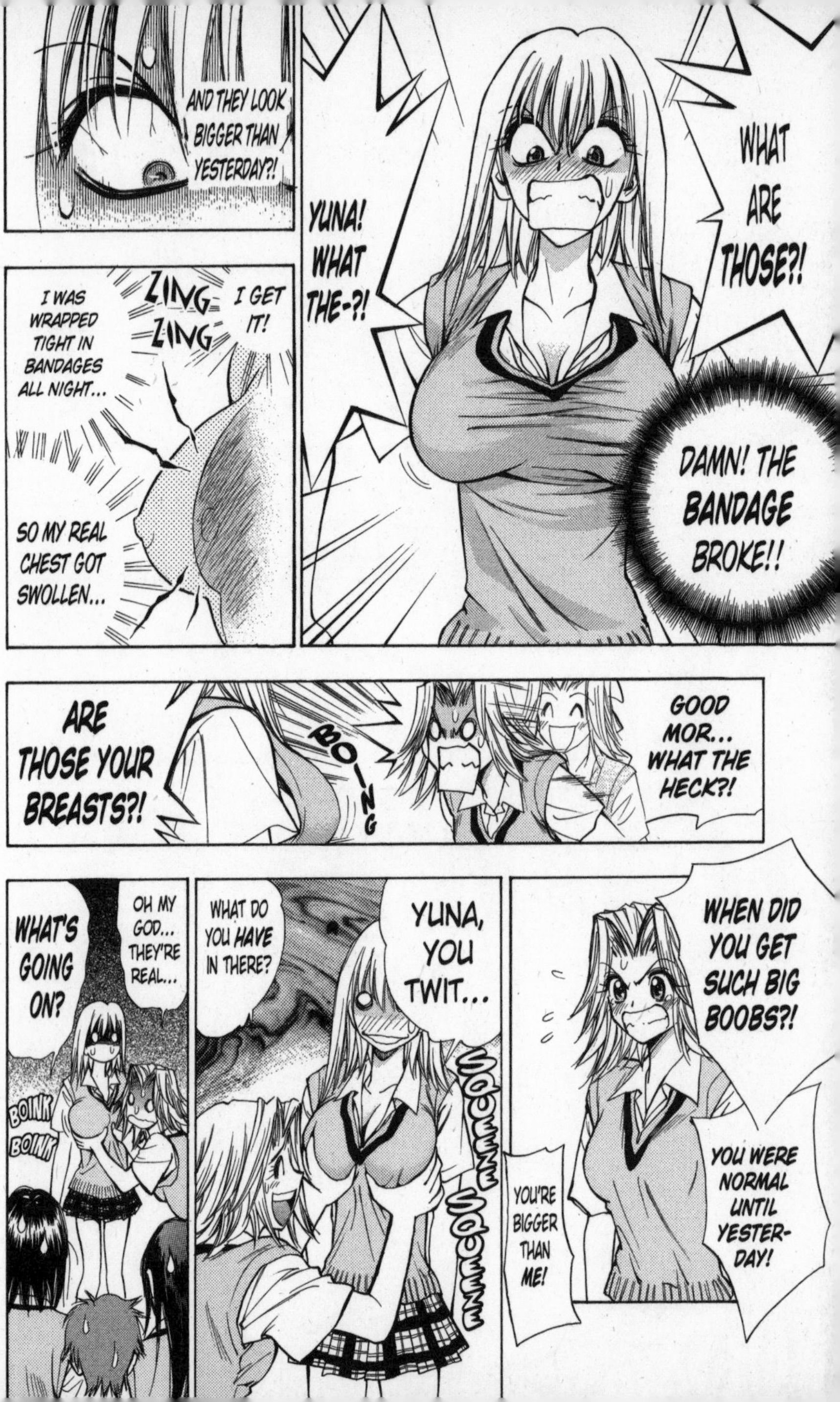
WHAT ARE THOSE?!
YUNA! WHAT THE-?!
DAMN! THE BANDAGE BROKE!!
AND THEY LOOK BIGGER THAN YESTERDAY?!
I GET IT!
ZING ZING
I WAS WRAPPED TIGHT IN BANDAGES ALL NIGHT...
SO MY REAL CHEST GOT SWOLLEN...
GOOD MOR... WHAT THE HECK?!
BO-I-N-G
ARE THOSE YOUR BREASTS?!
WHEN DID YOU GET SUCH BIG BOOBS?!
YOU WERE NORMAL UNTIL YESTER-DAY!
YUNA, YOU TWIT...
WHAT DO YOU HAVE IN THERE?
YOU'RE BIGGER THAN ME!
OH MY GOD... THEY'RE REAL...
WHAT'S GOING ON?
BOINK BOINK

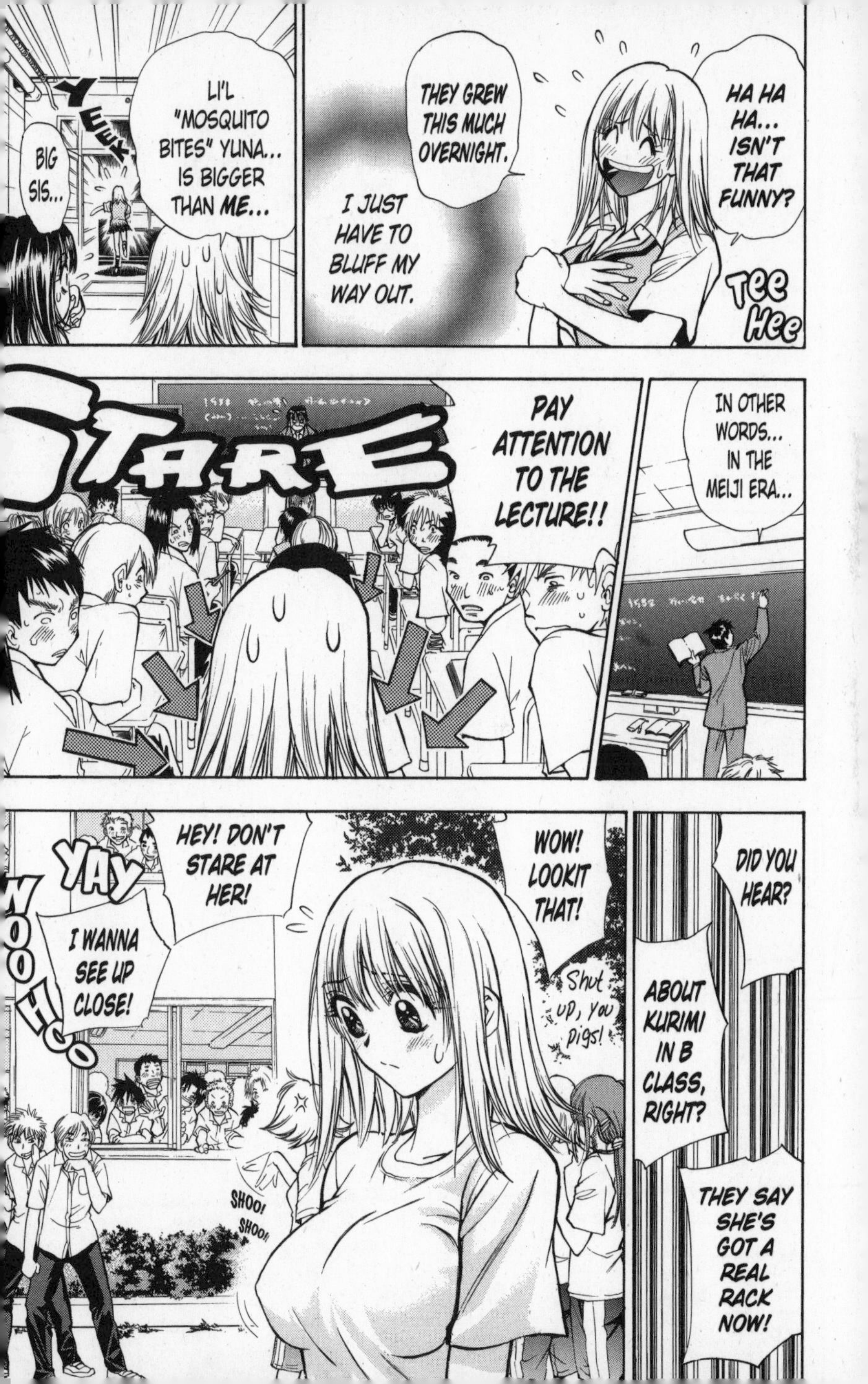

HA HA HA... ISN'T THAT FUNNY?
TEE HEE
THEY GREW THIS MUCH OVERNIGHT.
I JUST HAVE TO BLUFF MY WAY OUT.
LI'L "MOSQUITO BITES" YUNA... IS BIGGER THAN ME...
YEEK
BIG SIS...
IN OTHER WORDS... IN THE MEIJI ERA...
PAY ATTENTION TO THE LECTURE!!
STARE
DID YOU HEAR?
ABOUT KURIMI IN B CLASS, RIGHT?
THEY SAY SHE'S GOT A REAL RACK NOW!
WOW! LOOKIT THAT!
Shut up, you pigs!
HEY! DON'T STARE AT HER!
YAY
I WANNA SEE UP CLOSE!
WOOHOO
SHOO! SHOO!!

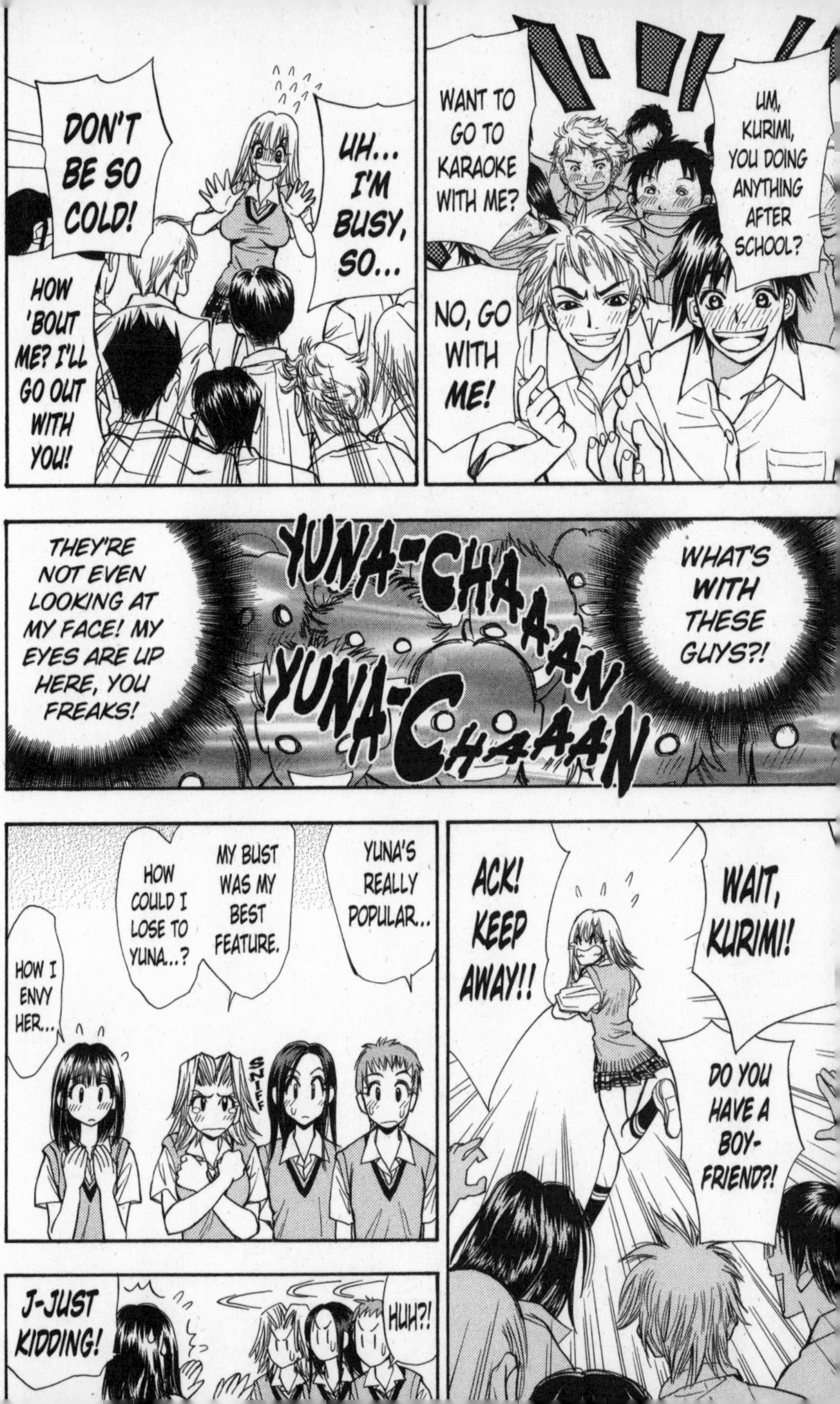
UM, KURIMI, YOU DOING ANYTHING AFTER SCHOOL?
WANT TO GO TO KARAOKE WITH ME?
NO, GO WITH ME!
UH... I'M BUSY, SO...
DON'T BE SO COLD!
HOW 'BOUT ME? I'LL GO OUT WITH YOU!
WHAT'S WITH THESE GUYS?!
YUNA-CHAAAN
YUNA-CHAAAN
THEY'RE NOT EVEN LOOKING AT MY FACE! MY EYES ARE UP HERE, YOU FREAKS!
WAIT, KURIMI!
ACK! KEEP AWAY!!
DO YOU HAVE A BOY-FRIEND?!
YUNA'S REALLY POPULAR...
MY BUST WAS MY BEST FEATURE.
HOW COULD I LOSE TO YUNA...?
HOW I ENVY HER...
SNIFF
HUH?!
J-JUST KIDDING!

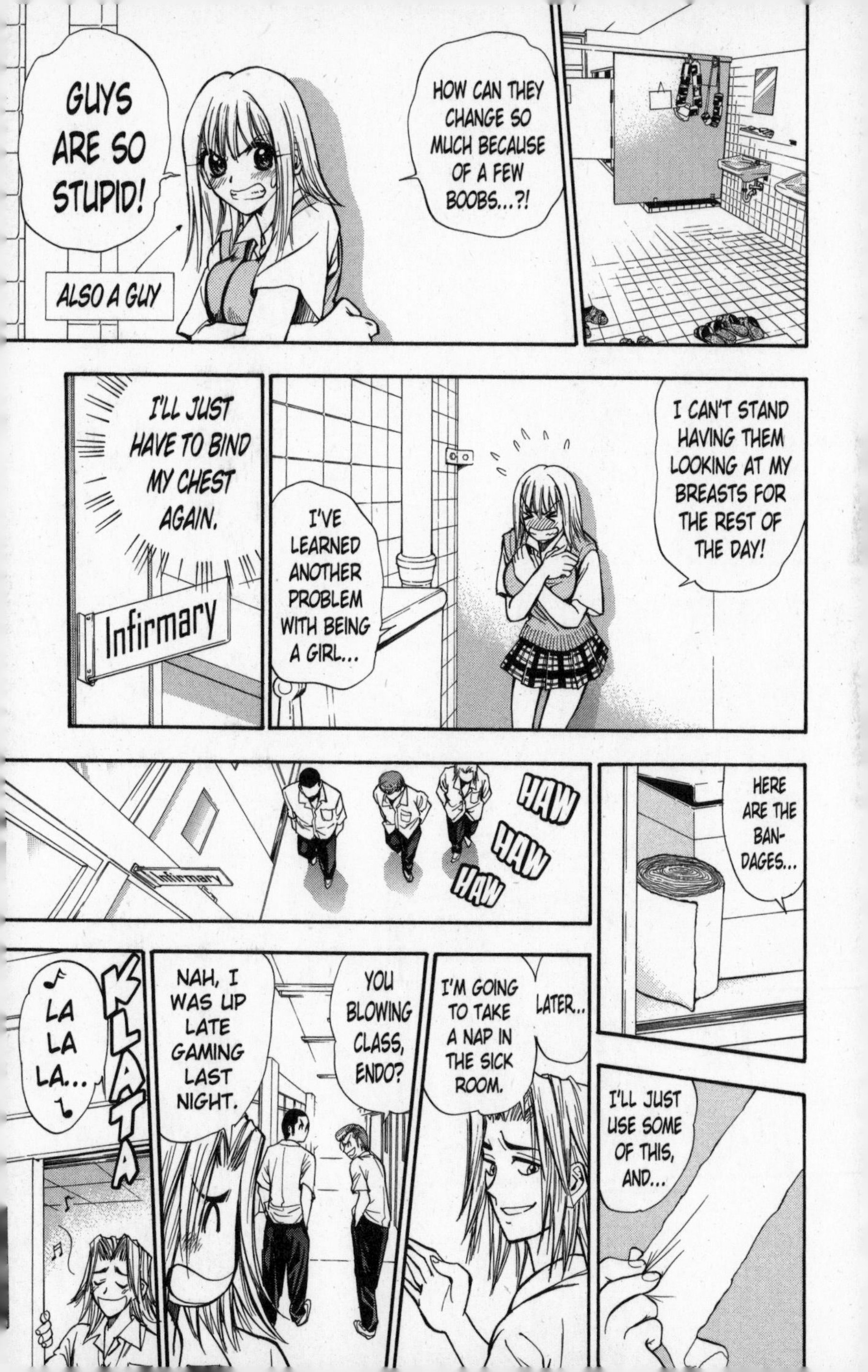

HOW CAN THEY CHANGE SO MUCH BECAUSE OF A FEW BOOBS...?!
GUYS ARE SO STUPID!
ALSO A GUY
I CAN'T STAND HAVING THEM LOOKING AT MY BREASTS FOR THE REST OF THE DAY!
I'VE LEARNED ANOTHER PROBLEM WITH BEING A GIRL...
I'LL JUST HAVE TO BIND MY CHEST AGAIN.
Infirmary
HERE ARE THE BAN-DAGES...
I'LL JUST USE SOME OF THIS, AND...
HAW HAW HAW
Infirmary
I'M GOING TO TAKE A NAP IN THE SICK ROOM.
LATER...
YOU BLOWING CLASS, ENDO?
NAH, I WAS UP LATE GAMING LAST NIGHT.
KLATA
LA LA LA...

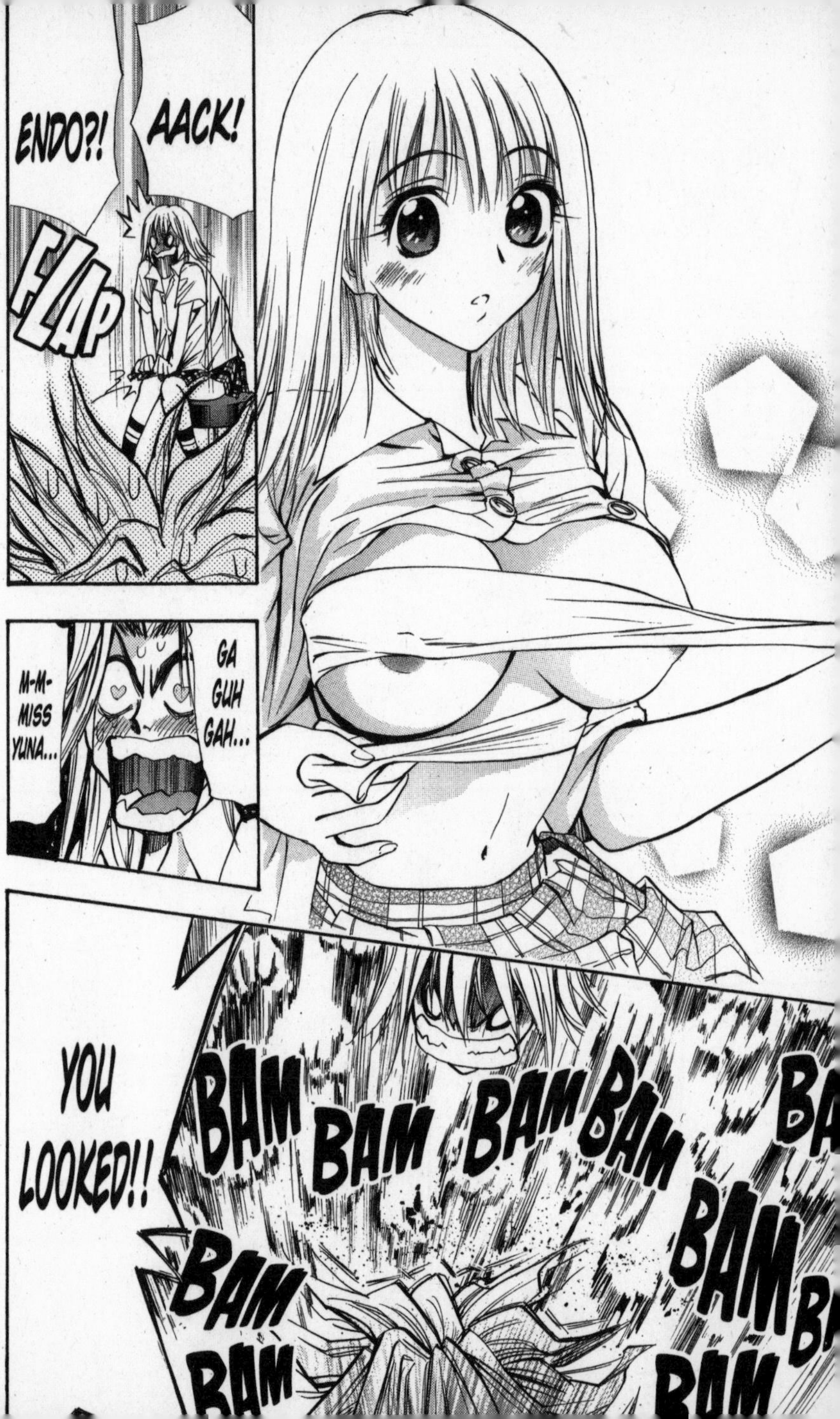
AACK!
ENDO?!
FLAP
GA GUH GAH...
M-M-MISS YUNA...
BAM BAM
BAM BAM BAM
BAM BAM BAM
YOU LOOKED!!
BAM BAM

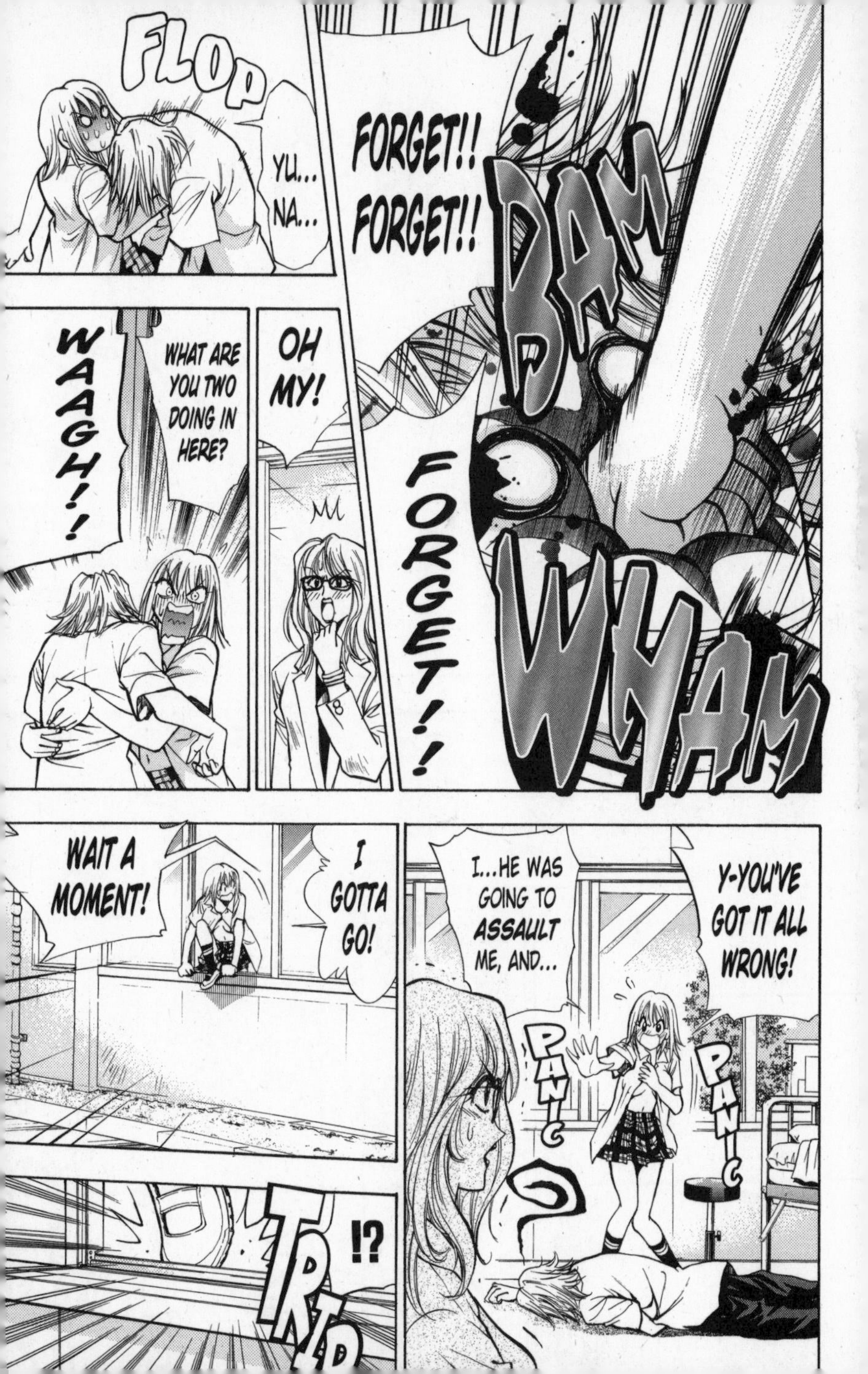
FORGET!! FORGET!!
BAM
FORGET!!
WHAM
FLOP
YU... NA...
OH MY!
WHAT ARE YOU TWO DOING IN HERE?
WAAGH!!
Y-YOU'VE GOT IT ALL WRONG!
I...HE WAS GOING TO ASSAULT ME, AND...
PANIC
PANIC
?
I GOTTA GO!
WAIT A MOMENT!
!?
TRIP

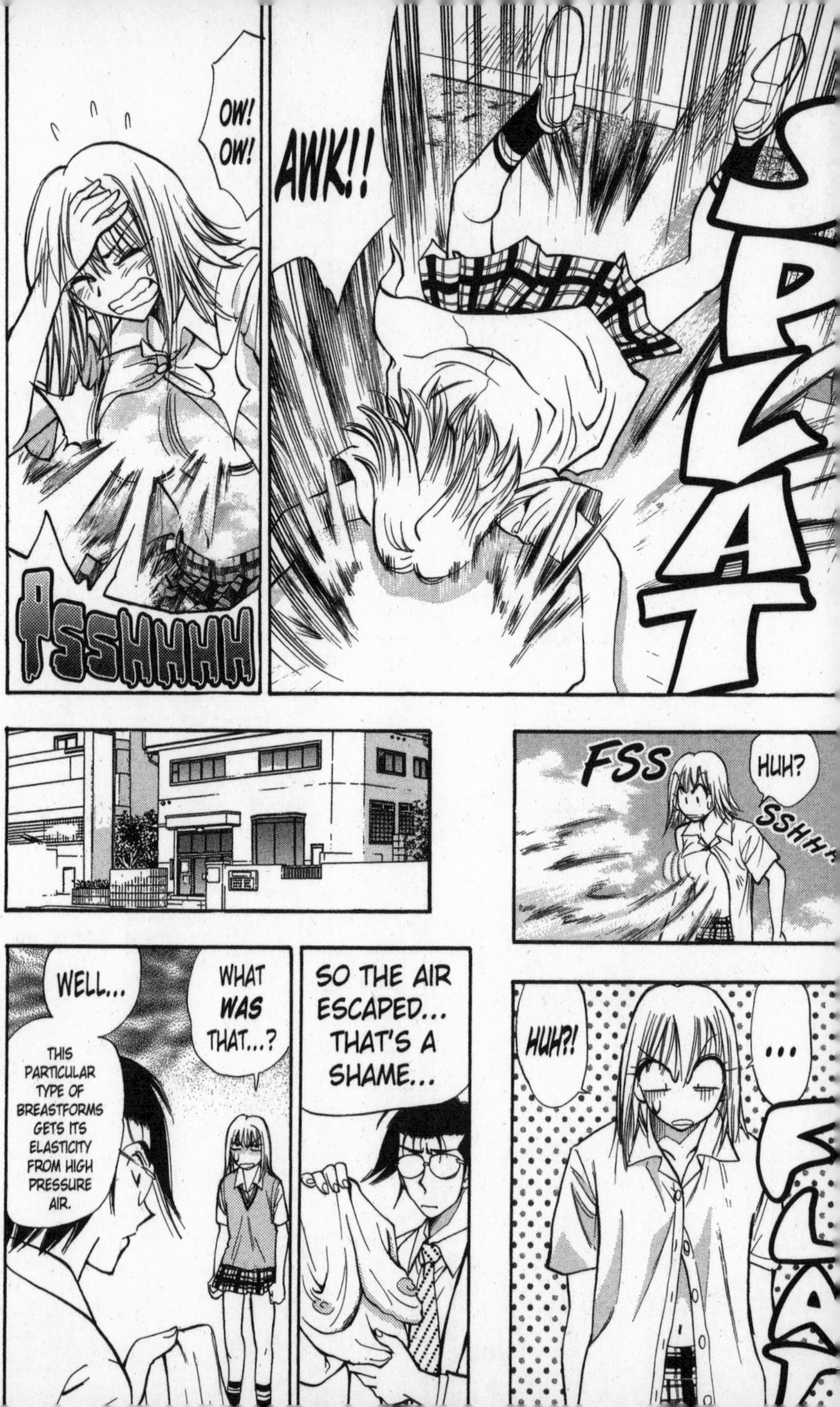
SPLAT
AWK!!
OW! OW!
PSSHHHH
HUH?
FSS
...
HUH?!
SO THE AIR ESCAPED... THAT'S A SHAME...
WHAT WAS THAT...?
WELL...
THIS PARTICULAR TYPE OF BREASTFORMS GETS ITS ELASTICITY FROM HIGH PRESSURE AIR.

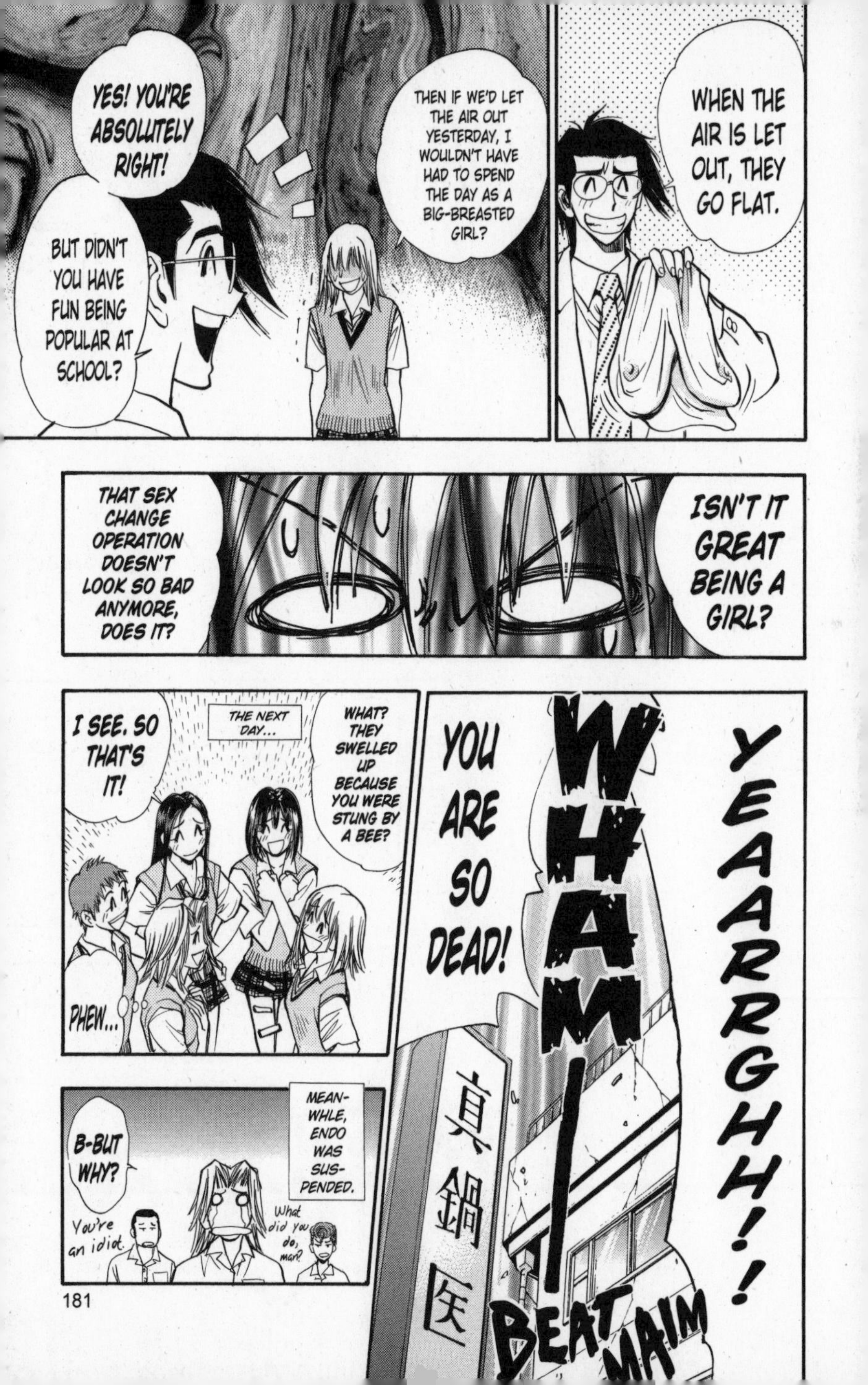
WHEN THE AIR IS LET OUT, THEY GO FLAT.
THEN IF WE'D LET THE AIR OUT YESTERDAY, I WOULDN'T HAVE HAD TO SPEND THE DAY AS A BIG-BREASTED GIRL?
YES! YOU'RE ABSOLUTELY RIGHT!
BUT DIDN'T YOU HAVE FUN BEING POPULAR AT SCHOOL?
ISN'T IT GREAT BEING A GIRL?
THAT SEX CHANGE OPERATION DOESN'T LOOK SO BAD ANYMORE, DOES IT?
YEAARRGHH!!
WHAM!
YOU ARE SO DEAD!
真鍋医
BEAT
MAIM
THE NEXT DAY...
WHAT? THEY SWELLED UP BECAUSE YOU WERE STUNG BY A BEE?
I SEE. SO THAT'S IT!
PHEW...
MEAN-WHLE, ENDO WAS SUS-PENDED.
B-BUT WHY?
What did you do, man?
You're an idiot.

Pretty Face

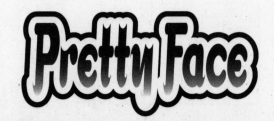

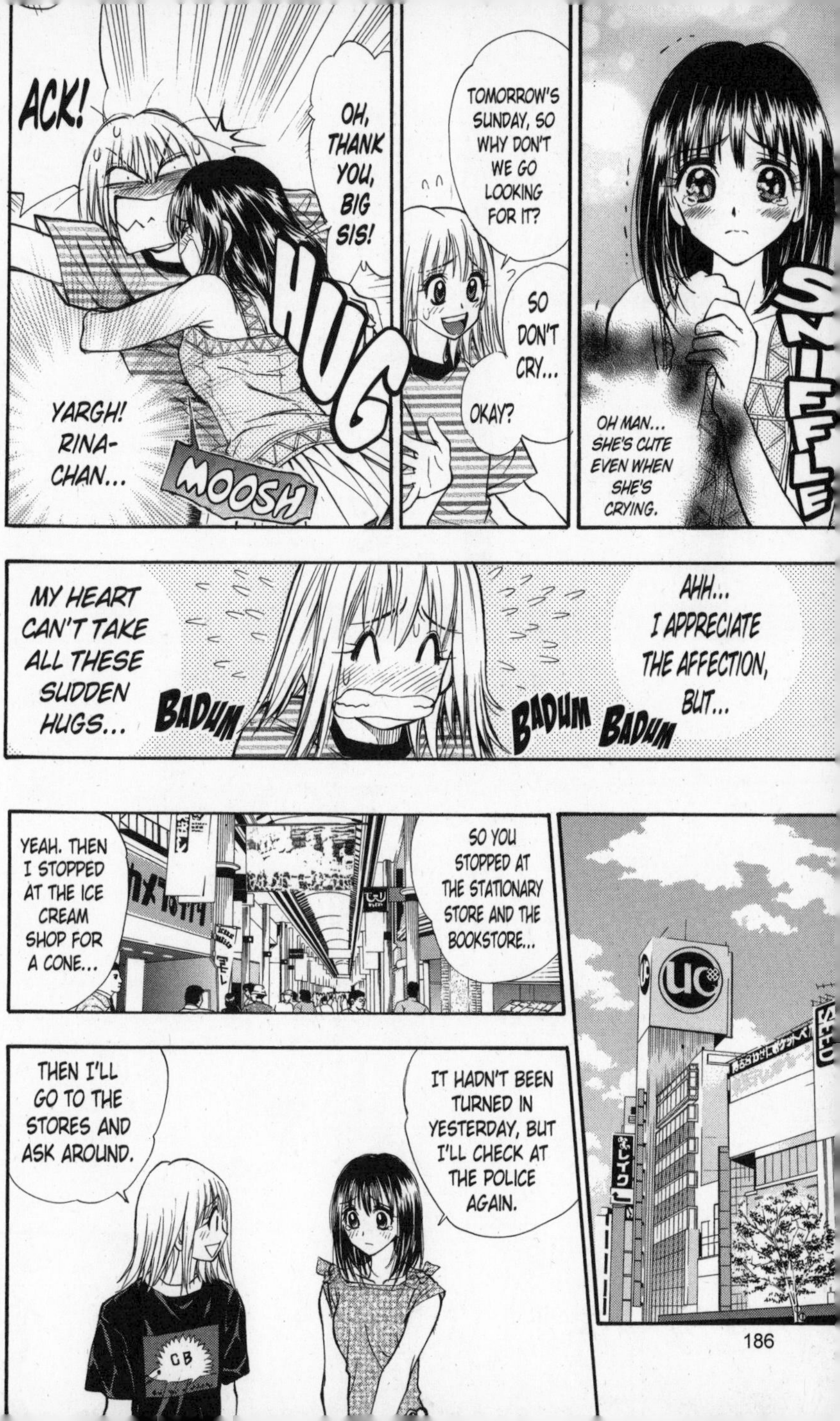
SNIFFLE
OH MAN... SHE'S CUTE EVEN WHEN SHE'S CRYING.
TOMORROW'S SUNDAY, SO WHY DON'T WE GO LOOKING FOR IT?
SO DON'T CRY...
OKAY?
OH, THANK YOU, BIG SIS!
HUG
ACK!
YARGH! RINA-CHAN...
MOOSH
AHH... I APPRECIATE THE AFFECTION, BUT...
BADUM BADUM
BADUM
MY HEART CAN'T TAKE ALL THESE SUDDEN HUGS...
BADUM
SO YOU STOPPED AT THE STATIONARY STORE AND THE BOOKSTORE...
YEAH. THEN I STOPPED AT THE ICE CREAM SHOP FOR A CONE...
IT HADN'T BEEN TURNED IN YESTERDAY, BUT I'LL CHECK AT THE POLICE AGAIN.
THEN I'LL GO TO THE STORES AND ASK AROUND.

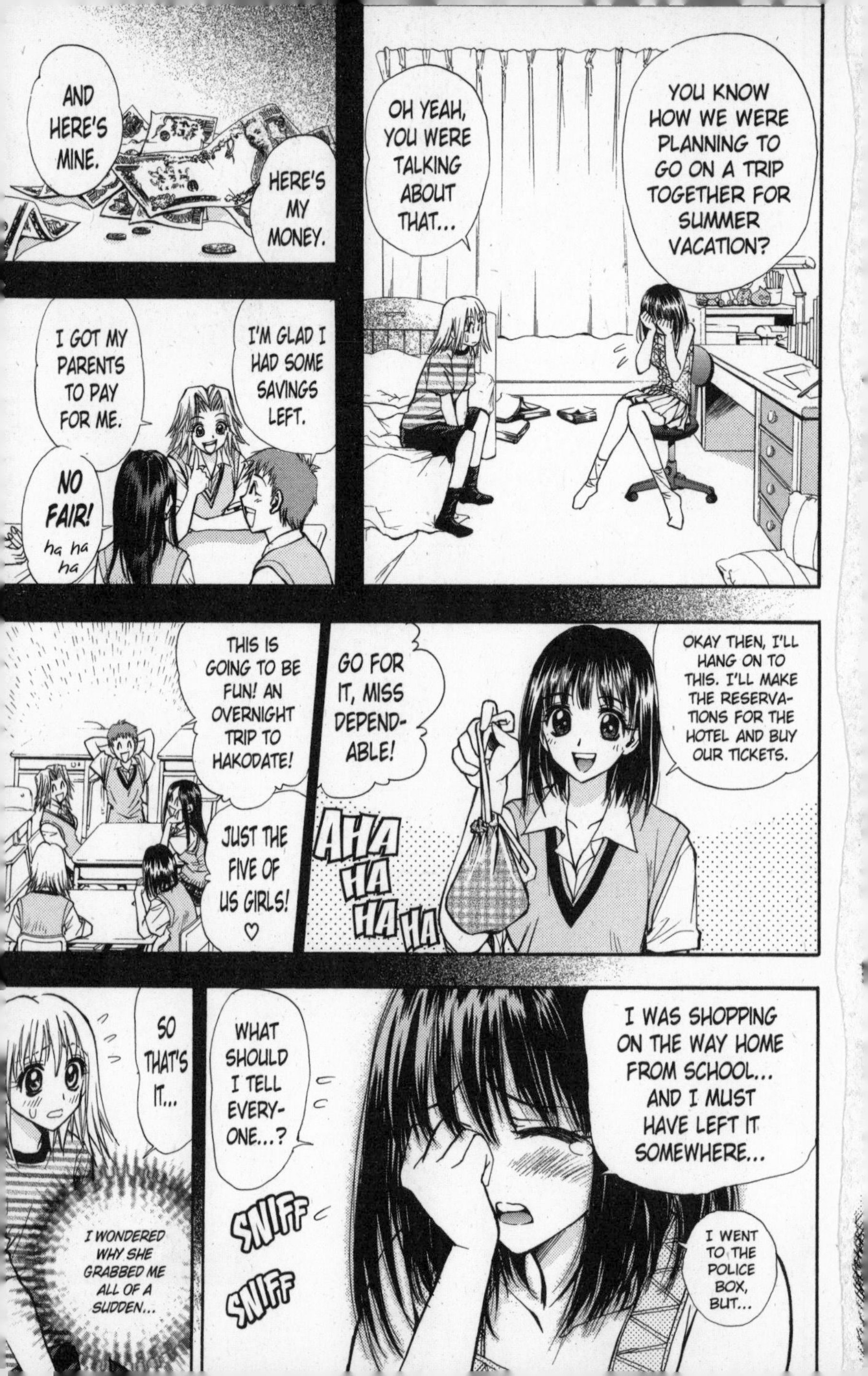
YOU KNOW HOW WE WERE PLANNING TO GO ON A TRIP TOGETHER FOR SUMMER VACATION?
OH YEAH, YOU WERE TALKING ABOUT THAT...
HERE'S MY MONEY.
AND HERE'S MINE.
I'M GLAD I HAD SOME SAVINGS LEFT.
I GOT MY PARENTS TO PAY FOR ME.
NO FAIR!
ha ha ha
OKAY THEN, I'LL HANG ON TO THIS. I'LL MAKE THE RESERVA-TIONS FOR THE HOTEL AND BUY OUR TICKETS.
AHA HA HA HA
GO FOR IT, MISS DEPEND-ABLE!
THIS IS GOING TO BE FUN! AN OVERNIGHT TRIP TO HAKODATE!
JUST THE FIVE OF US GIRLS! ♡
I WAS SHOPPING ON THE WAY HOME FROM SCHOOL... AND I MUST HAVE LEFT IT SOMEWHERE...
I WENT TO THE POLICE BOX, BUT...
WHAT SHOULD I TELL EVERY-ONE...?
SNIFF
SNIFF
SO THAT'S IT...
I WONDERED WHY SHE GRABBED ME ALL OF A SUDDEN...

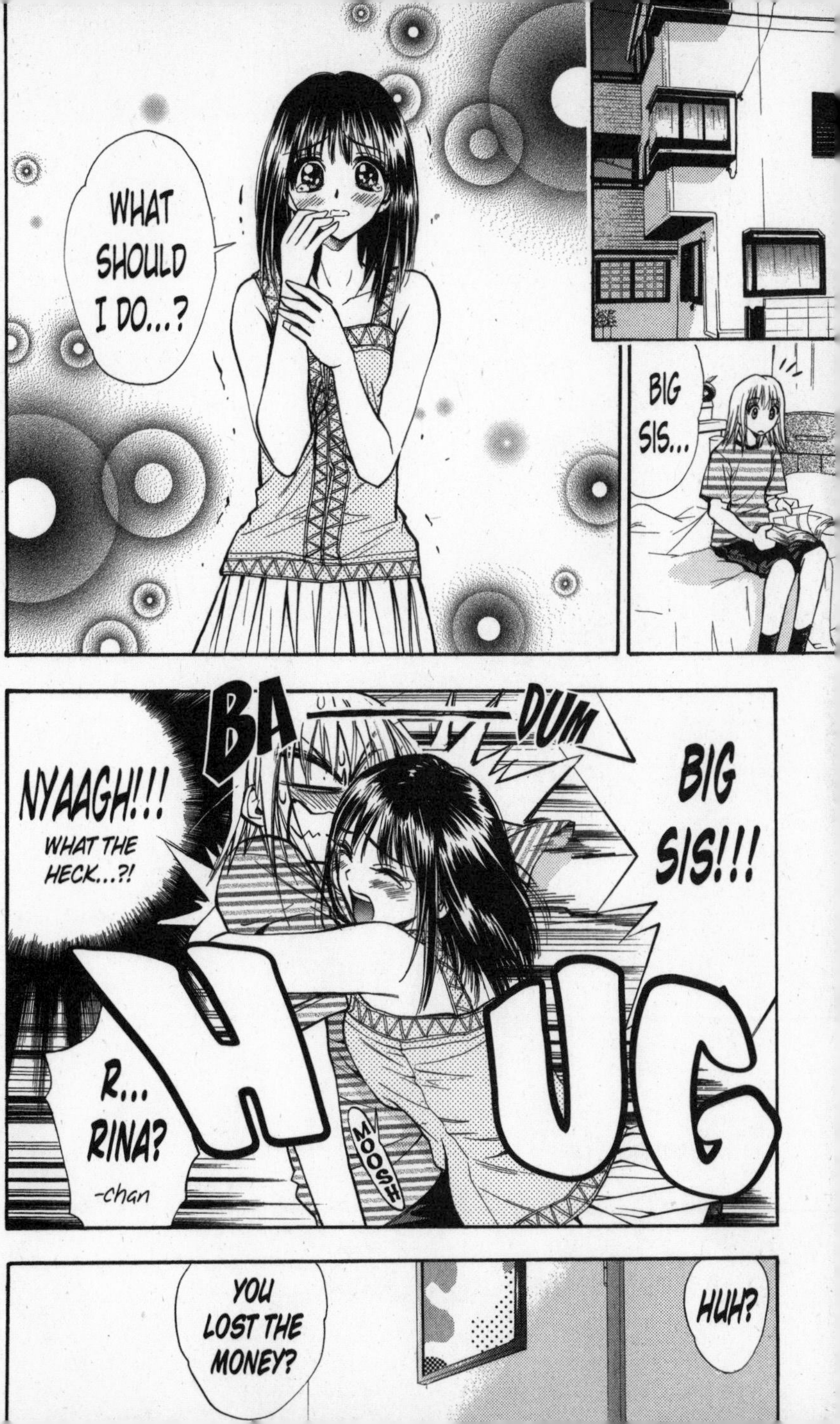
BIG SIS...
WHAT SHOULD I DO...?
BA—DUM
BIG SIS!!!
NYAAGH!!! WHAT THE HECK...?!
HUG
MOOSH
R... RINA? -chan
HUH?
YOU LOST THE MONEY?

Chapter 8: You Think You're Tough?

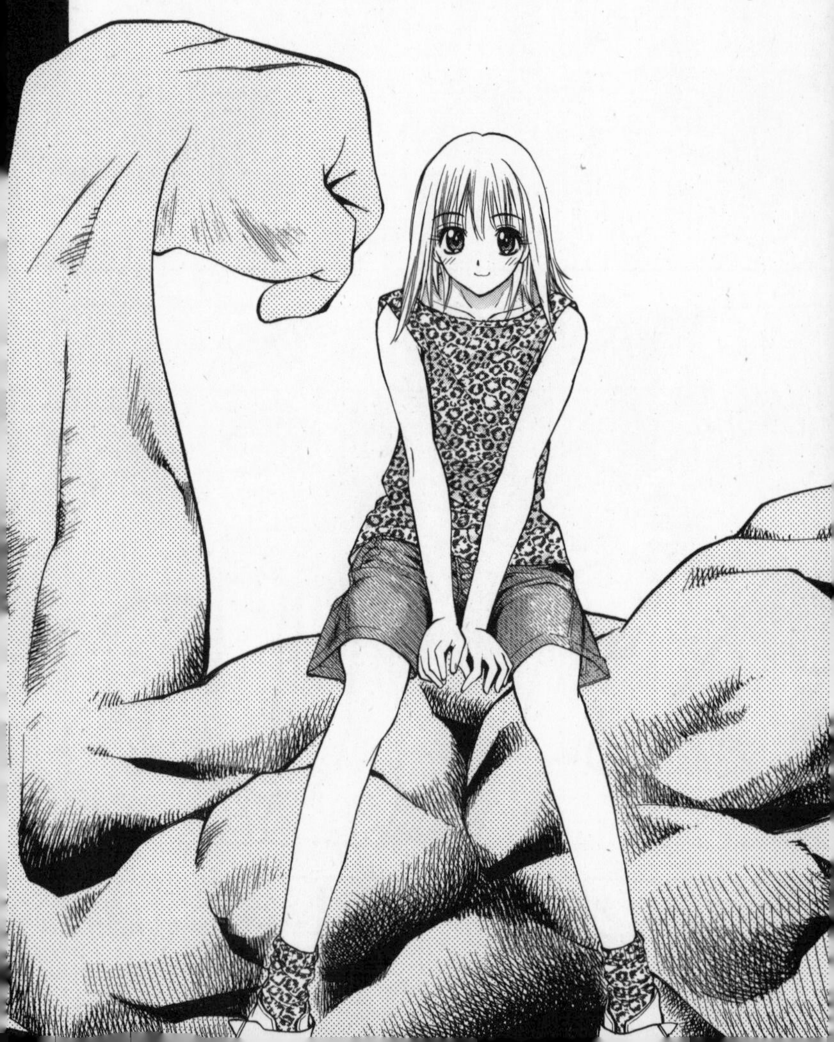

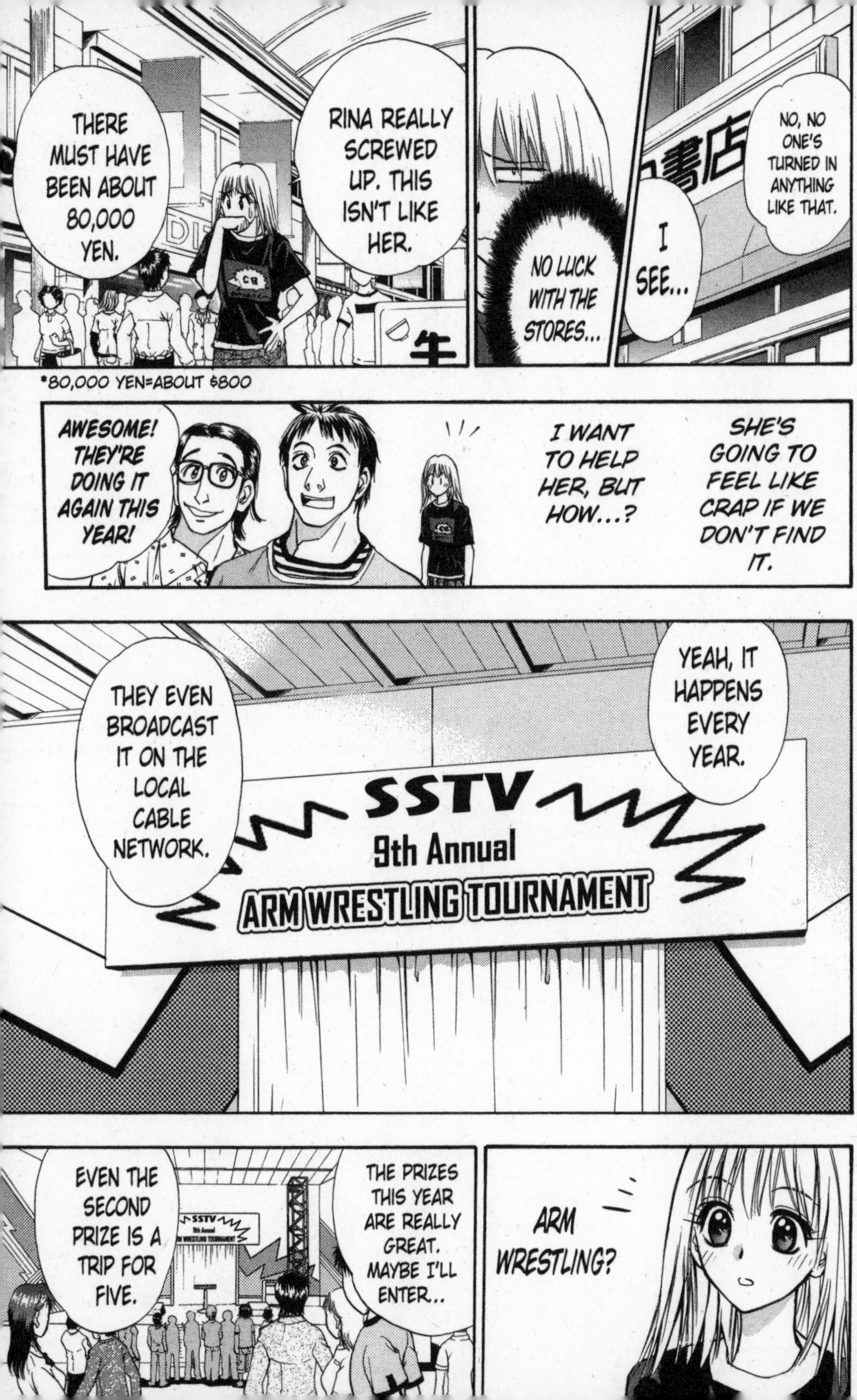
NO, NO ONE'S TURNED IN ANYTHING LIKE THAT.
I SEE...
NO LUCK WITH THE STORES...
RINA REALLY SCREWED UP. THIS ISN'T LIKE HER.
THERE MUST HAVE BEEN ABOUT 80,000 YEN.
*80,000 YEN=ABOUT $800
SHE'S GOING TO FEEL LIKE CRAP IF WE DON'T FIND IT.
I WANT TO HELP HER, BUT HOW...?
AWESOME! THEY'RE DOING IT AGAIN THIS YEAR!
YEAH, IT HAPPENS EVERY YEAR.
SSTV
9th Annual
ARM WRESTLING TOURNAMENT
THEY EVEN BROADCAST IT ON THE LOCAL CABLE NETWORK.
ARM WRESTLING?
THE PRIZES THIS YEAR ARE REALLY GREAT. MAYBE I'LL ENTER...
EVEN THE SECOND PRIZE IS A TRIP FOR FIVE.

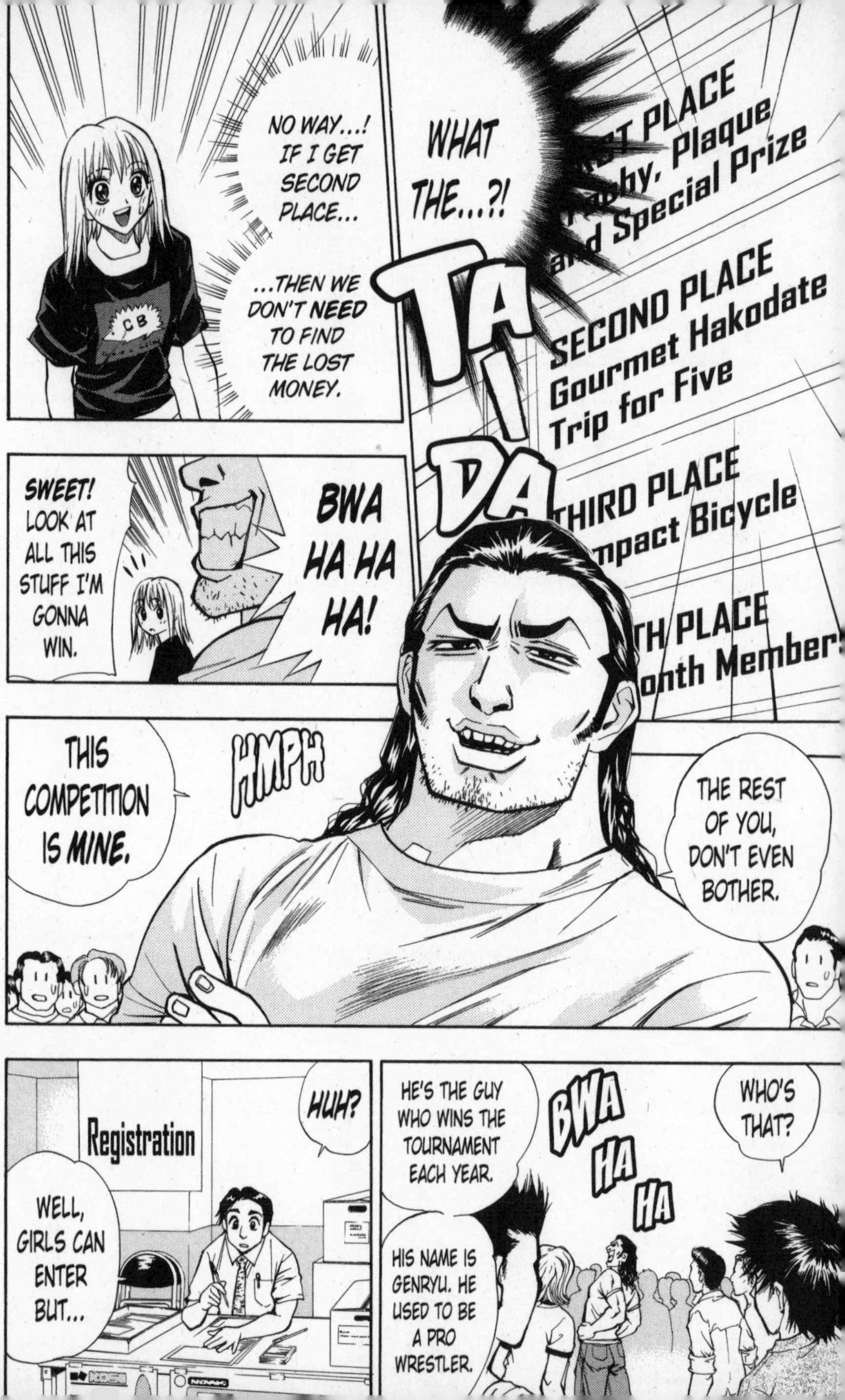
WHAT THE...?!
TA I DA
and Special Prize
SECOND PLACE
Gourmet Hakodate
Trip for Five
THIRD PLACE
NO WAY...! IF I GET SECOND PLACE...
...THEN WE DON'T NEED TO FIND THE LOST MONEY.
BWA HA HA HA!
SWEET! LOOK AT ALL THIS STUFF I'M GONNA WIN.
THE REST OF YOU, DON'T EVEN BOTHER.
HMPH
THIS COMPETITION IS MINE.
WHO'S THAT?
BWA HA HA
HE'S THE GUY WHO WINS THE TOURNAMENT EACH YEAR.
HIS NAME IS GENRYU. HE USED TO BE A PRO WRESTLER.
HUH?
Registration
WELL, GIRLS CAN ENTER BUT...

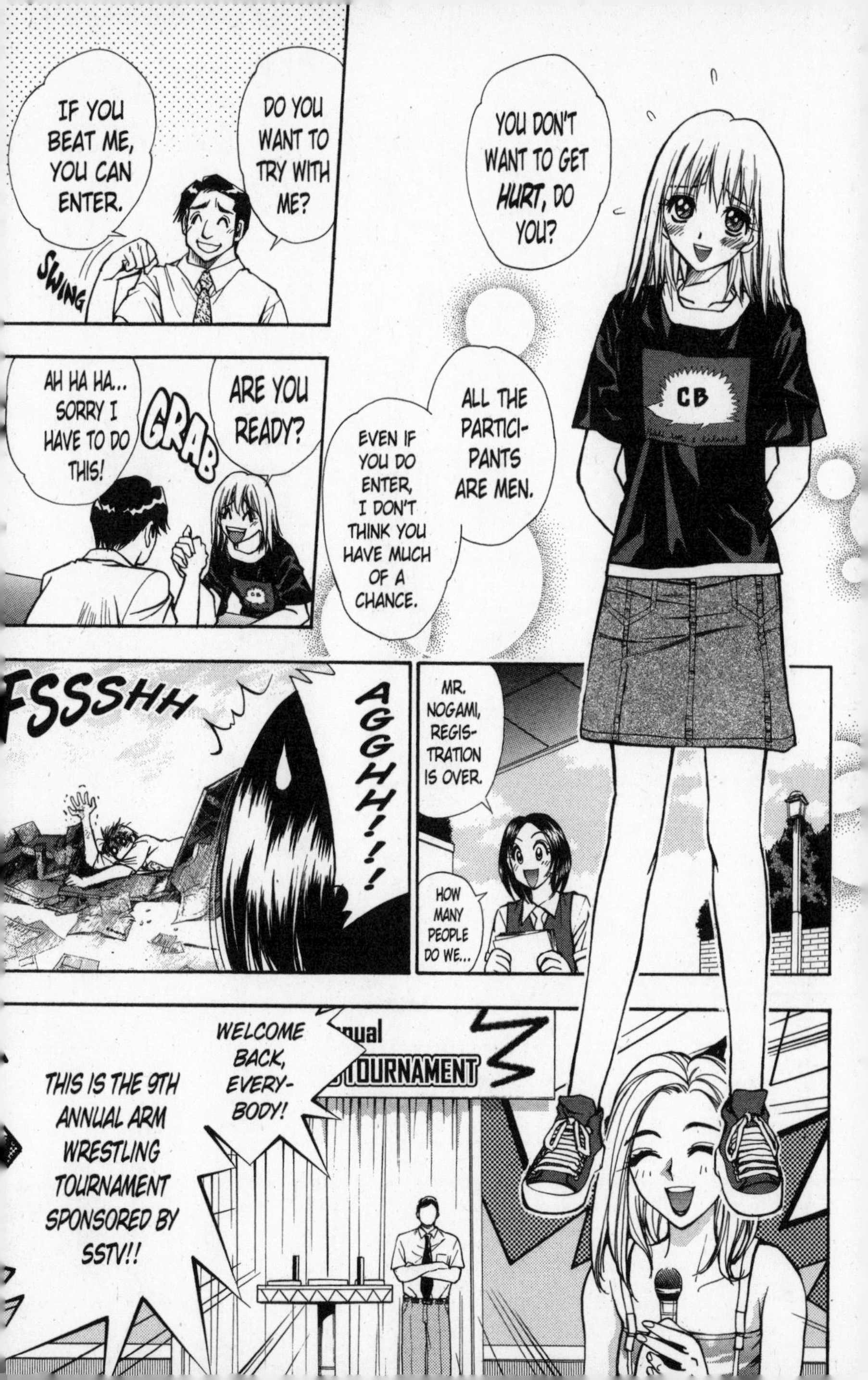
YOU DON'T WANT TO GET HURT, DO YOU?
ALL THE PARTICI-PANTS ARE MEN.
EVEN IF YOU DO ENTER, I DON'T THINK YOU HAVE MUCH OF A CHANCE.
CB
DO YOU WANT TO TRY WITH ME?
IF YOU BEAT ME, YOU CAN ENTER.
SWING
ARE YOU READY?
GRAB
AH HA HA... SORRY I HAVE TO DO THIS!
MR. NOGAMI, REGIS-TRATION IS OVER.
HOW MANY PEOPLE DO WE...
AGGHH!!!
FSSSHH
WELCOME BACK, EVERY-BODY!
THIS IS THE 9TH ANNUAL ARM WRESTLING TOURNAMENT SPONSORED BY SSTV!!

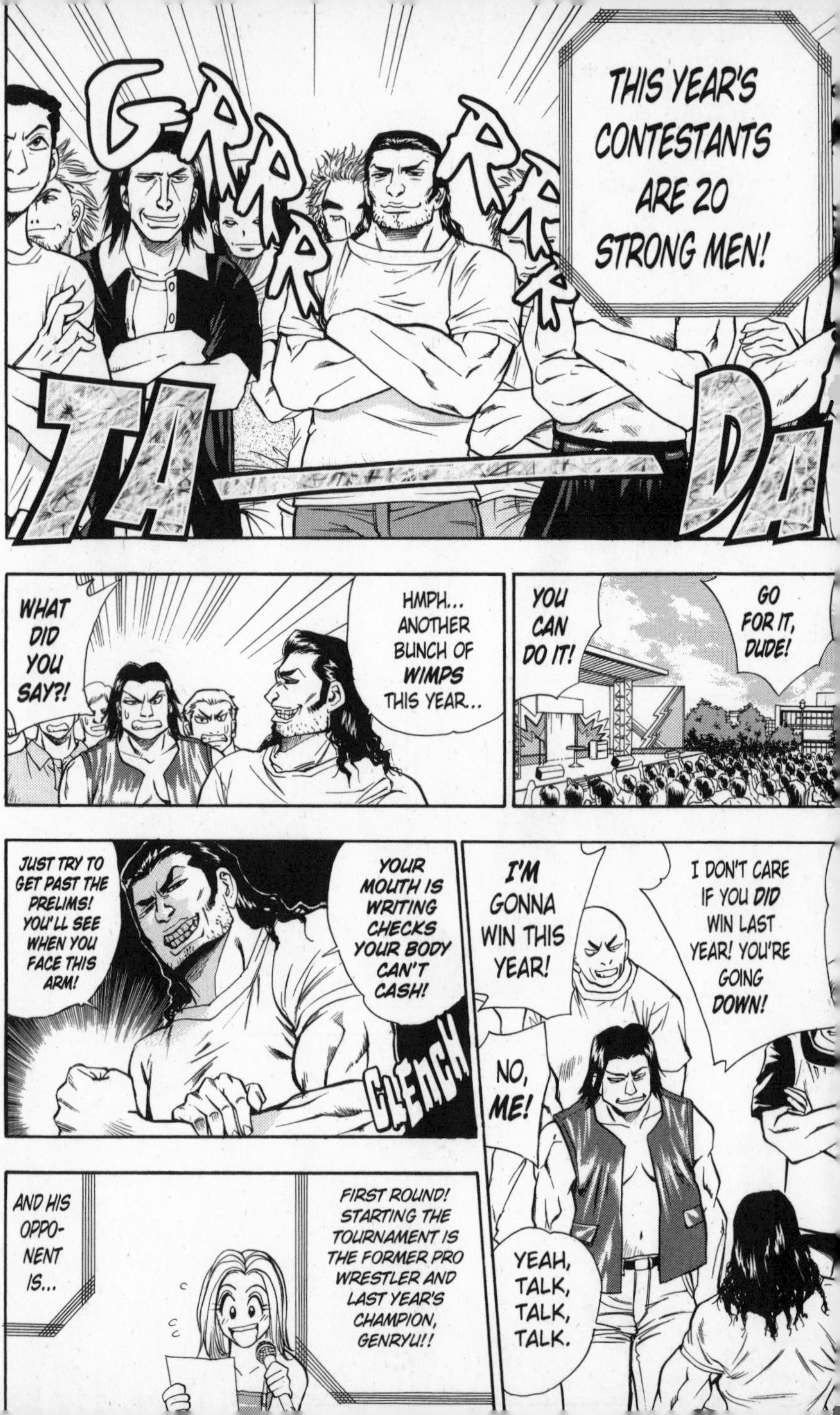
THIS YEAR'S CONTESTANTS ARE 20 STRONG MEN!
TA DA
GO FOR IT, DUDE!
YOU CAN DO IT!
HMPH... ANOTHER BUNCH OF WIMPS THIS YEAR...
WHAT DID YOU SAY?!
I DON'T CARE IF YOU DID WIN LAST YEAR! YOU'RE GOING DOWN!
I'M GONNA WIN THIS YEAR!
NO, ME!
YEAH, TALK, TALK, TALK.
YOUR MOUTH IS WRITING CHECKS YOUR BODY CAN'T CASH!
JUST TRY TO GET PAST THE PRELIMS! YOU'LL SEE WHEN YOU FACE THIS ARM!
CLENCH
FIRST ROUND! STARTING THE TOURNAMENT IS THE FORMER PRO WRESTLER AND LAST YEAR'S CHAMPION, GENRYU!!
AND HIS OPPO-NENT IS...

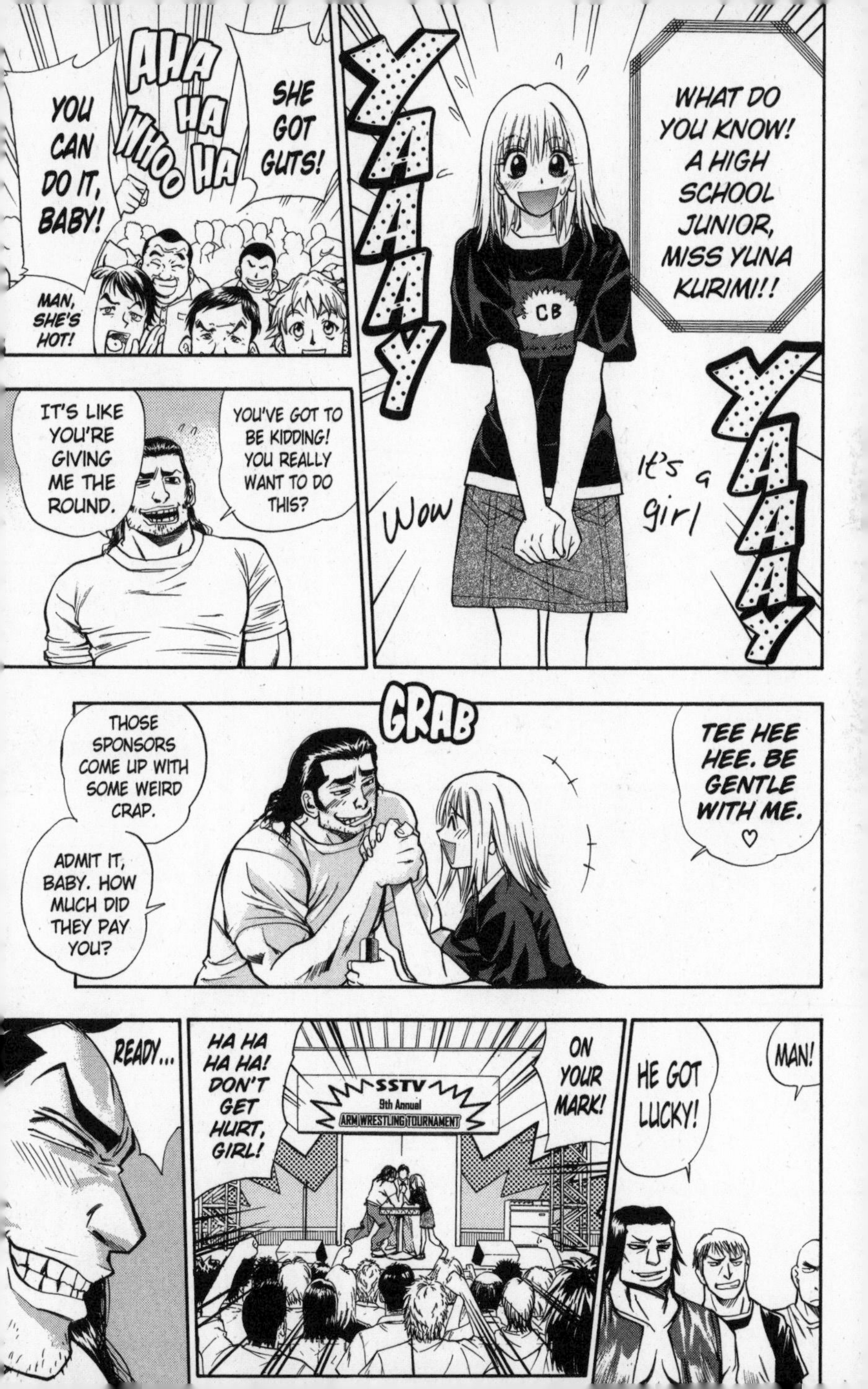
WHAT DO YOU KNOW! A HIGH SCHOOL JUNIOR, MISS YUNA KURIMI!!
YAAAY
YAAAY
It's a girl
Wow
SHE GOT GUTS!
AHA HA HA
WHOO
YOU CAN DO IT, BABY!
MAN, SHE'S HOT!
YOU'VE GOT TO BE KIDDING! YOU REALLY WANT TO DO THIS?
IT'S LIKE YOU'RE GIVING ME THE ROUND.
TEE HEE HEE. BE GENTLE WITH ME. ♡
GRAB
THOSE SPONSORS COME UP WITH SOME WEIRD CRAP.
ADMIT IT, BABY. HOW MUCH DID THEY PAY YOU?
MAN!
HE GOT LUCKY!
ON YOUR MARK!
SSTV
9th Annual
ARM WRESTLING TOURNAMENT
HA HA HA HA! DON'T GET HURT, GIRL!
READY...

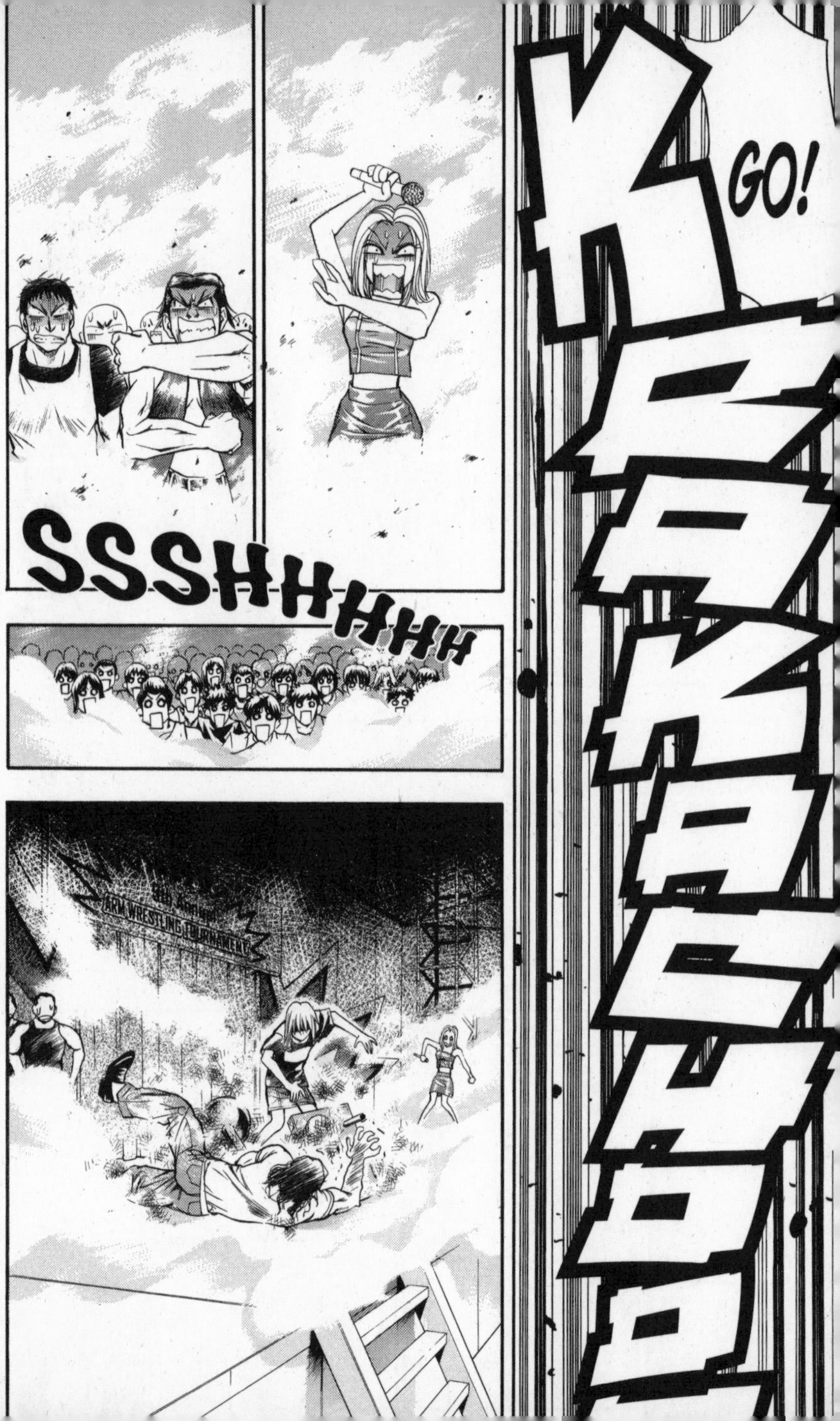
GO!
SSSHHHHHH
8th Annual
ARM WRESTLING TOURNAMENT

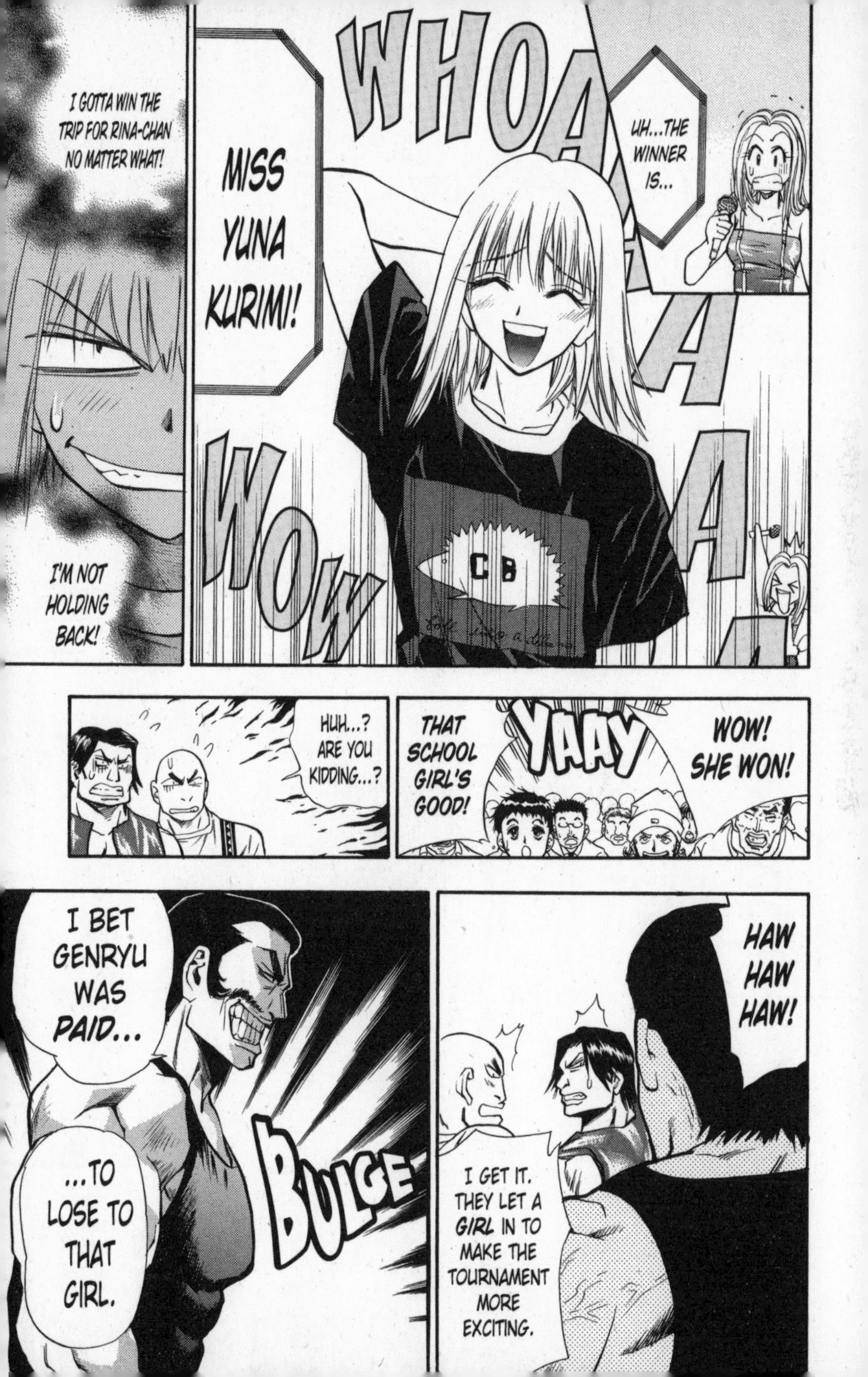
UH...THE WINNER IS...
WHOAAAA
MISS YUNA KURIMI!
WOW
I GOTTA WIN THE TRIP FOR RINA-CHAN NO MATTER WHAT!
I'M NOT HOLDING BACK!
WOW! SHE WON!
YAAY
THAT SCHOOL GIRL'S GOOD!
HUH...? ARE YOU KIDDING...?
HAW HAW HAW!
I GET IT. THEY LET A *GIRL* IN TO MAKE THE TOURNAMENT MORE EXCITING.
I BET GENRYU WAS *PAID*...
BULGE
...TO LOSE TO THAT GIRL.

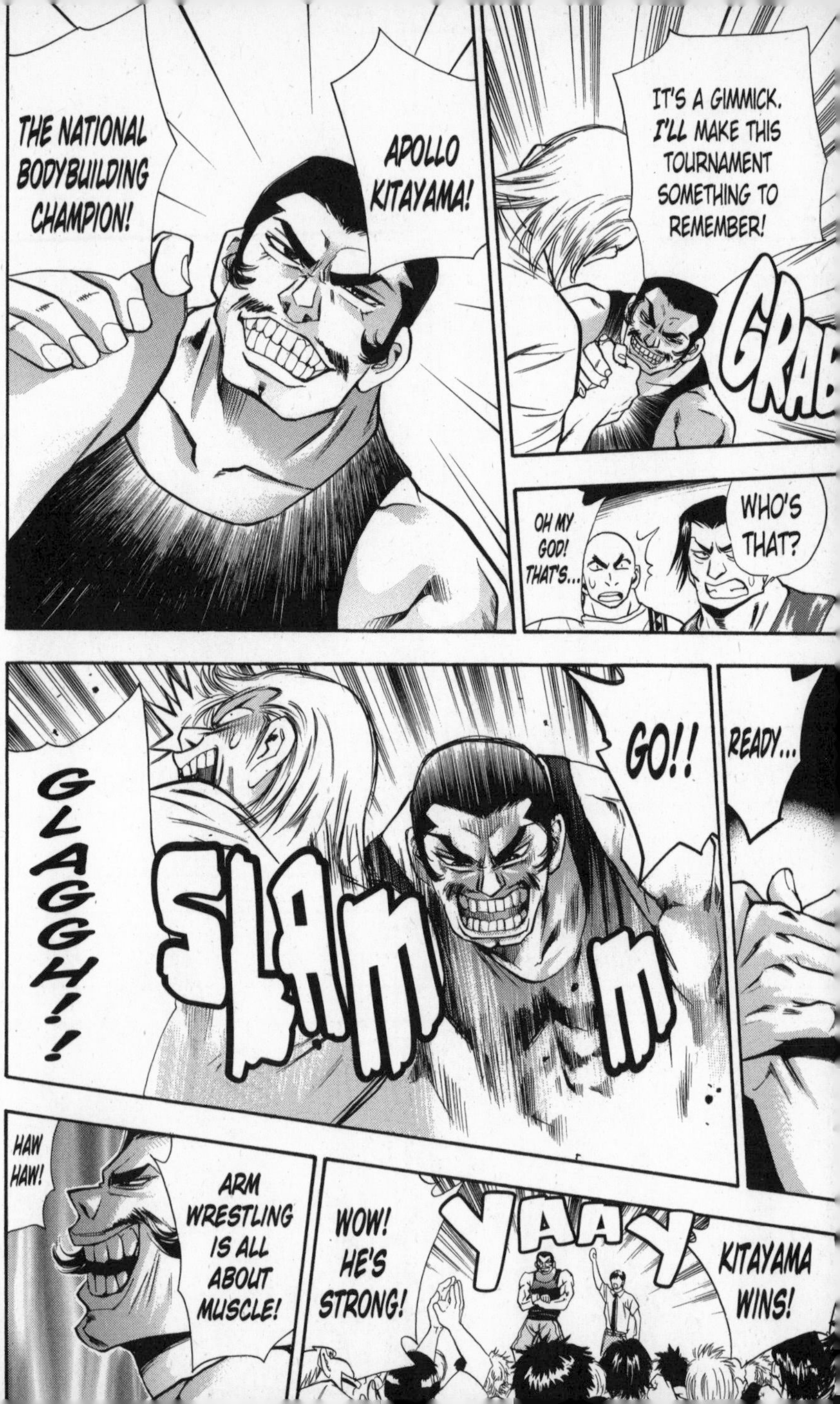
IT'S A GIMMICK. I'LL MAKE THIS TOURNAMENT SOMETHING TO REMEMBER!
GRAB
WHO'S THAT?
OH MY GOD! THAT'S...
APOLLO KITAYAMA!
THE NATIONAL BODYBUILDING CHAMPION!
READY...
GO!!
SLAMM
GLAGGH!!
KITAYAMA WINS!
YAAY
WOW! HE'S STRONG!
ARM WRESTLING IS ALL ABOUT MUSCLE!
HAW HAW!

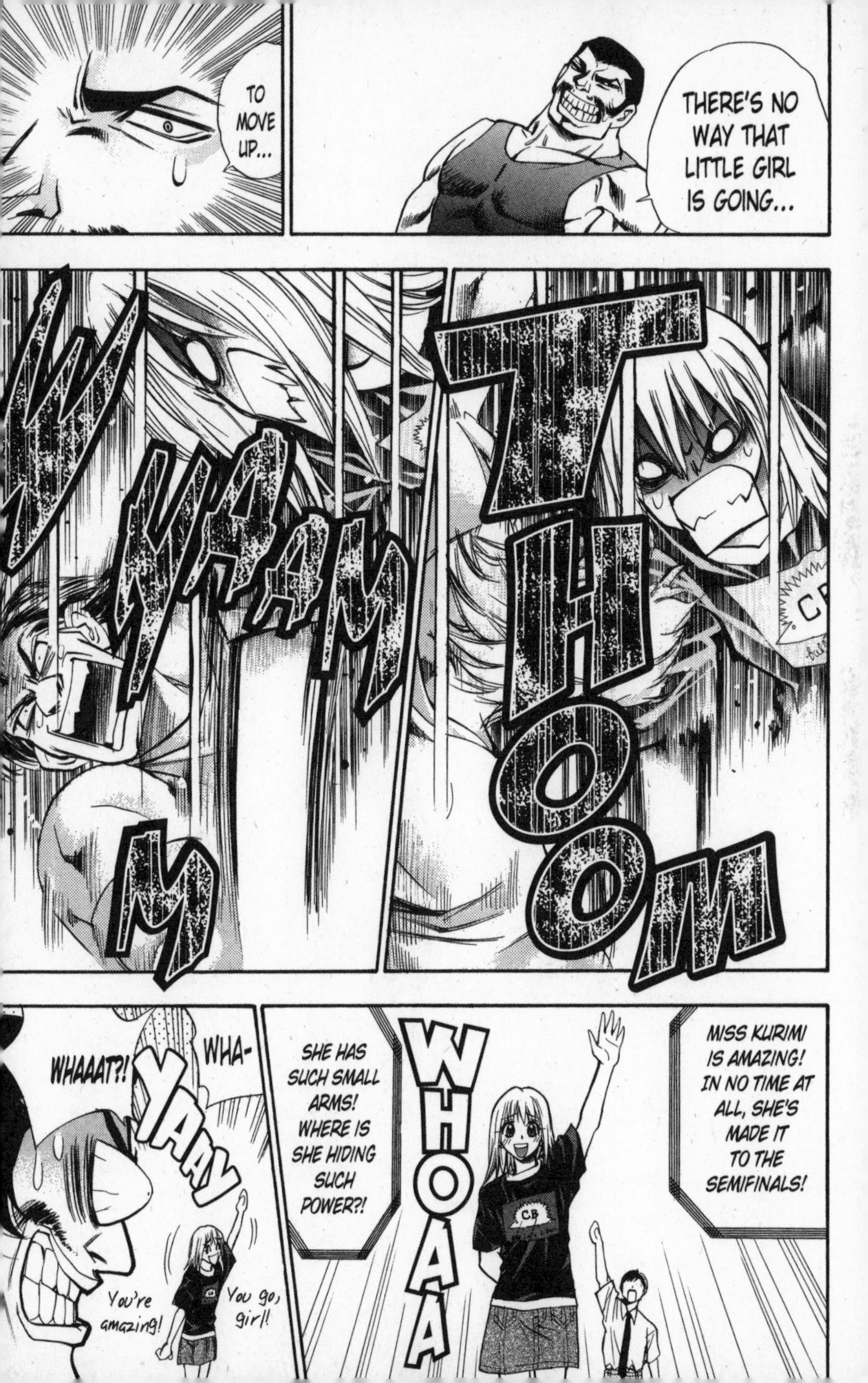
THERE'S NO WAY THAT LITTLE GIRL IS GOING...
TO MOVE UP...
THOOM
WHAMM
MISS KURIMI IS AMAZING! IN NO TIME AT ALL, SHE'S MADE IT TO THE SEMIFINALS!
WHOAA
SHE HAS SUCH SMALL ARMS! WHERE IS SHE HIDING SUCH POWER?!
WHA-
YAAY
WHAAAT?!
You go, girl!
You're amazing!

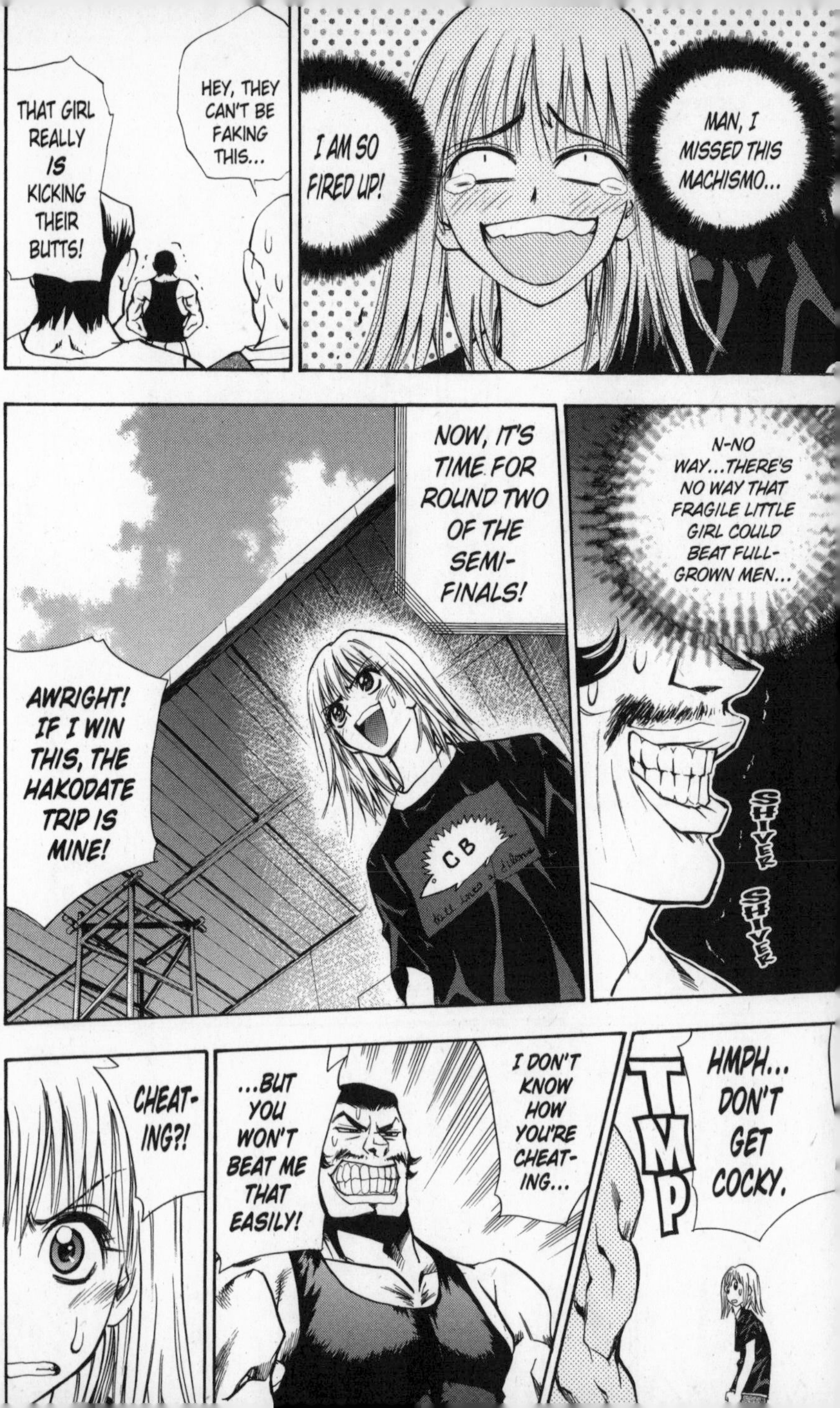
MAN, I MISSED THIS MACHISMO...
I AM SO FIRED UP!
HEY, THEY CAN'T BE FAKING THIS...
THAT GIRL REALLY IS KICKING THEIR BUTTS!
N-NO WAY...THERE'S NO WAY THAT FRAGILE LITTLE GIRL COULD BEAT FULL-GROWN MEN...
SHIVER SHIVER
NOW, IT'S TIME FOR ROUND TWO OF THE SEMI-FINALS!
AWRIGHT! IF I WIN THIS, THE HAKODATE TRIP IS MINE!
HMPH... DON'T GET COCKY.
TMP
I DON'T KNOW HOW YOU'RE CHEATING...
...BUT YOU WON'T BEAT ME THAT EASILY!
CHEAT-ING?!

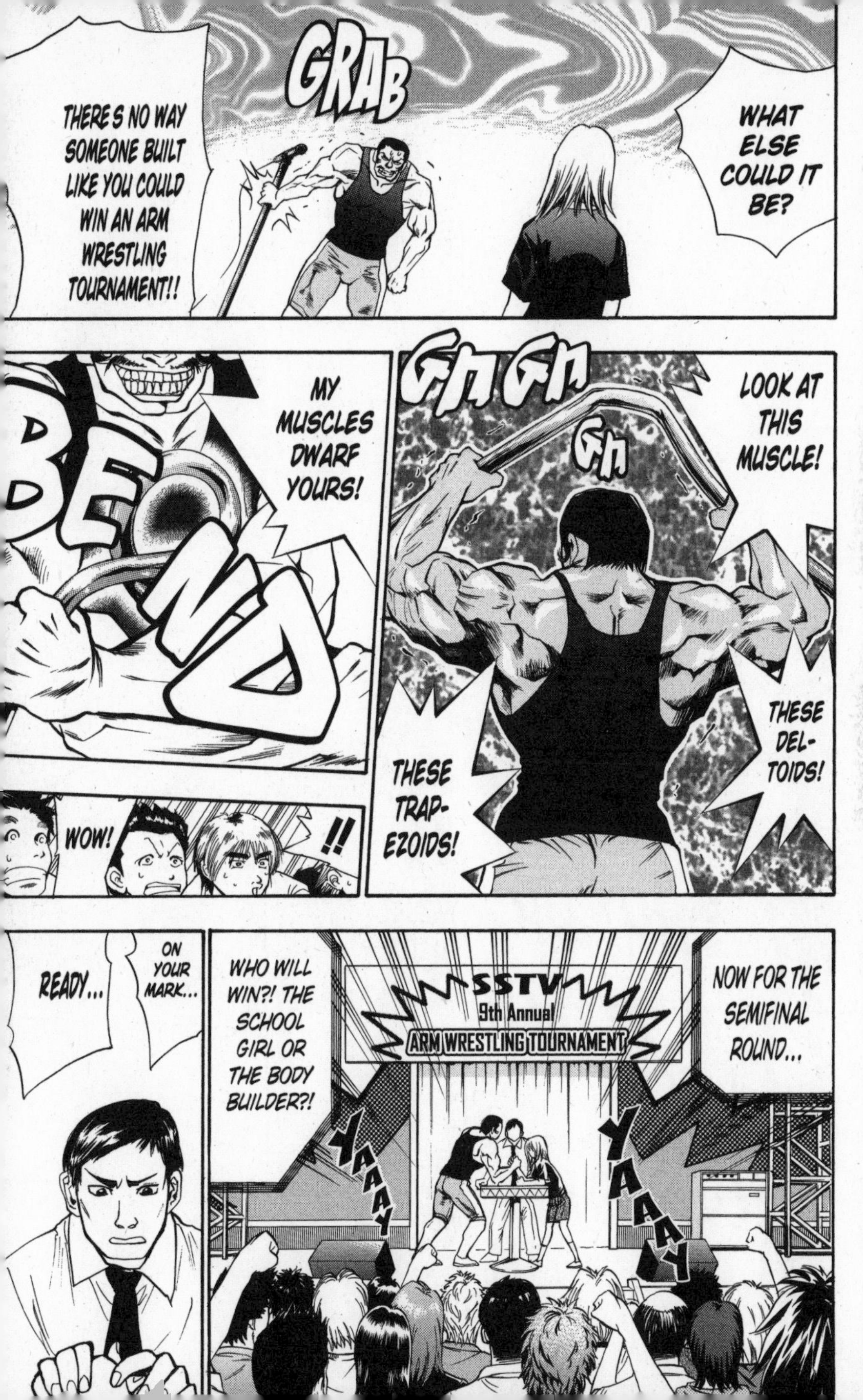
WHAT ELSE COULD IT BE?
GRAB
THERE'S NO WAY SOMEONE BUILT LIKE YOU COULD WIN AN ARM WRESTLING TOURNAMENT!!
LOOK AT THIS MUSCLE!
GM GM
GM
THESE DEL-TOIDS!
THESE TRAP-EZOIDS!
MY MUSCLES DWARF YOURS!
BEND
!!
WOW!
NOW FOR THE SEMIFINAL ROUND...
SSTV
9th Annual
ARM WRESTLING TOURNAMENT
YAAAAY
YAAAY
WHO WILL WIN?! THE SCHOOL GIRL OR THE BODY BUILDER?!
ON YOUR MARK...
READY...

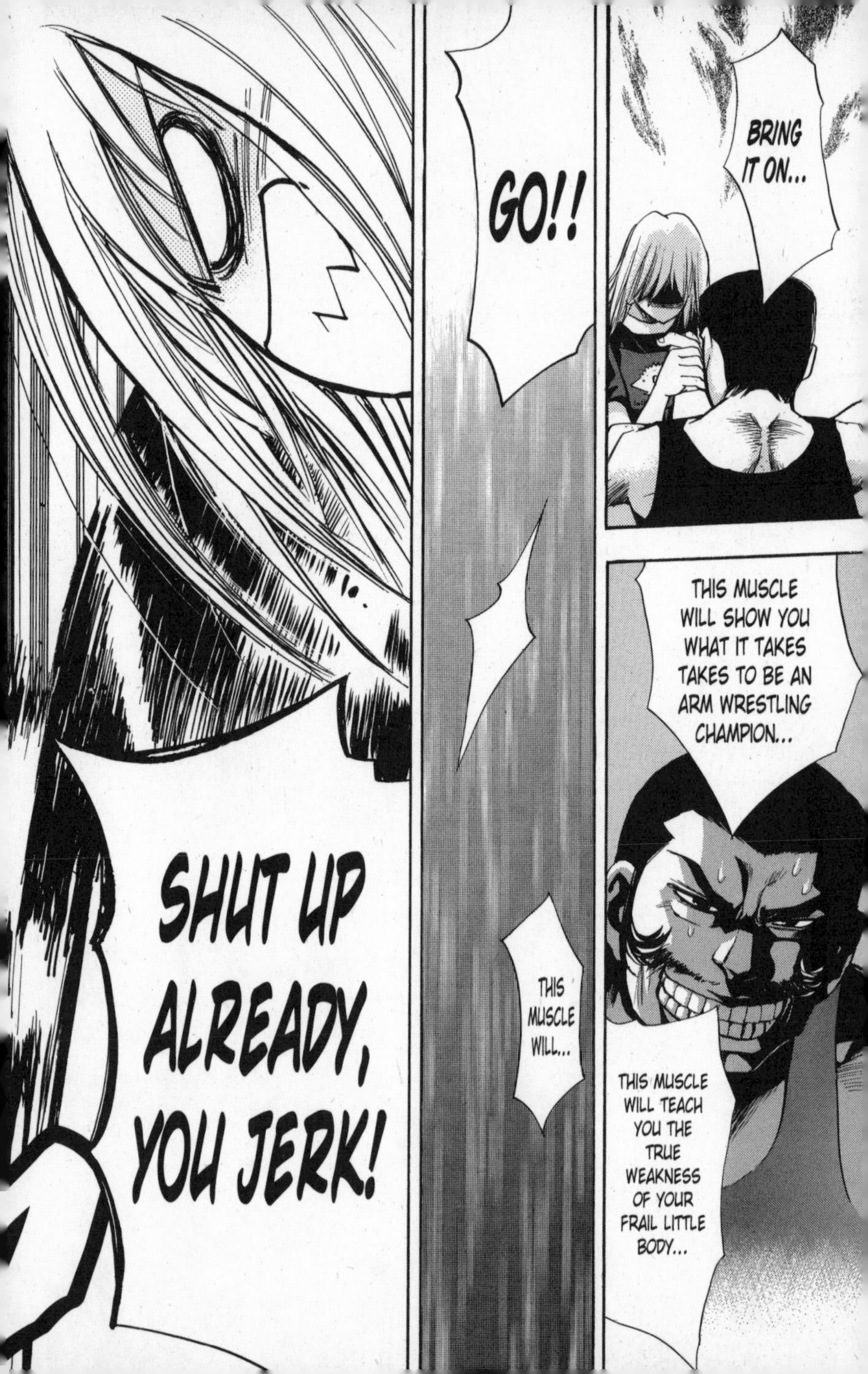
BRING IT ON...
THIS MUSCLE WILL SHOW YOU WHAT IT TAKES TAKES TO BE AN ARM WRESTLING CHAMPION...
THIS MUSCLE WILL TEACH YOU THE TRUE WEAKNESS OF YOUR FRAIL LITTLE BODY...
GO!!
THIS MUSCLE WILL...
SHUT UP ALREADY, YOU JERK!

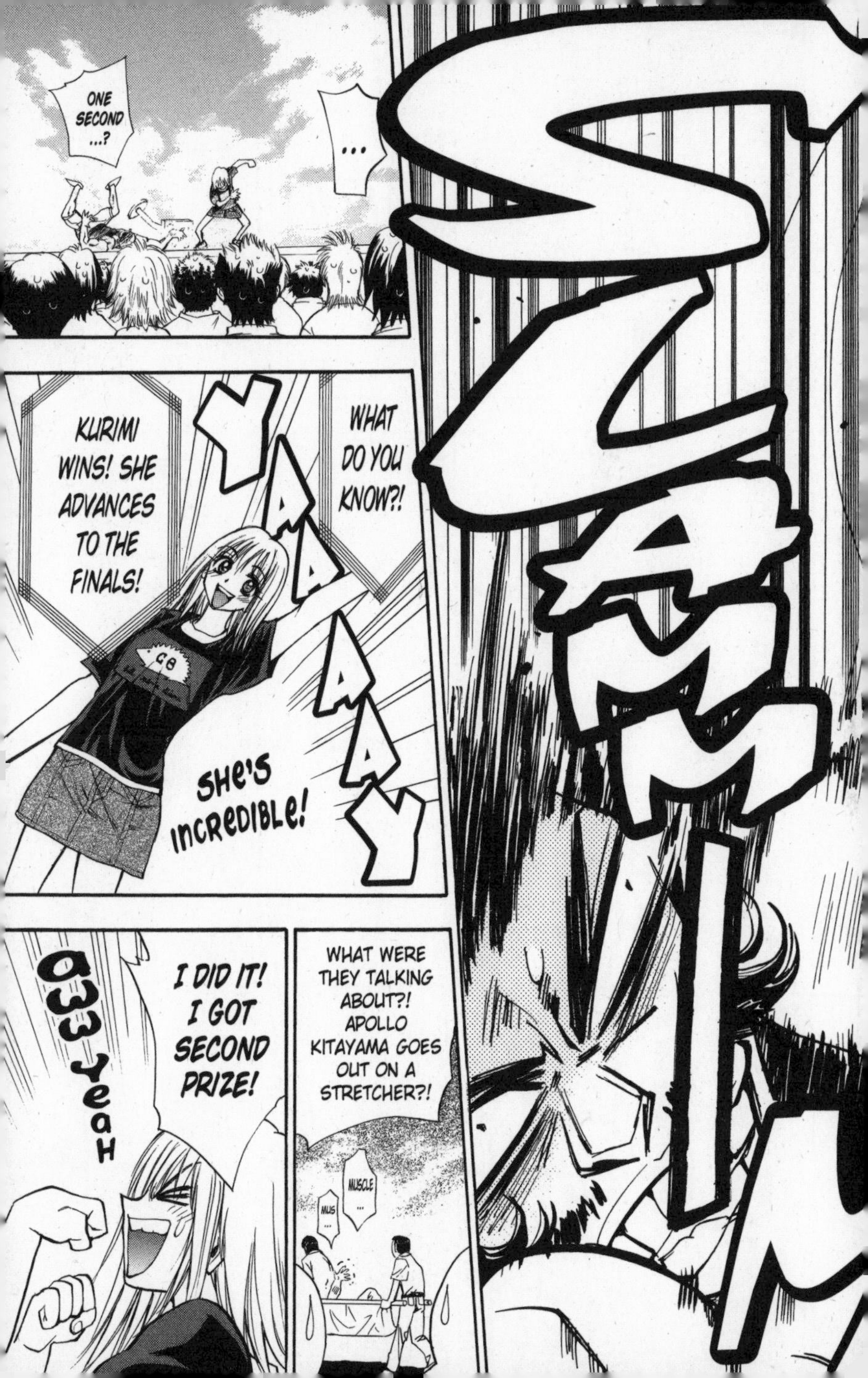

...
ONE SECOND ...?
WHAT DO YOU KNOW?!
YAAAAY
KURIMI WINS! SHE ADVANCES TO THE FINALS!
SHE'S INCREDIBLE!
WHAT WERE THEY TALKING ABOUT?! APOLLO KITAYAMA GOES OUT ON A STRETCHER?!
MUSCLE ...
MUS ...
I DID IT! I GOT SECOND PRIZE!
Yeah

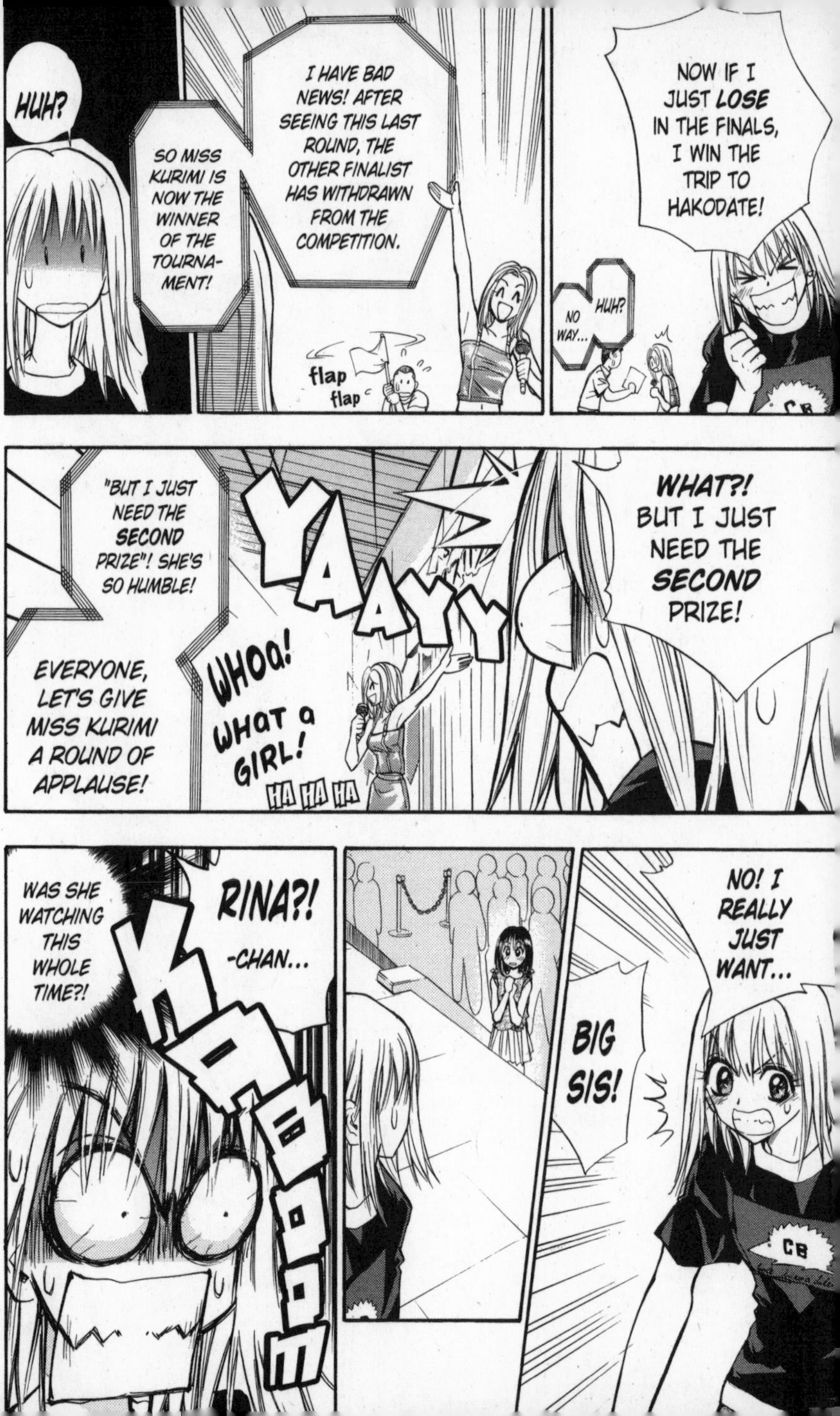
NOW IF I JUST LOSE IN THE FINALS, I WIN THE TRIP TO HAKODATE!
HUH?
NO WAY...
I HAVE BAD NEWS! AFTER SEEING THIS LAST ROUND, THE OTHER FINALIST HAS WITHDRAWN FROM THE COMPETITION.
flap flap
SO MISS KURIMI IS NOW THE WINNER OF THE TOURNA-MENT!
HUH?
WHAT?! BUT I JUST NEED THE SECOND PRIZE!
YAAYY
"BUT I JUST NEED THE SECOND PRIZE"! SHE'S SO HUMBLE!
WHOA! WHAT A GIRL!
EVERYONE, LET'S GIVE MISS KURIMI A ROUND OF APPLAUSE!
HA HA HA
NO! I REALLY JUST WANT...
BIG SIS!
RINA?! -CHAN...
WAS SHE WATCHING THIS WHOLE TIME?!
KA-BOOM

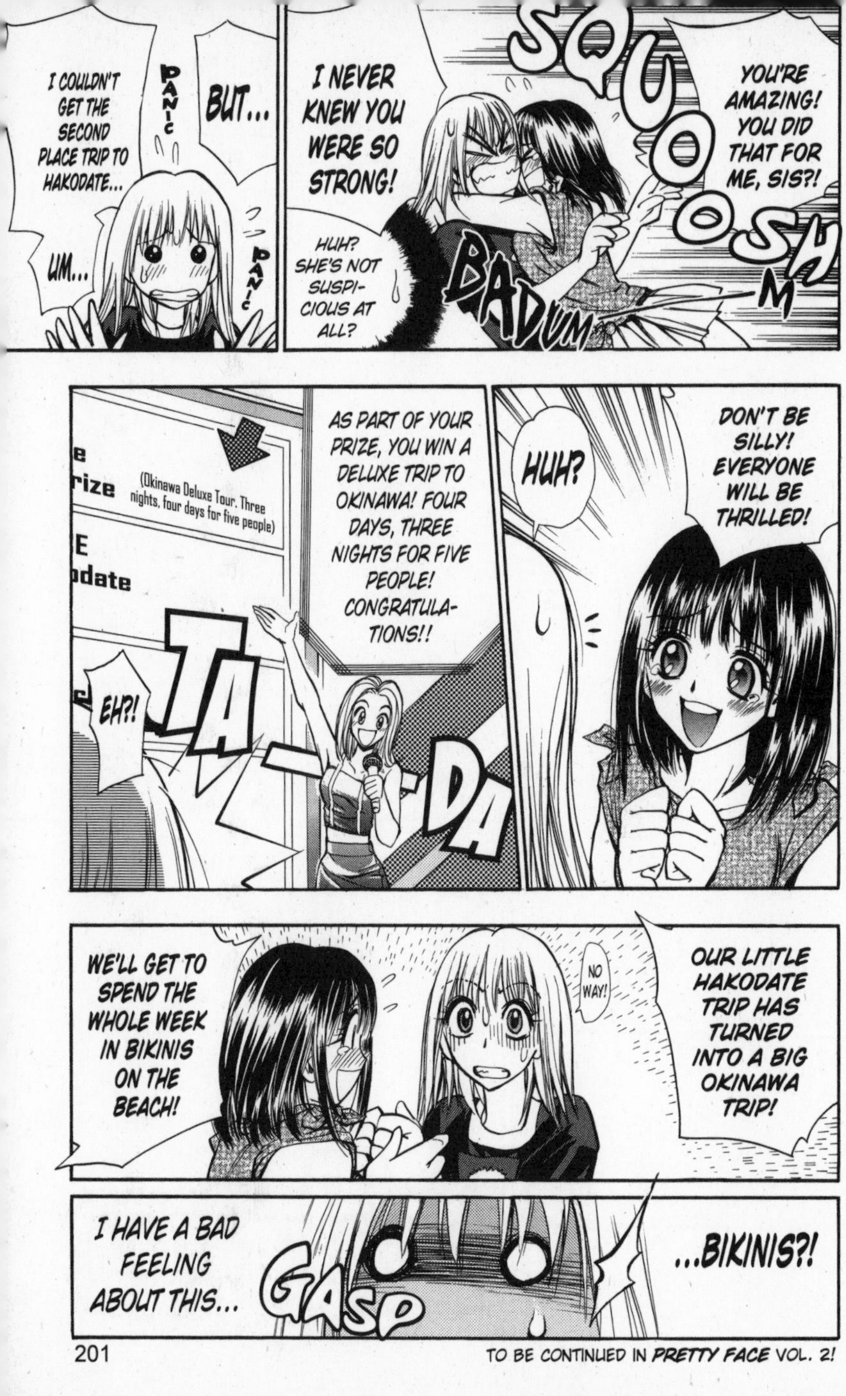
SQUOOOSH
M
YOU'RE AMAZING! YOU DID THAT FOR ME, SIS?!
I NEVER KNEW YOU WERE SO STRONG!
HUH? SHE'S NOT SUSPI- CIOUS AT ALL?
BADUM
BUT...
PANIC
I COULDN'T GET THE SECOND PLACE TRIP TO HAKODATE...
UM...
PANIC
DON'T BE SILLY! EVERYONE WILL BE THRILLED!
HUH?
AS PART OF YOUR PRIZE, YOU WIN A DELUXE TRIP TO OKINAWA! FOUR DAYS, THREE NIGHTS FOR FIVE PEOPLE! CONGRATULA- TIONS!!
(Okinawa Deluxe Tour. Three nights, four days for five people)
TA-DA
EH?!
OUR LITTLE HAKODATE TRIP HAS TURNED INTO A BIG OKINAWA TRIP!
NO WAY!
WE'LL GET TO SPEND THE WHOLE WEEK IN BIKINIS ON THE BEACH!
...BIKINIS?!
GASP
I HAVE A BAD FEELING ABOUT THIS...

TO BE CONTINUED IN *PRETTY FACE* VOL. 2!

Pretty Face

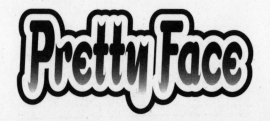

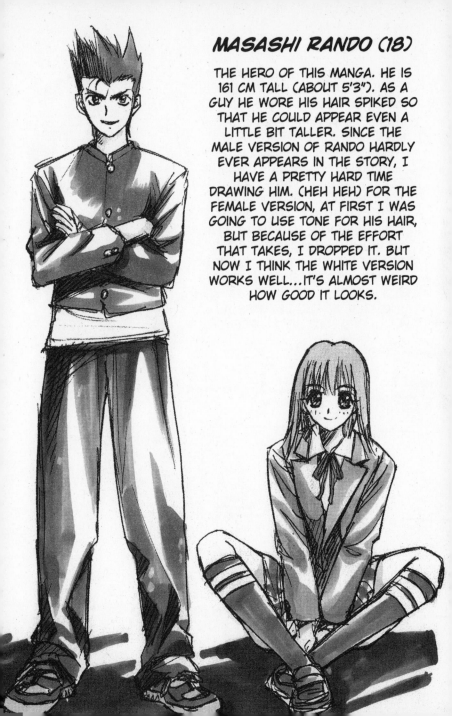

MASASHI RANDO (18)

THE HERO OF THIS MANGA. HE IS 161 CM TALL (ABOUT 5'3"). AS A GUY HE WORE HIS HAIR SPIKED SO THAT HE COULD APPEAR EVEN A LITTLE BIT TALLER. SINCE THE MALE VERSION OF RANDO HARDLY EVER APPEARS IN THE STORY, I HAVE A PRETTY HARD TIME DRAWING HIM. (HEH HEH) FOR THE FEMALE VERSION, AT FIRST I WAS GOING TO USE TONE FOR HIS HAIR, BUT BECAUSE OF THE EFFORT THAT TAKES, I DROPPED IT. BUT NOW I THINK THE WHITE VERSION WORKS WELL...IT'S ALMOST WEIRD HOW GOOD IT LOOKS.

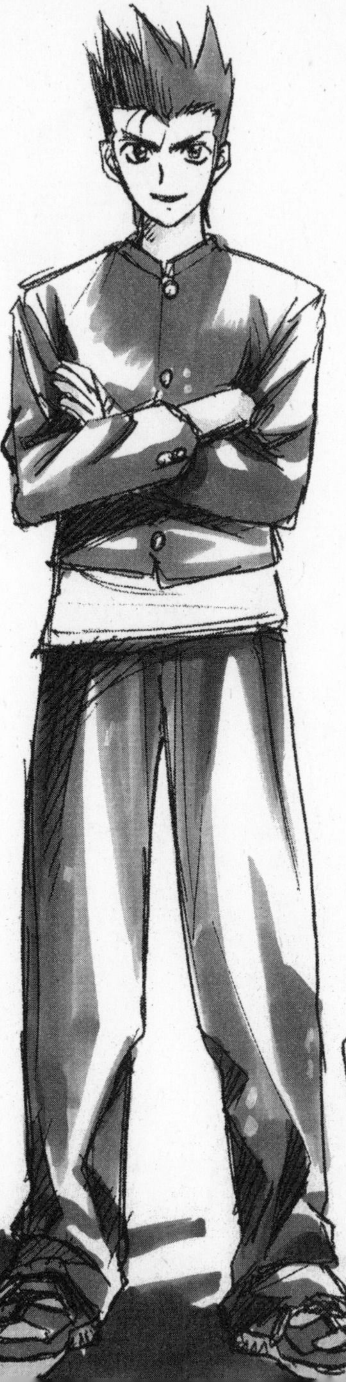

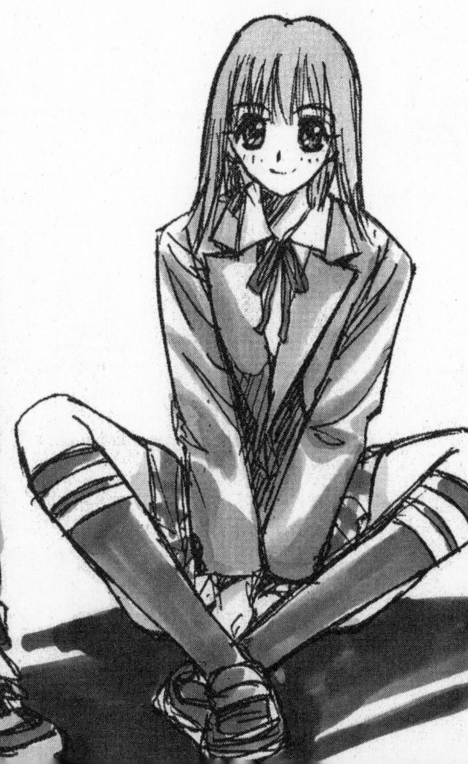

RINA KURIMI (16)

THE HEROINE OF THIS MANGA. SHE'S A BIT SHORTER THAN RANDO AT 159 CM (5'2"). SHE'S SMART AND DEPENDABLE, BUT SINCE SHE'S A CHARACTER IN A COMEDY, SHE'S GRADUALLY STARTING TO SHOW HER UNUSUAL SIDE. (HEH HEH) PERSONALLY I LIKE THE WAY SHE LOOKS WHEN SHE HAS HER HAIR TIED BACK. I OFTEN MISWRITE HER NAME WITH THE WRONG CHARACTERS (里奈). THE MISTAKES IN *WEEKLY SHONEN JUMP* ARE BAD ENOUGH, BUT PEOPLE GET IT WRONG IN A FAIR NUMBER OF FAN LETTERS AS WELL. IT'S RINA (理奈), PLEASE.

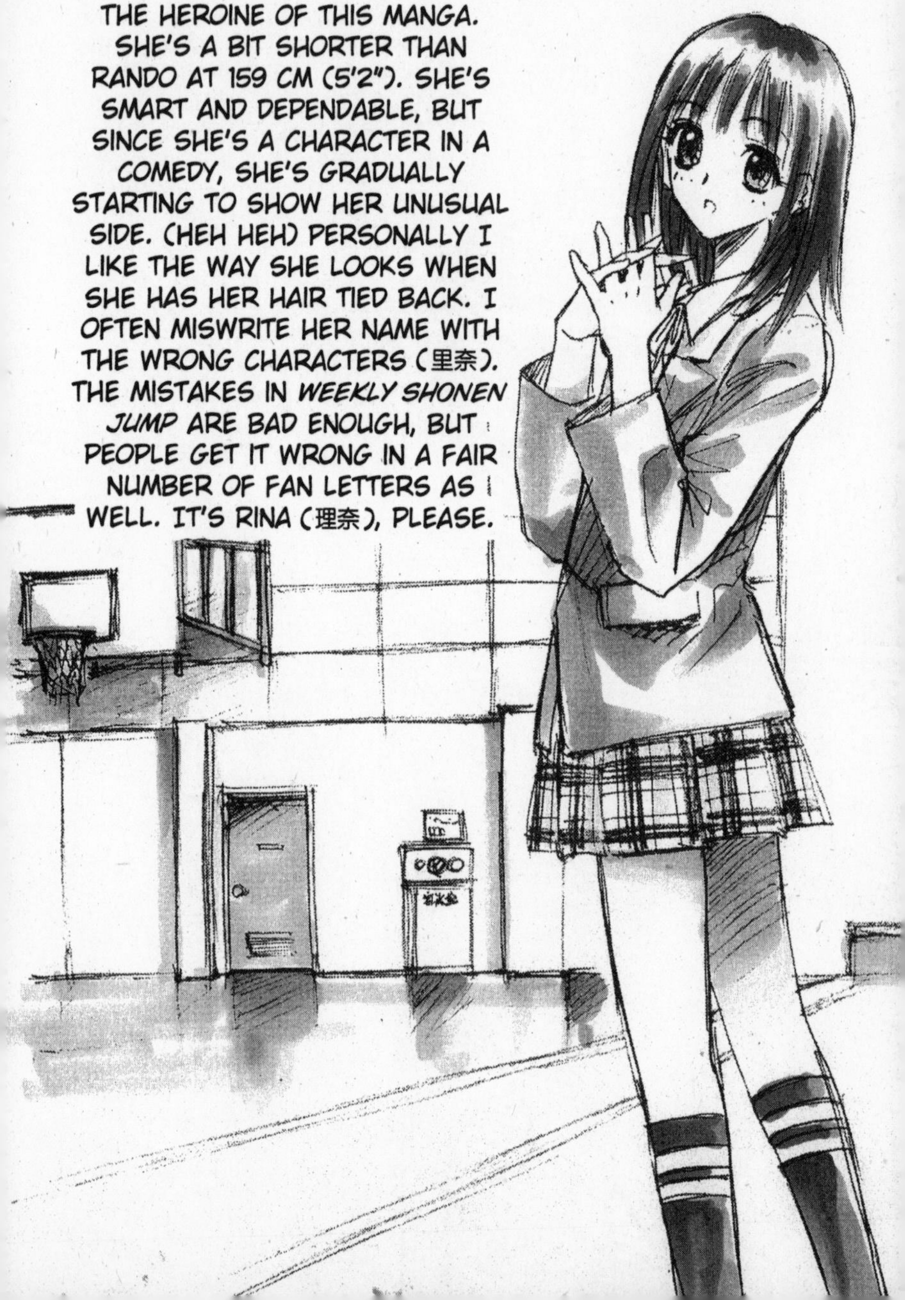

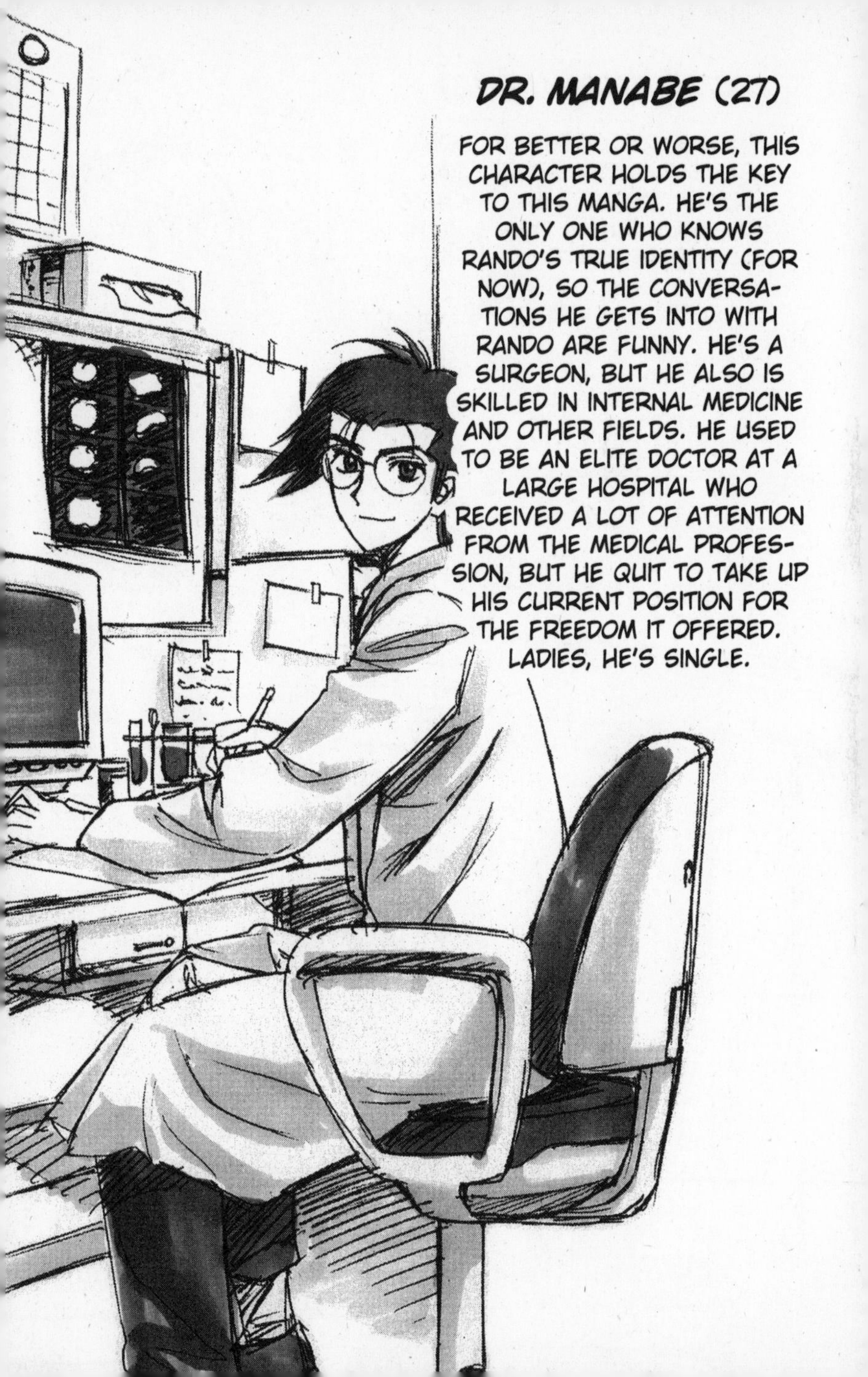
DR. MANABE (27)
FOR BETTER OR WORSE, THIS CHARACTER HOLDS THE KEY TO THIS MANGA. HE'S THE ONLY ONE WHO KNOWS RANDO'S TRUE IDENTITY (FOR NOW), SO THE CONVERSATIONS HE GETS INTO WITH RANDO ARE FUNNY. HE'S A SURGEON, BUT HE ALSO IS SKILLED IN INTERNAL MEDICINE AND OTHER FIELDS. HE USED TO BE AN ELITE DOCTOR AT A LARGE HOSPITAL WHO RECEIVED A LOT OF ATTENTION FROM THE MEDICAL PROFESSION, BUT HE QUIT TO TAKE UP HIS CURRENT POSITION FOR THE FREEDOM IT OFFERED. LADIES, HE'S SINGLE.

YUNA KURIMI (16)

RINA'S MISSING OLDER SISTER. NATURALLY SHE HAS THE SAME FACE AS RINA AND THE CURRENT RANDO. SHE'S RINA'S TWIN SISTER, BUT HER PERSONALITY IS DIFFERENT FROM RINA IN THAT SHE'S MORE ENERGETIC AND REFRESHING. HER CHARACTER WILL GRADUALLY COME OUT AS THE STORY PROGRESSES. SHE ALSO HOLDS THE KEY TO THIS MANGA.

THIS PICTURE IS FROM WHEN SHE WAS IN MIDDLE SCHOOL.

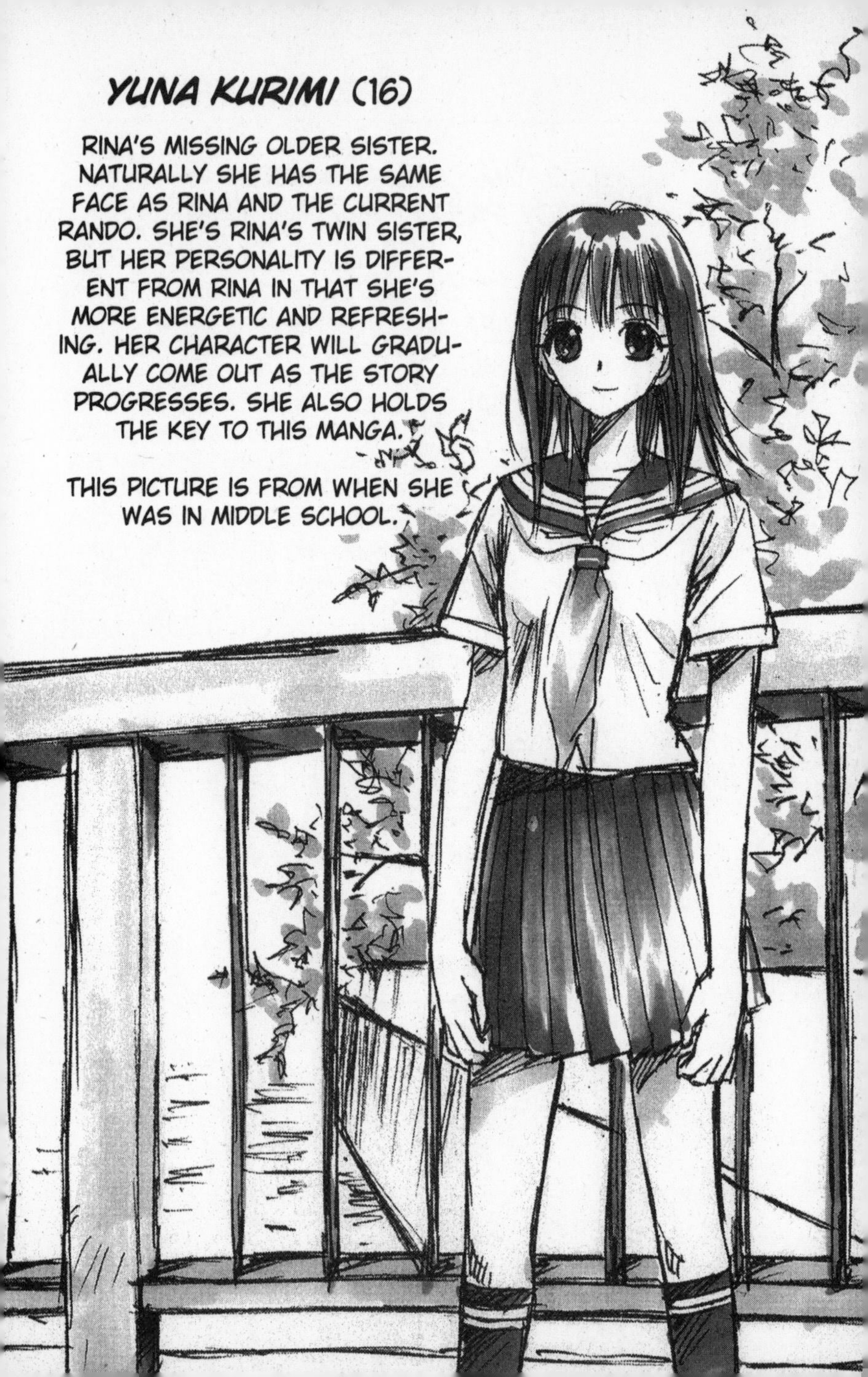

HELLO, I'M YASUHIRO KANO.
DID YOU ENJOY *PRETTY FACE* VOLUME 1?

I CAUSED A LOT OF TROUBLE FOR MY
EDITOR, MY STAFF AND A LOT OF OTHER
PEOPLE, BUT SOMEHOW I MANAGED TO DO
THIS SERIES. FINALLY, THE FIRST BOOK IS
OUT AND THE FEELING IS PRICELESS.

THE PACE OF A WEEKLY SERIES IS HARSH
AND I CAN'T PUT 100% OF MY POWER INTO IT.
I HAVE A LOT OF REGRETS AND DISSATIS-
FACTION, BUT I STILL KEEP WORKING HARD
SO THAT THE READERS WHO SUPPORT ME
WILL BE PLEASED! AT THE CURRENT TIME
(SEPTEMBER 2002), I DON'T KNOW HOW
LONG THIS WILL GO ON, BUT I REALLY WANT
TO TRY AND GET RANDO AND RINA TO A
HAPPY ENDING IN THE REAL MEANING OF THE
WORD. PLEASE LOOK KINDLY ON MY
EFFORTS.

OH, AND ONE OTHER THING...PLEASE DON'T
NOTICE THE LITTLE INCONSISTENCIES AND
QUESTIONABLE POINTS AS YOU READ IT!
DON'T POINT THEM OUT TO ME! THAT'S ONE
OF THE RULES OF *PRETTY FACE!* (HEH HEH)

SEE YOU AGAIN IN VOLUME 2!

Rando stru   les to be a   ood "bi   sister" to Rina as fate
conspires to put him in one disastrous situation after
another. When pants start comin   off and half-naked
    omen start cra   lin   all o   er him for the thinnest of
reasons, can our hero a   oid bein   exposed as a complete   eirdo   Will the mad Dr. Manabe succeed in his
plan to remo   e the last remnants of Rando's man-
hood...or   ill Rando remo   e Dr. Manabe's brains   ith
his fist   It's 7.5 inches of man   a   oodness!

AVAILABLE NOW!

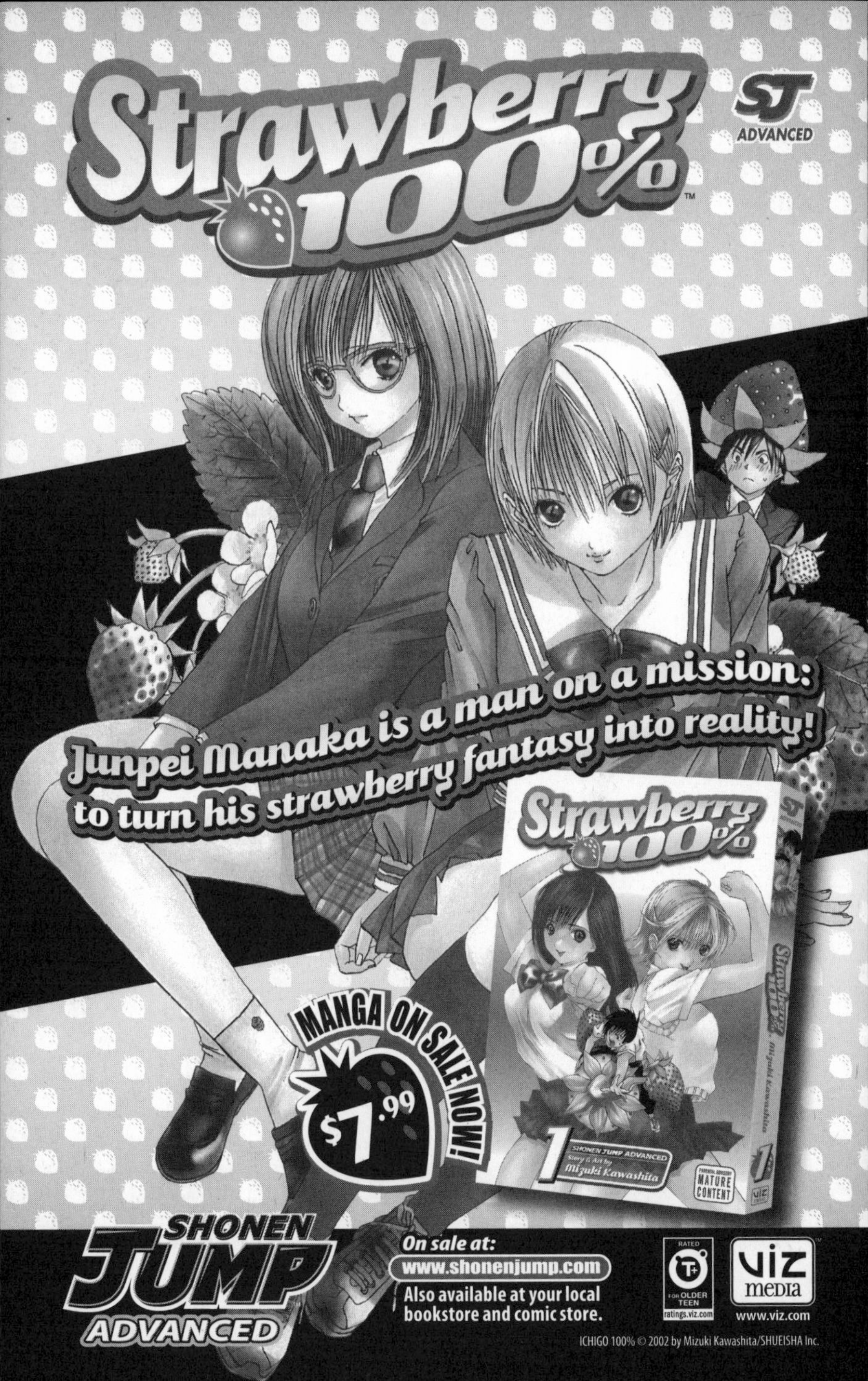
Strawberry 100%™
SJ ADVANCED
Junpei Manaka is a man on a mission:
to turn his strawberry fantasy into reality!
MANGA ON SALE NOW!
$7.99
Strawberry 100%
1
SHONEN JUMP ADVANCED
Story & Art by Mizuki Kawashita
MATURE CONTENT
SHONEN JUMP ADVANCED
On sale at:
www.shonenjump.com
Also available at your local bookstore and comic store.
RATED T+ FOR OLDER TEEN
ratings.viz.com
VIZ media
www.viz.com
ICHIGO 100% © 2002 by Mizuki Kawashita/SHUEISHA Inc.

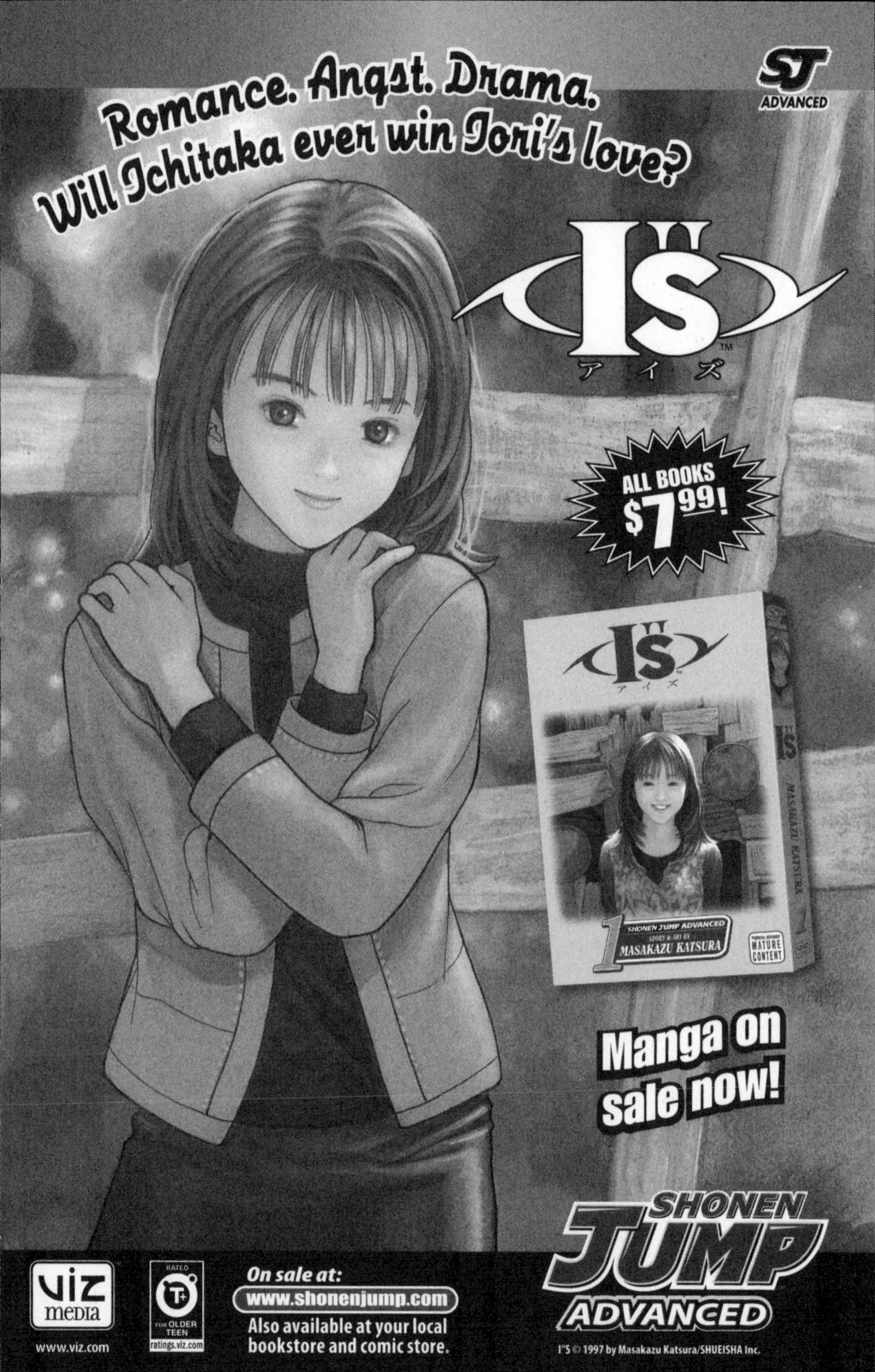
SJ ADVANCED
Romance. Angst. Drama.
Will Ichitaka ever win Iori's love?
I"S
アイズ
ALL BOOKS $7.99!
SHONEN JUMP ADVANCED
STORY & ART BY MASAKAZU KATSURA
MATURE CONTENT
Manga on sale now!
SHONEN JUMP ADVANCED
viz media
www.viz.com
RATED T+ FOR OLDER TEEN
ratings.viz.com
On sale at:
www.shonenjump.com
Also available at your local bookstore and comic store.
I"S © 1997 by Masakazu Katsura/SHUEISHA Inc.

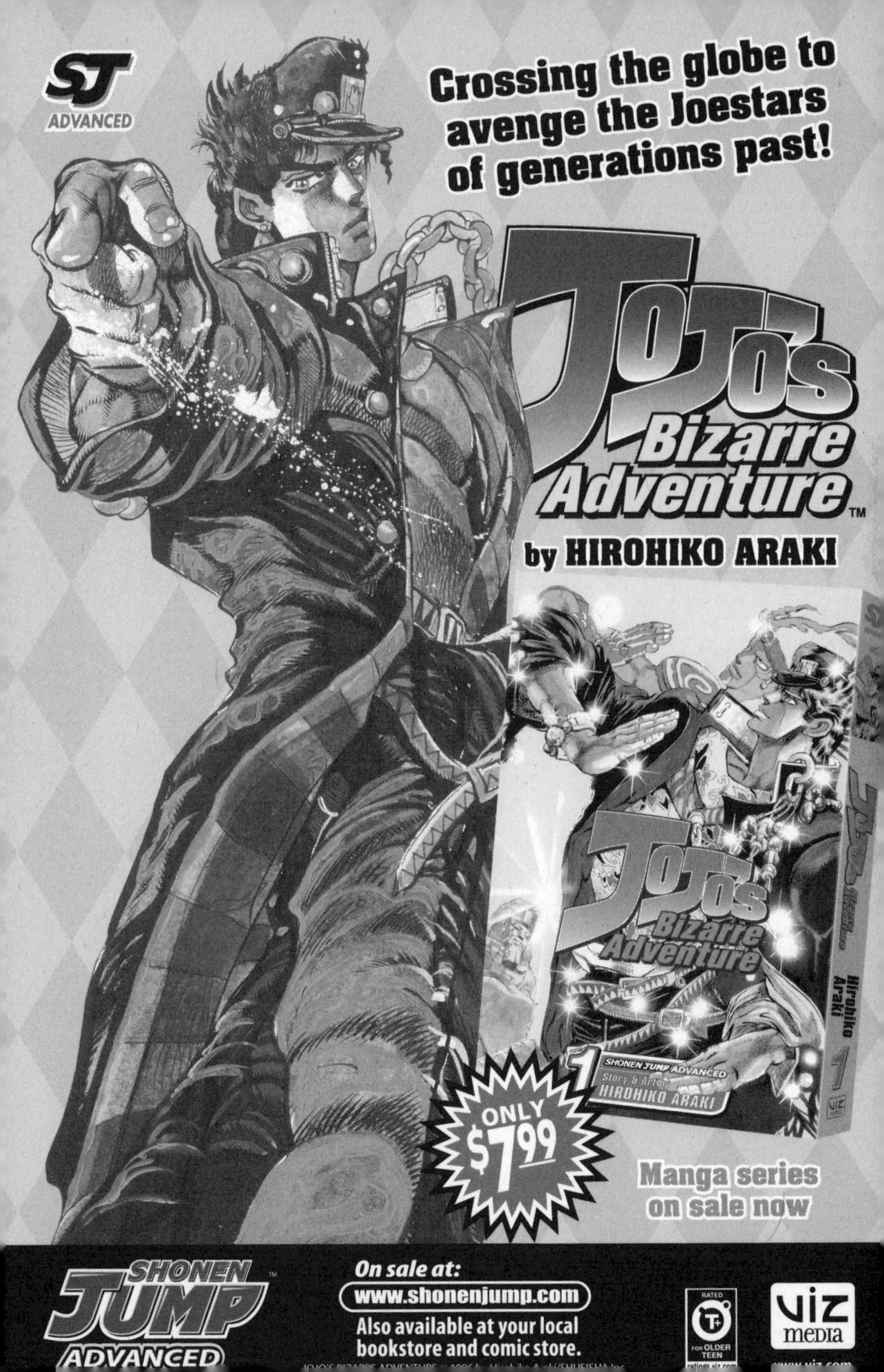

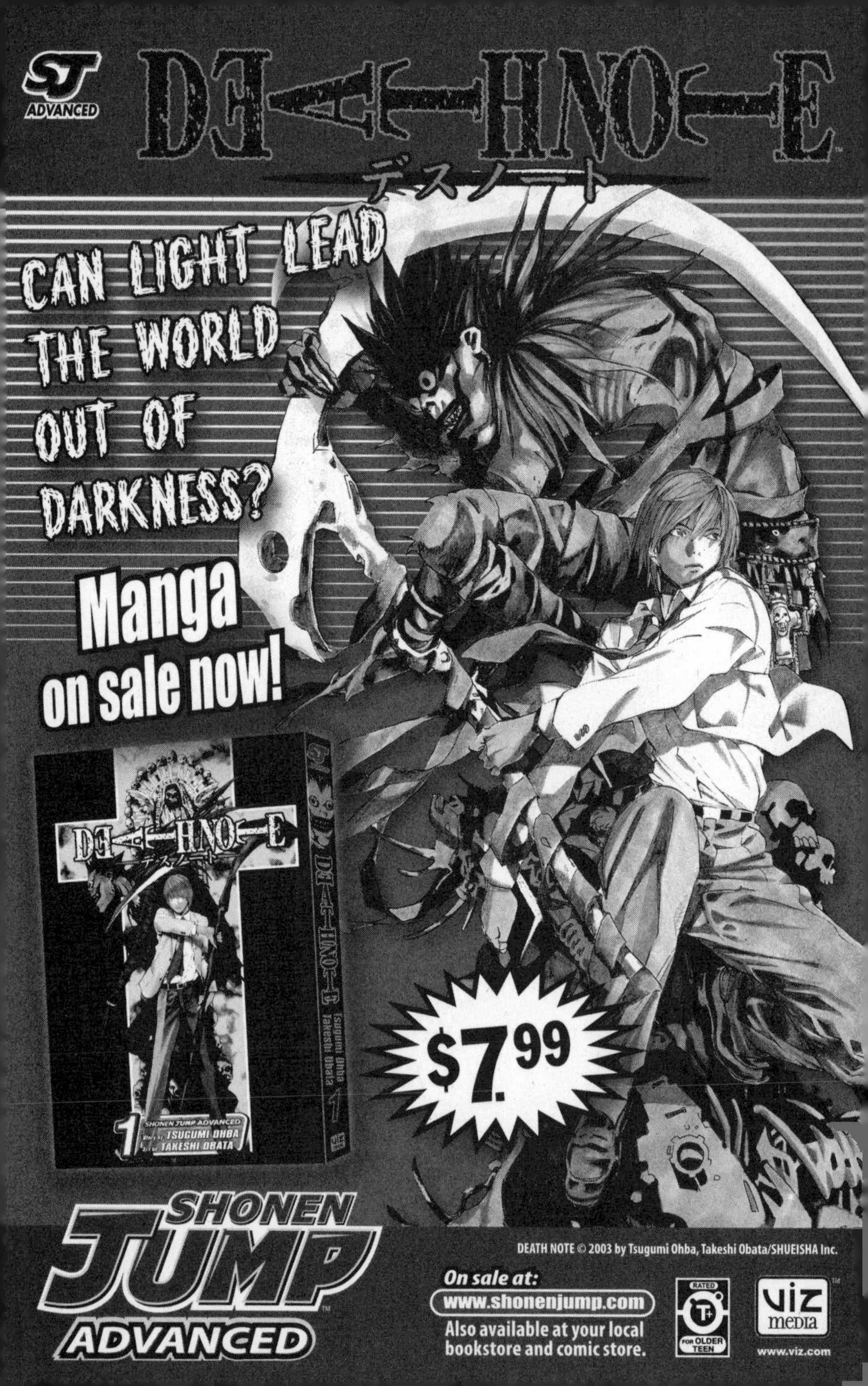
SJ ADVANCED
DEATH NOTE
デスノート
CAN LIGHT LEAD THE WORLD OUT OF DARKNESS?
Manga on sale now!
DEATH NOTE
デスノート
1 SHONEN JUMP ADVANCED
Story by TSUGUMI OHBA
Art by TAKESHI OBATA
DEATH NOTE
Tsugumi Ohba
Takeshi Obata
1
$7.99
SHONEN JUMP ADVANCED
DEATH NOTE © 2003 by Tsugumi Ohba, Takeshi Obata/SHUEISHA Inc.
On sale at:
www.shonenjump.com
Also available at your local bookstore and comic store.
RATED T+ FOR OLDER TEEN
viz media
www.viz.com

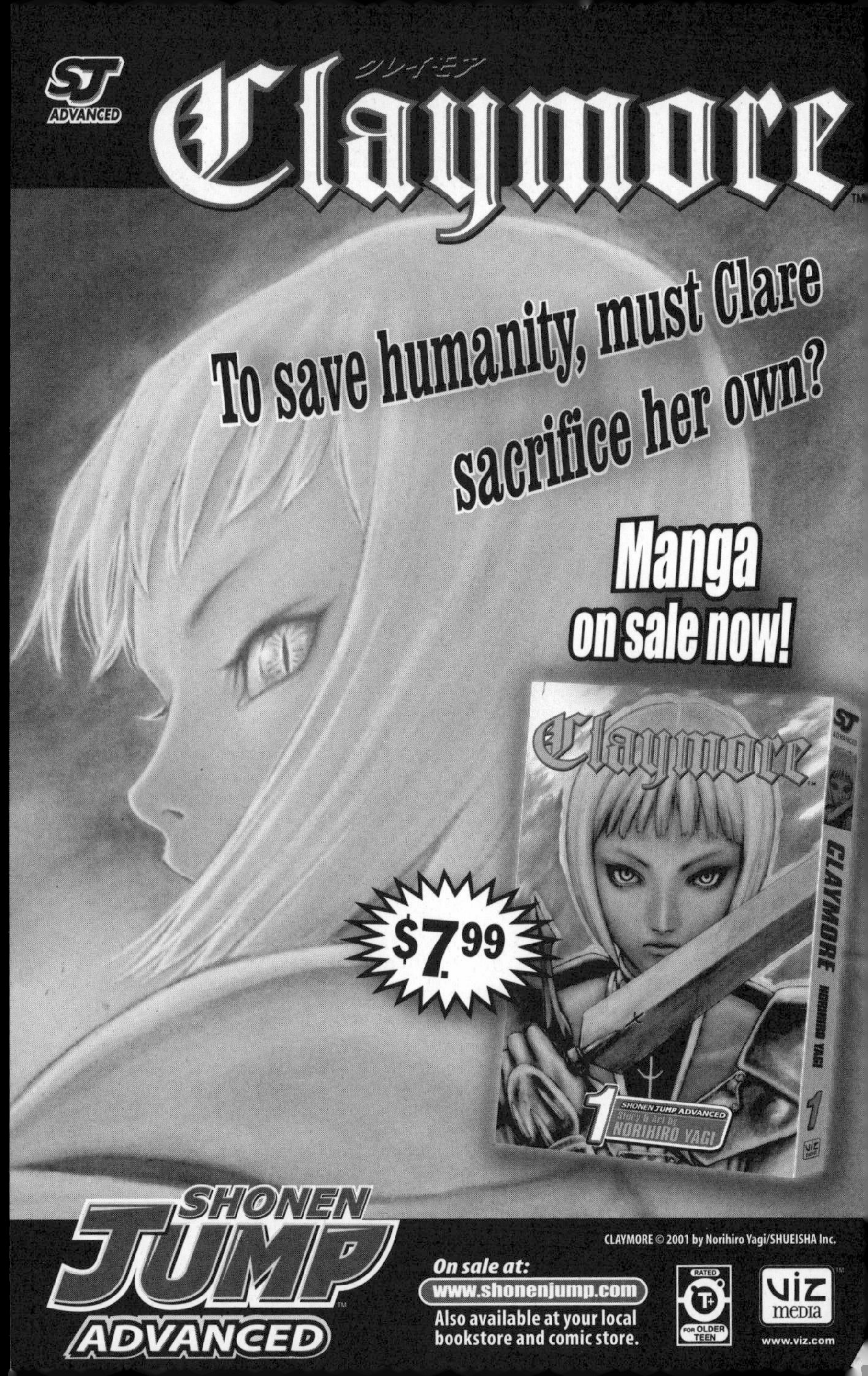

SJ ADVANCED
クレイモア
Claymore™
To save humanity, must Clare sacrifice her own?
Manga on sale now!
$7.99
Claymore
SJ ADVANCED
CLAYMORE
NORIHIRO YAGI
1
SHONEN JUMP ADVANCED
Story & Art by
NORIHIRO YAGI
SHONEN JUMP™ ADVANCED
CLAYMORE © 2001 by Norihiro Yagi/SHUEISHA Inc.
On sale at:
www.shonenjump.com
Also available at your local bookstore and comic store.
RATED T+ FOR OLDER TEEN
viz media
www.viz.com

Tell us what you think about SHONEN JUMP manga!

Our survey is now available online.
Go to: www.SHONENJUMP.com/mangasurvey

Help us make our product offering better!